KNOSSOS

KNOSSOS

MYTH, HISTORY AND ARCHAEOLOGY

James Whitley

BLOOMSBURY ACADEMIC

LONDON • NEW YORK • OXFORD • NEW DELHI • SYDNEY

BLOOMSBURY ACADEMIC
Bloomsbury Publishing Plc
50 Bedford Square, London, WC1B 3DP, UK
1385 Broadway, New York, NY 10018, USA
29 Earlsfort Terrace, Dublin 2, Ireland

BLOOMSBURY, BLOOMSBURY ACADEMIC and the Diana logo are trademarks of Bloomsbury Publishing Plc

First published in Great Britain 2024

Cover design: Terry Woodley
Cover image © Ashmolean Museum, University of Oxford

A catalogue record for this book is available from the British Library.

A catalog record for this book is available from the Library of Congress.

ISBN: HB: 978-1- 4725-2725-7
       PB: 978-1-4725-3284-8
       ePDF: 978-1-4725-2287-0
       eBook: 978-1-4725-2644-1

Series: Archaeological Histories

Typeset by RefineCatch Limited, Bungay, Suffolk

To find out more about our authors and books visit www.bloomsbury.com and sign up for our newsletters.

To my daughters, Isabella and Lilian

CONTENTS

Contents

TABLES

FIGURES

PREFACE AND ACKNOWLEDGEMENTS

I have a confession: my title is a little misleading. It suggests that myth is primary, that history flows from myth and that the archaeology is to be relegated to its traditional role within Classics – that of a handmaiden to History, Literature and Art. I do of course discuss myth; the aim of the book is historical (in the broadest possible sense of the term); and I do touch on textual and epigraphic topics which (in a traditional understanding of the division of labour within Classics) remain the preserve of the ancient historian. This book is however primarily and unashamedly *archaeological*: it is a work of archaeological synthesis and so of archaeological history. Most of the evidence we have for Knossos is material rather than textual. Much of that evidence was first generated by scholars working under the aegis of the British School at Athens, and subsequently published in several of its publications – principally its *Annual* (the *Annual of the British School at Athens*) as well as the *Supplementary Volumes* and *Studies* series. My debt to that institution should be obvious.

And it is a book about Knossos – Knossos as a major settlement and political community within a wider Eastern Mediterranean World. It takes the story of Knossos from its origins as a settlement in the Neolithic through its abandonment in Late Antiquity down to the present day. It is not principally about the Bronze Age or 'the Minoans': it is a diachronic history that tries to cross the great divide that has, for several decades, separated the study of Aegean prehistory on the one hand from the investigation of later (largely historical) periods on the other. The divide is largely conceptual, a 'green line in peoples' heads' (to use a term coined by my Cypriot colleague, Maria Iacovou). Just as the political 'green line' that currently divides the island of Cyprus corresponds to no natural divide (river or mountain), nor to any cultural, linguistic or ethnic boundary that might have existed before 1974, so the 'green line in peoples' heads' does not correspond to any particular divide that can be given a precise date (whether that be 1200, 1177, 1100 or 776 BC). It does not align with the end of prehistory and the beginning of history; it does not correspond to George Grote's distinction between a 'Time of Legend' and his 'Time of History' (Grote 1849a; 1849b); nor does it separate a division of labour between archaeologists (who work with material evidence) on the one hand and historians (who work with texts) on the other. This book then does not end with the Final Destruction of the Palace at the end of the Glorious and Heroic Age of Bronze – which I do not regard as a calamity that ought to be a perennial source of regret. Knossos of course remains central to the study of the Aegean Bronze Age; many may still feel that if all periods are equal, in Knossos at least some periods (the palatial) are more equal than others. I disagree. I discuss all periods during which the site was occupied. The two introductory maps (Figures 0.1 and 0.2) are there simply to provide some general geographical context; the plans relate to sites relevant not to one phase but to several.

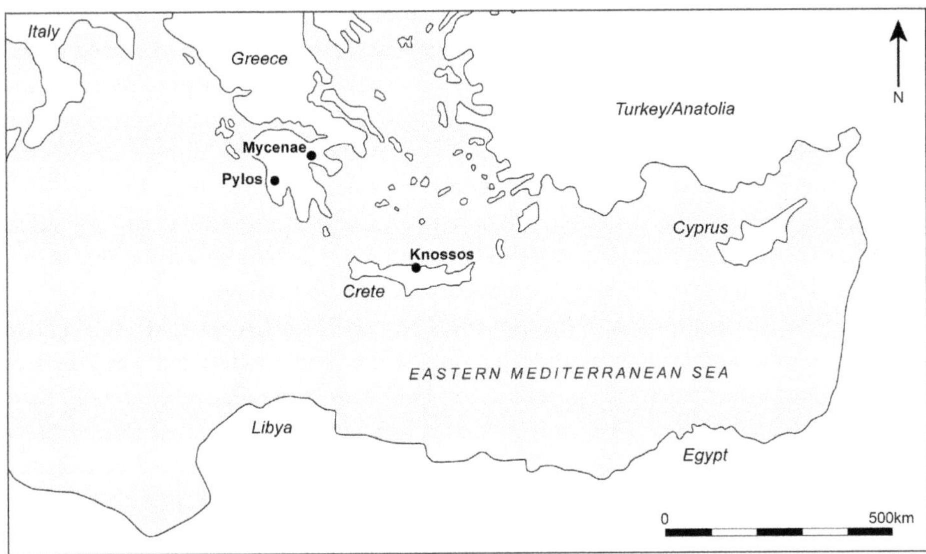

Figure 0.1 Map of the East Mediterranean, showing the position of Knossos.

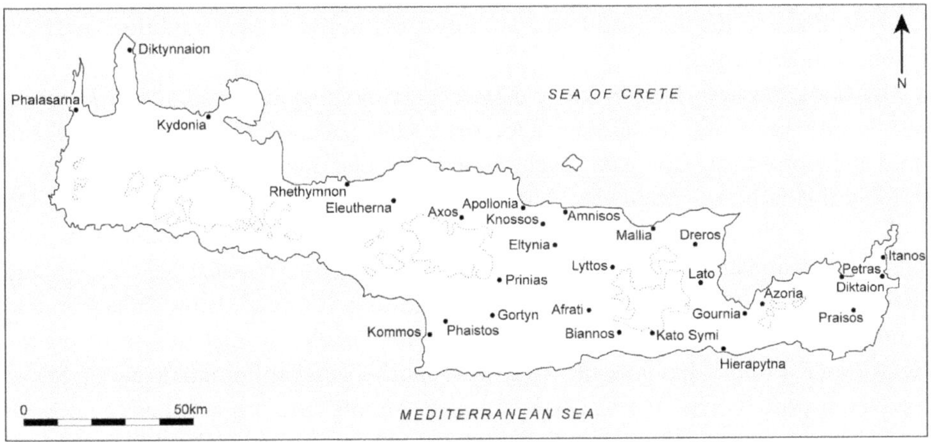

Figure 0.2 Map of Crete, showing sites mentioned in text.

The book of course touches on mythology. Knossos is far from unique in the Aegean world in that, without Greek myths, it would probably not have been the subject of serious investigation by archaeologists from the late nineteenth century onwards. But it is not a book about 'mythology'. What various archaeologists such as Minos Kalokairinos, Arthur Evans and others have revealed at Knossos is neither explained by nor explains myths about Minos, the Minotaur or the Labyrinth. Myths rather form part of the historiography of the site, to which two chapters have been devoted.

Who then is this book for? Primarily for students taking BA or BSc degrees in Archaeology, Ancient History or Classics (or equivalent) in the English-speaking world. I have taught various courses on Greek Archaeology covering all periods from the Neolithic to the Hellenistic in my time at Cardiff and have found that students in general (whether they are studying Ancient History or Archaeology, or some combination thereof) find Knossos very hard to understand. I hope, of course, that the somewhat legendary figure, the General Reader, will also find my book useful (not in the utilitarian but rather in the Reverend Awdry sense of the term), as will at least some of my professional colleagues in Classics, Ancient History and Archaeology.

I have a further confession: I am not really an expert on Knossos. My substantive contribution to an archaeological understanding of the site is modest. Nor am I the sole author. As I hope the reader will appreciate, this book arose through conversations I have either participated in (or eavesdropped on) with colleagues in Knossos, Athens, Palaikastro, Cambridge, Oxford, Cardiff and elsewhere over the course of several decades. This is not to implicate Jan Driessen, Florence Gaignerot-Driessen, Peter Callaghan, Colin Macdonald, Nicoletta Momigliano, Sandy MacGillivray, Peter Warren, Sinclair Hood, Hugh Sackett, Hector Catling, Alan Peatfield, Christine Morris, Don Evely, John Bennet, Antonis Kotsonas, Irene Lemos, Todd Whitelaw, Katerina Kopaka, Gerald Cadogan, David Wilson, Sara Paton, Eleni Hatzaki, Mieke Prent, Matthew Haysom, Rebecca Sweetman, Metaxia Tsipopoulou, Carl Knappett, Simone Todaro or Peter Tomkins in any of the opinions I may put forward. But this book would not have been written without them.

This book has been long in the making – I was first approached by Tom Harrison over twenty years ago. Publishers have since changed, and I would like to thank those at Bloomsbury (Georgina Leighton and Lily Mac Mahon) for their patience in bringing this book to completion. I would also like to thank Kirsty Harding for her work on the illustrations – which are, as ever, excellent. Todd Whitelaw has been assiduous in updating me on the progress of KULP (see abbreviations below), and I have had much useful correspondence with Antonis Kotsonas, Peter Callaghan and Conor Trainor on later periods in Knossos. Flint Dibble, through his work on the ZOOCRETE project, has provided me with much useful information about faunal deposits in post-Bronze Age Knossos. Nicoletta Momigliano has acted as the not-so-anonymous reviewer of the first draft of this book, and I have tried to incorporate many of her recommendations into my revised draft. Andrew Shapland of the Ashmolean Museum has been particularly helpful in advising on images from the Ashmolean Archive.

For permission to reproduce images I would like to thank the British Museum, the Ashmolean Museum (Oxford – in particular Ms Erica Martin and Dr Andrew Shapland), the British School at Athens (in particular the archivist, Ms Amalia Kakissis, and the Director, Professor John Bennet), Dr Georgios Papasavvas and Professor Jan Driessen (Louvain-la-Neuve). Fuller credits are given in the list of illustrations.

Finally, I would like to thank my family – my wife Christina (who shares my interest in Knossos, and with whom I have discussed many of the issues this book touches on over the years) and my daughters, Isabella and Lilian (who don't share my interest in this site and whose perspective provides a constant corrective to the archaeologically obsessed). My book therefore is dedicated to them.

A NOTE ON CHRONOLOGY FOR THE KNOSSOS SEQUENCE

Archaeological chronology is rarely straightforward. This is especially true for the chronology of Knossos, which has four successive chronological schemes based on slightly different principles. For the Neolithic we have one based on the excavation of defined strata within the tell of Knossos itself, tied into an Aegean-wide chronological scheme; for the Bronze Age we employ the term Minoan (rather than, say, Cretan Bronze Age). This Bronze Age scheme is based on a stratigraphic sequence of deposits both in the palace and the town tied in to changes in styles of painted pottery. It also has a slightly artificial 'tripartite' structure which has also been retained for the two other major regions of the Aegean Bronze Age (Cycladic and Helladic). An explanation of the overall chronology for the Aegean Bronze Age is given by Warren (Warren and Hankey 1989; Warren 2010). All the relevant terms are fully explained by contributors to the *Knossos Pottery Handbook* (Momigliano 2007b), who describe in detail the deposits on which the sequence is based. For the Iron Age (SubMinoan to Orientalizing) we employ a ceramic terminology used across the Aegean, though modified to suit the circumstances of Crete in general and Knossos in particular (Brock 1957; Coldstream 2001). For the Late Archaic through to Roman periods the terminology follows an Aegean- and even Mediterranean-wide scheme based on standard historical periodization (Whitley 2001, 60–71) – that is, the stately procession of Archaic, Classical, Hellenistic and Roman.

Radiocarbon dates have not been much used in the dating of the Knossian sequence, with the important exception of the study of the Neolithic. Readers should, however, be aware that the use of radiocarbon dating since the 1960s has created at least one major chronological controversy – the endless debate about the date of the eruption of the volcano on Thera (Santorini), which we know took place sometime within the Late Minoan IA ceramic phase. I myself agree with the revisionists on this (Bruins et al. 2008; Manning 2018; Manning et al. 2014). I prefer the higher (earlier) date in the seventeenth century BC to the 'lower' one in the sixteenth. Purely for convenience (as it does not affect my overall argument), I have none the less stuck with the standard chronology.

I have also used employed a standardized if also localized terminology for archaeological and historical periods. For the prehistoric periods down to the Late Orientalizing, these terms are usually based on the style or technique of (usually) painted pottery. These terms are usually abbreviated, with E standing for 'Early', M for 'Middle' and L for 'Late'; hence MM means 'Middle Minoan', LG means 'Late Geometric', and EO 'Early Orientalizing'. There are sometimes further subdivisions, marked by A, B or C, or even further subdivisions indicated by the numeral 1 or 2 – so LMIIIA2 means 'Late Minoan III A 2' (the second phase of Late Minoan III A). To the uninitiated, technical discussions about whether this or that deposit is MMIA or MMIB in date seem baffling – although in at least one case considered below (see Macdonald and Knappett 2007) the difference really does matter. MMIB stands for 'Middle Minoan I B', and MMIIA for 'Middle Minoan IIA', two successive phases in the ceramic chronology of the Bronze Age. For the Bronze Age, in addition to this ceramic-based periodization, there is also one based on institutional criteria. Hence the talk about 'pre-palatial', 'proto-palatial', 'neo-palatial' and 'final palatial' for most of the Bronze Age – though Dickinson (1994) prefers 'First Palace', 'Second Palace' and 'Third Palace'. Whether or not this institutional terminology is justified is a matter that will be discussed in the relevant chapters below.

For the Roman period and periods after the Roman, there is an established historical periodization. Here archaeological terminology follows the historical, the two being connected primarily through coin evidence (numismatics). The table below gives the relevant periodization with the standard abbreviations used.

Table 0.1 Chronological table – periods, terms used and abbreviations

Phase	Abbreviation	Date range (most probable)	Other terms	Events
Aceramic Neolithic (or Initial Neolithic)	IN	7000–6500/6400 BC	Stratum X	Colonization of Knossos from Anatolia (modern Turkey)
Early Neolithic (I and II)	EN I and EN II	6500–5900 BC	Strata IX–VIII	
Middle Neolithic	MN	5900–5300 BC	Strata VII–VIB	
Late Neolithic	LN	5300–4400 BC	Strata VIA–IV	
Final Neolithic	FN (I–IV)	4400–3100 BC	Strata III–I	
Early Minoan I	EMI	3100–2650 BC	Early Pre-Palatial	
Early Minoan IIA	EMIIA	2650–2450 BC	Early Pre-Palatial	Levelling of tell at end?
Early Minoan IIB	EMIIB	2450–2200 BC	Early Pre-Palatial	Levelling of tell at beginning?
Early Minoan III	EMIII	2200–2050 BC	Late Pre-Palatial	
Middle Minoan IA	MM IA	2050–1950 BC	Latest Pre-Palatial	
Middle Minoan IB	MMIB	1950–1900 BC	Old Palace (First Palace) – Protopalatial	Construction of First Palace?
Middle Minoan IIA	MMIIA	1900–1850 BC	Old Palace – Protopalatial	
Middle Minoan IIB	MMIIB	1850–1800 BC	Old Palace – Protopalatial	Earthquake at end

Table 0.1 Continued

Phase	Abbreviation	Date range (most probable)	Other terms	Events
Middle Minoan IIIA	MMIIIA	1800–1750 BC	Unclear. New Palace?	Earthquake at beginning
Middle Minoan IIIB	MMIIIB	1750–1675 BC	New Palace (Second Palace) – neopalatial	
Late Minoan IA	LMIA	1675–1580 BC	New Palace – Neopalatial	Thera eruption (1620 high chronology, 1520 low chronology)
Late Minoan IB	LMIB	1580–1490 BC	New Palace – Neopalatial	Fire damage to houses in town of Knossos
Late Minoan II	LMII	1490–1430 BC	Final Palace (Third Palace) – Final Palatial	Introduction of Greek-speakers to Crete
Late Minoan IIIA1	LMIIIA1	1430–1370 BC	Final Palace (Third Palace)	First phase of destruction of Final Palace (Chariot tablets)
Late Minoan III A 2	LMIIIA2	1370–1320 BC	Final Palace (Third Palace)	Final fire destruction of Palace at Knossos
Late Minoan IIIB	LMIIIB	1320–1200 BC	Post-palatial (at Knossos)	Final destruction of Mycenaean palaces on Greek mainland circa 1200 BC (Late Helladic IIIB)
Late Minoan IIIC	LMIIIC	1200–1050 BC	Post-palatial (latest Bronze Age)	
Subminoan	SM or SubMin	1050–970 BC	Transition to Iron Age	
Early Protogeometric	EPG	970–920 BC	Early Iron Age (EIA)	
Middle Protogeometric	MPG	920–875 BC	Early Iron Age (EIA)	
Late Protogeometric	LPG	875–840 BC	Early Iron Age (EIA)	

Protogeometric B	PGB	840–810 BC	Early Iron Age (EIA)	
Early Geometric	EG	810–790 BC	Early Iron Age (EIA)	
Mature Geometric	MG	790–745 BC	Early Iron Age (EIA)	
Late Geometric	LG	745–700 BC	Early Iron Age (EIA)	
Early Orientalizing	EO	700–670 BC		
Late Orientalizing	LO	670–630 BC (in cemeteries, some LO in other deposits later)		
Early Archaic	EA	630–525 BC		The 'Archaic Gap'
Late Archaic	LA	525–480 BC		
Early Classical		479–400 BC		
Late Classical		399–323 BC		
Early Hellenistic		323–146 BC		Sack of Lyttos 220/21, of Apollonia 171/70
Late Hellenistic		146–67 BC		Sack of Praisos 145–140 BC, conquest of Metellus 67 BC
Early Roman (Late Republic and Early Imperial)		67 BC to AD 96		Establishment of *Colonia Iulia Nobilis Cnossus* circa 27 BC by the first Roman emperor, Augustus
Middle Roman (Antonine to Severan)		AD 96–235		From the accession of Nerva to the murder of Alexander Severus

Table 0.1 Continued

Phase	Abbreviation	Date range (most probable)	Other terms	Events
Late Roman		AD 236–395		Christianity becomes state religion by 395. Empire divides into Eastern and Western parts at end. Gap in occupation?
Late Antique (Early Byzantine)		AD 395–827	Early Byzantine (Knossos now within Christian East Roman Empire)	Knossos abandoned by 650 AD?
Arab		AD 828–961		Arab conquest 828; Chandax (Candia or Heraklion) established as island's capital
Late Byzantine		AD 961–1204		Byzantine re-conquest by Nikephoras Phokas 961
Venetian		AD 1204–1649	Late Medieval to Renaissance	Venetian conquest 1204 (Fourth Crusade)
Early Ottoman		AD 1649–1821		Ottomans take Heraklion 1660; Greek Revolution (on mainland) begins 1821.
Late Ottoman		AD 1821–1898		
Modern		1898– present		Crete becomes first an International Protectorate and then part of the Greek state

ON THE SPELLING AND TRANSLITERATION OF ANCIENT GREEK NAMES

Here I have not been as consistent as some may like. This is partly because I don't think total consistency is either possible or desirable (see Whitley 2001, xxv). But it is also partly because preferred spelling depends on context. When citing Ovid in discussions of Daedalus or Icarus I use latinized conventions, but elsewhere use Daidalos. Clarification for those troubled by this can be found in the index.

ABBREVIATIONS

Abbreviations for chronological phases or periods have been given in Table 0.1 above. Below are other abbreviations, primarily bibliographic, which are used in this book. These principally relate to journals, some to publications of inscriptions or other corpora. They are generally compatible with those found in major works of reference (such as the *Oxford Classical Dictionary*) and in major journals in Classics and Classical Archaeology (such as the *American Journal of Archaeology* or the *Journal of Hellenic Studies*).

Bibliographic abbreviations

AJA
American Journal of Archaeology (Journal of the Archaeological Institute of America).

AR
Archaeological Reports (Supplement to the *Journal of Hellenic Studies* (*JHS*)), published jointly by the British School at Athens and the Society for Hellenic Studies).

Archaeologia
Archaeologia or Miscellaneous Tracts Relating to Antiquity (London, Society of Antiquaries of London).

BCH
Bulletin de Correspondance Hellénique (Journal of the École Française d'Athènes, the French School in Athens).

BCH **Suppl**
Bulletin de Correspondance Hellénique, Supplementary Volume (with number).

BSA
Annual of the British School at Athens (main publication of the British School at Athens).

BSA **Studies**
British School at Athens, Studies (with number).

BSA **Suppl**
British School at Athens, Supplementary Volume (with number).

CMS
Corpus der minoischen und mykensichen Siegel (Mainz and Berlin, 1958 onwards) – a corpus of Minoan and Mycenaean seals and sealings (seal impressions) now hosted by the University of Heidelberg.

IC
Inscriptiones Creticae (volumes I–IV, by Margerita Guarducci, Rome 1935–52) – a corpus of (almost) all Archaic to Roman inscriptions on Crete.

JHS
Journal of Hellenic Studies (Journal of the Society of Hellenic Studies).

SEG	*Supplementum Epigraphicum Graecum* (Leiden) – a supplement to *Inscriptiones Graecae* (the standard corpus of Greek inscriptions) and *Inscriptiones Creticae* – updated annually.
Suppl	Any supplementary volume to any journal (e.g. *Memnosyne, Hesperia*).

Other abbreviations (neither bibliographic nor chronological)

KMF	Crete Medical Faculty (area of excavation of the Knossos North Cemetery).
KNC	Object from the Knossos North Cemetery, published by Coldstream and Catling 1996.
KS	Knossos Survey, location of areas of investigated within the Knossos Survey area, following numbers given in Hood and Smyth 1981.
KULP	Knossos Urban Landscape Project.

CHAPTER 1
LEGENDS AND LABYRINTHS

Chapter abstract

After a brief personal introduction, this chapter looks at the place of Knossos in the Greek mythical imagination, and on its image in various Greek and Roman writers and artists. It then looks at how Knossos was viewed in the medieval world (e.g. the Labyrinth in the *Mappa Mundi*), by Venetian antiquarians, early modern and nineteenth-century travellers and scholars down to the time of the first archaeological investigations by Minos Kalokairinos. It looks briefly at the setting and topography of both ancient and modern Knossos.

1.1 Knossos: the view from the palace

The image of Knossos most people have today is one intimately connected to the Minoans. If you travel to Knossos today (or rather not today – at the time of writing, early 2021, no one is travelling to Knossos); that is, if you had travelled to Knossos in the recent past (say September 2019), you would have encountered a major structure of the Bronze Age set within a park planted with pines and cedars. If you had made the mistake of travelling in the morning – when the coaches from Heraklion arrive before eight o'clock to start their day's journey around Crete – then you would find the place crowded, noisy and almost impossible to understand. If you had instead come in the evening, you might be pleasantly surprised to find the place almost to yourself. Of course, your footsteps would be guided by the walkways now in place (for Knossos is, after the Athenian Acropolis, the most visited site in all of Greece, and its Bronze Age walls cannot bear the tread of so many tourist feet) – you would no longer be free to walk wherever you like, and you would find some parts (such as the Royal Road that leads from the Theatral Area) firmly out of bounds. On entering you would be greeted first by two bronze busts. One is of Arthur Evans, the man in British eyes most closely associated with uncovering the 'Minoan' past of Knossos. This statue has been a fixture for decades. More recently a bust of Minos Kalokairinos has been put up by the Greek authorities. Local guides, of course, are at pains to point out that Minos Kalokairinos, not Evans, was the first systematically to investigate the hill of Kephala (on which the palace stands). But if you are visiting by yourself and wander from the west court through to the central court by the south entrance, and from the central court descend the Grand Staircase, the vision of the Minoan palace you would get would be largely Evans'. It is of course a very strange kind of palace – like and yet unlike the residences of rulers we know from modern times (Buckingham palace), like and yet unlike the grand public buildings of

French and Italian towns (*palais* and *palazzi*), the work of a people ('the Minoans') now lost to history.

This vision is one, of course, reinforced by the popular books on sale at the entrance and by the choice (and order) of objects on display in the Heraklion Museum. The museum does contain some hints (notably finds from the Fortetsa cemetery) that Knossos persisted after the 'Minoans' – though you have to pay a great deal of attention to realize this. Elsewhere, signs of another (earlier or later) Knossos are hard to find. If you take the trouble to walk a little distance from the palace you will find that other Minoan buildings (the Little Palace, the Caravanserai) have been fenced off and are inaccessible; if you go a little to the south, you will find the gates of the Temple Tomb (the only tomb you are likely to see) firmly shut and locked. The palace is all and all of it is Minoan.

This impression is misleading at best (Whitley 1998; Kotsonas 2016a; 2018b) – though you have to go further afield to find signs of other periods. If you cross the Kairatos stream and go up the hill of Ilias, it is possible you might reach the cave of Mavro Spelio (black cave), which had some Geometric as well as Minoan burials; rock-cut features and the foundations of houses (largely of Bronze Age date) can still be seen on parts of this hill. Walking north up the hill you may pass the Taverna on your right and then proceed to the Villa Dionysos – the most substantial Roman monument in Knossos – which is fenced off from the public. If you walk further to the north and find paths along the Isopata ridge, you may come across the Kephala tholos tomb – also Bronze Age. If, however, you manage to make your way slightly to the west of the Isopata ridge (with difficulty, as many areas are now bounded by high wire fences), you might be able to find an area (usually locked) that contains the remains of several Roman buildings – and some Roman-built tombs. This is in the area of Teke, the former Muslim village now renamed Ambelokipi (vine-gardens). The fenced area is just to the north of the Crete Medical Faculty, built over the remains of Knossos' major North Cemetery from Early Iron Age to Roman times, and the site of the most magnificent early Christian basilica to have been built in Knossos. Nothing of this can now be seen – in 1985 some tombs (excavated by Iannis Sakellarakis) could still be glimpsed under some modern apartment blocks, but these have since completely disappeared. To gain any idea of later (post-Bronze Age) cemeteries, one has to retrace one's steps to the south, passing along a road by a modern cemetery. Here on the south-eastern slopes of the Acropolis are some Roman rock-cut tombs; if you proceed to the west over the Acropolis itself you may come to what is left of the Iron Age Fortetsa cemetery, represented by some unprepossessing depressions in the ground (the remains of collapsed chambers).

The casual visitor is highly unlikely to make such journeys. And, to speak truly, they are difficult to make unless you decide to stay in Knossos for several days. There are, of course, other rewards for wandering around the environs of Knossos – the Venetian and Egyptian (Ottoman) aqueducts are quite spectacular, even if they were designed to supply water to Heraklion (not Knossos). There are still pleasant walks to be had in early autumn, when the crocuses first start to flower. But to undertake such casual forms of exploration implies that you have a particular area or period of Knossos you wish to *research* – and for this you are likely to be staying in or around the Taverna.

1.2 Experiencing Knossos: the view from the Taverna

My first experience of Knossos was rather like this. I arrived as a prospective research student in the spring of 1982 to stay at the Taverna (or the Knossos Research Centre, as it is now called). I had absolutely no interest in 'the Minoans'. I visited the palace, of course, but was baffled by it. What fascinated me then was Knossos in the Iron Age and I was thinking about how I could best incorporate the material from the recently excavated (and, at that time, as yet unpublished) North Cemetery material into my PhD thesis (intended as a comparative study of Iron Age burials in Athens and Knossos). I was then a very junior scholar but I was warmly welcomed by the then Knossos Curator (Alexander 'Sandy' MacGillivray) and his then wife, Mary. Most people staying at the 'Taverna', however, were there to work – specifically on bodies of material from earlier excavations. These included material from the excavations of Arthur Evans and Duncan Mackenzie, such as Sandy's Middle Minoan sherds (that is, fineware pottery fragments from the Old Palace (protopalatial) period, later published as MacGillivray 1998), which were then laid out on strewing tables in the middle of Knossos' Stratigraphical Museum. At the time, these sherds were a complete mystery to me. Only later, through eavesdropping on conversations between the many Bronze Age specialists who visited the Taverna over the years, did the significance of such things become clearer.

And it was a great privilege to eavesdrop, especially at a time (the 1980s) when the food provided at the Taverna was so good (and so cheap). As a research student and subsequently holder of the School and then MacMillan-Rodewald studentships at the British School at Athens it was a great experience to listen in to Sinclair Hood and Peter Warren arguing over whether the Minoans were a peaceful or a warlike people (the iconography suggests the former, common sense the latter). Hugh Sackett's and Peter Callaghan's ruminations on the finds from the levels of the Unexplored Mansion were, at the time, of more direct interest, as were Hector Catling's thoughts on the bronzes from the tombs of the North Cemetery. My interest in 'Minoan' matters was, at the beginning of my stay, quite rudimentary – but gradually through listening in on conversations between Nicoletta Momigliano, Sandy MacGillivray, David Wilson, Colin MacDonald, Alan Peatfield, Jan Driessen and many others who came to stay I gradually learnt why distinctions between pottery phases might actually be important.

None of this was clear on my first visit, when I was mainly concerned with topography. Sandy advised me to go for a walk down the Isopata ridge (it's a nice walk, he said) which I did, as well as exploring the area of the Iron Age Fortetsa tombs (Brock 1957). Other residents were puzzled by my presence – Vronwy Hankey asked me (somewhat tartly, I thought at the time) what I was doing there (as I was clearly not working on sherds in the Stratigraphical Museum). For I was not (or at least not yet), at that time, a fully paid-up member of the Knossos club.

Whether or not you are looking at sherds 'in the Strat', the view from the Taverna is very different from that of the general visitor to the palace. For one thing, you can appreciate the depth of the deposits of post-Bronze Age material that overlies the foundations of the Little Palace, the Unexplored Mansion and the SEX (Stratigraphical Museum Extension) excavations. For another, you are more likely to encounter chance finds from the Knossos area – Corinthian columns of uncertain date, the statue of Hadrian that (until recently) stood in front of the Villa Ariadne and the *disiecta membra* of dismantled Roman buildings. More recently, when visiting the Taverna in 2011 I came across something even later and even less 'Minoan': these gravestones (Figure 1.1).

These marble slabs originally came from a cemetery in the village of Teke to the north of Knossos. They date to the eighteenth and nineteenth centuries when this village was predominantly Muslim. They are not objects that one would normally associate with Knossos – though they come from well within the area of the Knossos Survey (Hood and Smyth 1981). The slabs are inscribed in a cursive script that resembles Arabic. They are in fact written in Ottoman Turkish, a script that is now almost as strange (and inaccessible) as that of the still undeciphered scripts of Bronze Age Crete (Cretan Hieroglyphic and Linear A).

Viewing such things comes as a bit of a shock if your expectations have been framed either by notions of the 'Minoans' or by the legends that undergird this concept. They run against our ideas of what Knossos is all about, what we expect of it. For what we expect

Figure 1.1 Marble gravestones from Teke, inscribed in Ottoman Turkish, now lying outside the Stratigraphical Museum at Knossos. Photo by the author.

of it has been refracted through Western European ideas of what the place has meant. And for many centuries, 'Knossos' implied 'the Labyrinth'.

1.3 The view from Hereford: the Labyrinth in the *Mappa Mundi*

In an annex to the great gothic cathedral in Hereford (on the Marches of Wales) is one of the wonders of the medieval age. This is the *Mappa Mundi*, which dates to the late thirteenth century (the reign of Edward I of England). Several such maps exist, but this is the finest. The map shows a picture of the known world, as it was then understood by medieval monks and scholars. The world is divided into three continents (Europe to the West, Asia to the East and Africa below). At the centre of this medieval world is Jerusalem; and dividing Europe from Asia is the 'Middle Sea', the Mediterranean. Not too far from Jerusalem, in the middle of the Middle Sea lies (unmistakably) the island of Crete, marked by the sign of the Labyrinth.

Of course, the *Mappa Mundi* is not the kind of map one can readily use to find places in the real world. One cannot sail to the Uttermost East (to the top of the map) and find Paradise. Nor could one, in 1285 AD when the map was made, easily have found the Labyrinth itself, which ancient tradition locates at Knossos. Knossos in any case would have been difficult to find, as the (Orthodox) bishopric had by this date been moved to the village of Ayios Myron; and what remained of ancient Knossos, if it could be seen at all, would have been no more than a ruin. This difficulty in identifying the fabled ancient city was not because sailors from Western Christendom did not know Crete. Crete had been taken from the Byzantines by the Venetians in 1204 during the Fourth Crusade; its principal town (Candia/Heraklion, close to what we now know as ancient Knossos) was by 1285 AD a well-visited stop on the route of pilgrims, priests and knights on their journey to 'Outremer', the Holy Land. To think in this way is to mistake the purpose of the map.

It is not by accident that the Labyrinth is depicted, but not Candia (Heraklion). The map represents not a cartographically accurate but rather an idealized vision of the world. And the role of Crete in that world was summed up precisely by the Labyrinth, where, as everyone then as now knows, lived the monstrous Minotaur, offspring of Minos's wife Pasiphaë and a bull, slain by the Athenian Theseus. Both the Labyrinth and the Minotaur have a long and tangled cultural history (Kotsonas 2018a). Images of something like a maze appear in the Bronze Age (Evans 1921, 348, Figure 260), and 'the Labyrinth' later becomes the image of Knossian coins (Kotsonas 2018a, 377, Figure 7; see Figure 1.4 below).

This medieval vision also then represents a mismatch between the actual and the visionary. Knossos has always existed between these two poles. The role of Knossos in the twentieth and twenty-first centuries is in some ways no less fanciful than the depiction of the Labyrinth in the *Mappa Mundi*. This is not because, if you visit Knossos today, you will not see a genuine Bronze Age site – Arthur Evans' 'Palace of Minos'. Some of it is restored, some would say over-restored, but much of it is consists of blocks of stone and rooms placed there in the Bronze Age to form a large, complex and clearly important structure arranged around an interior court. But to call it a palace (that is, a residence of a ruler whether king or queen) and to associate it with the mythical King Minos is to make an imaginative leap that may not be fully justified by the actual evidence that we possess. To be sure, many visitors have found the site (with its narrow passages and confusing layout) to be 'labyrinthine'. And visitors too will find images of bulls – notably the (highly restored) bull fresco in low relief at the north entrance to the palace (Hood 2005, 56–8). But while there may be many frescoes of bulls, there are none of men with bull's heads (minotaurs) – though such things can be found in archaeological records of the Bronze Age.[1]

This mismatch survives in the modern folklore of the site, as recounted in the oral tradition of professional Greek guides. There is a story told at the British School at Athens, Knossos Taverna, of a time when British archaeologists under John Evans (no relation to Arthur) were excavating in the central part of the central court of the palace between 1957 and 1960 (Evans 1964). The team had dug down deep, excavating in 'Wheeler boxes' (5m x 5m trenches with 1m baulks), to reach the earliest Neolithic levels (around 7000 BC). By the time the team had reached the lowest levels (Stratum X), the trench was around 8m deep. Because Knossos is a major tourist attraction, the stream of visitors was not stopped simply because an excavation was taking place. Many of these visitors were accompanied by local guides. One of the excavators of these Neolithic trenches has a vivid memory a guide coming over, pointing down to these deep trenches and then stating (with the authority of a true expert) 'and this is where they kept the Minotaur'.

The story of the Minotaur in his Labyrinth is then the one that remains most indelibly associated with Knossos. Where and when does this story begin?

1.4 Myths and images

The story of the Minotaur is well known. Minos was the son of Europa and Zeus, who had appeared to his consort in the form of a bull. Minos became king of Crete and ruler of Knossos with the help of Poseidon, who sent the king a snow-white bull as a token of his support. In recompense, Poseidon expected Minos to offer up that same bull to him. Poseidon was to be disappointed; Minos instead chose to sacrifice one of his own bulls (as he prized Poseidon's bull so much), thinking Poseidon would either not notice or not mind. But Poseidon did notice and did mind. In revenge, he persuaded Aphrodite to cause Pasiphaë, Minos' wife and consort, to fall in love with Poseidon's bull.

By 'fall in love' I do not mean anything platonic. Pasiphaë desired to be mated with, that is penetrated by and physically joined with, Poseidon's bull, and Minos (realizing perhaps that this was a divine punishment) acquiesced to this. To fulfil her bestial desires, Pasiphaë had Daidalos, Minos' brilliant craftsman, make a contraption that mimicked the shape of a cow, and in this way Pasiphaë and Poseidon's bull were brought together in sexual intercourse. And they had a child. Their offspring was Asterios, the Minotaur, a creature normally depicted as having a man's body and a bull's head. Minos then had this monstrous offspring confined to the Labyrinth, a maze made for him by the master-craftsman Daidalos (whose name is forever associated with what is elaborate, cunning and Cretan; S. P. Morris 1992, esp. 150–94). It is here that the story intersects with that of Theseus.

Minos had had other children by Pasiphaë: Androgeus, Ariadne (Hesiod *Theogony* 948; Homer *Odyssey* 11.321–3) and Deucalion. Androgeus, the eldest son, had competed in the Panathenaic games, overseen by Aegeus, king of Athens. His success stirred the jealousy of the Pallantides (cousins if also enemies of Theseus, son of Aegeus), who murdered Androgeus. In revenge, Minos sailed to Athens and required of Aegeus that he hand over the murderers. This, Aegeus could not do, so Minos exacted another punishment. Every seven years the Athenians were to send their bravest and most beautiful to Knossos – seven youths and seven maidens. These youths and maidens were never seen again, and some said they were sacrificed to (and eaten by) the Minotaur. Theseus volunteered to go to Crete as one of the seven youths. With the help of Minos' daughter, Ariadne, he managed to enter the Labyrinth and slay the Minotaur (in some versions, cutting off its head). He then escaped with Ariadne (Homer *Odyssey* 11.321–4) and the other Athenian youths and maidens. So ended the Athenians' human tribute to the King of Crete.

The tale as told is irresistibly 'mythic'. With its bestiality and violence, the story has held great attraction to writers down the ages, particularly (or perhaps especially) in the twentieth century. There is, as far as we know, no early, complete version of this tale in Greek literature – it does not form part of an ancient epic called 'Minos' or 'Theseus'. The nearest we have to such an epic is a reference in Diogenes Laertius (writing probably in the second or third century AD) to the Cretan (and possibly Knossian) philosopher Epimenides (*c.* 600 BC), who is said to have composed 4,000 lines on 'Minos and Rhadymanthus' (Diogenes Laertius 1.112). The version of the Theseus story given above is one compiled from various sources. Though alluded to in the *Odyssey* (see above), the earliest of these we know of is in a poem by Bacchylides, probably first performed as a choral lyric in the festival of Apollo on the island of Delos. Bacchylides here tells a story of Theseus confounding Minos' sudden lust for the maiden Eriboia and alludes in passing to the seven Athenian youths and seven Athenian maidens whom Minos took as tribute.[2] Other early references include Pindar (e.g., *Paian* 4.35 (fr.38)) and references in Plutarch to plays (now lost) by Euripides.

Most the sources for the myth, however, are much later – many are Roman in date (Momigliano 2020, 25–9). Some were written the time of the Roman emperor Augustus, and some belong to the Graeco-Roman world of the second century AD. The Augustan sources comprise both Greek prose (the historian Diodorus and the geographer Strabo) and Latin poetry (chiefly Ovid). The story is later fleshed out in Plutarch's *Theseus* (15–20), where Theseus is treated as an historical figure like Solon or Pericles, and by various other Greek prose writers of the Second Sophistic in the second century AD, such as the periegete (traveller) Pausanias and the mythographer Apollodorus (or Pseudo-Apollodorus; *Bibliotheca* 3.1.1–4; *Epitome* 1.7–9; 1.12–15). In general, the Greek writers tend to 'side' with the Athenian version, where Theseus is the hero. Interestingly this is not true either of Plutarch or of Ovid, who is in many ways our most vivid source. Ovid tells it twice, neither from an 'Athenian' perspective: first in the *Heroides*, recounting the tale from the point of view of Phaidra (another daughter of Minos, but now married to Theseus); and in the *Metamorphoses* (8.152–82), a tale that segues seamlessly into the story of Daedalus and Icarus (*Metamorphoses* 8.183–235).

The story of Minos and the Minotaur has the apparent timelessness of a myth rather than of a story to which one can assign an author. How then do you date a myth? One method might be through a comparative analysis of myths and legends – as favoured by Martin West (2007). But if we look at the Theseus/Minotaur myth for themes that occur in various kinds of Indo-European poetry or song, we look in vain. Nothing like this occurs in Indian, Persian, Germanic or Celtic storytelling. This observation suggests that the 'myth of the minotaur' has a different origin, which may have little or nothing to do with Indo-Europeans. The other striking feature is the theme of the bull, which keeps on recurring (Europa and the Bull, Poseidon's bull and Pasiphaë, the Minotaur). The bull also turns up in the twelve labours of Heracles – the Cretan bull, the very same bull that impregnated Pasiphaë is one of those creatures that Heracles has to slay (Diodoros 4.13.4). Why bulls should be so associated with Crete is a bit of a mystery – the modern visitor to the island will find few if any cattle (and so no bulls), and it is difficult to imagine that the island ever had much in the way of low-lying, watery ground that cattle favour, even when oxen were needed as draught animals (Rackham and Moody 1996, 74–5). If ever such conditions existed, they must have been when the climate was very different from today.

Comparative analysis therefore seems to fail us. We have instead to turn to iconography. We should not expect that the iconographic record will match the textual. Both texts and images relate to various versions of 'myths' and tale-cycles whose expression was primarily and originally oral. We should not expect anything like a definitive version of a tale, or take it as read that versions attributed to famous figures such as Homer are those which are in any way *definitive* (Snodgrass 1998; Nagy 2020). The iconographic record, like the textual, is likely to record various, possibly incompatible versions of the same story.

There are many images of composite creatures on Bronze Age seal-stones (Simandiraki-Grimshaw 2010), an example being that to be found on the LMII-IIIA seal stone in the British Museum.[3] Some of these composite creatures appear to be minotaurs, having a man's legs and a bull's head, such as the agate example from Sellopoulo tomb I near Knossos.[4] Arthur Evans himself discovered a clay seal impression of a composite creature he initially thought was a minotaur in the early years of his excavation[5] – reproduced as Figure 1.2. But there are no large-scale (as opposed to miniature) depictions of composite creatures. When it comes to pots or frescoes, 'Minoan' iconography seems to have different concerns, and the earliest narratives from the Early Iron Age (e.g., those to be found in Teke tomb E at Teke; Sackett 1976; see Figure 6.7) seem to have nothing to do with the legend of the Minotaur, unless we assume that the depiction on the vase in Figure 2.7 represents Theseus taking leave of Ariadne (Schefold

Figure 1.2 Clay seal impression (sealing) of a 'minotaur' in the early years of Evans' excavation. After Evans 1901a, 18–19, Figures 7a, 7b and 7c. Redrawn by Kirsty Harding.

1966, 26). The earliest image we have that we can unambiguously associate with this myth was fashioned on the Greek mainland: an image thought to be that of a Minotaur appears on a seventh-century Boeotian relief amphora – but here he is shown as having the head of a man and the body of a bull (Carpenter 1991, 163; Simantoni Bournia 2013). The first instance of what comes to be the standard image of a bull's head on a man's body is to be found on a Corinthian gold band of the late seventh century (Payne 1931, 133), on a Cypriot seal (Brommer 1982, 62–3, Figure 8) and then on an early sixth-century Argive *Schildband* recovered from Olympia.[6] On all these objects, Theseus is shown killing the Minotaur, and this image first turns up on the surface of a vase on a Middle Corinthian cup (Payne 1931, 133, No. 986), datable to the early sixth century BC. Athenian versions soon appear, notably on a psykter-amphora by the black-figure vase painter Lydos.[7] These early images, of which there are quite a few (Brommer 1982, 35–64 and 77–92), follow a standard iconography: Theseus is shown slitting the Minotaur's throat, with the Minotaur on bended knee (having presumably been overcome), as in this example now in the British Museum (Figure 1.3). Sometimes (as in the vase by Lydos) there are onlookers, more often they are not. By the fifth century BC, another element has been added to this story: the Labyrinth itself. This is clearly signalled by two red-figure cups of the mid-to-late fifth century (one in London, one in Madrid), where the Labyrinth is indicated in the tondo (interior) of both cups by the use of a Greek key pattern.[8]

There are also early images of the Athenian youths and maidens, one on a seventh-century relief pithos now in Basel, another on the upper frieze of the François vase around 570 BC.[9] Other elements of the story appear only in Classical times. The first and only image of Pasiphaë cradling her monstrous son appears in the tondo of a red-figured Etruscan cup found at Vulci and dated around the early fourth century BC.[10] Later Italian versions of 'Theseus and the Minotaur', such as the mosaic to be found in Cremona, show

Figure 1.3 Theseus slays the Minotaur on a black-figure amphora by an unknown artist in the British Museum. BM GR 1920,0315.2. Courtesy British Museum.

Theseus in the very centre of the Labyrinth, slaying the Minotaur, in a pose that would not have been out of place on a black-figure Athenian vase. Iconographically at least, it is the 'Athenian' version that seems to have prevailed in the bulk of Graeco-Roman artistic representations.

But the Athenian version was not the only version. A more positive picture emerges if we turn away from the Minotaur to his stepfather, King Minos. If the standard version of the Minotaur/Theseus myth shows Minos as a stern patriarch, an unforgiving father and a cruel tyrant, there is another tradition that sees him (primarily) as a great king. Minos' first appearance in Greek literature is as the father of Ariadne, future wife of Dionysos in Hesiod's *Theogony* (948). Minos, along with other Cretan rulers, Rhadymanthus and Idomeneus, also turns up at several points in the Hesiodic *Catalogue of Women* (fr.

204.57), probably dating to the sixth century BC. In Homer's *Odyssey* (11.568–71), Odysseus recounts how he, in his journey to Hades, had seen Minos seated as one of the judges (or rulers) of the Underworld. Later, when Odysseus arrives in Ithaca, he first disguises his identity, claiming to be a Cretan, the grandson of Minos, son of Deucalion and the brother of Idomeneus (*Odyssey* 17.178–84). This passage also contains the first description of Crete: Crete of the ninety cities, the greatest being Knossos; and Crete of the five 'tongues', the Achaeans, Dorians, Pelasgians, Cydonians and 'great-hearted Eteocretans' (*Odyssey* 17.172–8). Of course, nothing in this (highly influential) passage can be taken at face value – Odysseus is lying, and, if we wish to believe that the *Odyssey* only reached its definitive form around the middle of the sixth century BC, as many scholars now do, then the author of the poem is a contemporary of Epimenides the Cretan, who famously said 'All Cretans are liars' (Diels-Kranz 1934, 32).

The role of Minos in the *Iliad* is quite different. Minos simply appears in genealogies – one recounted by his grandson, Idomeneus (*Iliad* 13.450–1), and another when Zeus is recounting his conquests (in this case of Europa) to Hera (*Il.* 17.322). Here Minos is paired with his brother Rhadymanthus. As a protagonist in the story, Idomeneus is much more prominent in the *Iliad* than Minos. He rules over Knossos, Gortys, Lyktos, Milatos, Lykastos, Phaistos and Rhytion (that is, central Crete) and, with another Cretan hero Meriones, leads the Cretan contingent to Troy (*Iliad.* 2.645–52). While both Idomeneus and Meriones are far from being the principal protagonists of the *Iliad*, they are more than minor characters is this tale. Meriones fights Aeneas in book 16 of the *Iliad*, where the main focus is on Patroklos (*Iliad* 16.603–31). Meriones is also strongly associated with the only Homeric description of an undeniably Bronze Age artefact, the boar's tusk helmet (*Iliad* 10.260–70), which he gives to Odysseus. Knossos then forms part of the background to the whole Trojan War Cycle and turns up in some unexpected places. One rather odd digression in this great tale is the description of the (circular?) dancing floor of Ariadne, which forms part of the decoration of the (second) Shield of Achilles (*Iliad* 18.590–4), made for him by Hephaistos. There is at least one credible archaeological candidate for this 'dancing floor' (Warren 1984).

Minos, however, remains indelibly associated with Knossos in the literature of the sixth century BC. In the Homeric Hymn to Delphian Apollo (Homer *Hymns* 3.393) the Cretan sailors who help to establish the cult come from 'Knossos of Minos'. Later, fifth-century historians tended to have a yet more favourable view. According to both Herodotus (1.171; 1.173; 3.122) and Thucydides (1.4), Minos was the first of the 'thalassocrats', the sea-rulers of the Aegean. By the fourth century, the Athens-based philosophers Plato and Aristotle put forward an almost wholly positive image of the great Cretan ruler. Minos was responsible for the laws of Crete that had endowed that island with its enviable stability (e.g., Aristotle *Politics* 1271b, 30–40; Ps-Plato *Minos*, 318d–321c; Plato *Laws*, 624). Minos is nonetheless a severely aniconic figure (Bažant 1992). Unlike Theseus, Ariadne or the Minotaur, he is hardly represented in vase painting or sculpture, though he sometimes appears in coins. Again, there is a curious mismatch between what our texts tell us and the images that caught the imagination of Classical Greeks and Romans.

There is also a difference of approach between various genres. The poet Ovid is, for example, just interested in the tale, and what he can do with it. He does not really care about when or where. But for Herodotus, Diodorus (e.g., 4.76–9) and even Thucydides, Minos was both an historical as well as a legendary figure, albeit one known (as Thucydides noted) entirely by repute. As historical figures, they could be placed in time. Just as Herodotus tried to date the Trojan War, so Minos could be placed earlier (about three generations) before that war. Diodorus did a more systematic job of trying to place these events in an overall chronology – both Herodotus and Diodorus produced what archaeologists would recognize as a relative chronology. Thence they tried, by a process akin to dead reckoning, to place them in some kind of absolute time.

So far we have had the story of Knossos, Minos and Ariadne as recounted largely by non-Cretans and non-Knossians – we have had Athenian, Sicilian and even Roman views. But what of the view from Knossos itself?

1.5 The view from the city

It is easy to forget, in all this, that Knossos was a functioning city – an independent *polis* – throughout Archaic, Classical and Hellenistic times (Perlman 2004, 1169–70, No. 967). It was a substantial settlement with an ancient name, a name found on one of the Linear B tablets from the palace itself and mentioned in an Egyptian stele that dates to the reign of Amenhotep III (1386–1349 BC).[11] Even after it became a Roman colony, it continued to function as a political entity until the seventh century AD. Did not Knossians themselves have a view of how their past was represented?

There is no specifically Knossian view recorded in any surviving literary text. Diogenes Laertius (1.109–15) recounts the story of the shadowy (if historical) Knossian 'philosopher' Epimenides, who is said to have written several poems in hexameters; none of these survive. The nearest thing to a Cretan view on King Minos is contained in a story that Herodotus recounts (7.170–1). The Cretans were consulting the Delphic oracle about whether they should join the Spartan–Athenian alliance against the Persians. The Pythia advised caution and reminded them of what happened the last time the Cretans went on a major expedition to foreign shores. This was an expedition to Sicily, to avenge the death of King Minos himself. The expedition, which consisted of everyone apart from the Praisians and the Polichnitai, ended in disaster (see also Diodorus 4.79). The centre of the island was deserted, and was settled by other peoples, including 'Hellenes' (i.e., Greeks). Or at least, Herodotus says, this is the story according to the people of Praisos, who lived at the extreme end of the island. This tale is the nearest thing we have to a Cretan view and was to be enormously influential in later attempts to understand Cretan ethnicity in the Bronze Age. But it does not concern Knossos as such. For a Knossian view we have to turn to iconography.

Around 470–450 BC the Knossians began to mint their own silver coins, mainly to an Aeginetan standard (Stefanakis 1999). One of the earliest (around 450 BC) is this silver stater, now in the British Museum (Figure 1.4), showing a Minotaur (bull's head,

Figure 1.4 Fifth-century coin of Knossos showing Minotaur and Labyrinth. BM GR 1895, 1002.6. Courtesy British Museum.

man's body) on the obverse and a stylized Labyrinth on the reverse. The legend on the obverse reads 'ΚΝΟΣΙ' retrograde. The image of the Labyrinth continues. On a later (*c.* 350–300 BC) silver coin (BM G.2022), there is a female head (Ariadne? Pasiphae? Europa?) on the obverse and a more conventional square Labyrinth on the reverse. Here the legend reads more clearly 'ΚΝΩΣΙΩΝ' (roughly translatable as 'of the Knossians'). All these coins were struck in Knossos. Clearly the image of both the Labyrinth and the Minotaur were not images of which Classical Knossians were in any way ashamed. The stories these images represented were rather celebrated, a source of local pride. The Labyrinth in particular (depicted both as a square or rectangle, and in a circular form) became a standard image on Knossian coins throughout the Hellenistic period and even into Roman times (when Knossos became a Roman colony) – there is even an issue with the Labyrinth on one side and the Emperor Augustus on the other (Mielczaruk 2013). These associations with the myth lasted for as long as the city itself lasted as a viable social and political unit in the ancient world.

What then does this Labyrinth – or this image of a Labyrinth – represent? It is of course possible to have a representation of something that, strictly speaking, doesn't exist – what, after all, are images of pagan gods? But it is rarer to have a representation of something that people do not believe to exist or ever to have existed. These labyrinths depicted on coins must represent something that Classical, Hellenistic and Roman Knossians believed either existed (in their time) or had existed (at some point in their past). Belief in an actual Labyrinth is confirmed by Roman writers. Vergil alludes to it (*Aeneid* 5.588–91), and the elder Pliny (*Natural History* 36.19.85) describes it at some length.

1.6 Roman to medieval

The Labyrinth and the Minotaur remained one of the most recognizable images of Graeco-Roman culture for quite some time. The graffiti of the Labyrinth that appears on a wall in Pompeii just before 79 AD perhaps represents the image at its most popular. Elsewhere the story continues to appear in Roman art. When Theseus slays the Minotaur on the face of Roman (Antonine) marble sarcophagus now in the Metropolitan Museum of Art in New York (90. 12a.b),[12] his pose and the Minotaur's recalls some of the earliest images we have. On Roman mosaic floors, sometimes the Minotaur (or his head) simply appears in the centre of a Labyrinth; more frequently, Theseus slaying the Minotaur continues to be the focus of these Labyrinth mosaics (Woodford 1992, 578). As late as the fourth century AD, a mosaic floor from the province of Rhaetia (modern Austria), now in the Kunsthistorische Museum in Vienna, shows Theseus slaying the Minotaur in the very heart of an elaborate Labyrinth.[13]

A local antiquarian tradition also seems to have flourished in Roman times. Diodorus (5.79.4) notes that the Cretans could point to the tombs (marked by an exemplary epigram in elegiac couplets) of Meriones and Idomeneus at Knossos, heroes mentioned in the *Iliad* (*Iliad* 2.645, 651; Kotsonas 2018b). In the early third century, Flavius Philostratus recounts that his protagonist (Apollonius of Tyana) visited Knossos, specifically so that his companions could gaze upon the Labyrinth that had once held the Minotaur (*Life of Apollonius* 4.34; see D'Agata 2010, 60). An even more bizarre story is the one recounted by the Roman, L. Septimius in 376 AD, who dedicated a Latin translation of a lost Greek epic by Dictys of Crete to one Q. Aradius Rufus. The Greek original from which this was translated was purported to have originated in Knossos itself, found in a tomb, written on bark in Greek but in Phoenician characters (by which is probably meant early Greek letters; see Gainsford 2012). This was said to be an eyewitness account of the Trojan War. That noted philhellene, the Emperor Nero himself (it was said), ordered that they be edited and transcribed. No one of course now believes that there was ever a Bronze Age epic of this kind – 'the work itself . . . belongs to [the] class of literary impostures' (Evans 1909, 109; see Alcock 2002, 124).[14] But it does testify to a continued Roman antiquarian interest in a distant past, and of Knossos' centrality to that lost heroic age.

But after the fourth century, with the gradual Christianization of the Eastern Empire, this antiquarian interest both in the site itself and in the overtly pagan iconography of the Minotaur and the Labyrinth begins to fade from view. Like many other Mediterranean cities, Knossos too was Christianized. At least two Christian basilicas were built there in the fifth century (see Chapter 5), and Knossos became the seat of a bishop (that is, the centre a bishopric or diocese named after the town). This did not lead immediately to a complete loss of Knossos' connection to Minos, the Minotaur and the Labyrinth – indeed the connection survived, as the *Mappa Mundi* shows. But Knossos was at a considerable disadvantage vis-à-vis other Greek cities when it came to the retention of social memory.

It is easy for us to underestimate, in the modern world, how closely memories are connected to things – to statues, or to other objects with distinct associations. Social memory is a theme that runs through Pausanias' *Guide to Greece*, much more so than 'art'.

Social memory could inhere in quite humble objects (linen corselets captured from Himera, Spartan shields captured from Pylos) – they need not be sculptures. When the first Christian emperor, Constantine, decided to decorate his new capital, he transferred a selected number of these objects with considerable social memory from famous Greek pagan sites to his 'New Rome' (Constantinople, Istanbul) and set them up in the hippodrome. At least one of these objects – the serpent column from Delphi that commemorates the victory of the Greek allies over the Persians at Plataea in 479 BC – survives today. But there was nothing that Constantine could usefully take from Knossos. The coins were too small, and the Labyrinth (if it was indeed the ruins of the palace) was simply too big.

The East Romans (Byzantines) then had nothing in their capital to remember Knossos by, apart from the stories in the Greek texts that they preserved (Momigliano 2020, 30–3). And Knossos was soon placed on the periphery of the East Roman world. In the seventh century, Crete became a border province with the Arab Muslim Caliphate to the south. More significant than this, however, is the abandonment of the site. Sometime between 650 AD and the Arab occupation of the island around 828 AD the city of Knossos was deserted. The Arab (or Spanish) invaders established a new capital for their Emirate in Chandax, medieval Candia (and ancient and modern Heraklion). When, in 961 AD, the East Romans reconquered the island under Nikephoros Phokas, they did not reoccupy Knossos, but tried to established an inland capital at Temenos (Kanli Kastelli, ancient Lykastos; Tsoungarakis 1988, 58–74, 312). By this time Knossos was too small to remain the seat of a bishop – the bishopric of Knossos was moved to the village of Ayios Myron, a fact which was to confuse some later antiquaries (D'Agata 2010, 62). After the Venetian conquest of 1204, the capital of Crete remained (as it effectively does today) the coastal city of Candia (Heraklion). Knossos itself had become a ruin and may even have lost its name. Whether this weakened or strengthened its association with the various myths and legends of Minos, the Minotaur and the Labyrinth in the eyes of either Venetians or Byzantines can be debated. There is in any case no more sign of such legends playing a role in local (Cretan) identity.

But the myth itself survived. In the East it did so through various learned commentaries on Greek texts, particularly in the *Suda* (Chaniotis 1992a; 1992b). The story of 'Dictys Cretensis' moreover remained unaccountably popular in the Byzantine world. There were, however, no monuments to Minos or the Minotaur – and there is no evidence (so far as I know) that the Theseus/Minotaur iconography survived in any of the trophies from Classical Antiquity that Constantine set up in the Hippodrome of Constantinople.

But if Knossos gradually slipped away from the consciousness of Greek-speaking Eastern Romans, the Fourth Crusade (and subsequent Venetian occupation of the island) brought Knossos and the Labyrinth back for a time into the imagination of Western Christendom. Whether or not there was anything for the Western traveller to see in Knossos in 1285 AD cannot now be determined. It is likely that any memory of the place (and of the Minotaur and the Labyrinth) survived, not in the form of any ruin or in any particular image, but simply in the stories that Ovid had retold and which were preserved in turn in the libraries of monasteries (and later universities) in Western Europe. The role of the universities was to increase in later medieval times, and especially during the Renaissance. This in turn was to change how Knossos was both seen and remembered.

1.7 The Renaissance and after

Both antiquarianism and Classical scholarship are products of the Renaissance. By 1650, Classical scholars had produced scholarly versions of ancient Greek texts that had been lost to the West in medieval times. In this way Greek as well as Latin versions of the stories of Minos, Theseus, the Minotaur and the Trojan War became better known to scholars and travellers. In Italy, early antiquarian investigations of Rome and other ancient sites eventually developed into something we would recognize as Classical Archaeology. And there were some Venetian antiquaries who, before 1649, took a lively interest in the island of Crete and its remains. The Florentine monk Cristoforo Buondelmonti, had visited the island in the fifteenth century. In 1586 the Venetian scholar Onorio Belli undertook a much more systematic assessment of the surviving ruins of Knossos, noting amongst other things a large Early Christian basilica and the remains of a (probably Roman) theatre or circus (Kopaka 2004, 501–3; Spratt 1865, 60). These early antiquaries have one major achievement to their credit: they correctly identified ancient Knossos (and the Labyrinth) with the hamlet of Makryteicho (D'Agata 2010, 63–5).

Political necessity, however, cut short any archaeological interest the Venetians may have had in Knossos. When they were constructing the great fortifications of Candia (Heraklion) against the Ottoman Turk, the largely Roman ruins of Knossos provided a useful source of building material. These walls managed to fend off the first Ottoman assault in 1649. Eventually, however, the Ottomans took the city in 1660; in doing so they gained control of the whole island.

The Ottomans retained a firm grip on Crete throughout the later seventeenth and eighteenth century. They had no particular regard for pagan legends and no particular interest in Knossos. Candia served as their provincial capital, as it had the Venetians before them. The number and frequency of visits to Crete from Western Europe declined, and the nationality of such visitors changed. Increasingly the French, Dutch and then English (after 1707, British) displaced the Italians (Loy 2019), as French, Dutch and British shipping gradually replaced that of the Italian city states of Venice and Genoa. The few Westerners with antiquarian interests (such as Richard Pococke and Claude Etienne Savary) had little impact on how the island was viewed in Western Europe (Farnoux 1996). They came to see Knossos and the Labyrinth, and local guides made sure that their expectations were met. They did, nonetheless, maintain the tradition of antiquarian enquiry linked to topography that had already been established by the Venetians.

In Western Europe the intellectual landscape changed radically during the eighteenth century. J. J. Winckelmann had turned traditional antiquarianism (or at least that branch of antiquarianism focused principally on Classical Antiquity) into a more systematic discipline, Classical Archaeology, which German scholars (such as Gerhard) were to refine in the early years of the nineteenth century (Whitley 2001, 20–5). One effect of the rise of Classical Archaeology and of a more systematic 'science of antiquity' (*Alterthumswissenschaft*) was that the iconographic record of the Theseus legend (evident both in coins and in the vases that came to be excavated in Italy) became better known. Similarly, German philologists began the systematic application of source criticisms to ancient texts, including those relating to Minos, Knossos and the Minotaur. The variety of ancient stories began to become apparent, and Ovid's versions came to be seen as unusual. For Crete, all the ancient sources and legends were collected together by the German scholar Karl Hoeck in the spirit of the new 'science of antiquity'. Hoeck published the results of his research in three volumes. The first dealt with topography, and inevitably discussed where the Labyrinth might be found (Hoeck 1823, 56–68); the second volume was subtitled *Das Minoische Kretas* and is the first recorded use of the term 'Minoan', later popularized by Arthur Evans (Hoeck 1828a); the third volume covered 'Dorian' Crete (Hoeck 1828b). Hoeck, at this time, did not mean by Minoan what Evans and other came to mean by the term – namely that Bronze Age Crete was rather special and distinct. The term here just means 'pertaining to Minos' (Karadimas and Momigliano 2004; Momigliano 2020, 33–6). He did, however, treat Minos as an historical person, and the period of his rule one that preceded 'Dorian' Crete. This is the first appearance of this tripartite structure of Cretan history (pre-Minoan, Minoan and Dorian) which persists to this day. Though Hoeck's history is critical, he did not yet, like many later nineteenth-century historians (Grote in particular) divide antiquity between a time of history (beginning in 776 BC), where we had reliable sources, and a time of legend, where we could not really distinguish between story and fact (Grote 1849a; 1849b). As in Plutarch, the one segues seamlessly into the other.

1.8 Crete: the contested island

By 1830, Crete was in an awkward position vis-à-vis other provinces of the Ottoman Empire. Though the Greek Christians of the Peloponnese had eventually been successful in their bid for independence, the Cretan uprising of 1821 had been ruthlessly suppressed (Mazower 2021). While Orthodox, Greek-speaking Christians were always in the majority, many Cretans (both Greek and Turkish speakers) remained faithful Muslims throughout the nineteenth century, forming at times as much as one-third of the island's population. The Christians, however, increasingly looked to Greece and to the philhellenic Great Powers (Britain, France and Russia) through whose intervention Greek independence from Ottoman Turkey had been secured. The cultural politics of Muslim–Christian relations were to be crucial to the story of the excavation of Knossos.

The number of Western visitors to Crete increased in the early nineteenth century. In 1834, Robert Pashley, a fellow of Trinity College Cambridge, arrived on the island. Pashley travelled across the whole of Crete, making observations on its antiquities, its customs, its language, its history and its current state. In one sense, Pashley was simply continuing the antiquarian tradition of Belli, Pococke and Savary. But in other respects he represents a new departure, and forms a link to modern scholarship. Pashley was perhaps one of the most perceptive of all the nineteenth-century traveller-scholars. His style is sharp and his observations acute. He was fully aware of the condition of the island (Pashley 1837, xx–xxiii). He was also fully cognisant of the disparity between Knossos' past glory and present wretched state:

> The natural caverns and excavated sepulchres seen in the immediate neighbourhood of the site of Cnossos call to mind the well-known ancient legend respecting the Cretan labyrinth, the locality of which is uniformly assigned to this city. It was described as a building, erected by the celebrated artist Daedalus and designed as a dwelling for the Minotaur. There is however no sufficient reason for believing that the Cretan labyrinth ever had a more real existence than its fabled occupant. Much as is said, in the Homeric poems, of Daedalus, Minos, Ariadne, and other Cretan worthies, it is in vain that we search, to find in them any evidence of the material existence of this monument. Hesiod and Herodotus are equally silent on the subject of the imaginary edifice, and the latter author, who compares the Egyptian labyrinth with the temples of Ephesus and Samos, could hardly have avoided mentioning the labyrinth of Crete, if there had been any such a building in existence. It is scarcely necessary to add, that I found no traces of any such monument in the neighbourhood of Mákro-Teíkho.
>
> *Pashley 1837, 208*

Pashley then went on to describe the coins (many of which he then collected; Pashley 1837, 208): 'The forms of the mythical labyrinth, as exhibited on the coins of Cnossos, are naturally varied, since they represent not a material edifice, but a work of the imagination.'

Pashley was critical of the work of earlier travellers, whom he suspected (with some justice) of simply wanting their expectations to be fulfilled. He suggested that the name Knossos or Gnossu had not really survived to his day – most of the inhabitants refer to the hamlet which now occupied the remains of the ancient city as 'Makry Teicho' – big wall. Insofar as the name survived, it was only as a bishopric, which had in his day been incorporated into a larger Orthodox archdiocese. Pashley grimly recorded that the population of the area around Knossos had been almost halved since the uprising of 1821. Knossos or Makryteicho was then too small even to rate an estimate. He noted only that there were a total of twenty-six Christian and ninety-four Muslim families in 'ten or twelve other hamlets' in the district of Temenos in 1834 (Pashley 1837b, 318). The largest town, Megalo Kastro (Heraklion or Candia), had a population of 12,000. In the end, Pashley bade farewell to:

> … this capital of ancient Crete, which, even after the Roman conquest, remained for some time a considerable city, but, under the Venetian and Turkish rule, has dwindled down into this miserable hamlet, and the few shapeless heaps of masonry, which alone recal [sic] to the remembrance of the passing traveller its ancient and bygone splendour.
>
> *Pashley 1837a, 209*

This contrast between present wretchedness and bygone splendour is a persistent trope of early nineteenth-century travel literature (Whitley 2001, 44–7; cf Hamilakis 2007). Interest in the inherent romanticism of ruins anticipates in some ways an archaeological sensibility, if not archaeological practice. Pashley too is influenced by German scholarship in his historical scepticism. In some ways he anticipates Grote in his incredulity towards the legends of Minos and the Labyrinth, while accepting that material evidence supports the notion that Knossos must have been a considerable city in Greek and Roman times.

Pashley certainly stimulated greater interest in ancient Crete. He had a worthy British successor in Captain T. A. B. Spratt, who travelled around the island in the early 1860s and who explicitly set out to remedy the 'deficiencies' of Pashley (who had never got round to providing a detailed description of the eastern part of the island). Like Pashley, Spratt too visited Knossos (Spratt 1865, 58–76) and, like Pashley, was struck by the disparity between past glory and present poverty. Minos and the Labyrinth were, again, sought but not found. Spratt did, however, comment on the fame of Cretan artists in antiquity and managed to secure for himself a marble 'Venus' (Spratt 1865, 72–3). This sculpture, undoubtedly a work of Roman date, made his journey worthwhile. There now could be no doubt at least that 'Makro Teicho' was the site of Greek and Roman Knossos.

So far, the history of the exploration of Knossos was one of foreign travellers trying to relate the ruins they saw with the legends they knew from ancient texts. The relative wealth and political power of the Western European powers (particularly France and Britain) and the weakness of the Ottoman state throughout the nineteenth century made this appear a natural development. But neither the Ottoman authorities nor the local Cretans saw it quite that way. One of the consequences of Great Power rivalry of the nineteenth century was the competitive acquisition of Classical antiquities, particularly sculptures, to grace the great museums of London, Paris and Berlin. The Ottoman Empire still saw itself as a Great Power and so as the equal of other Great Powers (Britain, France, Prussia/Germany, Austria-Hungary, Russia and increasingly Italy and the United States). In 1869 the Ottomans founded their own Imperial Museum in Istanbul. Once this museum became firmly established (after 1872), its explicit mission was to collect all notable antiquities within the empire and gather them together in the imperial capital – Istanbul.

1.9 The first excavations: Minos Kalokairinos and his peers

Up until this time, antiquities meant largely Greek and Roman objects and buildings from known (that is, historical) periods. But within the boundaries of the Ottoman Empire, Heinrich Schliemann had in 1871 demonstrated that significant antiquities could date before Classical times. His excavations at Troy (the mound of Hissarlik) revealed a pre-Classical, prehistoric Aegean civilization. Subsequent investigations (with Dörpfeld) of Orchomenos (1875) Mycenae (1876) and Tiryns (1882–3) in the Greek mainland demonstrated that this civilization had both elaborate tombs and splendid palaces, whose interiors were decorated with frescoes (Fitton 1995, 48–103; Momigliano 2020, 37–49). All these sites were associated with Greek legends; Grote's 'time of legend' (1849a; 1849b) came to have a material basis; Greek legend might then contain a grain of historical truth. And, if this was true of Agamemnon's Mycenae and Priam's Troy, might it not also be true of King Minos' Knossos?

Why then not excavate Knossos? This question immediately raised another: who was to excavate and where would the finds end up? The Ottoman authorities were not pleased that Schliemann had neglected to give most of his finds from Troy to the museum in Istanbul. The educated Greek Orthodox Christians of Heraklion and other major towns on the island feared exactly that – that any finds from Knossos would go to form part of an Imperial Collection in the Ottoman capital. The location of art and artefacts from a major Cretan prehistoric civilization in a museum in Istanbul would be an outward and visible sign of the island's subjugation to Ottoman rule; it would fly in the face of any aspiration to join with Greece.

But, for a time at least, the interest that Schliemann had inspired in Aegean prehistory outweighed such political scruples. A local merchant from Heraklion named Minos Kalokairinos (1843–1907) had already shown some interest in the antiquities of Greek and Roman Knossos (Kotsonas 2016b), recording such things as the so-called 'Tomb of Caiaphas' (probably of Roman date) before its demolition by Ottoman soldiers. In 1878 he began some small-scale excavations at the hill of Kephala above the hamlet of Makry Teicho. Excavations revealed large walls and some other finds which were clearly older than Classical Antiquity. Kalokairinos appears then to have reached a part of what later came to be known as the west magazines. Finds included fineware pottery, chiefly drinking wares, of clearly 'Mycenaean' shapes belonging to the so-called 'Palace Style' of LMII and LMIIIA (Kopaka 1993); and some large storage vessels (pithoi). Publication of these discoveries by French and German scholars in established journals (Hassoullier 1880; Fabricius 1886) brought Bronze Age Knossos to the attention of the international scholarly community. Some of these finds, Minos Kalokairinos kept for himself; others, clearly prehistoric, such as this pithos (now in the British Museum; Figure 1.5), he sold to foreign museums partly to defray the costs of excavation. He had clearly found a major Bronze Age site (Kopaka 1993) – a Cretan answer to the Homeric glories of Mycenae and Tiryns uncovered by Schliemann. Minos Kalokairinos was not able to continue, because he did not have the means to buy the land from its Muslim owners nor the funds to support several seasons of large-scale excavation. He had, however, demonstrated, beyond any reasonable doubt, that a prehistoric civilization had once existed on Crete. A new term for this new civilization ('Minoan') began to come into use (Karadimas and Momigliano 2004).

Kalokairinos is in many ways a liminal figure – lying somewhere between antiquarianism and the self-consciously 'scientific' endeavours of the twentieth century. For in his time it was still quite common to come to Knossos in search of the Labyrinth. Kalokairinos thought he had found the site of this legendary structure either in the cave of Agia Irene or the caverns of Spilia (see Kotsonas 2018a, 387–9), both near Knossos. He

Figure 1.5 Late Bronze Age pithos from Knossos, from the excavations of Minos Kalokairinos, now in the British Museum. BM GR 1884, 0807.1. Courtesy British Museum.

later went on to make other explorations of the Knossos area, whose significance for our understanding of Greek and Roman Knossos has only recently been appreciated (Kotsonas 2016b). Kalokairinos' discoveries quickened foreign interest in the island. This interest had in part been stimulated by other finds on Crete, notably Federico Halbherr's discovery of the Gortyn Law Code in 1884. Halbherr's excavations in 1885 at those most distinctively Cretan of sites, the Idaean and Psychro caves, began to reveal the richness and antiquity of ancient Crete in both the Bronze and Iron Ages. In the same year, Halbherr excavated and explored Knossos itself (Morgan 2009). He recovered a fragment of an Archaic law code (*IC* I.8.2 = Gagarin and Perlman 2016, 472–3, K2) from the house of Konstantinos Koukourakis in the village of Makryteichos. He also explored an area just west of the Civil Basilica before it too was dismantled and its members used as building material by Ottoman troops. From the Roman Civil Basilica itself he excavated parts of a third-century BC legal text (*IC* I.8.5 and 5bis). But he did not have a powerful backer who could help him pursue these investigations any further.

There were other factors at work. The 1870s and 1880s were the period of Great Power rivalry in Greek Archaeology. The Great Powers scrambled not only for colonies in Africa but for great archaeological sites in Greece. Though the French had been in possession of their own *École Française* in Athens since 1846, the establishment of a German Institute (in 1872), then an American (in 1884) and then a British School (1886) in Athens increased both the number of foreign scholars coming to Greek lands looking for new discoveries and the sense of cultural, ostensibly philhellenic, rivalry between these Great Powers: all wanted to make some great archaeological, as yet unexpected, discovery on the soil of Greece. The German investigations of Olympia had also shown what very large, well-funded, systematic excavations could achieve; in the 1880s it was German archaeological and scholarly expertise that set the standard for others to follow. Knossos was clearly in need of a foreign patron. Who was it to be?

The site had no lack of suitors. Inspired by Kalokairinos' finds, the British consul in Khania had written in 1879 to the British Museum suggesting that the museum sponsor excavations (Hood 1987). In 1880 and 1881, the American William Stillman made a visit and attempted to obtain rights to excavate on behalf of the newly formed Archaeological Institute of America, but his efforts came to naught. Schliemann himself visited in 1886, as did his more scientific collaborator, Wilhelm Dörpfeld. Schliemann wanted to excavate what was (by this time) clearly an important Bronze Age site, but first he had to buy the land. He was frustrated, partly by the complexities of the Ottoman land law and the problem of multiple ownership. But he also failed to obtain the wholehearted support of local Cretan antiquaries and the Christian population, who feared that any finds would not stay in Crete but would be taken to Constantinople.

Local Cretan antiquaries were to play a key role in this game of who was to woo and win Knossos. Local Christians had set up a Society for the Promotion of Learning in the 1880s, and two of its members, Josef Hazzidakis (1848–1936) and Stefanos Xanthoudides (1861–1928) were central in creating a distinctive Cretan archaeology. Other foreign suitors came to share Schliemann's frustration. In 1891 the Director of the French School, Th. Homolle, sent his colleague André Joubin to negotiate purchase of the site with a view to excavation. But again these efforts led nowhere. The local Christians in particular did not appreciate Joubin's work in cataloguing the marble sculpture held in the museum in Constantinople. The French had shown themselves insufficiently partisan in the cause of Cretan freedom.

What then was needed was an archaeologist, scholar and philhellene who had considerable knowledge of Balkan politics and Balkan intrigues, the means to fund large-scale excavations, and the patience to deal with local (largely Muslim) landowners. Such a person was to make his appearance in 1894. But before we come to the man who, after Minos, is most strongly associated with modern-day Knossos, it is worth pausing to describe what the site would have looked like in the late nineteenth century. The topography of Knossos plays an important role in our story and hence requires some attention.

1.10 The topography of Knossos

Knossos, when compared to Athens with its Acropolis or with Delphi, set against the limestone cliffs of Mount Parnassus, has little drama in its setting. To be sure, seen from the north, that is from a ferry arriving in the port of Heraklion at dawn, it can seem suitably picturesque – being framed by the cone of Mount Jouktas. This in some ways is an illusion; for Knossos is not defined by its hills but by a stream, the Kairatos, which runs below the hill of Kephala and (until the demands for water to supply the growing city of Heraklion became too great) used to flow year-round.

The supply of water seems to have been a perennial concern for the people, first of Knossos and then Heraklion. The countryside around Knossos bears witness to this (see Figure 1.6). Let us begin at the Egyptian (i.e. Ottoman) aqueduct about 1km to the south of the present village. Starting from this aqueduct, we proceed north along the current road and ancient route to the west of the Kairatos. Here, above the road to your left rises the hill of Gypsades, whose low summit is referred to as Upper Gypsades, the flatter slope running down toward the palace. This hill, as its name suggests, is the source for the gypsum which adorned much of the ancient palace, and on it have been found both Bronze Age houses, an Archaic to Hellenstic sanctuary (to Demeter) and Bronze Age to Iron Age tombs. To your right and to the east of the stream rises the hill of Ailias, a much higher, harder limestone hill, which still retains the prickly vegetation characteristic of the island. After a while you reach the site of the Temple Tomb (see below, Chapters 2 and 5) and then the hill of Kephala (Κεφάλα του Τσελεμπή), the site of the palace, appears framed by cypress trees. To reach the present village, however, you veer slightly to the left, past the 'Caravanserai' to where the Kairatos is joined by another stream, the Vlychia (also sometimes spelt Vlikhia). From here the road takes you to the present village, with its bus stop and restaurant, which in the late nineteenth century was nothing more than a collection of houses called Bougada Metochi (the hamlet of Bougada). To your right is now the site of the palace (which is not just the palace but includes a large part of the ancient town). For much of the settlement's history, this was the very centre of the city of Knossos. Proceeding a little further and passing the path of the 'Royal Road', there is a modern road to the right (and east) that takes you to the heart of the modern village with its modern church, the hamlet (Metochi) of Makry Teichos ('big wall').

Returning to the village, just before the Royal Road another modern road (very steep) to the left and west leads you behind Bougada Metochi along the borders of the 'Evans estate', defined by a modern wall. If you continue this way you will reach the so-called Acropolis, a hill formed of neogene marl, which (if you have any expectations that it might resemble the Acropolis of Athens) is bound to disappoint. The western edge of this hill defined the western boundary of the city in ancient times. From the peak of the hill, to the west, you can see the village of Fortetsa (Fortezza), the site of an Ottoman fort used in the siege of Heraklion (1649–60). In the valley between the Acropolis and the village of Fortetsa is an Iron Age cemetery ('Fortetsa), of which more below.

Let us go back to the car park just outside the palace. If you continue north on the road to Heraklion, on your left you pass by a large wall and fence. Behind this fence

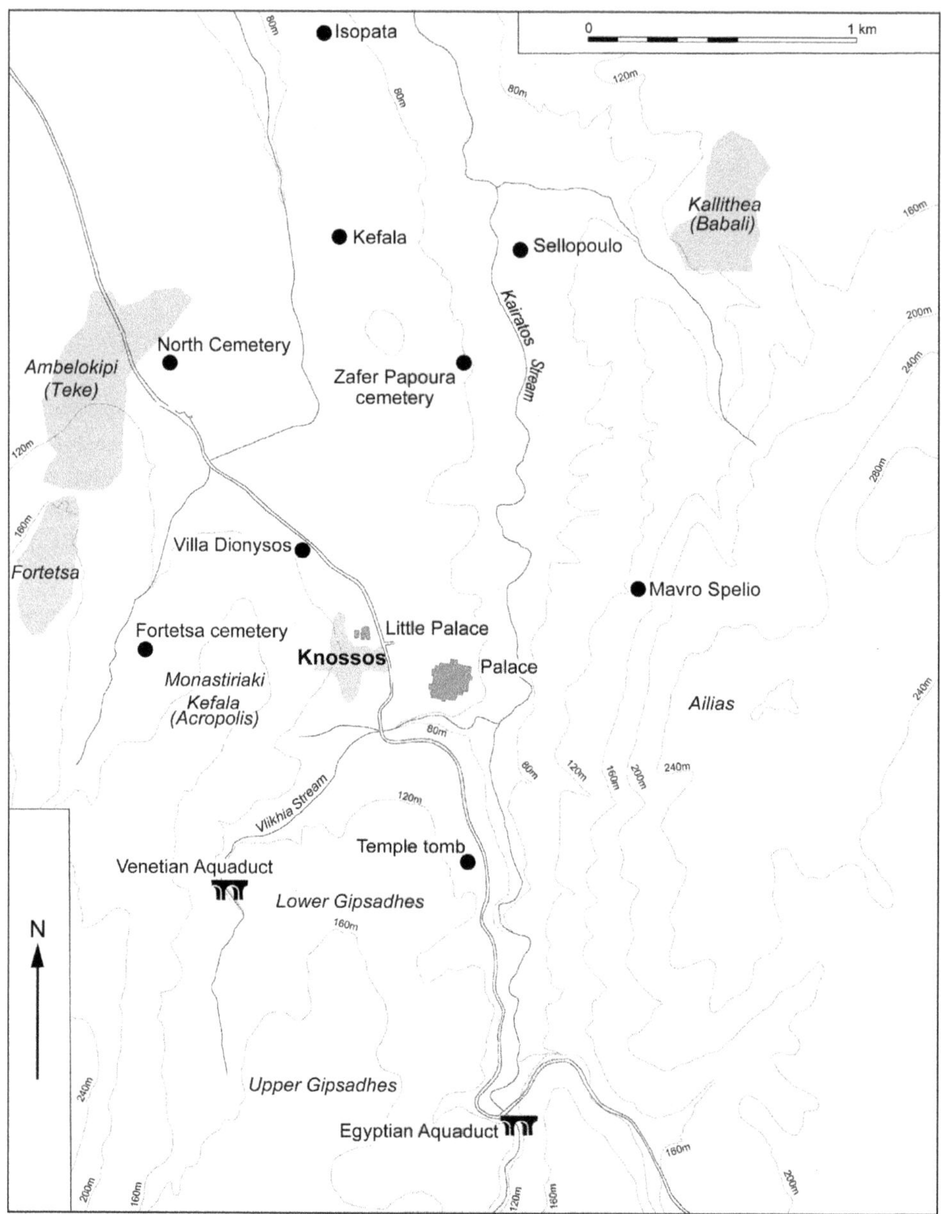

Figure 1.6 Map of the Knossos area, showing local toponyms. Redrawn by Kirsty Harding.

(opposite the Royal Road) is the so-called Little Palace, and further behind it the 'Unexplored Mansion' (now thoroughly explored) and the Stratigraphical Museum. This is where much of the work and study of Knossos takes place today. Next to the museum, to the north, is the Villa Ariadne, from which a driveway leads down again to the main road, past the British School at Athens' taverna. Joining the road again, the Evans' estate is here marked by a row of Aleppo pines. About 100m further on, you reach the Villa Dionysos to your left, and to the right on the other side were some Roman remains noted by Halbherr (see above). Continuing along the road, you reach first the hospital (the Venizeleion), where the road veers to the left. Here is the modern village of Ambelokipi, until recently known as Teke, a Turkish word that testifies to the presence here in the 1890s of a community of Sufis and whirling dervishes. The original 'Teke' is now a museum. To the right above you is the Medical Faculty of the University of Crete, a modern construction built over the largest Early Iron Age cemetery on the island. In general, tombs of all dates from the Early Iron Age until the Early Christian period have been found in and around this village, now clearly a suburb of Heraklion. To the left of Teke is the village of Fortetsa (or Fortezza, so named after an Italian word for little fortress). In between this village and the Acropolis hill of Knossos to its east was the site of an important Early Iron Age cemetery (named after the village; see above).

To find the tombs of the Bronze Age we have to retrace our steps. Overlooking Knossos to the east is the limestone hill of Ailias (Elias), and to reach this, one has to go back to Makry Teicho and ford the stream of Kairatos (dry in summer, but sometimes in spring you still have to wet your feet). Bronze Age tombs are to be found dug into the eastern face, the most spectacular being at the 'black cave' of Mavro Spelio. Other Bronze and Iron Age tombs are to be found to the north, and again here we have to retrace our steps. We return to the main Heraklion–Knossos road to just before the Venizeleion hospital. Here a road turns off to the right, down the hill. Taking this road, and then turning northward leads you along the ridge of the Kephala (another one, distinct from the hill on which the palace lies). To your left is the great cemetery area of Zafer Papoura, and along the ridge itself some Late Bronze Age and Iron Age tombs (some excavated by Hogarth). Eventually you reach the site of Isopata, where once stood the 'Royal Tomb'. This point, at the edge of the ridge, provides the best view, over the sea first to the island of Dia and (on a clear day) to the faint outline of the volcanic island of Thera, the southernmost of the Cyclades.

Walking this landscape is a very different experience today than it was in (say) 1890. For one thing, there are now many more people, and Knossos is being encroached upon from the north by the growing city of Heraklion. For another, the landscape is much less open – there are many more fences and many more trees (Rackham and Moody 1996, 118). Some species, such as eucalyptus which is such a prominent feature of both urban and suburban areas in Crete, were then unknown on the island. The toponyms, which were never completely consistent, have changed much since the late nineteenth century (Vasilakis 2004). But the main differences are ethnic and political. For, in 1890, the island was still Ottoman, and many of its inhabitants still Muslim. It was into this world that, in 1894, a middle-aged Englishman with a Welsh surname made his first dramatic entrance.

CHAPTER 2
INVENTING THE MINOANS: ARTHUR EVANS AND AFTER

Chapter abstract

This chapter describes the history of archaeological investigation at Knossos from 1900 (when Evans first broke ground) until the turn of the millennium. The central figure in all this is of course Evans, and much space will be devoted to a close analysis of how and why the term 'Minoan' came to be so widely used, and to Evans', Ventris' and others' attempts to decipher and interpret Hieroglyphic, Linear A and Linear B. The chapter will discuss post-war work in Knossos up to 2000, including accounts of the investigation into the Neolithic, Iron Age, Classical and Roman periods (e.g., Payne at Fortetsa, the Villa Dionysus).

2.1 Arthur Evans and Crete

In the English-speaking world, Knossos is forever associated with Sir Arthur Evans. Through his excavations at the 'Palace of Minos', Evans revealed the lost civilization of the Minoans to the modern world. Evans' interpretations (and reconstructions) certainly retain a strong hold over popular views of the 'Minoans' – books that contain the word 'Minoan' or 'Minoans' in the title continue to sell (and generally to sell well). But in key respects this view is both inaccurate and unfair.

First, it is unfair to Knossos itself, which had existed both before the Minoan period and persisted long after it. It is unfair to the modern Cretan view of this, the principal archaeological site of the island – for Cretans, it is Minos Kalokairinos who is justly famed for first revealing this Bronze Age palace to the world. It is unfair to our contemporary understanding of Bronze Age Crete, which is the result of the labour of scholars of many nationalities (Greek, Italian, French, German, American as well as British) over the course of the twentieth and into the twenty-first century. And, perhaps most surprisingly of all, it is unfair to Evans himself.

Arthur Evans (1851–1941) was, from an early age, steeped in archaeology (MacGillivray 2000, 11–66). His father, Sir John Evans (1823–1908) had been instrumental in 1859 in establishing that humankind had been on this earth for many hundreds of thousands (and not a few thousand) years. Like many of his generation, Evans' education had a Classical flavour – though Classics was not the degree he took at Oxford, his *alma mater*. His education and upbringing coincided with the formation of archaeology as a distinct discipline with claims to scientific status. At this stage, however, there was no profession of archaeology as such; the term could embrace a variety of interests we might classify as anthropology or folklore (Alcock et al. 2001).

Arthur Evans, as a young scholar, also took a broad view of what 'archaeology' might entail. His youthful experiences included spending time in a Norwegian cave (Bradley 2000, 3–5, 18–19), and in so doing, attempting to understand how the shamans of the Saami (the indigenous peoples of northern Norway) might have felt the underworld in microcosm. This experience may underlie his interpretation of 'pillar' cults and pillar crypts in ancient Crete (Evans 1901b, 200–4). His interests embraced both the coinage of Classical Sicily and Roman silverware and coins found in southern Scotland (Traprain Law in East Lothian). He made pioneering contributions to the study of the ancient Celts through his study of the 'Aylesford–Swarling' cremation burials of the later Iron Age of southern Britain (Evans 1890). As a young man, he travelled across the Balkans on foot. In these travels, and in his later role as a correspondent for the *Manchester Guardian*, his interests in local culture and politics overlapped with his study of the Roman milestones on the *Via Egnatia*.

Evans' most important work, before coming to Crete, was as Keeper of the Ashmolean Museum in Oxford (MacGillivray 2000, 67–108). Here, from 1884 onwards, he built up the archaeological collections, showing an interest not only in the Mediterranean lands but also in British and European prehistory. He was a firm advocate of the unity of archaeology as a science – there should be no separate 'Classical' archaeology, as archaeology was the study of the whole of the human past through its material remains. It was through his work on the Ashmolean collections, and his correspondence with others in the museum world, that he first became aware of the potential significance of Crete. German scholars had proposed that the origins of the civilization that Schliemann had revealed at Mycenae and Tiryns should be sought on that island (Evans 1894, 273–4). Evans' interest was also piqued by a four-sided agate prism, at first thought to be from Sparta but later found to be from Crete (Figure 2.1).[1] Seal-stones inscribed not only with images but with something that looked like writing had been acquired by German and British museums. These had been studied by Adolf Furtwängler, who engaged in producing a vast catalogue of all known ancient gems. Furtwängler exchanged notes with Evans and their investigations revealed that the provenance of many of these seals with a previously unknown ancient script could be traced to Crete.[2] Hitherto, the works of Schliemann and Dörpfeld, while they had found both splendid tombs and equally splendid palaces decorated with elaborate frescoes, had not found much to indicate that this Aegean Bronze Age civilization was literate.

Evans proposed that the symbols to be found on these Cretan seal-stones were part of a pictographic script which 'is itself of independent growth and, though perhaps modified by Egyptian influences, is not a mere copy of Egyptian forms' (Evans 1894, 371). The search for more such inscribed gems prompted Evans' first visit to Crete in 1894. Though he did begin to investigate the possibility of further excavation at Knossos, his search for inscribed gems led him to explore the island as a whole, returning on several occasions to the 'Eteocretan' territory of eastern Crete, where legend suggested a remnant of Crete's original (i.e., pre-Greek) population had survived into historical times (MacGillivray 2000, 109–68). The expedition of 1894 was the first of six undertaken every year until 1899 (Brown and Bennet 2001); by 1894, Evans had sufficient new information to publish his first systematic account of ancient Cretan seals and scripts (Evans 1894). On several occasions he was accompanied by other scholars, notably (in 1895) his protégé J. L.

Myres, who had made notes on finds from the excavations of Minos Kalokairinos (Kopaka 1993). These expeditions were certainly successful in recovering many more gems engraved with possible hieroglyphs (Figure 2.1), most of which found their way into the Ashmolean's collections. These finds provided evidence to support Evans' idea that Crete was the home of at least one ancient Bronze Age script. Evans' interests were not at this stage confined to the Bronze Age – archaic terracotta plaques and pithoi (storage jars) are amongst the many ancient Cretan objects that found their way back to Oxford (Boardman 1961; Brown and Bennet 2001).

Evans' deepening knowledge of the archaeology of the island convinced him that Knossos was the key to Crete's ancient secrets. Negotiations to buy the land had been underway since 1894, but was only due to the help of other foreign scholars, as well has his own determination and private wealth, that Evans was finally able to buy the land that was later to become the Knossos estate: the hill of Kephala itself (where Kalokairinos had dug) as well as a plot further to the north and west (where the Villa Ariadne, Knossos taverna and Stratigraphical Museum now stand; Panagiotaki 2004). By 1898 the political situation had changed in his favour. Insurrections by the Christian population from 1896 onwards had prompted attempts at repression by the Ottoman authorities – attempts which, though brutal, were largely ineffective (Beaton 2019, 177–83). The powers (Britain, France, Italy and Russia) intervened, and from 1898 Crete became an international protectorate under the regency of Prince George (heir to the Greek throne). Many Muslim landowners now realized that they faced a grim future if they remained in Crete. The two 'Moslem Beys of an exceptionally intractable disposition' (Evans 1909, 17) were now willing to sell; and Evans was both able and more than willing to buy.

Figure 2.1 Engraved gem with possible hieroglyph from Crete, now in the Ashmolean Museum (acquired by Evans). This is Ashmolean 1889.998 (*CMS* VI, 1, No. 104 = Hughes Brock and Boardman 2009a, 242–3, No. 104); see Evans 1894, 294, Figure 32; 1909, 8–10. Redrawn by Kirsty Harding.

2.2 The palace revealed 1900–10

Though Evans was an excellent all-round archaeologist – his knowledge of finds and his eye for iconographic detail was probably unrivalled – his skills as an excavator were limited. He realized he needed the services of someone who had greater experience in the investigation of stratigraphically complex, multi-period sites in the Aegean. Such experience was to be found in the person of Duncan Mackenzie, who had (with R. M. Dawkins) undertaken the difficult task of investigating the Bronze Age settlement at Phylakopi on Melos. The pairing of a 'cautious, canny Highlander' (Momigliano 1999), a man of modest means and humble background (whose first language was Scots Gaelic) who had taken the trouble to acquire a proper PhD in philology and archaeology at the University of Vienna, and the wealthy and privileged 'amateur' Englishman may have seemed unpropitious. But it was to be a successful partnership. Mackenzie supervised the day-to-day excavation, oversaw the local workmen and took detailed notes of the contexts of the objects being found; Evans studied the finds and maintained overall direction of the project.

Excavation on the hill of *Kephala tou Tselembi* (Κεφάλα του Τσελεμπή) began on 23 March 1900. Preliminary results were published in the *Annual of the British School at Athens* between 1900 and 1905 (MacGillivray 2000, 169–241). Work initially concentrated on the western part of the hill and moved east and south in later seasons. The first excavation season did not disappoint: spectacular finds came to light less than 30cm from the surface. That the hill of Kephala had been the site of a Bronze Age palace was confirmed by the discovery of a 'throne room' (Figure 2.2) (Evans 1900, 35–45), steatite vases with figures in relief and fragments of frescoes. More large storage jars (pithoi), similar to those found by Minos Kalokairinos, were found in the west magazines, which lay behind a gypsum façade facing a west court. These pithoi were larger than contemporary mainland examples, and the several magazines in which they were found were more extensive. More surprising was the discovery of written documents, some in a Linear and others in a 'Hieroglyphic' script (Evans 1900, 25, 59–63). The next two seasons in 1901 and 1902 revealed the extent of the palace structure, arranged (unlike mainland examples in Tiryns and Mycenae) around a large open central court (roughly 50m by 25m). Confirmation that this palace had some connection with the legends of Minos and the Minotaur was provided by clay seal impressions (Evans 1901a, 18–19).

Excavation of the slopes of the eastern side of the hill was a more difficult operation, as this 'domestic quarter' had several surviving storeys, some large halls (Hall of the Colonnade, Hall of the Double Axes), light wells and a monumental staircase (Evans 1901a, 102–17; 1902, 39–87, Figures 30–32; 1904; 1905; Brown 1983). Here excavation had to follow consolidation (and so partial restoration) of the existing structures.

Perhaps the most striking feature was the length of occupation of the mound itself. It was realized almost immediately (Evans 1901c) that the succession of palace complexes overlay much older strata, which seemed to go back to the Stone Age. These strata were composed of the debris from earlier houses, which Evans speculated were made of wattle and daub. Knossos was thus the first Neolithic tell site known in Greece outside of Thessaly.

Figure 2.2 Photo of early excavation of the throne room (Ashmolean). Image courtesy of the Ashmolean Museum, Oxford. GB 1648 AJE/3/1/12/26/1.

The earliest reports of the excavation had recorded a Mycenaean palace. The implication of this term is that the structure at Knossos was similar in both function and design to the palaces revealed at Tiryns by Schliemann and Dörpfeld and at Mycenae by Tsountas. But it soon became apparent that the structure (the latest palace) was only the last in a series of courtyard complexes whose dark-ground pottery (initially dubbed 'Kamares' after a cave in Crete where examples of these pots had been found) bore little relation to known mainland Mycenaean pottery types (Mackenzie 1903; 1906). Quite apart from its size (at over 1ha in extent, this was overall about four times larger than the megaron structures found at Mycenae and Tiryns), this large structure had other features which were quite un-Mycenaean. The whole complex was arranged around a central court much larger than anything found in these 'Mycenaean' palaces. The irregular, gypsum-built western façade of the palace faced an outside court (a west court) – another feature not paralleled on the mainland. Immediately inside the building were magazines devoted to storage in large vessels (called pithoi, singular pithos; see Figure 1.5). Pithoi in these west magazines were both more numerous and much larger than those to be found in other known Mycenaean palaces – and even larger vessels of this type were to be found in rooms on the north-eastern corner of this structure (Figure 2.3).

No mainland parallels moreover could be found for the semi-subterranean rooms with a central pillar dubbed 'pillar crypts' (Evans 1901b) nor for the lustral basins (so-called even though they were not built to retain water), such as the one found near the throne room.

Figure 2.3 The west magazines as found. Image courtesy of the Ashmolean Museum, Oxford. GB 1648 AJE/3/1/4/25/1.

The religious iconography too seemed to be different from anything encountered in historical Greek polytheism. An impression of a signet ring (Evans 1901a, 28–30, Figure 9) seemed to show that female deities were more important than male. What we would now call 'depositional practices' were also different. Nothing from either the Bronze Age or the Archaic period on the mainland at all resembled the curious assemblage of faience figurines, tablets and other curiosities in the so-called Temple Repositories in the central part of the palace sanctuary (Evans 1903, 35–94). Two faience female figures with breasts bared, elaborate dresses and even more elaborate headgear had no obvious parallels in later Greek art (Figure 2.4). They seemed to hint at religious practices that could not be interpreted in the light of what we knew of later Greek polytheism. The use of the phrase 'Temple Repositories' for these finds moreover hinted that the purpose of the structure Evans was excavating remained a puzzle – for how could it both be palace (residence of a ruler) and temple (the centre of a cult)? Though Evans' first attempt at interpretation for the 'tree and pillar cult' (Evans 1901b) did retain the term 'Mycenaean', his preference for ethnographic analogy over standard philological method underscores how unusual these practices were. By 1903, Evans and Mackenzie had abandoned the term Mycenaean and substituted Minoan in its place, thus emphasizing Crete's and Knossos' distinction from the mainland Bronze Age (Momigliano 2020, 49–59).

Evans did not invent the term Minoan (Karadimas and Momigliano 2004) but he did popularize it, and by 1909 (the time of the publication of *Scripta Minoa*) it had become

Figure 2.4 Finds from the 'Temple Repositories' at Knossos, including the two faience snake goddesses. Image courtesy of the Ashmolean Museum, Oxford. AN _ C_ 1490-a.

generally accepted. Evans' justification for the term was that, because it was in origin *dynastic* (referring to a mythical king), it would not have the misleading ethnic connotations of the names of known historical groups (such as Achaeans, Pelasgians or Eteocretans; Hom. *Odyssey* 17.172–8). It was intended to denote a cultural difference, not an ethnic one. In using the term, however, Evans did leave the door open to the idea that 'Minos' was an historical figure – and a king. This idea underpins his interpretation of the structure as a palace – the residence of a ruler and perhaps a dynasty.

Most exciting of all perhaps was confirmation of Evans' suspicion that this Bronze Age civilization had been literate. Though some stirrup jars (large transport vessels) with signs had turned up on the mainland in sites such as Menidi in Attica, the excavation at Knossos revealed many more. Clay tablets, roundels and bars were uncovered in three ancient scripts which Evans arranged in an evolutionary sequence: Hieroglyphic, Linear A and Linear B. Evans inferred that the Linear scripts must be related to a known Iron Age script from Cyprus, which (being a form of Greek) had already been deciphered (Evans 1909). Evans recognized that these scripts were syllabaries, using a set of signs for vowel/consonant combinations (syllables). In fact, they were mixed scripts, using both signs for syllables and 'pictographic' signs for things (such as chariots or sheep). Evans could not fail to notice that some of these pictograms had signs indicating numbers beside them. These documents also hinted at a distinct system of weights and measures, which Evans tried to reconstruct. Did these tablets then serve an administrative purpose?

Figure 2.5 The Linear B Pp series as found, a nest of tablets (photo from Evans 1909, 45, Figure 21). Reimaged by Kirsty Harding.

But if they were, both they and the palace they were housed in came to a violent end. Some of the Linear B tablets had been found in what appear to be groups and seem to have fallen from an upper floor (Figure 2.5). They appear to have been burnt in a conflagration that brought the palace to an abrupt end at some point in the Late Bronze Age. Did Minoan civilization then go down in flames?

2.3 Museums, finds and fakes

Archaeological excavation on this scale generates large numbers of finds. It also immediately raises the question of where they are to be stored (if they need to be studied), or where they should be displayed (if they are of any aesthetic interest). For finds that simply needed to be studied for understanding the sequence and nature of deposits, Evans and Mackenzie early on established a local 'Stratigraphical Museum'. But this clearly would not do for the gemstones, ivories, decorated steatite vases, frescoes, bronzes, gold rings and faience figurines – to say nothing of the finer examples of painted pottery, such as those in the Palace Style. Art, after all, requires a museum.

Since 1883 a 'Syllogos of Candia' had been established for archaeological objects found on the island. But the scale of discoveries from both Knossos and Phaistos underscored the inadequacy of this small museum. Between 1904 and 1912, Joseph Hazzidakis and Stephanos Xanthoudides established a proper museum to ensure that finds from Crete would, in general, stay in Crete and that the beauties of Minoan civilization could be properly displayed. This was, in a sense, to be a kind of Cretan 'national museum', and their inspiration seems to have been other well-established national museums – not only the National Museum in Athens but also the paradigmatic National Archaeological Museum in Copenhagen.

This does not quite mean that everything excavated in Knossos stayed in Crete. In this era it was quite common for excavators based in museums to be allowed to keep a proportion of the finds for that museum – an arrangement known as *partage*. So, outside of Heraklion, a significant proportion of finds excavated by British archaeologists in Crete (and particularly from Knossos) in this period are to be found in Oxford (Galanakis 2013; Hughes, Brock and Boardman 2009a; 2009b), where Evans remained Keeper of the Ashmolean until 1909. Nor was this traffic in finds entirely one way. The ideal behind *partage* was one of exchange and was undertaken in an international spirit of research into prehistory in general; for example, the Heraklion Museum also acquired a small collection of prehistoric objects from Scandinavia.

Objects once excavated had to be first conserved and then (in some cases) restored. The need for this was particularly pressing in the case of the frescoes. Evans employed the Gilliérons (*père et fils*) for this purpose (Brown 1983). Their restorations in some ways reflect the expectations of the time – not simply in naming one female figure *La Parisienne* but also in the colours they used. Deep Pompeian reds give a very dark and heavy feel to many of these original (if highly restored) frescoes, and in the copies that soon began to proliferate.

The distinctive iconography and high quality of workmanship of the objects selected for display was, of course, central to Evans' developing notions of Minoan civilization. That civilization clearly had its own distinctive style and iconography. The female figures, such as the 'snake goddesses' from the Temple Repositories, hinted at a religious and political order that was (as we might put it now) much more gynocentric (women-centred) than that of the Homeric world. Evans began to interpret the female figures as representing a major female deity, a Mother Goddess with a younger male consort (as there seemed to be no images of middle-aged or older men). Other objects that seemed to support this hypothesis were soon to come to light.

Museums not directly connected to the excavations at Knossos now wanted to get a piece of this newly discovered art. In the early years of the twentieth century, American museums, such as the Metropolitan Museum of Art in New York and the Boston Museum of Fine Arts, were flush with the riches of the Gilded Age. In 1914 the Boston Museum of Fine Arts acquired a gold and ivory statue of a female goddess (Boston 14.863). Some years later, just after the publication of volume III of the Palace of Minos (Evans 1930), with its extended discussion of sport in the palatial Bronze Age of Crete, another chryselephantine statue of the 'Lady of the Sports' was acquired by the Toronto Museum (Evans 1935a, 28–34). Both small statues, whose provenance was something of a mystery, nonetheless exactly fitted the expectations captured in the phrase 'Minoan art'. Indeed, both had been explicitly manufactured with these expectations in mind. Nowadays we would call them fakes. Insofar as they both purport to be prehistoric objects when in fact they are both modern, this characterization is fair. But in another sense, since both art and the Minoans are entirely modern concepts, both represent perfect specimens of 'Minoan Art' as the term would be understood in the early twentieth century (Lapatin 2006).

In any case, by the early 1920s, demand for Minoan Art from museums and private collectors had outstripped supply. At least one workshop, specializing in 'distressed ivory', was set up in Heraklion to meet these expectations, and tomb robbers (*archaiokapeloi*) had organized themselves to strip the Tombs of the Mesara of their engraved gems. Both the systematic faking and the systematic theft continue to this day.

2.4 Knossos: town, cemeteries and Minoan civilization 1900–14

As soon as Evans started excavating the palace itself, Hogarth (1900) had begun to look at the substantial town around the palace. He soon discovered at least two substantial structures on the Gypsades hill, which seem to have both 'Kamares' and 'Mycenaean' pottery. Hogarth also began to investigate the cemeteries, finding Roman cemeteries to the west and north-west of the site, and abundant evidence of an extensive Roman town. Not to be outdone, after the major phase of excavation of the palace was over, Evans excavated the largest of these Bronze Age cemeteries, that of Zapher Papoura, considerably to the north of the palace area. Excavation here revealed a range of collective burials from the Late Bronze Age. Three forms of tomb architecture were revealed: the pit cave (where several small chambers are grouped around a central pit); the shaft grave (with deliberate overtones of Mycenae); and chamber tombs (tombs with a central chamber, a narrow entrance and a long *dromos*) for which there were good mainland parallels. Many of the later burials (e.g., grave 36, the 'chieftain's grave'; Evans 1905b, 441–9) were extended inhumations with weapons.

These burials did not really answer one of Evans' burning questions. If Knossos was ruled by a royal dynasty (based on a palace), where were the tombs of the kings? One possible answer was 'the Royal Tomb of Isopata', further to the north of Zapher Papoura (Evans 1905b, 526–62; 1935b, 771–6), which, Evans speculated, might have been the tomb of Idomeneus mentioned by Diodorus (5.79.4; Evans 1905b, 561; see now Kotsonas 2018b). Another candidate for a royal tomb was the 'Tomb of the Double Axes' (Evans 1914, 33–59).

Evans' excavations before 1910 had also extended further west into the town. In 1905, workmen had, starting from the Theatral Area, followed the Royal Road westward, downward and into the side of the hill. Here, excavation began to resemble mining. Workmen encountered later 'Geometrical' finds and Roman-era structures, which were not investigated with any great care. Excavation ended when they reached another large 'Villa', so large (with a façade 85m long) it was dubbed the 'Little Palace' (Evans 1905a, 2–3; 1914, 59–94; 1928b, 515–24). Like the palace itself, this 'Little Palace' had a number of features which were difficult to explain in domestic terms – that is, if the structure were simply a house or residence. It had ashlar masonry and columns. It had underground structures, 'lustral shrines' and 'pillar crypts', which hinted at some kind of religious function. Analogies with what was known from Egypt, the Near East or later periods in Greece seemed to be inadequate to explain what this structure was for.

Evans' discoveries stimulated widespread interest in the civilization of the Cretan Bronze Age. Other British archaeologists had investigated the Kamares Cave on the south face of Mount Ida, the Bronze Age towns of Zakro and Palaikastro in the far east of Crete, and sites on the Lasithi plateau (including the 'Dictaean Cave' at Psychro). The Italians under the direction of Federico Halbherr had already (before 1900) begun investigation of a very similar structure at Phaistos, soon too interpreted as a palace. But we can glimpse here the beginnings of a debate about the significance of these finds. Mackenzie had published a series of papers which placed the palace at Knossos within a wider, Aegean frame (bringing to bear his experience of working at Phylakopi on Melos). The thrust of Evans' scholarship was to make Bronze Age Crete become 'Minoan' Crete. This view has much to recommend it. The prevalence of female images over male and the complete absence of scenes of warfare (if not quite of hunting) in Cretan iconography mark a sharp break with the mainland. Crete seemed much less 'Homeric' than either Tiryns or Mycenae. Crete in the Bronze Age was somehow *sui generis*.

Evans had now partially settled in Knossos, in the middle of his estate. Between 1906 and 1907 he built a fine villa for himself (the aptly named Villa Ariadne) equipped with the latest modern conveniences (including tennis courts) on the low rise above the palace, where he stayed for much of the year. This villa was decorated in a suitably grand style, with a (headless) statue of the Roman emperor Hadrian set up next to the entrance. Evans began improvements, building walls and planting Aleppo pines. He graciously allowed Mackenzie to stay there to oversee matters when he was back in England.

By this time the initial exuberance of discovery had waned a little. There had always been factions within both the British School at Athens and the Hellenic Society in London who had argued that the School ought to concentrate on more traditional subjects – that is, on Classical archaeology proper rather than prehistory. In the years before 1914 the main energies of the School were directed towards Laconia. Just as other schools had focused their efforts on Olympia, Delphi, Athens and Corinth, so the British School needed a major Classical site, and what could be better than Sparta? In 1912, in his presidential address to the Hellenic Society, Evans had to put up what amounted to a defence for the study of Aegean prehistory – we must study the roots in order fully to appreciate the fruits of Hellenic civilization (Evans 1912). This again raised the question of how 'Hellenic' Cretan Bronze Age civilization actually was. If it was truly *sui generis* (that is, essentially different from later Greek civilization), then how could 'Minoan' Crete provide the roots of Hellenic civilization? Was Bronze Age Crete truly Hellenic, or somehow pre-Hellenic (that is, pre-Greek)?

Liberal belief in progress had helped to foster research in Bronze Age Crete in the years before 1914. Evans had co-operated with great figures such as Federico Halbherr, and Greek scholars such as Joseph Hazzidakis and Stephanos Xanthoudides. A spirit of international co-operation among European nations and European scholars had vastly accelerated the progress of research, still in large part conducted in the spirit of German *Altertumswissenschaft* (the scientific study of antiquity). War, appearing like a thunderstorm out of a clear blue sky, was to change all this.

2.5 A decade of wars 1912–22

The year 1912 marked the beginning of a decade of war for Greece. This decade was to bring both victory and defeat. It began with victory over the Ottoman Empire in the first Balkan War, after which Greece was enlarged and Crete became legally and permanently part of Greece. It ended in 1922 with defeat at the hands of the new Republic of Turkey. This defeat in turn led to a major displacement of people – the so-called exchange of populations between 'Turks' (that is all Muslims, apart from those in Thrace) in Greece, and 'Greeks' (that is all Orthodox Christians, apart from those in Constantinople) in Turkey.

At first these wars merely dented the progress of international research into Minoan Crete. Crete was far from any front line. In 1915, Hazzidakis began to excavate a third Bronze Age Palace at Mallia (later to become the responsibility of the French School). A. J. B. Wace, as director of the British School, and George Karo, as director of the German, expressed their desire to maintain cordial and scholarly relations between their respective schools as late as Christmas 1914, when hostilities in France had been underway for several months (Clogg 2009, 165). Evans, too, tried to resist the demonization of German and Austrian scholars (MacGillivray 2000, 261–2). But as Greece was gradually dragged to the Allied side, archaeologists too were co-opted by the war. D. G. Hogarth became an intelligence officer (based in Cairo), and J. L. Myres performed wonders in the Royal Navy.

After 1918, relations between scholars from Allied countries and those from the former Central Powers were soured. Worse still was the fate of the refugees. The Greek–Turkish war spelled the end of Muslim Crete, though Muslims had been leaving the island since 1898. After 1923, most (but not all; see below) 'Turks' were expelled, to be replaced in many cases by Christian (but not necessarily Greek-speaking) refugees from Asia Minor. This was not welcome to Evans or Mackenzie, who had been scrupulous in employing both Christians and Muslims as workmen (and, if anything, regarded the Muslims as more trustworthy).

2.6 After the war: the Palace of Minos

Excavation in and around Knossos was slow to resume after the war. The main efforts of the British School at Athens, under Wace's directorship, were concentrated on that other great Bronze Age site, Mycenae. Parallel investigations of Knossos and Mycenae were to raise questions of the relationship between these two major Bronze Age seats of power, and between Minoan and Mycenaean civilization (MacGillivray 2000, 272–3). Evans and Mackenzie did not return to Knossos until 1922. Here, Mackenzie concentrated on studying and cataloguing what had already been excavated and identifying important assemblages for later study (Momigliano 1999, 123–32).

Evans' priorities were different. Though he did begin another excavation (the 'House of the Frescoes') in 1923 and explored the so-called 'Caravanserai' in 1924 (Evans 1928a, 106), it was the publication of the palace that became his main concern. Before 1910 (Evans 1906) he had already begun to develop his famous tripartite chronological scheme (Early, Middle and Late Minoan, subdivided into I, II and III). Building on this and on *Scripta Minoa* (Evans 1909), he began to write up his findings in a series of synthetic volumes, which began to appear from 1921 onwards (MacGillivray 2000, 270–2). The title – *The Palace of Minos at Knossos* – suggests that these were site reports, a genre that had already become established in Greek archaeology after the German excavations at Olympia. *The Palace of Minos*, however, is far from being a catalogue of finds arranged by period and type (as the Olympia reports had been). Its aim was not only to synthesize but also to compare. It is anything *but* a straightforward site report. The clue is in the subtitle: *A Comparative Account of the Successive Stages of the Early Cretan Civilization as Illustrated by the Discoveries at Knossos*. Its first volume begins chronologically by looking at the earliest occupation of the Kefala hill, a hill which had been, for many millennia during the Neolithic era, a tell site – a settlement built up by a process of continuous rebuilding over the detritus of previous layers of occupation. This type of settlement had many good parallels (and antecedents) in the ancient Near East. For many years the tell of Knossos was the only Neolithic site known on Crete (Evans 1921, 32–55). Over, or rather around, this tell were layers of Early Bronze Age (Early Minoan) occupation.

This strictly chronological order was not maintained in later volumes (Evans 1928a; 1928b; 1930; 1935a; 1935b). The *Palace of Minos* turns both in on itself and out towards the rest of Bronze Age Crete, prehistoric Europe and ancient Egypt. Some have compared its spiralling structure to Proust (it is certainly long enough). It is full of iconographic and functional parallels, taken from Malta, Villanovan Italy, Old Kingdom Egypt and even Britain. It is also informed by ethnography, drawing examples from as far afield as Somaliland. One of its obsessions was prehistoric religion, and the possibility that both cult and politics in the Bronze Age must have had a primarily female focus. And it was influential, promoting the idea that Minoan Crete was the first European civilization, one that bridged the divide between the ancient civilizations of the Near East and Egypt on the one hand and the barbarian societies of European prehistory on the other (Momigliano 2020, 94–103). This idea informs other works of synthesis that began to appear at this time – most strikingly so in Gordon Childe's *The Most Ancient East* (Childe 1929) and *The Dawn of European Civilisation* (Childe 1925). They also informed that great comparative study of civilizations, Arnold Toynbee's *A Study of History*, whose first volumes began to appear in the early 1930s (Sherratt 2006).

When major excavation did resume in the late 1920s it was not led by either Evans or Mackenzie. Evans had in any case handed over – gifted – the Knossos estate (and thus the rights to excavate on it) to the British School at Athens in 1924 (MacGillivray 2000, 280–1). He continued to reside there and to direct operations at a distance; for a brief time, Mackenzie served as curator (and so was accountable to the School rather than to Evans himself). Neither Evans nor Mackenzie, however, were directly involved in all major excavations in the broader area of Knossos. Forsdyke (of the British Museum) explored the cemetery of Mavro Spelio (Forsdyke 1927), which revealed multiple tombs of types not paralleled at Zapher Papoura.

Evans' last hurrah came with the excavation to the south of the palace. This was stimulated by the discovery of the mysterious 'Ring of Minos', a large gold ring with a very distinctive iconography (Evans 1935b, 947–56). Evans suspected something truly 'royal' must lurk near where this ring had been discovered, and his efforts were rewarded by uncovering (in 1931) the 'Temple Tomb' (Evans 1935b, 957–87, 991–1018). At last he had found a sepulchre worthy of King Minos himself.

This excavation was the first undertaken without Mackenzie. By 1929, Evans was an old man, and Mackenzie not much younger. Mackenzie, the first Knossos curator, had by 1929 (in the view of both Evans and the Managing Committee of the British School) become unemployable, having been badly affected by the death of the Muslim foreman, Ali Agha or Ali Baritakis, in 1927. The circumstances of Mackenzie's departure from Knossos have remained a matter of controversy (Momigliano 1999, 132–42; Grundon 2007, 110–13). He died in Italy soon after leaving Knossos for the last time. Knossos was now to witness its first 'changing of the guard'.

2.7 The new brooms: Pendlebury, Payne and the women of Knossos

Before 1922 the excavation of Knossos had been a male-only affair. It had also been almost entirely focused on the Bronze Age – on prehistory. To be sure, Hogarth had come across some Geometric tombs in 1900 (Hogarth 1900, 82–5; Coldstream 2002), and Evans had noted 'Geometrical' finds in the layers he dug through to get to the palace itself. That the ashlar walls of the Little palace were used as foundations for Roman houses was not, however, of very much interest to him. In 1929 and 1930, one Dorothy Hartley, a student both of Girton College Cambridge and of the School, turned up at the Villa Ariadne and expressed an interest in publishing these 'Geometrical' finds from around the palace (Hartley 1931). At little earlier (1928), another young scholar, Humfry Payne, had gathered together Evans' 1909 excavations of 'Geometrical' tombs from around Knossos, and conducted some excavations of his own (Payne 1928), excavations which brought to light Knossos' distinctive 'Orientalizing' style of the seventh century BC

(Figure 2.7). Soon Payne was to become the School's youngest director. Between 1933 and 1935, Payne and Alan Blakeway conducted the excavation of the Fortetsa Cemetery to the west of the Acropolis hill. The finds here yielded a continuous series of tomb deposits of the Early Iron Age (from around 1100 to 600 BC).

These excavations and reappraisals formed part of the general reorientation of interest towards the Archaic period that took place in the 1930s. This new focus was particularly noticeable in the fieldwork conducted by the British School at Athens. Payne's excavations, first at Eleutherna in Crete, at Knossos and then at Perachora near Corinth, revolutionized our understanding of this period. Blakeway's work placed Iron Age Knossos in a pan-Mediterranean perspective, connecting it to wider processes such as trade and colonization (that is, the establishment of Greek communities outside of the Aegean).

Figure 2.6 Orientalizing style funerary pithos from Payne's excavations. After Payne 1928, Plate XII.

More important for the study of the Bronze Age was the appearance of another ambitious young scholar, John Pendlebury, who first arrived at Knossos with his young wife Hilda in 1928. Pendlebury was to have a varied career, juggling his various Cretan interests with excavation at the major New Kingdom site of Tell-El-Amarna in Egypt. In 1929 he was appointed Knossos curator to succeed Mackenzie. He set up house not in the grandeur of the Villa Ariadne but in an old taverna (soon to become 'The Taverna'), closer to the main road to Archanes. His job as curator was to look after the estate, manage excavations and publicize the site to potential tourists (who would pay to see the palace).

But to whom was he accountable? The School's director, or to Evans himself? The then School director, Humfry Payne, also had a young wife (Dilys Powell, later film critic for *The Observer*). But Evans was still around, still engaged in excavations around Knossos (such as the Theatral Area and the Kouloures in the west court) and he still expected Pendlebury to act as his new Mackenzie.

Pendlebury was soon put to work. With his wife Hilda (also an archaeologist) he undertook the excavation of some Middle Minoan houses below the west court (Pendlebury and Pendlebury 1930). By 1931, Pendlebury was also in effective charge of the excavations of the Temple Tomb. His job as Knossos curator involved not only maintaining the estate and supervising the excavations but also making the estate pay. Evans had by this time gone to considerable trouble and expense to reconstruct much of the site and its frescoes, and these restorations had gone far beyond straightforward consolidation of existing walls. They represented an interpretation in themselves. Some have seen these restorations as being a touch 'art deco' in style. Evans felt strongly, however, that a ruin was simply not intelligible to visitors – restoration was a necessity. Moreover, the site had to be promoted for tourism, monies from which would help support the activities of the British School. To this end, Pendlebury put together a guide to the site. Written in 1932, this is nothing like the *Palace of Minos*. It is a succinct summary of the architectural and stratigraphic phases of the palace and of its dependencies.

> The Palace of Knossos is not an artistic unity. As a Greek Temple reveals the spirit of the people caught at a particular moment, so the Palace, like a Gothic cathedral or the temples of Karnak or Luxor, reveals the history and progress of its builders. Older structures are adapted to a new plan; old foundations, once built over, lie in what at first seems a confusing labyrinth ...
>
> *Pendlebury 1954, 26*

Pendlebury, however, did not here take issue with the general tenor of Evans' interpretation in *the Palace of Minos* – that the building was a palace and that it represented a lost civilization uniquely attuned to the lands of Crete. Others were not so positive. The palace continued to confound some visitors. Evelyn Waugh, visiting the site in 1929 while on a cruise around the Mediterranean, was not impressed by what he saw. He noted:

. . . something fearful and malignant in the cramped galleries and stunted alleys, these colonnades of inverted, conical pillars, these rooms that are mere blind passages at the end of sunless staircases; this squat little throne, set on a landing where the paths of the palace intersect; it is not the seat of a lawgiver nor a divan for the recreation of a soldier; here an aging despot might crouch and have borne to him, along the walls of a whispering gallery, barely audible intimations of his own murder.

Waugh 1985, 112–3

This was not the lost aristocratic Eden that others wanted to find in Bronze Age Crete.

A sunnier picture is provided by life at Knossos. The 'Taverna' was much more hospitable to young women than the Villa ever had been, something brought out vividly in Dilys Powell's *The Villa Ariadne* (Powell 2003). Two of these young women, Edith Eccles and Mercy Money-Coutts (later Seiradaki), sometimes joined Pendlebury (and his wife Hilda) in exploring Crete on foot. Sometimes these women even went exploring on their own. The results of these later explorations, and of a more concentrated period of joint research on sites on the Plain of Lasithi (including the type-site of a 'Cretan refuge settlement', Karphi), were to form the backbone of Pendlebury's *Archaeology of Crete* (Pendlebury 1939). This book provides a period-by-period catalogue of sites and archaeological synthesis of all periods from the Neolithic to the Roman, informed by autopsy. It is still in use today and can be seen as the spiritual ancestor of large-scale, regionally focused and multi-period archaeological surveys.

By 1934, however, Pendlebury had found the task of juggling his commitments to Knossos and Tell-El-Amarna to be impossible. He resigned, to be succeeded by R. W. ('Squire') Hutchinson in the role of Knossos curator. Hutchinson continued to investigate the Knossos area but engaged for the most part in rescue rather than research excavations. When, for example, the road around Knossos was widened, he noted the finds that turned up. The major excavation in this period (1935 and 1937) was the investigation of the Villa Dionysos, a large Roman villa arranged around a central courtyard. It had some spectacular mosaics, which attracted the interest of the then assistant director of the British School at Rome (Ralegh Radford). These excavations, a new focus on rescue and Evans' advanced age took Knossos yet further away from 'the Minoans'.

The 1930s was also a decade of assertive nationalism, in Greece as elsewhere in Europe (Beaton 2019, 256–63). A new generation of younger Greek archaeologists had taken over from Hazzidakis and Xanthoudides. Spyridon Marinatos (later succeeded by Nicolas Platon) took over at the Heraklion Museum. Marinatos himself excavated several Minoan villas in north-central Crete, notably at Amnisos and Vathypetro.[3] He was much concerned with the gradual theft of Cretan prehistory. The very things that had brought Evans to Crete, engraved gemstones, were often to be found in tombs, which were being systematically looted by *archaiokapeloi* (tomb robbers). These finds had sometimes found their way into foreign museums, and Marinatos (not without reason) suspected that some foreign archaeologists were complicit in this illegal trade.

This sometimes led to tension between the British at Knossos and the Greek authorities. Certainly, this was a sign that the easy internationalism of Edwardian times was now a thing of the past.

Though Hutchinson continued to excavate around Knossos (notable discoveries being the Late Bronze Age tholos tomb at Kephala[4] in 1938–9, and the even more spectacular Iron Age tombs at Khaniale Tekke in 1940), by the end of the decade the mood around Knossos had darkened. Evans, having completed the *Palace of Minos*, had left for good in 1935 (MacGillivray 2000, 299). In 1936 both Payne and Blakeway died when still in their thirties. War was looming. Pendlebury's notion that Karphi was a 'city of refuge' (Pendlebury et al. 1938) – that is, a city inhabited by refugees who had fled from war – reflects the spirit of the times. Pendlebury now began to conceive of Cretan archaeological history not only in cultural but in racial terms (Grundon 2007, 229–30). The peaceful Minoans were displaced in the first instance by the more war-like (if Greek-speaking) Achaeans, who took over the palace of Knossos in its final phase. These were in turn displaced by the even more austerely war-like Dorians. The Achaeans (and remnants of the Minoans, the 'Eteocretans') now took to the mountains – mountains in which others were soon to seek refuge.

2.8 The 1940s: the Second World War and its aftermath

On the 28 October 1940 the Greek dictator Metaxas memorably said no (*Ochi*/Οχι) to Mussolini's suggestion that he might like to let the Italians occupy his country (Beaton 2019, 263–70). Greece was dragged into the Second World War on the Allied side, as it had been in the First World War – its only allies at this stage being the British Empire and Commonwealth.[5] At first the Greeks prevailed against the Italians in Albania but could not hold off a simultaneous combined German–Bulgarian attack on Greece's north-east flank. By 1941, Allied (and Greek) forces had retreated to Crete.

As in the Great War, so in the Second World War, archaeologists with local knowledge and linguistic ability were recruited as intelligence officers by British forces. Pendlebury's knowledge of Crete was particularly appreciated, and he was given the task of building up a network of local resistance should the Allies fail to hold the island. The Battle of Crete in May 1941 (Beevor 1991, 61–230) was one of the fiercest fought in the Mediterranean. Eventually, after heavy losses, German forces prevailed. The Allies withdrew, leaving the Cretans to endure German occupation. Casualties included Pendlebury himself, who was first wounded and then (on 22 May 1941) shot in cold blood by three German soldiers.[6] Back in England, having heard of Pendlebury's death, Evans himself passed away soon after, at his home at Youlbury on 11 July 1941 (MacGillivray 2000, 304–5).

The Villa Ariadne and Taverna at Knossos itself were taken over by the German military, serving as the residence of German general in command of Central Crete until the German withdrawal to Khania in late 1944. With the German army came German and Austrian archaeologists. The Germans had, before the war, been unsuccessful in gaining an archaeological toehold on the island. Archaeological prestige, and the idea that the modern martial Germans had something in common with the agonistic ancient Greeks (Myron's *Discobolus* was, after all, Hitler's favourite 'work of art') is an under-appreciated aspect of Nazi ideology. The Nazi state continued to support major excavations at Olympia until after the Battle of Stalingrad had been well and truly lost. *Forschungen auf Kreta* (Matz 1951) is the record of the relatively brief period when German soldier-archaeologists could safely explore Crete without fear of assassination. It includes a record of excavations at the unusual Middle Minoan administrative centre of Monastiraki in the Amari valley (Matz 1951, 27–71). Friedrich Matz and the Austrian Fritz Schachermayer (who had made a Pendlebury-like exploration of the island in 1938; Schachermeyer 1938) were later to make major contributions to the study of the Aegean Bronze Age. The Germans also expressed a strong interest in excavating the only site in Crete which could equal Olympia – Knossos. In 1941 the University of Graz (in Austria) set up a research institute on the island. Small excavations of post-Minoan levels around the Villa Ariadne were undertaken and various artefacts stored in the Villa Ariadne found their way to Graz (Flouda 2017). Finds from Knossos of Neolithic to Roman date remain there to this day.

But further German efforts to undertake more extensive excavations were firmly resisted by the Greek authorities in the persons of Spyridon Marinatos and Nicolas Platon. The Greeks' priority was to preserve what they had from the depredations of the war. Marinatos had fortunately commissioned an entirely new museum in Heraklion, constructed in the entirely modern material of reinforced concrete between 1937 and 1940. This robust structure, though damaged, thankfully proved to be bomb-proof. The tomb at Isopata was not so lucky, and slit trenches dug by German soldiers damaged some of the Early Iron Age tombs in the Teke area (Tzorakis 2021).

But if Cretan (and Knossian) archaeological finds largely escaped unscathed, the island itself did not. The Battle of Crete had been fierce; the Cretan resistance was fiercer still (Beevor 1991, 239–352). German reprisals for such embarrassments as the kidnapping of General Kreipe from the Villa Ariadne in 1944 (the famous 'Hussar Stunt', led by Patrick Leigh Fermor) included the wholesale destruction of the large village of Anoyeia. The memory of such atrocities lives on – German archaeologists have never been allowed to lead archaeological projects in Crete since the war (though German scholars have made major contributions to the study of Crete in all periods). British and Australian archaeologists were involved in the resistance, largely organized from the SOE side by the Australian T. J. Dunbabin (who managed to make some observations on the Amari valley while hiding from German soldiers). It was Dunbabin who oversaw the formal surrender of the German forces in Crete, which took place at the Villa Ariadne on 9 May 1945.

In Greece the war against the Germans was succeeded almost immediately by a Civil War (Beaton 2019, 286–305). On one side were Soviet-backed communists and on the other, first British- and then American-backed constitutional (and so, 'democratic') royalists. The latter eventually prevailed, and for the next two decades Greece was run by a succession of centre or centre-right parties (communism being outlawed). The country became a nation firmly aligned with NATO and 'the West' (Beaton 2019, 306–42). This was to affect Greek archaeology in subtle and not so subtle ways – Greece's importance as the cradle of 'the West' gradually became identified with Greece as the cradle of democracy; some wanted to find this cradle further back in time than the Classical period, in Minoan Crete (Hamilakis 2007). The Civil War itself, however, did not much affect Crete, and in late 1945 Hutchinson returned to Knossos to resume (albeit briefly, until 1947) his duties as curator.

2.9 The post-war era I: the legacy of Evans, Linear B and the destruction of the palace 1947–67

The post-war archaeological era in Crete appears to us in a much less heroic light than the first forty years of the twentieth century. In 1947, British scholars were faced with two legacies. The first (see below) was the legacy of the Knossos estate, and the excavations of the 1930s. The second was Evans' intellectual legacy.

For Evans' influence did not die with him. For one thing, many of the finds from the palace of Knossos remained unpublished. The Linear B tablets from Knossos had only received cursory notice in *Scripta Minoa I* (Evans 1909). Oxford University Press persuaded J. L. Myres (who had survived both world wars) to bring the second volume of *Scripta Minoa* to press, relying on Evans' notes. *Scripta Minoa II* (Evans 1952), which details (almost) all the Linear B tablets from Knossos, is the last publication to bear Evans' name; it retains Evans' view that the script represents a pre-Hellenic Cretan language.

This view was rapidly became untenable. French and Italian excavations at Mallia and Phaistos respectively had established that Knossos was not alone – there were Cretan palaces with large central courtyards in both these sites (Fitton 1995, 140–80). These palaces were both smaller than Knossos and appear not to have lasted until the very end of the Bronze Age (being destroyed at the end of the so-called neopalatial era, in Late Minoan IB). Though they had documents in other scripts, they had none in Linear B. Excavation on major mainland sites – notably at Mycenae by A. J. B. Wace and at Pylos by Carl Blegen – had by 1953 established that Knossos was not alone in possessing Linear B documents (Fitton 1995, 150–65). Wace had long ago crossed swords with Evans over the extent of Minoan influence on the Mycenaean mainland. Evans believed that Mycenae and other major mainland centres were, at some point, dependencies of a great thalassocracy (sea empire) based on Knossos. Wace acknowledged that there was a general Aegean style that was shared between the mainland and Crete, but pointed out that the differences in the design and size of the palaces in the two regions, and the fundamental differences in tomb architecture, suggested that Minoan and Mycenaean remained distinct cultures (which in turn represented distinct peoples) throughout the Bronze Age. The Mycenaean world, with its elaborate warrior tombs and iconography of warfare and hunting, seemed much more 'Homeric' than the Minoan. Wace also believed that the convergence in styles (and in the appearance of mainland tomb architecture and mortuary practices in Knossos at the very end of the Bronze Age) supported some notion of an 'Achaean' takeover at around the time of the Trojan War (ideas that had already been mooted by Pendlebury).

The excavation of the 'Palace of Nestor' at Pylos in Messenia (investigated from 1939 onwards by Carl Blegen of the American School and resumed shortly after the war) seemed to support the Wace thesis. At Pylos, Blegen uncovered a megaron-centred palace which was nonetheless decorated with frescoes similar in style (if not always in iconography) to those at Knossos (Blegen 1966). Furthermore, a cache of Linear B tablets, a veritable archive of documents, found at this palace and apparently used for administration, underscored how very unlikely it was that this script was purely Minoan. The script must also be Mycenaean – that is, they must belong as much to the 'Helladic' tradition as to the 'Minoan'. These tablets (around 600 of them, just over half the number from Knossos) were transcribed and published very rapidly in 1951 by Emmett Bennet Junior. The similarity between the Linear B archives of Knossos and Pylos was undeniable. But if Linear B was a syllabary (and so phonetic), what language was it the script of? Enlightenment was to come from an unlikely quarter.

In 1936 a young schoolboy called Michael Ventris (1922–56) attended a lecture given by Arthur Evans on excavations at Knossos. At that moment (so it is said) this fourteen-year-old determined to solve the puzzle that Evans had so far failed to do – to decipher Linear B (Chadwick 1967, 1). An architect by profession, Ventris devoted his spare time to this now well-established conundrum. Others had claimed to decipher Linear B before; a notable breakthrough had been made by Alice Kober, who had demonstrated that the script must represent an inflected (and so probably Indo-European) language (Chadwick 1967, 35–6). That Greek, too, was an inflected, Indo-European language did not escape Ventris, and after his war service he began to trawl through the evidence in his spare time. The near simultaneous publication of the Linear B finds from both Knossos and Pylos provided the critical mass of documents that enabled decipherment. In 1953, Ventris joined up with the professional philologist John Chadwick to put forward his hypothesis that Linear B was used to write an early (archaic) form of Greek (Ventris and Chadwick 1953; Fitton 1995, 171–8). Despite some initial scepticism (Linear B had always been thought to be pre-Hellenic, not Hellenic), over the next five years the decipherment became generally accepted amongst (almost) all scholars (but see Thompson 2019). But by that time, Ventris would be dead, killed in a car accident.

Linear B provided a new picture of a Late Bronze Age, 'Mycenaean' world (Ventris and Chadwick 1973; cf. Chadwick 1976). But it was a view from the archives, a clerk's perspective on how the palaces were run. It gave a view of a highly stratified political and social order, with a *wanax* and *lawagetas* at the apex, and various officials below. It provided a glimpse of a palatial economy, the distribution of raw materials (copper, tin, flax) to workers; for Knossos it showed a great 'palatial' interest in the management of flocks of sheep (Killen 1964).

If this decipherment had overturned Evans' initial hypothesis, it had not – initially at least – overturned his scholarship. But it did create an inconsistency. The Linear B tablets from Knossos and Pylos had only survived because they had been baked hard in a great conflagration – the final destruction of both palaces. The language of the tablets from both sites was very similar, suggesting that they came from the same broad linguistic horizon. But the relative archaeological dates assigned by their excavators were quite different. Pylos was destroyed at the end of a phase known as Late Helladic III B, conventionally dated around 1200 BC. Evans and Mackenzie had, however, dated the final destruction of the Knossos palace (which they associated with King Minos himself, someone not normally considered to be Mycenaean) to Late Minoan III A – a hundred or more years earlier. Some philologists had great difficulty in believing that documents which, in both linguistic and epigraphic terms, were so similar could be so far apart in date. One scholar – Leonard Palmer – for one could not (Palmer 1963; 1969). He began to trawl through Evans' account of the evidence for the final destruction, putting forward an archaeological argument that the final destruction of Knossos must be broadly contemporary with the final destruction of Pylos. This prompted a thorough re-examination of Evans' and Mackenzie's notes and documentation – a reappraisal which (eventually) vindicated both archaeologists (Palmer and Boardman 1963; Popham 1964; 1970). The final destruction of the palace of Knossos took place substantially earlier than that of Pylos. The implications of this have taken several decades to be properly appreciated.

Apart from scripts, Evans' other main interest had been in engraved gems – seal-stones or glyptic. This was continued, in the post-war era, not by British but by German archaeologists. Barred from excavating on Crete, Friedrich Matz could at least continue his interest in the island by studying the extensive museum collections. In 1958 he initiated the *Corpus der minoischen und mykenischen Siegel* – a comprehensive catalogue of all seal-stones (engraved gems) from the Bronze Age Aegean (Pini 2010). In this way the principles of *Altertumswissenschaft* could be brought to bear on Minoan archaeology.

2.10 The post-war era II: investigating Knossos 1947–67

In 1947, Hutchinson was replaced by Piet de Jong as Knossos curator. De Jong is perhaps the best-known illustrator of the Aegean Bronze Age – his watercolour reconstructions provide a picture of that era that words cannot. But he was to be the last curator, at least of the whole of the archaeological site that Evans had given to the British School.

Despite the best efforts of successive curators, the site of Knossos and the Evans estate had never been able to pay its way. It was also something of an embarrassment for the Greek state that a major site of this kind should remain the possession of a foreign school. All other major sites, from Delphi to Olympia to the Acropolis of Athens, were now owned and managed by the Greek state. Moreover, around this time, the British School itself was being reorganized. All the British Schools and institutes abroad were now brought under the umbrella of the British Academy, and so financed (indirectly) by the British state. The British School should then (it was argued) not need any income from Knossos. So, in 1952, as part of these new arrangements, the Knossos site and Evans estate (including the Villa Ariadne) were handed over to the Greek government, to be managed in future by the Greek archaeological service.

The British School, however, maintained some rights: rights of residence in the Taverna, and of excavation within the area of the estate. From 1957 until 1961, a new director of the School, Sinclair Hood, exercised these rights by excavating both to the north and the south sides of the Royal Road. This revealed a series of deposits going down from the 'Greek' period (Classical and Hellenistic) to the earliest part of the Bronze Age (Early Minoan). Hood (with Nancy Sandars) had earlier excavated a number of Late Bronze Age graves – including 'warrior graves' on the upper slopes of the Gypsadhes hill (Hood et al. 1959). Investigation of the lower slopes of this hill (already known for the frequency of its terracottas; see Kotsonas 2016b, 307–15) led to the discovery of a later Greek sanctuary to Demeter (Coldstream 1973b). Hood and Sandars were part of a post-war generation that had few links either to Evans or to Pendlebury. With Myres' death in 1954 and Dunbabin's in 1955, only Hutchinson provided any kind of link with earlier generations of investigators.

This does not quite mean that Evans' legacy was forgotten. Hood's championing of the notion of warrior graves was at odds with Evans' picture of the peaceful Minoans, but Evans' vision was given new life through Jacquetta Hawkes' *Dawn of the Gods* (Hawkes 1968). Hawkes saw the Minoans as being un-warlike; 'the Minoans' were a culture which exhibited 'feminine' principles; 'the Minoans' lived in harmony with the natural world, unlike the 'masculine' Mycenaeans (Momigliano 2020, 137–85). Hawkes' view chimed in with a reappraisal of the frescoes from the palace by another young scholar, Mark Cameron (Cameron 1968). Cameron criticized the Gilliérons' 'Pompeian' interpretation of the frescoes' colour scheme. Minoan frescoes were lighter in tone, more in tune with nature, less heavy in their effect. Cameron's reappraisal of the frescoes was to find dramatic confirmation when Spyridon Marinatos' excavations at Akrotiri on Santorini (Thera) became more widely known – for here too were Aegean (if not Minoan) frescoes with a light and airy feel to them, somehow reflecting the deep blue of the Aegean Sea.

The post-war generation included John Boardman and J. N. Coldstream. These scholars were more interested in what came after 'the Minoans' than in the Bronze Age. Boardman cooperated with Hutchinson in the publication of the Iron Age tombs of Khaniale Tekke (Hutchinson and Boardman 1954; Boardman 1967) and collected scraps of material relating to Archaic Knossos (Boardman 1962). Coldstream published the Iron Age and Orientalizing material from Hood's excavations along the Royal Road (Coldstream 1972; 1973a), as well as several well deposits (that is, wells that had been filled in with later material after they had fallen out of use) of the same date (e.g., Coldstream 1960). This renewed interest in the Iron Age was partly prompted by James Brock's study and final publication of the Fortetsa tombs originally excavated by Payne and Blakeway (Brock 1957). This publication provided a viable ceramic sequence and relative chronology from the so-called Subminoan through to the Orientalizing periods.

Knossos

This period also witnessed renewed interest in the Neolithic of Knossos. John Evans (no relation to Arthur) of the Institute of Archaeology in London sunk several 5x5m trenches in the middle of the central courtyard of the palace in two major seasons (1957–60 and 1969–70), with a focus on the formation and development of the tell settlement (J. D. Evans 1964; 1971; Warren et al. 1968). All these excavations generated many new finds, and this necessitated a reconsideration of how they should be stored. The answer was a new, enlarged Stratigraphical Museum, completed in 1967 and built over Evans' tennis courts. This was to serve the British School well in the years to come.

2.11 Great excavations: the second major phase of exploration at Knossos 1967–85

If Evans' excavations at Knossos can be seen (in retrospect, and from a largely British perspective) to have been a golden age of exploration, then the silver age was late in coming. But if any period can be so called it is the phase of major excavations that took place from 1967 onwards. In that year both Greek and foreign archaeologists experienced the shock of a military coup – the colonels (not the generals) took over the government; democratic politicians and eventually the king (Constantine) went into exile. Greece was subject to seven years of military rule; with the junta came a backward-looking cultural nationalism focused on the glories of Classical Greece.

This coup did not adversely affect foreign archaeologists. The colonels were committed to NATO and 'the West' and were supported by other Western powers (principally the United States) as a bulwark against communism. Indeed, the work of the foreign schools flourished, and nowhere more so than in Knossos. New research excavations were initiated. The first of these (from 1967 to 1973) was the exploration of the Unexplored Mansion (Popham 1973; Sackett 1973), whose impressive façade and foundations Evans had reached in 1910. The term 'Unexplored Mansion' is now of course a misnomer – no Bronze Age structure in Knossos has been more thoroughly explored. The publication is indeed unusual in that it gives equal weight to the Late Bronze Age villa or mansion and to the later accumulation of deposits (sub-Minoan through to Roman) on top (Popham 1984–5; Sackett 1992a).

In retrospect, it is extraordinary how much was excavated during this period. British archaeologists at Knossos were, in practice, used as rescue archaeologists, and treated as something akin to an archaeological unit (in the British sense) in these years. Their excavations extended far beyond the estate, where they had rights. So, more Bronze Age tombs were found at Sellopoulo; Iron Age tombs on the Lower Gypsades (Coldstream et al. 1981); Middle Minoan villas were explored just south-west of the estate area; and a Classical 'Shrine of Glaukos' was investigated within the village itself (Bougada metochi; Callaghan 1978). All these investigations, however, pale beside the major enterprise that British archaeologists were invited to undertake on behalf of the Greek state.

Greece in the 1970s had very few universities, and Crete had none. The new conservative (centre-right) government that came into power in 1974 wished to remedy this situation. It planned a vast new medical and scientific campus outside Heraklion, next to the major Venizelion hospital (whose foundations had been investigated by Piet de Jong). But this proved also to be the site of the largest cemetery in ancient Knossos – not so much Minoan as Iron Age, Hellenistic, Roman and (early) Byzantine. The then Ephor of Central Crete and director of the Heraklion Museum, the distinguished scholar Stylianos Alexiou, invited the British to excavate the site. The study of the finds was to occupy several scholars for several years.

This huge increase in finds had to be housed somewhere, so a decision was made to enlarge the Stratigraphical Museum. This entailed another rescue excavation to the west of the structure – the Stratigraphical Museum Extension (SEX) excavations. These began in 1978 under the direction of Peter Warren (Warren 1981; 1983). The results proved to be very similar to those of the Unexplored Mansion – there was a major overlay (several metres thick) of Roman, Hellenistic, Classical, Archaic and Iron Age material over some major Minoan structures. These included platforms interpreted, perhaps not seriously, as 'dancing floors' (Warren 1984). More controversially, finds included Bronze Age children's bones with unusual cut marks. Could the peace-loving Minoans also have been cannibals?

These finds were of sufficient importance to put a stop to any talk of extending the museum. This overcrowded space would now have to serve as the study area for the avalanche of finds that these excavations had revealed. The political mood had also changed. In 1981, Greece elected a new socialist (PASOK) government under the leadership of Andreas Papandreou (Beaton 2019, 347–55). This government was much less committed to the notion that Greece was part of the 'West'; members of this government remembered that NATO and 'the West' had continued to support the colonels, and that the British had done nothing in 1974 to forestall a Turkish invasion (and subsequent occupation) of northern Cyprus. The 'rights' of British excavators to investigate Knossos were now interpreted in a harsher light. The Archaeological Service (under its new Ephor for Central Crete, Iannis Sakellarakis) made it clear that, in future, it alone would undertake all rescue excavations in the Knossos area. This point was clarified when more Iron Age tombs just north of the North Cemetery came to light. Sakellarakis made it plain that these were his to excavate and rebuffed a suggestion that it might be best if all these finds (which after all came from one cemetery) should be published together.

2.12 Back to the palace 1978–2000

If the days of the British at Knossos as 'rescue' archaeologists were now over, there was still plenty there to study. During the 1960s and 1980s, Sinclair Hood (with David Smyth) had been engaged in major works of synthesis – first a survey of all the finds in the Knossos area and then a new plan of the palace (Hood and Smyth 1981; Hood and

Taylor 1981). In 1978, Hood (and others) undertook a systematic study of the mysterious masons' marks which were to be found in large numbers on the limestone ashlar blocks of the palace and other buildings (Hood and Bendall 2020, xix). A new generation of scholars – J. A. MacGillivray, Nicoletta Momigliano and David Wilson – found that much could be learnt about the Bronze Age through a reappraisal of deposits which, though excavated by Evans and recorded by Mackenzie, had never been completely published. John Bennet began a reappraisal of the Linear B archives, which gave a good idea of the political and geographical reach of the final 'Mycenaean' palace. All this prompted a re-evaluation of the palace itself. Many scholars of many nationalities had long been fascinated by the enigmatic structure at Knossos. In 1984 they met in Athens, in a symposium organized by the Swedish institute, on the topic of 'the function of the Minoan palaces' (Hägg and Marinatos 1987). Numerous papers in this conference expressed a degree of scepticism about the term 'palace' and suggested that at its acme this structure was more temple than ruler's residence.

Just as the political climate had changed, so had the intellectual. The British School (like other foreign schools in Greece) had hitherto been sheltered from the academic storms that had, since the 1960s, raged in anthropological archaeology on the other side of the Atlantic. Theory had, up to 1970 or so, been kept at arm's length. But not for much longer. New or processual archaeology had arrived in the study of Aegean prehistory in the form of Colin Renfrew's *Emergence of Civilisation* (1972). By the 1980s, graduate students had arrived in Greece with research projects which had 'an anthropological or sociological tinge' to them (Waterhouse 1986, 50). Processual and post-processual archaeologies were thereafter to affect how Knossos was to be interpreted.

In 1985, some of these younger scholars (who had barely completed, or even begun, their doctorates) were given a chance to explore the palace – or at least its drains (Macdonald and Driessen 1988). They are seen in tank tops below (Figure 2.7). In 1987 a more systematic reinvestigation of the palace took place in three locations with undisturbed deposits under the general direction of Sinclair Hood. This was to be the first of many small tests that were made, especially in the 1990s during Colin MacDonald's tenure of the Knossos curatorship. Excavations focused in particular on the south-west area of the palace and the area of the south-west houses (Coldstream and MacDonald 1997). These highly targeted excavations were intended to resolve outstanding stratigraphic problems – problem-focused in other words. One of the results of these new tests was to re-emphasize the role of commensality (communal consumption) in some of the earlier phases of this great structure (MacDonald and Knappett 2007).

The Greek Archaeological Service also took a renewed interest in the palace. By 1990, Knossos had become the one of the most visited archaeological sites in Greece, second only to the Acropolis of Athens. It had to endure millions of footfalls a year. Up until this time, tourists had been free to wander over the site at will, but this was no longer sustainable. The service commissioned a new, more accurate plan of the palace and its immediate environs. The aim here was to provide the basis for walkways that would guide tourists around the palace and conserve the existing walls. Walkways would have to be supported by foundations, and to this end, deep shafts were excavated. Greek

Figure 2.7 The 'tank top' photo (from left to right, Jane Cocking, Colin MacDonald, Jan Driessen and Cyprian Broodbank) at the Knossos Taverna, 1986. Courtesy Professor Jan Driessen, Louvain-la-Neuve.

archaeologists (such as Nikos Efstratiou from Thessaloniki) were brought in to do this work in 1997 (Efstratiou et al. 2013), work which revealed new information on the earliest Neolithic phases of the hill of Kephala.

The year 2000 also marked the centenary of Evans' original excavations. A celebratory conference was held in Heraklion, organized jointly by the British School and the Greek Archaeological Service. Contributions were in both English and Greek. This conference and subsequent conference volume (Cadogan et al. 2004; see also *Cretan Quests* (Huxley 2000)) provided an occasion for reflection on what one hundred years of investigation had achieved. It was not just about Evans and the Bronze Age – there was much on Neolithic and 'post-Minoan' Knossos. There was also a degree of reappraisal of the historiography of the site, of the guiding assumptions and interests of its investigators (whatever their nationality). Neither theory nor politics could continue to be set to one side.

For the investigation of Knossos is no simple narrative of discovery. To be sure, new facts come to light, largely through new excavations. But these facts are constantly being reappraised and were moreover always interpreted within a particular intellectual framework – something which in other archaeologies is called a paradigm. That we continue to use the term palace for the major, central courtyard structure is testament to this fact – palace is a highly loaded term, as is Minoan. Nor can the work of foreign archaeologists working in Greece be considered as taking place outside of politics. If the account I have given of the work of (largely) British archaeologists over the twentieth century sometimes reads like diplomatic history, that is because that is exactly what it is. Archaeology in foreign lands is always a form of cultural diplomacy, just as archaeology undertaken within Britain is always connected to that species of cultural nationalism that goes by the name of 'heritage'.

It is this far from neutral process – a process where theories are continually both tested and contested – that eventually produces knowledge about the past. And it is this process that has also produced a peculiar set of terms by which we place the phases of Knossos's history in chronological order (see chronological note). The terminology of pre-Minoan (Neolithic), Minoan (Bronze Age) and post-Minoan (Iron Age to Roman) creates expectations about the kinds of narrative we can write. That these terms are far from being simply descriptive will become clear in subsequent chapters.

CHAPTER 3
FROM VILLAGE TO PALACE: NEOLITHIC AND EARLY BRONZE AGE (EARLY MINOAN) KNOSSOS

Chapter abstract

This describes Knossos' development from the arrival of the first settlers from Anatolia at the beginning of the Neolithic, through the Early Bronze Age (Early Minoan period) down to the immediately pre-palatial period in the traditional account of things. It will end with a consideration of a new proposal that a palace (or central courtyard structure) was first built in Knossos in the middle of the third millennium BC, and what archaeologists have normally come to expect were the major indications of state formation.

3.1 Knossos begins: early human settlement in Crete

For most of its existence – from the turn of the eighth and seventh millennium BC down to around 2000 BC – Knossos might appear to us to have been little more than a very small human settlement. It started out as a hamlet, became a village and only after several millennia (just before 2000 BC) did it acquire the dimensions of a small town. Whatever its absolute size, its status relative to other settlements on the island was one of primacy. It was probably the earliest and almost always the largest community on the island. It was also long thought that Knossos was not only the first agricultural settlement on Crete but also that the site itself represented the first signs of any human presence on this substantial Mediterranean island. This view is no longer tenable. Research on the south of the island by an American team (Strasser et al. 2010) has found evidence of Lower Palaeolithic and Mesolithic habitation in the Plakias region. Whereas the Lower Palaeolithic hominids who lived in this area may not have been human in the full sense of the term (they were not representatives of *homo sapiens*), the early Cretans of the Mesolithic (or Epipalaeolithic) certainly were. How these gatherer-hunters interacted (if they did) with the first Neolithic people to arrive on the island we do not yet know.

The environment (not so much the climate) that greeted these new arrivals was very different to what it is today. Pollen and plant remains from a deep sounding in the palace made in 1997 (Efstratiou et al. 2004; Badal and Ntinou 2013) indicate that the surrounding area was a mix of evergreen forest and shrub, dominated by oak trees with some pine and juniper. There were as yet no olives or vines. The continuous supply of water provided by the Kairatos stream, and the easily tillable soft marls in the surrounding area (identifiable through the vegetation which grew on them), must however have made the area an attractive one to early agriculturalists.

These people, who arrived in Knossos around 7000 BC, seem to have come from southern Anatolia (modern Turkey). The evidence for this lies in the varieties of cereals these early Knossians made use of. In addition to the usual 'primitive' varieties of wheat (such as emmer), these early Knossians seem to have used more developed forms (bread wheat, *triticum aestivum*; J. D. Evans in Warren et al. 1968, 269; Sarpaki 2013, 69–73). Such varieties are not found until very much later in the north of the Aegean (Macedonia and Thessaly, the two most densely settled regions of northern Greece) but are very similar to those to be found at contemporary major Anatolian sites (such as Çatalhöyük). Their material culture, too, was different from that of the Thessalian or northern Greek Neolithic (see below). The settlement of Crete then follows a pattern we see elsewhere in the Mediterranean: larger islands are settled before smaller ones, because larger islands have a more diverse ecosystem (Cherry 1981; 1990). Whereas a drought can devastate a small island like Thera, ecological diversity allows for more risk buffering – if the harvest fails in one part of the island, you can gather some plants from another part. You might (in principle – but see below) also do some hunting.

The subsistence practices of these early agriculturalists in most respects followed the usual pattern for Neolithic Greece. The main domestic crops were wheat (several varieties, including einkorn and emmer), barley and pulses such as lentils, supplemented by fruits (figs) and nuts (almonds) (Sarpaki 2013). Faunal remains for the succeeding ENI period (Perez Ripoll 2013) also indicate that the usual domestic animals had been brought in – cattle, pigs, dogs, sheep and (probably) goats. More intriguing is the suggestion that the earliest Neolithic settlers might have been, directly or indirectly, responsible for the reintroduction onto the island of species we might consider wild – badgers, hares and pine martens (Moody 2012; Perez Ripoll 2013, 162–4). Of these, it is now only hares that you can still hunt on Crete.

These new human arrivals from Anatolia, who cannot have numbered more than one hundred (and possibly as few as twenty-five) individuals, seem to have settled down to create a small settlement on a kidney-shaped knoll to the south-east of the hill of Kephala (Evans 1964, 140–2; 1994, 2–5; Tomkins 2008, 31) – exactly where the slopes of this small hill were steepest. This early settlement can have been no more than a hamlet, being less than 0.25 hectares in size. Nonetheless, that these people were predisposed to live cheek-by-jowl in a collection of small houses built of unbaked mud-brick in a sedentary community, rather than living in a more dispersed pattern across a wider area, is in itself an interesting fact. Sedentism is a necessary but hardly sufficient condition for a way of life based on agriculture, and when we call these early settlers farmers, that statement has to be qualified. To be sure they made extensive use of the cultivated cereals (chiefly wheat and barley) that had been domesticated in the Near East and had been spread by human migration. They also relied for their meat primarily on domesticated animals, chiefly sheep and goats (less so pigs and cattle in the earliest phases) – whether they ate the dogs they kept is less certain. However, they probably did not cultivate large fields but small plots which they worked by hand-using stone hoes (celts). Gardening with some sheep and goats (rather than agriculture proper) might be a better description than farming of what these people were up to.

Even to call these people Neolithic is perhaps to give the wrong impression. For at this very early stage (J. D. Evans' Stratum X) they lacked one of the key features of the Neolithic – pottery. This early phase is therefore labelled 'Aceramic' (without pottery).[1] However, while they had no pottery, they did make tools from local chert (flint), animal bone and imported obsidian. Study of the chipped stone (chert and obsidian; Conolly 2008), however, indicates that this community was under considerable 'resource stress'. The local chert (flint) is of very poor quality, and the obsidian (obtained probably from Melos) has been highly worked and reworked. Obtaining and retaining good quality tools was a real challenge for these early settlers. Life in this early post-colonization phase was precarious for other reasons. This small community cannot have been self-sustaining (that requires a population of over 300) – marriage partners would have to be sought from elsewhere (Tomkins 2008, 31). It is possible that, during trips to Melos to obtain obsidian, Knossians might have encountered people travelling in the other direction from (say) Franchthi Cave in the southern Argolid – which might help to explain similarities in their lithic assemblages (Conolly 2008).

Table 3.1 gives the dates for this Neolithic period in tabular form. Plenty of radiocarbon dates were produced as a result of the excavations in the late 1950s and early 1960s (J. D. Evans 1994, 20 Table II). These have now been supplemented by more recent dates from further excavations of Neolithic levels in 1997 (Efstratiou et al. 2013; Facorellis and Maniatis 2013). Many of these, however, are 'charcoal' or 'charcoal mixed samples'. The most useful are from the earliest phases, and these are the only ones given here.

By 6400 BC then, at the latest, a solid start had been made. An indication of the establishment of a permanent community is perhaps the practice of burying children

Table 3.1 Phases of the Neolithic in Knossos, with approximate calendar dates and the most useful radiocarbon estimates

Phase	Abbreviation	Principal stratum (after J. D. Evans)	Date range	Radiocarbon
Aceramic Neolithic	IN	X	7000–6500/6400 BC	BM-124 charcoal from oak stake 8050 +/- 180 BP; BM-278 same, 7910 +/- 140 BP; OxA-9215, wood charcoal (*quercus*) 9000–8730 BP
Early Neolithic	EN (I and II)	IX–VIII	6500–5900 BC	BM-436 carbonized grain 7740 +/- 130 BP
Middle Neolithic	MN	VII–VIB	5900–5300 BC	
Late Neolithic	LN	VIA– IV	5300–4400 BC	
Final Neolithic	FN (I–IV)	III–I	4400–3100 BC	
Early Minoan I	EMI	Knossos FF 4	3100–2650 BC	

within the fabric of the settlement (Evans 1964, 139–42), which (even before the end of this period) had begun to take on the properties of a tell.

3.2 The earlier Neolithic (Early Neolithic to Late Neolithic II): the growth of a settlement

Evans and Mackenzie recognized, in the first few years of the excavation of Knossos, that the palace was built over (and into) an earlier Neolithic tell. Most of what we know of the settlement derives either from Mackenzie's and A. J. Evans' excavations in the West (Evans 1921, 32–55) and Central Courts (Evans 1928a, 1–21); and J. D. Evans' later investigation of the Central Court (Evans 1964; 1971; Warren et al. 1968), supplemented more recently by a test to the north-east of the Central Court in 1997 (Efstratiou et al. 2013) and one in the throne room area of the palace in 1987 (Manteli and Evely 1995). These excavations provide us with our basic sequence, subsequently modified by Peter Tomkins (2007).

In the Early Neolithic (stratum IX), pottery was introduced into the settlement.[2] The shapes were mainly bowls and jars (often with lugs or handles), whose outer surfaces were either polished or burnished. Other decoration was incised or *pointilliste* – never painted (in contrast to the Neolithic of Thessaly). Pottery is a new technology, and probably an imported one, since as J. D. Evans pointed out (1994, 7), the shapes 'are not the initial experiments of beginners but belong to an already established tradition of potting'.

The shapes in question seem to relate to food preparation and serving (not so much to drinking). Since the easiest way in which new technologies are introduced is through the arrival of new people, we cannot rule out the possibility that this new technology was introduced by a second wave of immigrants, also from Anatolia. It was Arthur Evans (1928a, 4), after all, who remarked that the 'Neolithic culture of Crete was fundamentally Anatolian'. There is no better testimony to this than the terracotta anthropomorphic (human-shaped) figurines which begin to proliferate in this period (Mina 2008). What these figurines were for – whether they were predominantly male or female (or neither), whether they had something to do with fertility of a primordial Neolithic 'Mother Goddess' – has been long debated, but no consensus has emerged. They may be related to another peculiar practice which also has parallels in Anatolia – burials within the settlement mound. It was once thought that it was simply children or neonates (new-borns who probably died in childbirth) who were so interred, but recent study (Triandaphyllou 2008, 143–5) has shown that parts of the long bones and crania of adults were also incorporated within the fabric of the mound (there being no positive evidence for a separate cemetery at this stage). Might both human bones and anthropomorphic figurines therefore represent the same thing – the incorporation of past generations into the fabric of the community which the tell mound came to represent?

Certainly the settlement grew during this period. It became both higher and wider. By the time of the Middle Neolithic (stratum VII), the houses had become more complex. Structures were built with multiple rooms and were often constructed on stone foundations. The material used for the walls was now the more durable *pisé* – no longer

Figure 3.1 Knossos – Neolithic terracotta figurine. British Museum GR 1934.0115.2, 142800 jpg. Licenced under Wikimedia Commons.

the simple unbaked mudbrick but rather rammed earth with an admixture of lime, partially baked. By the end of stratum IV (Tomkins' Late Neolithic II), the site had grown to cover at least 2ha. This is not to say that it was densely occupied, as excavations within the Central Court seem to give evidence of empty spaces between houses. But generations did tend to live on the detritus of earlier generations and so the tell gradually built up.

How much did the settlement and so the population expand? J. D. Evans (1971; 1994) and Broodbank (1992) argued for a slow and steady increase, the site reaching the size of

3ha by the end of the Late Neolithic (stratum IV) and the population perhaps amounting to more than 1,000 inhabitants. Tomkins (2008, 30–5) and Isaakidou (2008, 102–3) have both argued that these figures are overestimates, that the tell grew more slowly, and the population in the Neolithic never exceeded 750 persons at any one time. Moreover, the undoubted increase in the size of the site was not so much one of steady expansion as of something little short of an explosion during the Late Neolithic (5300–4500 BC) – and only at this point did it reach 2ha.

This debate is important for two reasons. First there is the question of when the community could have become self-sustaining. By Isaakidou's reasoning (Isaakidou 2008), this could only have been achieved at some point in the Late Neolithic. The capacity to sustain oneself matters, as a self-sustaining community necessarily has different relations with other communities from one that is not. The second point is that there is, also necessarily, a relationship between population size and politics. As the population expanded, so the structure of the community must have changed. Whereas a community of 100 requires no formal process of decision-making – it remains a face-to-face society – a community of 800 to 1,000 requires some mechanisms by which at least disputes between households could be managed. This need not have led to a formal hierarchy – the much larger Anatolian Neolithic site of Çatalhöyük has absolutely no evidence of formal ranking either between or within households (Hodder 2006). But if there is no hierarchy there may have to be more ritual (though there is no clear evidence for this at Knossos), or at least something (such as forms of commensality) to provide the social glue that all communities require. While hierarchy is not inevitable in communities of this size, some form of politics certainly is.

The use of animals also changed. Gradually the proportion of sheep fell and the proportion of cattle grew during the Middle and Late Neolithic (Isaakidou 2008; but see Perez Ripoll 2013). This increasing emphasis on cattle in the bone assemblages is anomalous when compared to other Aegean Neolithic sites (Isaakidou 2008, 101–7). This emphasis cannot be attributed to any kind of 'feasting' (as the bone deposits are too scattered) but must rather be the outcome of using either cows or castrated bulls (oxen) for traction – that is, ploughing. Such a use of oxen within a highly intensive agricultural regime must then represent a very early (indeed the earliest) indication of what has been called the 'secondary products revolution' (Sherratt 1981), whereby animals are used not only for meat but also for traction, milk and wool (secondary products). Further evidence of this revolution can be found in stratum IV (Late Neolithic II, around 4400 BC). Here we have our first sign of the use of textiles in the form of loom-weights and loom-shuttles (Evans 1921, 43, Figure 10). Were they weaving wool or flax? It could have been both, since flax (Sarpaki 2013) has been found as early as ENI.

Another intriguing feature of the faunal assemblage, from MN onwards, is the proportion of wild (or rather feral) species. Finds in the MN and LN levels include both wild boar and *agrimi*, the Cretan wild goat (*Capra aegagrus*: Perex Ripoll 2013, 152–5, 162–5). These goats are not native to Crete but were the descendants of domestic goats that came over with the first Neolithic settlers on the island (Bar Gal et al. 2002; Moody 2012, 246). Both *agrimi* and boar here are not so much wild as feral – species once domesticated that have now grown wild. Such animals have to be hunted, and in the case of the *agrimi* this would probably have involved hunting with dogs.

There is also growing evidence of Knossos' wider Aegean connections. If the settlement ceased to be unique – there are about six other Early Neolithic settlements, and many more datable to Late Neolithic times (Tomkins 2007, 28–30) – it for long remained the largest such settlement on the island, being much bigger than its nearest neighbour, the hamlet of Katsambas (Galanidou and Manteli 2008) and the cave at Amnisos (Marinatos 1929), which may have been used for burial. Knossos' connections extended to Melos in the Cyclades, the volcanic island which is the source for most (if not quite all) the obsidian found at Knossos, and to other parts of Crete. A male figurine from stratum VIII may also have had a Cycladic origin (Evans 1994, Plate 3c). Sources for the celts (the stone tools used as both adzes and axes) were various (Strasser 2004; 2008). Materials included periodotite (from the Anoyeia area on the slopes of Mount Ida and parts of south-central Crete) and granodiorite, which is only found in the Mirabello area of the island. Granodiorite is also found in pottery from as early as the Early Neolithic period – and this too seems to represent pottery manufactured in that area and then brought to Knossos itself (Tomkins et al. 2004, 56). Painted pottery from the Peloponnese is also found on the site as early as the Middle Neolithic (just before 5300 BC).

By the end of the Late Neolithic period, then, Knossos was part of a mosaic – or network – of Neolithic sites on the island. It remained the largest of these sites, and (as the first Neolithic settlement that we know of) might well have retained an aura of primacy – as the *original* settlement. Indications that relations between these communities were not always peaceful may be found in the appearance of stone mace heads in Late Neolithic times (Evans 1994, Plate 4c) – though of course we cannot be absolutely sure that these objects really were 'weapons of war'.

3.3 The Final Neolithic

After 4400 BC the number of known sites of human habitation in Crete increases exponentially. Most of these sites are very small, and many are in upland and sometimes inaccessible locations, locations which are often (much later) used for 'refuge settlements' at the end of the Bronze Age. Some scholars (Nowicki 2002; 2008; 2014; but see Tomkins 2008, 35–40) have seen this increase in settlement, and the marked preference for 'defensible' locations (where natives could defend themselves against invaders), as evidence of a new wave of incomers (again from Anatolia). But if so, we see very little evidence for 'new people' at Knossos. The pottery (Tomkins 2007, 32–8) represents a straightforward development from the Late Neolithic. Continuity is much more apparent than change.

There are some terminological problems with the notion of the 'Final Neolithic'. While this phraseology does bring Crete in line with the rest of the Aegean, it also creates difficulties if we look at the Neolithic in a wider frame. For in the Balkans and in Anatolia we are now in the 'Chalcolithic' (i.e., bronze/stone age) or 'Aeneolithic' (Sherratt and Sherratt 2008). The term 'Chalcolithic' could be justified at least for Knossos, since a flat copper axe was found in one of the Final Neolithic houses excavated by Evans and Mackenzie (Evans 1928a, 14). We get a much better picture of houses for this final phase of the Neolithic, principally through the houses in the Central Court (Evans 1928a, 1–21). These substantial structures testify to the architectural and social solidity of what remained the largest settlement in Crete.

How large then was this settlement? J. D. Evans (1971; 1994; supported by Whitelaw et al. 2019) believed that the settlement – and the population – continued to expand, reaching a size of 5ha and a possible population of 2,000 by the end of the period. Tomkins (2008, 36) sees the period as largely static – neither the site nor the population increased by much if at all. But if it did not expand it still retained its relative position within the island – Knossos remained Crete's 'super site'.

Evidence for structural change within the community is harder to discern. There are some straws in the wind – changes in the ceramic assemblage. For the first time we have evidence of a *drinking* vessel from the Final Neolithic IV period (Tomkins 2007, 42–4, Figure 1.15, No. 18). The significance of this will be discussed in the next section. Generally, however, the transition between 'the Neolithic' (where Knossos is just part of a much wider field of discourse) and 'the Minoan' (where Knossos is, by definition, central) is smooth. There is no marked break. After a stratum identified as 'sub-Neolithic' (Tomkins 2007, 44–8), we enter 'Early Minoan' without really noticing very much change.

3.4 The coming of metal? The earliest Bronze Age, the earliest 'Minoan' (EMI)

The move from Neolithic to 'Minoan' implies two major transformations (Evans 1921, 56–70). The first is technological – as we enter the Bronze Age (and so the age of metals), humans develop a means of transforming the material world. Smelting and casting copper alloys represents a new alchemy of transubstantiation, which goes beyond the chipping, polishing and shaping of stone. The second transformation could be described as 'ontological': from being merely a local example of a certain technological stage (the Neolithic), the inhabitants of Knossos become central to the 'coming into being' of a new era, a new cultural essence. With the coming of metallurgy came also 'the Minoans'.

Of course, it is not quite that simple. Many scholars would argue that, while the Bronze Age is a bit of a misnomer (since there is not that much actual bronze, as opposed to copper, in this early period), the term 'Minoan' is simply a convention; that is, a convenient cultural and chronological marker, no more. Only Nowicki (2002; 2008) would argue that this cultural change (such as it was) was caused principally by the coming of a new people – the Minoans – introducing their distinctive new culture into the island of Crete. This is not to say that there might not have been immigrants coming into the island at this time – the cemetery at Ayia Photia on the north coast of east Crete is full of Cycladic objects which seem to indicate something more than trade connections (see Day et al. 1998). And immigrants, as we all now know, affect patterns of culture (cooking, burial and so forth) in the host community. But the evidence for the wholesale replacement of one population by another just is not apparent. This controversy continues to divide scholars (Hood and Cadogan 2011, 281–5; Whitley 2006).

Whatever the scale and impact of (a probably small) number of immigrants, the move from 'Neolithic' to 'Minoan' represents a change in what might be called the discursive frame. Since the time of Gordon Childe, scholars of the Neolithic have seen it a long-term process that plays out on a wider (European or Mediterranean) stage (e.g., Whittle 1996; Broodbank 2013, 148–248). Study of 'the Minoans' is, by contrast, necessarily confined to Crete. Whereas scholars of the Neolithic are therefore almost forced to be comparative, scholars of 'the Minoan' can sometimes convince themselves that, since their case is unique, it is also incomparable. Advances in Cretan Bronze Age scholarship can therefore be advanced solely (it is thought) through uncovering more 'Minoan' facts from the island of Crete.[3] This is reflected in the chronology and phasing for this period (see below).

One cannot ignore comparisons when it comes to metallurgy however. Of all the regions of the Aegean, the island of Crete is perhaps the poorest in metal ores in general and copper ores in particular. That is not to say that there might not have been some usable deposits to be found somewhere on the island, but in comparison to the quantities of copper ore to be found in southern Attica (around Laurion and Thorikos) and on islands in the Western Cyclades (such as Siphnos) these deposits were insignificant. Copper – whether as ingots, or as ore, or as finished products – would have to be imported. So the flat copper axe found in one of the Final Neolithic houses excavated by Evans and Mackenzie (Evans 1928a, 14) must have been brought to Knossos from elsewhere. This axe nonetheless remains the only identifiable copper object in Knossos for some time. If we want evidence of copper in the earliest part of the Cretan Bronze Age (EMI) we have to look outside of Knossos – to eastern Crete. Several copper artefacts have been found in the Ayia Photia cemetery close to Sitia, and copper daggers have been found in many Early Minoan tomb contexts (mainly EMII–III) elsewhere in Crete (Branigan 1967; 1968, 185–6). But nothing like this has been found in Knossos. To be sure, there are some signs of copper-working during the second millennium BC at the nearby site of Katsambas (just

Table 3.2 Chronological terms for the 'Early Minoan' or pre-palatial period (based on Momigliano 2007b) at Knossos

Phase (ceramic)	Calendar date BC (High chronology)	Calendar date BC (Low Chronology)	Architectural or institutional phase	Events
EMI (Early Minoan I)	3000–2650	Same	Early pre-palatial	
EMIIA	2650–2450	Same	Early pre-palatial	Levelling of tell?
EMIIB	2450–2200	Same	Early pre-palatial	Levelling of tell?
EMIII	2200–2050	Same	Late pre-palatial	Levelling of tell?
MM IA (Middle Minoan IA)	2050–1950	Twentieth century BC	Late pre-palatial	

to the east of modern Heraklion) which later served as the port of Knossos. Further to the east on the island, at Chrysokamino near Kavousi, a full-scale workshop for the smelting and casting of copper objects datable to the end of the Early Bronze Age (EMIIB or EMIII) has been found (Betancourt 2006, esp. 179–89; Muhly 2006). While the traces of smelting that have been found only date to the end of the Early Bronze Age in Crete, sherds of Final Neolithic date beneath the furnace hint at the possibility of earlier activity. In any case, at this stage most copper alloy objects on the island (mainly in the form of daggers or flat axes) would have been 'arsenical copper' and other alloys rather than tin-bronze proper. If we take copper smelting as our criterion, it is only really by 2300 BC that the island enters the 'Bronze Age'. EMI and EMII are then, in a sense, 'Chalcolithic'.

The immediate effects of this new technology – especially in terms of boosting the 'productive forces' of the community– would have been minimal. There is little or no copper in EMI Knossos, and throughout the Early Minoan period most tools were made of chipped or polished stone. There is certainly none to be found in 'the palace well, whose finds represent the earliest (EMIA) ceramic assemblage in "Minoan" Knossos' (Hood and Cadogan 2011, 21–73; Wilson 2007, 49–56). It is worth looking at the finds from here in some detail.

At first sight it might seem strange that the only major deposit for this first 'Minoan' phase takes the form of a well. In fact, in many sites which have had long occupation, and where settlements have been extensively built over and modified, this is not at all unusual. Most of what we know about (much later) Early Iron Age settlement deposits in both Knossos and Athens comes from wells which have been filled in after their proper use – as a means of supplying drinking water – comes to an end. Such wells often have very small 'use' deposits (representing parts of broken vessels, such as amphoras, used to draw water from the well), and much larger 'dump' deposits. These last represent material taken from middens or households and just considered (it is thought) rubbish – bits of broken crockery and other detritus taken from everyday life and no longer of any practical use. Most of the finds from this well comprise such a 'dump' deposit. The exception are the fragments of a pithos – a storage vessel – from the very lowest levels (Hood and Cadogan 2011, 52–4, esp. no. 133).

Pithos is a term used by Aegean prehistorians and Classical archaeologists for a certain type of ceramic storage vessel, often used to hold grain. If sealed with clay, such vessels can keep grain fresh for a very long period of time. Pithoi (plural of pithos) represent the Aegean world's technological solution to the problem of storing grain and forestalling famine in lean years. Pithoi are still produced by specialists in Crete today – their production usually involves the use of special clays and inclusions. The example from the palace well (no. 133) is one of the earliest such from the Aegean Bronze Age, being 0.68m high. This size indicates use at household rather than community level, but (as you will see) pithoi could get a lot bigger.

The rest of the ceramic assemblage from the well comes from the 'dump' fill – a deposit full of ceramics, spindle whorls, bone and stone tools and imported obsidian. Though for the most part this assemblage represents a logical development from the latest Neolithic (and so testifies to the essential continuity of the life of the community), there are some

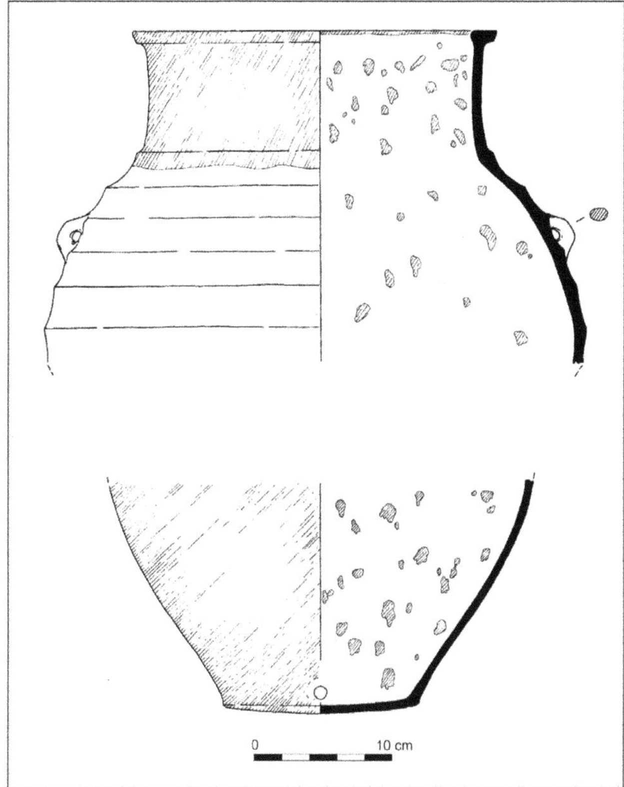

Figure 3.2 Early Minoan pithos. Hood and Cadogan 2011, 53, Figure 3.10. No. 133 from the palace well. Redrawn by Kirsty Harding. Courtesy British School at Athens.

changes. First, pouring vessels (jugs) become more distinctively jug-like, and drinking vessels more closely linked to drinking. Jugs, especially the 'jugs with cutaway spout', are now painted and their shapes more distinctive (Hood and Cadogan 2011, 42–4, Plate 9). A similar pattern can be observed with the drinking vessels. The chalices, with their high feet (Hood and Cadogan 2011, 31–4, Plate 3), become more elaborate and more frequent. Specialized forms of cooking vessel – in particular the 'Minoan' baking plate (Hood and Cadogan 2011, 41–2) – make their appearance. Both cooking and storage vessels (pithoi) now come in distinctive fabrics. Not all pottery fabrics are local, with petrographic analyses (Wilson and Day 1994) indicating that imports from south-central Crete (the Mesara) begin to appear in Knossian assemblages from EMI onwards, as do some Cycladic imports.

The faunal and floral remains from the well are of greater interest. Isaakidou (in Hood and Cadogan 2011, 63–7) detected relatively high levels of cattle bones in deposits dominated by sheep and goat – and no obvious evidence for feasting. Jane Renfrew (in Hood and Cadogan 2011, 67–9) detected some new additions to the flora – some olive stones and some indications of vine cultivation. Neither olives nor vines had formed a significant component of the diet of Neolithic people – indeed archaeobotanical studies (Sarpaki 2013) and analyses of wood charcoal (Badal and Ntinou 2013) had revealed no evidence for the presence of olives in earlier levels during the Neolithic (or at least between ENI and LNII). Olives and vines are not simply an addition to the range of foodstuffs consumed, since they require a different kind of cultivation (involving pruning) from grains and pulses. They are tree crops, and in Colin Renfrew's (1972) view provide the basis for characteristic Mediterranean 'polyculture'. This is a practice whereby two crops (wheat, say) can be grown in the same field as one of these tree crops (the olive). For this to work properly on an uneven and dissected landscape such as Crete, slopes have to be terraced – and at this stage there is no evidence for that. Vine cultivation is also the necessary condition for wine production – whether grapes were just (at this stage) simply a kind of fruit, or whether the grape's full potential was already being realized cannot as yet be determined. But it does raise the possibility that the elaborate chalices were for drinking something more substantial than water.

Deposits (with pottery) have been found beyond the palace well, of course – tests from the palace indicate continuing occupation of this area during EMI (Wilson and Day 2000). There is not much to say about the next sub-phase. EMIB deposits are even scrappier than those of EMIA. The relative scarcity and elusiveness of EMI

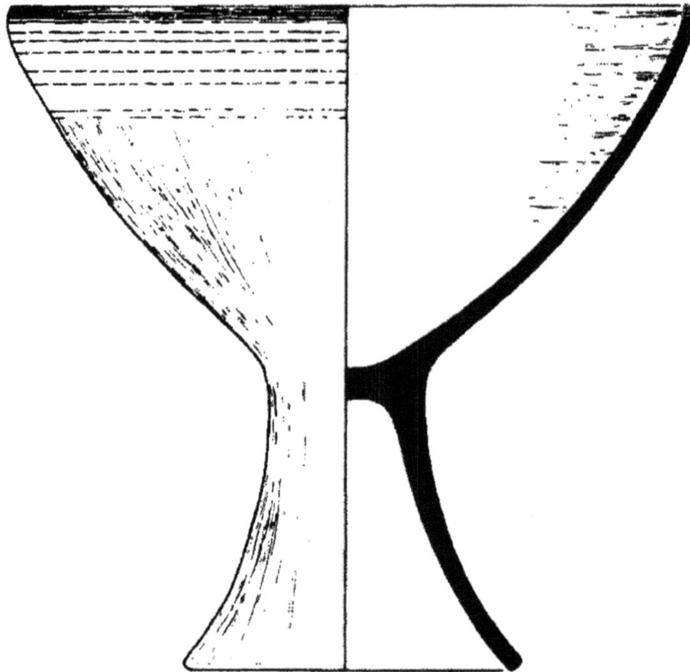

Figure 3.3 Early Minoan 'chalice' (drawing). Hood and Cadogan 2011, 32, Figure 3.4. Redrawn by Kirsty Harding. Courtesy British School at Athens.

deposits is a bit of a puzzle. If we had more such deposits we might be able to settle a major disagreement about the size of the settlement at the very beginning of the Bronze Age. In J. D. Evans' and Broodbank's view, the relentless expansion of the settlement seems to have come to a halt – it may even have contracted during this period. Tomkins (2008, 36), however, sees this period as witnessing a very rapid expansion in the size of the settlement – moving from 2 to 5ha within a few generations. Whether through rapid expansion or contraction, the community may well have been confronted with a crisis. If so, a solution of kinds was reached in the subsequent, EMII period.

3.5 Early Minoan II: a community reformed?

Early Minoan II (EMII) is the longest part of the Early Bronze Age in Knossos (Evans 1921, 71–102). It has two, very clear ceramic sub-phases (EMIIA and EMIIB), which have been much studied over the past few decades.

EMII also has much more concrete evidence for architecture than EMI. This takes the form, in EMIIA, of the 'West Court Houses' (Wilson 1985; 2007, 57–61; J. Evans 1972), houses found in excavations under the west court during excavation by John Evans in 1969. These houses (or at least one multi-roomed house) are quite substantial and built on stone foundations. The pottery assemblages from the houses continue the trends established in EMI. There are many drinking vessels – goblets with high stems, the descendants of EMI 'chalices'. There are more jugs (including beaked jugs) and more examples of painted wares (including a very elaborate spouted bowl; Wilson 1985, 308, No. P93; Figure 3.4).

Other areas with clear EMIIA phases have scrappier deposits. The finds from the north-east magazines group show some development over the west court house assemblage (Wilson 2007, 61–70). The two principal areas, however, where we now have abundant EMIIA–EMIII material are the Royal Road – particularly the Royal Road North – and the 'Early Houses to the South of the Palace'. Finds from these two areas (both of which have been investigated in fits and starts over several generations) have recently been published in synthetic form (Hood and Cadogan 2011, esp. 75–94), where the two areas are referred to as 'Area A' (Royal Road) and 'Area B' (Early Houses). Of these two areas, we only really have significant EMIIA deposits from the Royal Road. The pottery from here reveals little change from EMI – the only addition to the assemblage being the mysterious horned stands (Hood and Cadogan 2011, 264–6), which seem to have had some role in cooking (and which do not outlast the phase).

EMIIB marks a clearer ceramic break. The Mesara and Cycladic imports characteristic of EMI and EMIIA are no longer to be found. More prominent are the footed goblets – drinking vessels with much lower feet than the earlier chalices, which seem to come in uniform size and shape (Hood and Cadogan 2011, 142–6, 268–70). Some of these goblets represent examples of 'Vasiliki ware', whose origins are to be found in sites near the Ierapetra isthmus on Crete. Some are imports, others local imitations of a certain type of 'mottled' decoration that Knossians at this time found attractive. It is in EMIIB,

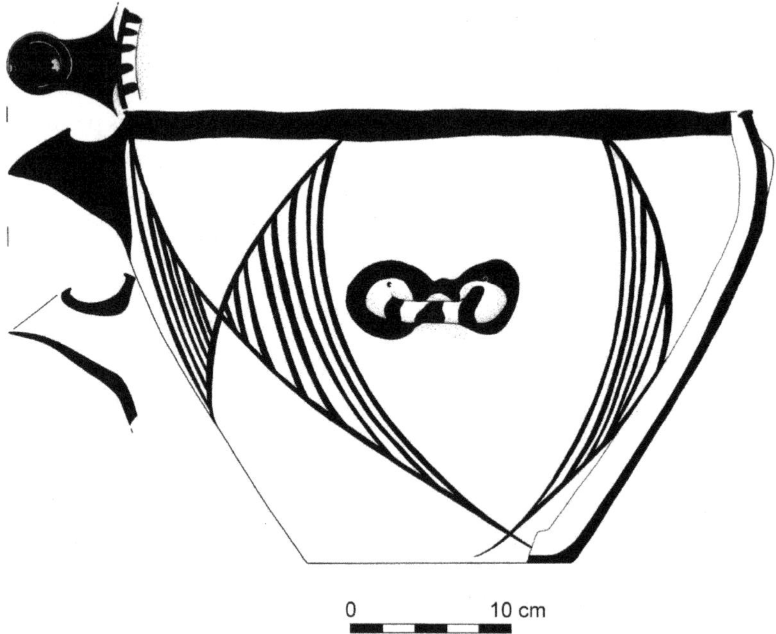

Figure 3.4 EMII spouted bowl. Wilson 1985, 308, No. P93. Redrawn by Kirsty Harding. Courtesy British School at Athens.

moreover, that perhaps the most unassuming, if also the most distinctive, 'Minoan' vessel first makes its appearance – the tripod cooking pot (Hood and Cadogan 2011, 116–17, 139, 152–3). This shape was to remain in use in Knossos down to Geometric times.

What underlying social processes underlay these changes? Since the 1990s there has been much talk about commensality as something that provided the social glue that kept the Knossian community together. Sometimes people talk of feasting. But if by feasting we imagine that Knossians at this time were slaughtering and then consuming large animals (pigs, sheep, goats or cattle) in a manner reminiscent of the feasts that accompanied animal sacrifice in Classical times, then the evidence just isn't there. Feasting implies a degree of ostentatious consumption of large cuts of meat – involving practices like spit-roasting. Valasia Isaakidou's detailed examination of the faunal assemblages from EMII deposits (Isaakidou in Hood and Cadogan 2011, 229–33, 237) seems to indicate small-scale domestic consumption. Moreover, the appearance of the tripod cooking vessel runs against the notion of 'feasting' on large cuts of meat. Such vessels are best suited for stews – which, if they involve meat, indicate a concern with 'calorific maximization' – getting the most out of your animal – rather than ostentatious consumption of large domesticates in a public setting.

Against this must be set the evidence for the goblets (or 'eggcups') – their uniform size, the fact that they are made in a variety of 'fine' wares (Wilson and Day 2000, 6–8) and their frequency. None have yet appeared in clearly definable sets, but their appearance

Figure 3.5 EMII goblets. Hood and Cadogan 2011, 269, Figure 10.13. Redrawn by Kirsty Harding. Courtesy British School at Athens.

does hint at perhaps more communal forms of drinking practice, or at least uniformity of drinking practices between different households.

Whatever the role of commensality, there are indications that the settlement continued to expand. EMIIB deposits have been found south of the palace (Momigliano and Wilson 1996). As the settlement expanded, and as more people were living 'cheek by jowl' in a densely occupied, nucleated settlement, the shape of that settlement changed. Excavations around the west court houses hint at the construction of dry-stone walls to form terraces – terraces constructed so that one house could and would overlook another (Wilson 1994). If one house (or household) overlooks another, does this imply some kind of ranking of households? If so, there is little else that indicates ranking or hierarchy, and little to show that the community was transformed in EMII.

This statement, however, overlooks one important fact about the deposits from this period. For, as we know, at some point the tell of Kephala was levelled to create a platform for the 'palace'. These operations 'removed not only the Early Minoan levels but a great deal of the Late Neolithic ones also over a wide area of the centre of the mound' (J. D. Evans 1972, 115; see also Efstratiou 2013). This fact creates what archaeologists call 'problems of taphonomy' – archaeologists need to account for site formation processes (both natural and cultural) when they try to make social sense of their evidence (such as pottery deposits). The levelling of the mound, of course, would explain why so many of the deposits are disturbed and why so much EMIIB material has been found near the edges of the palace area (such as the Royal Road and south of the palace). It may account for the apparent absence of sets of drinking vessels (if these are indications of commensality). But what is curious is that so much of the mound was levelled – as John Evans says, not merely to the Early Minoan but in many places to the Neolithic levels. This is a point to which we will return.

3.6 Early Minoan III–Middle Minoan IA: Knossos just before the palace?

This phase (EMIII–MMIA) in Knossos' history is known as 'pre-palatial' – the phase just before the construction of the palace. This rather begs the question of what kind of structure the 'palace' was, and what kind of institution it may have represented. The question of the date of the earliest 'palace' – or rather the date of the laying out of the first building with a large central court– has become more complicated in recent years. There is a strong argument for a much earlier date, which will form the end of this chapter.

In ceramic terms, this phase has long been elusive. While MMIA is reasonably well defined (Momigliano 1991), Arthur Evans did not really define 'EMIII' very closely, and some scholars have doubted its existence. Recently, Momigliano (2007a; see also Wilson 1994, 33–5) has argued strongly that a ceramic phase of EMIII does exist. The phase can be identified in key deposits such as the upper east well Group. The distinction between EMIII and MMIA is that while EMIII is not simply a 'light-ground' style, MMIA is the first style that is consistently polychrome and largely dark-ground. Characteristic of this phase is that the standardized drinking vessel – the EMIIB 'eggcup' – gradually becomes taller and turns into a goblet.

The ceramic assemblage changes in other ways as well. The deposits from the 'Room of the Jars' within the area of the palace form a more coherent 'drinking assemblage' than anything to be found in earlier levels (Momigliano 2000). This deposit may then relate to some genuine commensal practice involving drinking and fine pouring vessels.

Hitherto the architecture of the various phases of the settlement at Knossos has taken the form of houses. These gradually become more sophisticated over the course of the Neolithic and Early Bronze Age, with stone socles being introduced in EMII; but they are still houses – and houses moreover that are much less sophisticated than their contemporary Early Helladic II equivalents (the corridor house) at Lerna and Aegina. The 'protopalatial' (MMIA) houses excavated in the west court (Pendlebury and Pendlebury 1930) may (just) fall into this category – if they do not belong more happily

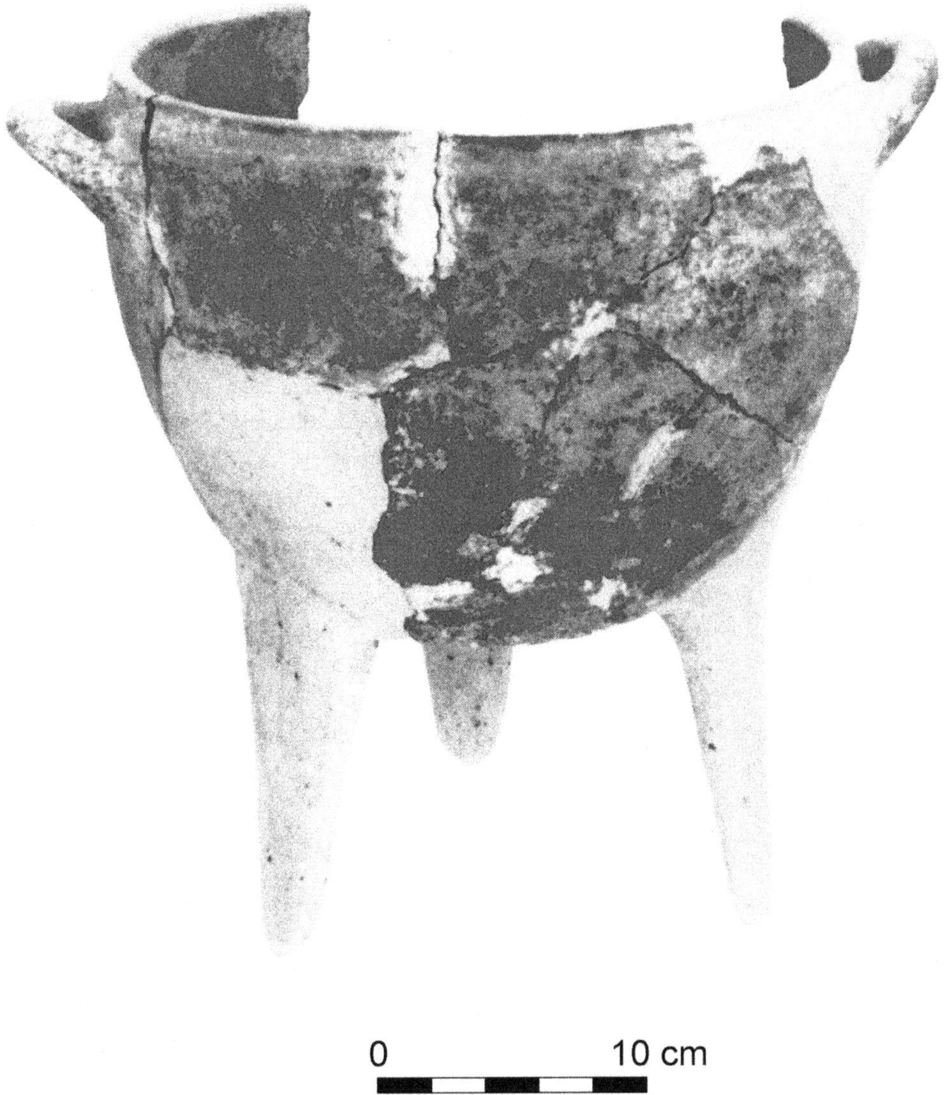

Figure 3.6 Restored EMII tripod cooking vessel. Momigliano 2007b, 92, Figure 3.10, No. 5. Courtesy British School at Athens.

to 'protopalatial' proper. For this phase in Knossos we have, for the first time, structures which are not simply domestic. First are the two rather mysterious 'hypogea' (underground buildings), one in the south-east corner of the palace, and the other the 'Early Hypogaeum beneath the South Porch' (Evans 1921, 103–7). This last hypogeum is an elaborate, circular structure cut into the soft rock. It was never fully excavated. We only have Evans' plan to go on, but it appears to have had a rock-cut entrance and a rock-cut spiral staircase, of which Evans says, 'The staircase itself, in combination with the great bee-hive chamber, suggests analogies with the spiral staircases enclosed in the Nuraghe of Sardinia or the brochs of Scotland . . .'

Both Late Bronze Age Sardinian Nuraghe and Late Iron Age Scottish brochs are much later in date than this hypogeum, and if we are to seek contemporary parallels in the Mediterranean for elaborate rock-cut structures of this early date, we probably have to look to the funerary 'temples' of Malta. Evans was puzzled by this hypogeum and thought it may have served some defensive purpose. Most scholars nowadays (following Renfrew 1972) would prefer to see it as having been used for storage (presumably of grain). If so, its size indicates it must have served the community as a whole, rather than a single household. The second new, non-domestic structure is the so-called 'keep' found to the north-west of the later Central Court, which Evans (1921, 127–50) originally dated to MMI. Recently, Hood and Bendall (2020, 138–40; *contra* Branigan 1992) have suggested that this structure might be even earlier – EMIII. The keep incorporates several large ashlar blocks with masons' marks. This then represents the first use of a symbolic system that may be linked to early forms of writing at Knossos (Hood and Bendall, 52–4). Finally, there is the north-west platform or north-west terrace wall (see Figure 3.7).[4] This is an exterior façade, built of carefully shaped if rather small stone blocks. Its date (EMIII) and its later incorporation in the larger structure has always prompted speculation that it may represent the earliest phase of the palace. The platform was last investigated in 1987 in a small trial excavation undertaken by Alan Peatfield under the general direction of Sinclair Hood (results of which have yet to be published).

If there were architectural changes, there were also major changes to the structure of the settlement. During EMI–II, the size of Knossos changed little from that of the

Figure 3.7 North-west platform/north-west terrace wall (EMIII). Photo by the author.

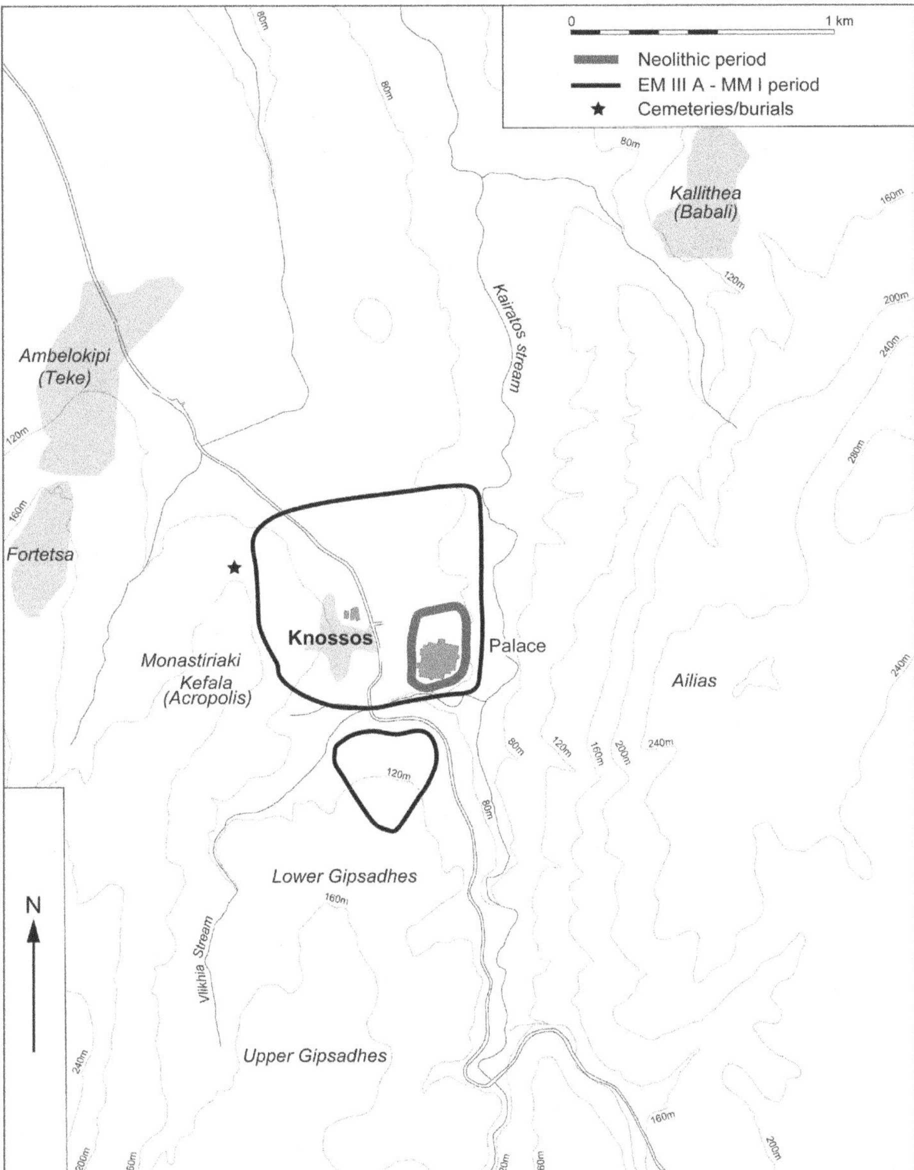

Figure 3.8 Expansion of the settlement area from Neolithic times until immediately pre-palatial times EMIII/MMIA. Information from Whitelaw et al. 2019, Figures 2 and 3. Drawn by Kirsty Harding.

Neolithic tell – it remained around 5ha, and certainly no more than 8ha. The latest estimates for the EMIII–MMIA settlement (Whitelaw et al. 2019) indicate a dramatic increase in size – to at least 20ha and possibly 40ha. This is large enough to be called 'urban' by some measures – it is certainly within the range of many of the forty-nine Archaic to Classical *poleis* of the island (Perlman 2004). So the population of this community must have more than doubled over a period of little less than two centuries. This is a remarkable development – even more so if we consider that it seems to emerge with little or no warning. For millennia, Knossos seems to have been a stable village community. Suddenly it became something else.

3.7 States, urbanism and Crete: Knossos in a wider frame c. 2000 BC

Anthropologists and archaeologists have long puzzled over the emergence of states. Particularly perplexing are 'pristine' states, that is political communities with central authority that emerge from less complex political orders. For these states could not have been influenced in any way by their neighbours. 'Minoan' states are, strictly speaking, not pristine, since in the third millennium BC the kingdom of Egypt lay to the south-east, and palace states (such as Ebla) could be found in Syria. Ebla at least had a complex social order and administrative system that fully justifies the term state (Archi 2015).

But what is a state, as distinct from a polity or a political community? Scholars have scoured the ethnographic classics and archaeological literature to come up with some general principles. The veteran Mesoamerican and Mesopotamian comparative specialists, Kent Flannery and Joyce Marcus, have come up with some general material correlates that characterize early (pristine) states across the globe, from early Mesopotamia to the nineteenth- and early twentieth-century Swazi Kingdom (Flannery and Marcus 2012, 422–34; Marcus 1998). The main characteristics of states are:

1. Evidence of permanent hierarchy, in the form of temples, palaces or elaborate tombs. These mark the fact that a stratified hierarchy, where wealth, power and status is ascribed and not achieved, has emerged.

2. An urban centre (of at least 40 ha in extent) that forms the capital of a state's territory.

3. This territory is sufficiently large for a four-tier administrative hierarchy (however defined) to have emerged (see Flannery and Marcus 2012, 422–74).

4. A monopoly of force – the state controls a police force or an army.

5. A monopoly of legal authority – the state sets laws (written) or monopolizes legal authority in the person of a king or ruler.

The traditional picture, painted by Evans, of 'Minoan' Crete as a kingdom with a ruler called Minos would certainly conform to this stereotype. But here we are getting ahead of ourselves, for we cannot see anything like this around 2000 BC. Anthropological archaeologists such as Flannery and Marcus agree that a precondition of a state emerging is the development of a hierarchy that goes beyond ranking – that is, beyond social stratification. Where should we look for signs of such stratification?

Archaeologists have long been accustomed to look for ranking in burials. Regional traditions in burial and in funerary architecture are a very prominent feature of the Early Bronze Age in Crete as a whole (Herrero 2009). There is plenty of evidence for possible 'ranking' in the elaborate forms of burial we find in the tholos tombs of the Mesara (Branigan 1998a), or the house tombs of Mochlos or the elaborate burial architecture at Phourni (near Archanes; Murphy 1998; 2011b). Some have argued that the funerary feasts focused on ancestors; feasts that took place around the Mesara tholos tombs must have provided some of the social glue that helped reorganize Cretan communities in the Early Bronze Age (Hamilakis 1998). Surely, then, something like this must have been found at Knossos, the largest site on the island?

Well, the answer to this proposition is no. We do not know for sure where Knossian bodies were buried after they ceased to be incorporated in the fabric of the tell at some point in the Neolithic. Desperate attempts have been made to find EM to MMI tombs in the area of the later North Cemetery (Teke), or on the Gypsadhes hill to the south (Herrero 2014, 236). On the Acropolis there is the tomb at Monastiriako Kephali (Preston 2013b) where remains of twelve individuals have been found. The age/sex ratios of the bodies seem skewed, with women outnumbering men by a factor of 2:1 and few if any children or sub-adults. The associated pottery, comprising numerous cups, appears to date to late EMIII or MMIA. This is the first clear example of the practice of collective burial which perhaps represented kin groups of some kind.

There is no other clearly attested Early to Middle Minoan I burial or tomb near Knossos, nor any evidence of elaborate tomb architecture. There is little to indicate social ranking in burials, and the close attention given to possible hierarchies in pottery shapes and assemblages (e.g., Day and Wilson 2002) could be seen as a proxy for this lack of funerary evidence. Such a search for 'ranked commensality' in ceramic forms would provide an alternative model, one that would have some support in the ethnographic literature (see Dietler 2001).

Many scholars find this puzzling. Flannery and Marcus (2012) omit the Aegean from their global survey – it just doesn't seem to fit. Aegean scholars are equally perplexed by the absence of evidence for an emerging hierarchy in Crete in the third millennium BC. For, what we would expect if we follow Renfrew (1972) is the gradual accumulation of traits that characterize states (sometimes called complex societies). Against this gradualist view, other scholars (notably Cherry 1984; 1986) have put forward a 'catastrophist' alternative – complex societies emerged suddenly just before 2000 BC. Certainly, the evidence I have given above favours the 'catastrophist' view. But, even if this is correct, it does not explain how or why it happened. We may point to increasing contact with Egypt (Bevan 2004), whose polished stone vessels find their way into later contexts at Knossos, as providing an external stimulus. But even if we allow for this kind of stimulus, we still have to explain how one thing (say the existence of a palace-state at Ebla in Syria) stimulated the emergence of another (say a 'palace' at Knossos). But are we framing the question in the right way? Many scholars think not. Consider this statement of perplexity by one of the most distinguished 'Minoanists' of his generation:

> The regional dynamics and different trajectories [in Minoan Crete] … make me wonder whether … we are not trapped into established theoretical models and definitions of political and territorial organization. The scarcity of fortifications, an absence of overt royal iconography and the difficulty of tying the Cretan situation to territorial organizations known from the Bronze Age Mediterranean leaves me frustrated.
>
> *Driessen 2001a, 65*

We may be too obsessed with hierarchy. There are other paths to complexity. One means of organizing complex systems such as societies is not so much through hierarchy as through *heterarchy* (Schoep and Knappett 2004). Heterarchy is a term devised to cover systems with overlapping different and competing loci of authority (religious, political, etc.) within a particular social order. So the apparent absence of hierarchy within EMI–II Knossos is not therefore conclusive evidence of the absence of complexity.

Which brings us back to the 'palace'. Our ideas of what constitutes a palace still owe much to Evans. Even if we allow for the fact that Cretans in the third millennium BC may have known about developments in Egypt and in Syria (where recognizable palaces did exist), this does not mean that they would immediately find a use for such a structure. And even if emulation, or the diffusion of ideas, is at work, we still have to think about the local context. For emulation (of a palace in Syria) may not entail imitation. Certainly, at some point in the third or early second millennium BC Knossians constructed a large monumental structure with a central courtyard. Indeed, it is this central courtyard that Driessen (2002; 2004) has argued is the essential feature of a so-called palace. But this palace, in its earliest form, was clearly not the 'palace' of Evans.

Whatever we call this structure, the inhabitants of Knossos first had to level the tell – a tell which was necessarily associated with generations of previous occupation. Most discussion of this has simply accepted this 'levelling' exercise at face value – as perhaps an inevitable result of the kind of explosive settlement and population growth we witness in EMIII–MMIA. What these discussions omit is how unusual this practice is. Most Neolithic and later Iron Age tells in much of the Balkans were simply abandoned as settlements (Whitley 2017b); some went out with a bang, in violent fire destructions (Tasić et al. 2015). No others that I know of were *levelled*. Recently, too, scholars have noticed that the earliest phases of Malia and Phaistos seem to be much earlier than previously thought. A settlement of the size of 'late pre-palatial' Knossos – at least 20ha (Whitelaw et al. 2019; see also Whitelaw 2001; 2004) – must be called urban, and it would be extremely unusual for an urban settlement to lack a central structure.

Recently Peter Tomkins (2016) has argued that the earliest 'palace' must have dated to long before the so-called protopalatial period in MMIB (*contra* MacGillivray 1994). Building on John Evans' (1972) observations as to the depth of the disturbance in Neolithic strata, Tomkins argues that a courtyard – or at least a defined and bordered open space – must have been erected for the first time in EMII. This space would have served as a 'gathering place' for several corporate groups who made use of (but may not have actually lived in) Knossos. These groups would have erected some small buildings (one for each group) around this defined space. This communal ritual space preceded anything like 'urbanism' in Knossos. If this is so, it would be around this courtyard space that the EMIII–MMIA town grew. This structure can hardly, at this stage, be called a palace – a residence for a ruler or an elite group. Its function must have been more communal.

Such a proposal remains controversial; the matter is far from settled, and we can probably look forward to decades of debate on this issue. But this is in many ways an attractive hypothesis. It helps to explain the expansion of settlement in the final pre-palatial phase; it brings Knossos into line with Malia and Phaistos; and it helps to explain the absence of burials.

Whenever the first 'palace' or 'courtyard structure' (Driessen 2002) was created, it certainly marked a sharp break with what had gone before. For millennia (between 7000 and 2000 BC) Knossos had been, in many respects, a fairly typical east Mediterranean tell settlement, where people had lived out their lives in ways that would have been familiar to their neighbours in the Aegean and Anatolia. After the erection of the first monumental structure the character of Knossos shifts decisively as the pace of change accelerates.

CHAPTER 4
PALATIAL KNOSSOS: THE 'PALACE OF MINOS'?

Chapter abstract

This chapter will look specifically at the period most people associate with Knossos, the palatial, when Knossos formed the largest city in the Aegean world. It will begin with what most scholars still call the 'first palace' (formed around 1900 BC) through to what are called the neopalatial (New Palace) and final palatial periods, down to the destruction of this structure around 1300 BC. During these periods the palace formed the centre of a large urban complex, whose size peaked around 1500 BC. It will argue that it is only in the final palatial period that the palace was indeed a palace – the residence of a ruler and the centre of a form of centralized administration.

4.1 On palaces

This chapter covers the shortest period in this history of Knossos – when the town was dominated by that large building and institution we call 'the palace'. In most standard accounts, this lasted (in calendar years) from 2000 to 1325 BC, a period of less than 700 years. This is a much shorter period of time than the five millennia of the Neolithic and pre-palatial 'Minoan' phases (on the one hand) and the three millennia of the post-palatial and historical periods (on the other). But while it may be the shortest period in Knossos' history, it is (in the eyes of most scholars, and of most people who have visited Knossos) also the most glorious. For this is the period of Evans' 'Palace of Minos', a period when the social, cultural and political life of the town was dominated by the palace. It was also a period when the town of Knossos – at between 90 and 120 hectares at its greatest extent – was one of the largest in the Eastern Mediterranean. We are now dealing with an urban, literate civilization which was (in many ways) the equal of the palace states of the Near East, if not quite the great Kingdom of Egypt to the south and east (Cline 2015).

Yet the term 'Palatial Knossos' or 'the palace of Minos at Knossos' presents us with several problems. It is not just that Minos may not have been an historical person. It is also that the structure (and institution) we called a 'palace' may not have been the same structure and institution when it was first constructed as when it was finally destroyed. When it was finally brought to an end, 'the palace' was certainly a residence of a ruler, the centre of administration and the locus of political power for the whole of central Crete. It is tempting to work back from what we know of its final phase and interpret its earlier phases in the same light. But what Evans called 'the Palace of Minos' was destroyed, modified and rebuilt on several occasions, and during these phases of rebuilding, the

Table 4.1 Terms and dates for the Bronze Age, particularly the palatial Bronze Age, in Knossos

Phase (ceramic)	Calendar date BC (High chronology)	Calendar date BC (Low Chronology)	Architectural or institutional phase	Events
MM IA (Middle Minoan IA)	2050–1950	Twentieth century BC	Late pre-palatial	
MMIB	1950–1900	Nineteenth century	Old Palace (First Palace) – protopalatial	Construction of palace? Earthquake
MMIIA	1900–1850	1800–1750	Old Palace – protopalatial	
MMIIB	1850–1800	1750–1700	Old Palace – protopalatial	
MMIIIA	1800–1750	1700–1640	Unclear. New Palace?	Earthquake
MMIIIB	1750–1675	1640–1600	New Palace (Second Palace)–neopalatial	
LMIA	1675–1580	1600–1510	New Palace – neopalatial	Thera eruption (1620 high, 1520 low)
LMIB	1580–1490	1510–1430	New Palace – neopalatial	Fire damage to houses in town of Knossos
LMII	1490–1430	1430–1390	Final Palace (Third Palace) final palatial	
LMIIIA1	1430–1370	1390–1360	Final Palace – final palatial	Final destruction of palace at end of this?
LMIIIA2	1370–1320	1360–1330	Post-palatial?	Or here?
LMIIIB	1320–1200	1330–1190	Post-palatial (in Knossos)	Final destruction of Mycenaean palaces on Greek mainland c. 1200 BC
LMIIIC	1200–1100	1190–1100	Post-palatial	
Sub-Minoan	1100–950		Transition to Iron Age	

structure was extensively modified. In brief, there was never a single 'Palace of Minos'; rather, there were several successive structures built over one another. This process of architectural change also reflects institutional change. For this reason, scholars refer to several palaces – the Old Palace, the New Palace and the Final Palace in one scheme,[1] or (in another) the seven or so phases of rebuilding that took place over these 700 years. These changes are reflected in the chronology and terms we use for this period.

Part of the problem lies in the term 'palace'. For British readers the term 'palace' implies a rather splendid residence of a king or queen. This is also how 'palace' is understood by North Americans – even if Caesar's Palace in Las Vegas is not an actual residence of a Caesar, the name would mean nothing if it did not allude to an original building on the Palatine Hill in Rome. In Italian, however, *palazzo* does not necessarily imply a ruler's residence – every substantial Italian town has several *palazzi*; some of these might still be residences of important families, but they are more likely to be municipal buildings with splendid rooms (often used for academic conferences). Similarly, in France, a *palais* is no longer the residence of a king, but often simply a large building with an important civic or legal function (as in *Palais de Justice*). In France, however, they still remember that the very large structure at Versailles was once a ruler's residence (and the centre of state power); it is only recently that the 'palais' that is the Louvre has lost all of its administrative roles. Meanings and functions can change. Bearing this in mind, let us look at the first of the 'palaces' uncovered at Knossos.

4.2 Protopalatial Knossos: the construction of the First Palace?

The construction of a central courtyard building underneath the later 'palace' is probably the single most important event in Knossos' history. Most scholars (*pace* Tomkins 2016) still believe this took place around 1950 BC. They disagree profoundly, however, as to what this palace looked like, and what buildings it incorporated. Evans' original idea was that the original palace was a series of large buildings – which he called *insulae* (a Latin term designating a block of houses, used by Roman archaeologists to designate regions in Pompeii and other major Roman sites) – grouped around a central court. At this stage, then, there was no 'palace' as such – the main feature was the court (Driessen 2004; Graham 1987, 73–83). According to Evans (1921, 127–50, 203–24), it was only during the Middle Minoan period that these various 'insulae' became a single structure, a structure which (Evans 1921, 225–30) was also equipped with a system for drainage and sanitation (MacDonald and Driessen 1988). MacGillivray (1994) has cast doubt on Evans' 'insula' hypothesis. He argues that it is more likely that a central courtyard structure was erected as an architectural whole from the very beginning (if, that is, the beginning dates to *c.* 1950 BC). This new structure, of course, incorporated some older buildings – the EMIII north-west palace angle, the MMIA monolithic pillar (MacGillivray 1994; 2007, 107) and perhaps, too, the 'keep' (Branigan 1992), which is more likely to have been used for storage than for defence (for location, see Figure 4.1). It is unclear whether either of the earlier 'hypogea' (see Chapter 3) continued to be used, or, if so, what they would be

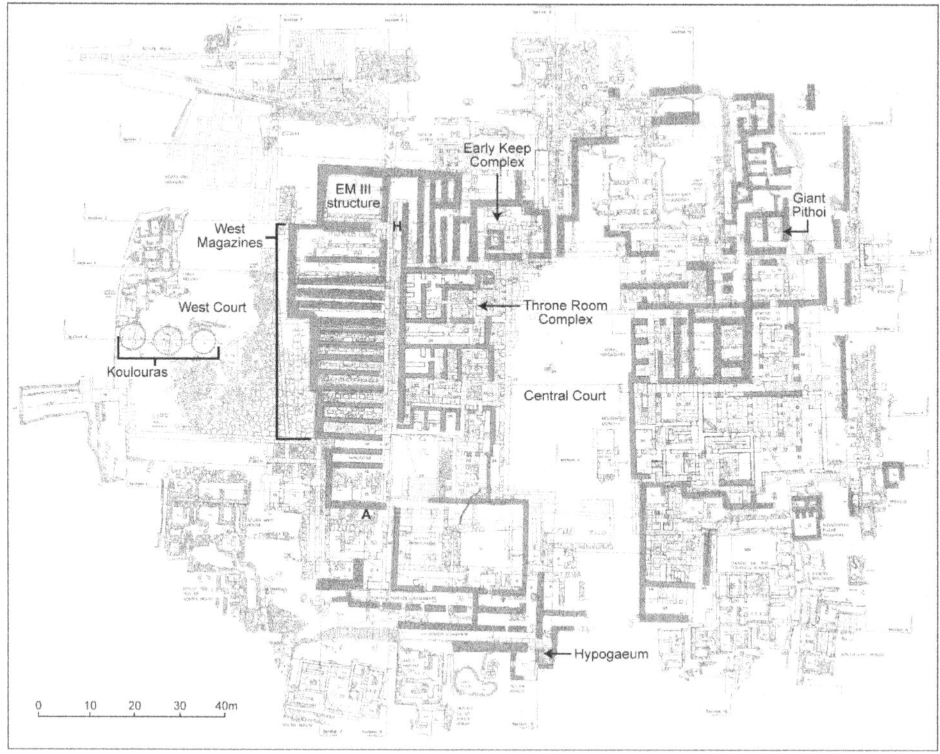

Figure 4.1 Hypothetical plan of the Old Palace at Knossos. Drawn by Kirsty Harding. Based on Hood and Taylor 1981. Key: **A** indicates the location of Deposit A (see Figure 4.3 below and Knappett and MacDonald 2007); **H** indicates the location of the Hieroglyphic Deposit (see Figure 4.4 below).

used for. This new MMIB structure made extensive use of ashlar blocks, many of which appear to have been inscribed with masons' marks (Hood and Bendall 2020, 39–44). Over 1,600 such marks have been found in Knossos, and most are found in or on the walls of the palace. The purpose of such marks has been much debated. Are they practical? Or are they essentially magical, a way of marking out certain buildings as special and ensuring that their construction will be, in every sense, fortunate? Hood (Hood and Bendall 2020, 81–91) argues strongly that such marks are not to help with quarrying, nor are they marks of contractors, nor can they be interpreted as providing guides for the positioning of blocks. They must, by default, be interpreted as ritual or magical, as a means of marking out this new structure as special.

If this structure were a palace (in any sense) it would have had to have had a fitting façade. We do know that, along with the construction of the central court and the buildings around it, a west court outside the palace was laid out at this time. Central courts and west courts seem to be feature of all Minoan palaces. Today the side of the palace facing the west court has cut ashlar blocks built over a layer of gypsum – most scholars think that these are MMIIA in date (see MacGillivray 1994). Evans (1921, 127–

31) had argued that the foundations of the 'west wall' must have represented an earlier, suitably monumental façade facing the west court (whose earliest phase must be contemporary with the central court). Momigliano (1992), however, has looked at the evidence for this so-called 'proto-palatial façade' and found it wanting. Certainly there was nothing monumental about some of the earlier structures (the EMIII north-west angle) incorporated into this 'palace'. And fairly soon – during MMII – a monumental façade facing the west court was constructed, built of ashlar blocks of gypsum quarried from the local hill to the south (Gypsades). This irregular wall (Figure 4.2) remained a constant feature of all subsequent phases of the 'palace'.

The structure, then, lacked a convincing 'front' in its earliest (MMIB) phase, a phase in which there is obviously nothing grand or monumental, but rather narrow entrances and no ashlar façade. In other respects, however, it was quite carefully conceived. Its central feature was the court (Driessen 2004; Palyvou 2000), whose long axis (approximately

Figure 4.2 The gypsum façade of the 'palace' facing the west court, constructed in MMII. View from the south. Photo by the author.

54m × 28m) was aligned north–south. This is one of the reasons that Driessen (2002) prefers to call this and related structures not palaces but court-compounds. For to reach the various parts of the palace, one has to go through the court around which all other structures are arranged. There are other features of the court that recall the cosmological alignments we find in Early to Middle Minoan tombs, whose openings are set to coincide with the rising and setting of the sun at solstice and equinox. Lucy Goodison (2004) has explored this dimension of 'palatial' architecture in some detail and suggested that there were other cosmological features to be found in the throne room. MacGillivray (2004) proposed that the first (that is, the MMIB) palace referenced the surrounding landscape in its overall architectural design. Clearly within sight of the central court would have been Mount Juktas. This was not merely a prominent mountain but also a 'peak sanctuary', whose earliest phases seem to date to this period (Evans 1921, 151–63). These inferences have largely been drawn on the later palace. Given, however, that the north–south alignment must have been present in the 'Old Palace', it is likely that these cosmological features must have been present from the very beginning. Such observations have lent support to the idea that the primary purpose of this 'palace' was as a gathering place (MacGillivray 2007, 106), a setting for communal and seasonal festivals whose character must, in part, have been religious. Does this then make this structure not so much a palace as a temple? Or should we look to another, near contemporary, analogy closer to home – the Knossos palace as a kind of henge?[2]

Henges are a feature of the later Neolithic (late third to second millennium BC) in Britain. Recent reinterpretations of the most famous henge – Stonehenge (Parker Pearson 2012) – have emphasized two associations: its connection with the dead and with ancestors; and its link to communal and seasonal feasting (which took place, not at Stonehenge, but at nearby Durrington Walls). We can, I think, rule out any ancestral or funerary functions for the protopalatial palace – there are no bodies, nor fragments of bodies, nor anything that might serve to commemorate one's forebears. But feasting has been of considerable interest to scholars. What we lack from Knossos in this period is any quantity of animal bones – bones of large domesticates such as sheep, goats, pigs or cattle – that would suggest slaughter for a 'feast' (see Isaakidou 2007). There is nothing like the deposits we find in some later Greek sanctuaries (e.g., at Eretria; see Verdan 2013) and nothing to indicate that consumption was as ostentatious as the feasting that accompanied later Greek sacrifice certainly was.

Does this then disconfirm the 'henge' hypothesis? Perhaps it is worth looking at what structures or rooms surrounded the central court. Of course, here we do not really know for sure what the earliest function of a room was, since many were modified or built over in later periods. There seems to have been a 'lustral basin' in the north-west corner of the palace (by the north entrance), which could (conceivably) have been related to an initiatory ritual. There is as yet no 'domestic quarter', no set of apartments that could have served as the residence for a king or ruler. Vast areas (including the west magazines) were devoted to the storage of foodstuffs in large pithoi. But most of what we find seem to be pantries, or rooms full of elaborate, painted fineware pottery. It is for this reason that discussion of feasting has concentrated not on animal bones but on ceramics.

Here there were certainly major changes from the previous period. For one thing we have well defined deposits – 'The Early Chamber beneath the West Court Group', 'The Royal Pottery Stores Group', the 'Trial KV Group' and the 'West and South Polychrome Deposits' (MacGillivray 2007; see also Evans 1921, 164–90, 231–70) through which we can trace, successively, the typological development of MMIB, MMIIA, MMIIB and MMIIIA. Both the ceramic sequence and the stratigraphy is eminently clear, and equally mark a sharp break with what had gone before (MacGillivray 1998). While all these styles are, like MMIA, 'dark ground', the vessels are more highly decorated than before with light (and sometimes) red paint, giving a very rich effect, perhaps reminiscent of metalwork (or textiles, or both). The fineware shapes are dominated by drinking and pouring vessels. The drinking vessels display an enormous variety of cups (angular, tall rimmed, rounded, carinated), with some goblets. Pouring vessels include jugs and the bridge-spouted jar. These vessels now have much thinner walls – the thickness of the drinking vessels is sometimes no more than 3mm or so. It requires a new technology to produce such effects.

Scholars have long argued that this new technology must have been the potter's wheel. Knappett (1999; 2004; Macdonald and Knappett 2007, 23–55), however, has argued that the wheel was introduced slowly, beginning in MMIA. By MMIIA it was being used to produce smaller vessels, including cups, in large numbers; by MMIIB, larger, pouring vessels were being made using this new technique. The technology of the potter's wheel comes from the East, as perhaps does the 'metallic' inspiration for the polychrome decoration, which many have seen as evoking the effects of metalwork (though whether at first- or second-hand we cannot say).

Not all these very fine cups – and many have walls less than 2mm thick – were produced near Knossos. Mackenzie and Evans were not mistaken when they referred to the earliest palatial phase as 'Kamares', named after a cave high on the heights of Mount Ida which overlooks the Mesara plain in south-central Crete (where the contemporary 'palace' of Phaistos is to be found). Petrological and chemical investigation (Day and Wilson 1998; 2002) seems to indicate that quite a large proportion of these painted fineware cups were produced somewhere on the Mesara plain and imported to Knossos. But if they were manufactured by Mesara potters, the manner in which these cups were used seems to be peculiarly Knossian. In and around the palace there are a number of 'pantries' – places where large numbers of drinking cups were stored (MacDonald and Knappett 2007). In one of these pantries (deposit A, datable to MMIB; MacDonald and Knappett 2007, 57–68, 161–5; for location, see Figure 4.1), a clearly 'hierarchical' structure seems to be apparent in what most scholars still think is the earliest phase of the 'palace'. Figure 4.3 shows the cups themselves from deposit A.

Table 4.2 gives the estimated proportions of the participants, based on the numbers of cups found (see below).

Of course several caveats need to be entered here before we infer that this apparent hierarchy of drinking cups represents a permanent hierarchy of persons. First, if this represents a hierarchy, it does so only for the relevant occasion. It then may well be as consistent with a rotation of the duties (and privileges) of office holders or magistrates as

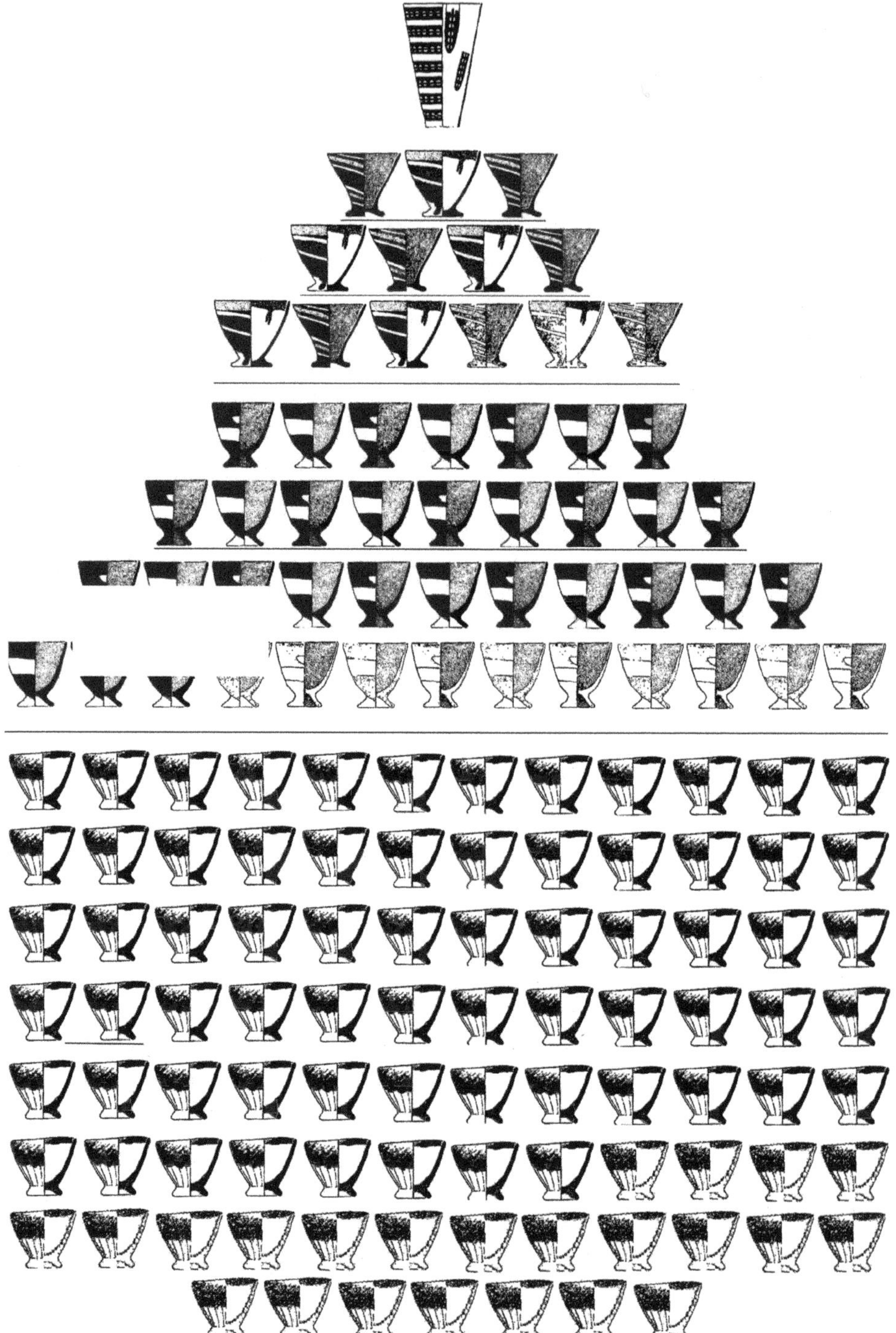

Figure 4.3 Pyramidal hierarchy of MMIB goblets from deposit A. After Macdonald and Knappett 2007, Figure 6.1. Redrawn by Kirsty Harding. Courtesy British School at Athens.

Table 4.2 Estimated number of participants in cup-based commensality within the courtyard complex at Knossos

Participants	Minimum	Maximum
Grade A	1	1
Grade B	11	13
Grade C	34	40
Grade D	78	91
Total	124	145

Source: MacDonald and Knappett 2007, 57–68, 161–5.

with a more established and permanent pyramidal social order. And second, these deposits just relate to drinking – and is drinking that important?

Drinking only becomes socially important if it relates to feasting. And here another feature of the early palace is significant – the space devoted to storage. One of the main architectural peculiarities of both the 'palace' at Knossos and the palace at Phaistos is that large parts of both structures are devoted to magazines – corridors alongside which very large storage vessels (pithoi) were placed. In Knossos, these series of narrow corridors with storage vessels are referred to as the west magazines (Evans 1921, 449–62) – they lie immediately behind the irregular west front of the palace (whether or not it was, at this stage, lined with gypsum blocks) that faces the west court. This seems to be a general feature of all early palaces. Some of these storage vessels are very large, standing over 2m in height – higher than most people both in the Bronze Age and today. These pithoi were normally used to store grain – more rarely oil or wine. Most of the time they would have remained sealed with clay, which was an effective means of protecting the grain from rats or mice ('commensals') and for storing grain over long periods (to offset the risk of famine). Breaking the seal on such a vessel would imply that all of the contents would have to be consumed very quickly.

The pithoi now preserved in the west magazines at Knossos are largely of late Bronze Age date (Christakis 2005), but evidence from Phaistos suggests that these storage areas had been in place since the very beginning of the 'Old Palace' period. In architectural terms the west magazines as we see them today (Hood and Bendall 2020, 156–71) date from after MMIIB (that is, after the first architectural phase of the palace); there are other smaller protopalatial magazines (Hood and Bendall 2020, 153–4) which indicate that most of these storage areas must have their origin in protopalatial times, even if the 'Room of the Giant Pithoi' seems to date from a later phase (MMIIB) of the Early Palace (Hood and Bendall 2020, 128–30). Estimates of their total capacity vary – one (Moody 1987) suggests that the capacity (at 1713m^2, 12 per cent of the ground floor) was very much greater in MMII than in MMIII (1250m^2, 9 per cent of the ground floor) or LMI (850m^2, 9 per cent of the ground floor).

The magazines – and storage – are central to a debate about what the 'palace' was for. In the 1970s the tone of that debate was set by Colin Renfrew (1972), who argued that

Bronze Age palaces (both Cretan and Mycenaean) were central to a redistributive economy. The palace – and the palace elites – both managed the storage of the produce of the Cretan peasantry and arranged for its redistribution for the common good: from each according to his means; to each according to his deserts. Communal storage is something we find elsewhere in the Eastern Mediterranean from the Bronze Age onwards (Strasser 1997) – think of the biblical story of Joseph interpreting Pharaoh's dream (Genesis 41.17–37). In addition to the magazines, the three MMIB *kouloures* in the west court of the palace might conceivably have functioned as granaries in this period (Strasser 1997) – although it seems more likely that they were just pits, later covered over. Since Renfrew, however, other scholars have cast doubt on this notion of 'redistribution'. Paul Halstead (1989) has shown that there are other means by which farmers can engage in 'risk-buffering' against the prospect of major crop failure, by planting cereals in small plots widely distributed over the terrain at different altitudes. The Cretan terrain is certainly well suited to such practices. Crop production geared towards surpluses, moreover, usually entails the use of large fields – which in turn run a greater risk of catastrophic crop failure than do the practices of traditional Greek farmers (Halstead 1993; 2001). And Strasser (1997) has shown that not all early state societies are 'redistributive', nor do all redistributive hierarchies become states.

We have to look at more particular explanations for this investment in large-scale storage than 'redistribution'. One feature of many of the early inscriptions in Hieroglyphic and Linear A from many of the palaces is that they seem to involve the movement of large quantities of something (we haven't deciphered what) at very infrequent intervals (Olivier 1990). These documents would, however, be consistent with the idea of provisioning for occasional, seasonal gatherings involving large numbers of people using both the central and west courts of the palaces. Large gatherings require that large numbers of people be fed.

This brings us back to the question of feasting. I prefer the term 'gatherings' to that of feasts, since 'feasts' implies the provision of special foods (usually from slaughtered animals, whether domestic or hunted). Feasts in an anthropological sense (Dietler 1996; 2001) are also great occasions – such as the feasts that accompanied the act of sacrifice that took place in the great festivals of the Classical world. These certainly merit the term. But there is as yet absolutely no positive evidence from the bioarchaeological record for a large-scale, seasonal slaughter of animals at Bronze Age Knossos that would be a necessary feature of such feasts (Isaakidou 2007). How then should we interpret these documents, and the investment in storage that we find in the west magazines and in other parts of the earliest palace (see Evans 1921, 203)? Perhaps it is time to turn to the documentary evidence.

4.3 A literate civilization? Scripts and seals in protopalatial Knossos

With the palace appear the first scripts in Bronze Age Crete. These scripts were used primarily in administration (hence their recovery from archives). 'Minoan' Crete therefore was Europe's first literate civilization (as in Childe 1925).

These statements represent the *communis opinio* of many scholars who draw on the evidence of Knossos to compose a broader picture. These pictures may have several subjects: the Mediterranean world in the Bronze Age (e.g., Broodbank 2013); the development of Europe in prehistory; or, more narrowly, the succession of cultures within the prehistoric Aegean. They do not necessarily represent the views of the experts on Cretan script and seal use in this period. The picture that Crete in general and Knossos in particular presents is messier and more complex than these statements allow.

The study of Cretan Bronze Age scripts begins with Evans. In *Scripta Minoa*, Evans (1909) identifies three scripts from Knossos. These he places in an evolutionary sequence: Cretan Hieroglyphic, Linear A and Linear B. Evans recognized that all three scripts were 'mixed': primarily syllabaries, but also retaining features of ideographic or pictographic systems. They were also much simpler – in that they made use of a much smaller number of signs – than contemporary scripts in the Near East and Egypt (cuneiform and Egyptian Hieroglyphic respectively). We now know that 'Cretan Hieroglyphic' is not simply the first script in this sequence: at Phaistos, Linear A and the (still mysterious) 'script' of the Phaistos disk were in use in protopalatial times; and closer to Knossos, scholars have identified an 'Archanes script' (Decorte 2018; Ferrara et al. 2021), which, though it may not be a script in the strict sense of the term, is certainly a coherent symbolic system. It is the Cretan 'Hieroglyphic' script, however, that is most closely associated with protopalatial Knossos since the discovery, by Evans, of the 'Hieroglyphic Deposit' within the palace itself. This script is quite complex (Olivier and Godart 1996, 12–17). There are ninety-six phonetic signs that represent syllables (vowel–consonant combinations – syllabograms); eighty-two that represent whole words or things (such as cattle) – so-called logograms; four that represent numbers on a decimal scale (1, 10, 100 and 1000) – 'arithmograms'; and nine for various fractions ('klasmatograms'). Some of the signs of these early scripts seem very similar, if not identical, to masons' marks (Hood and Bendall 2020, 52–4; Salgarella 2021).

The Hieroglyphic script itself has yet to be deciphered – we cannot read it, and we do not know what family of language (Indo-European? Semitic?) the inscriptions might belong to. But we can add up the numbers – and numbers seem to be a key feature of the documents we do have. Some of these numbers are quite large – in the thousands (Olivier 1990). Documents in 'Cretan Hieroglyphic' come in several forms (Olivier and Godart 1996): there are small nodules; there are medallions (sometimes referred to as Hanging Nodules, as they have a hole for suspension); there is one three-sided and many more four-sided bars; and there is at least one tablet. There are no lengthy texts on any of these documents – generally there are no more than three signs, and the sole tablet from Knossos (Olivier and Godart 1996, 122, No. 068 **KN Hi 01**) has many more numerals than either 'logograms' or 'syllabograms'.

Knossos is nonetheless fairly rich in these documents, as the table below shows.

The bulk of these documents come from the Hieroglyphic deposit, which many have interpreted as an archive. In this light it is odd then that the first written document from Knossos (indeed from the whole of Crete) is neither palatial nor forms part of an

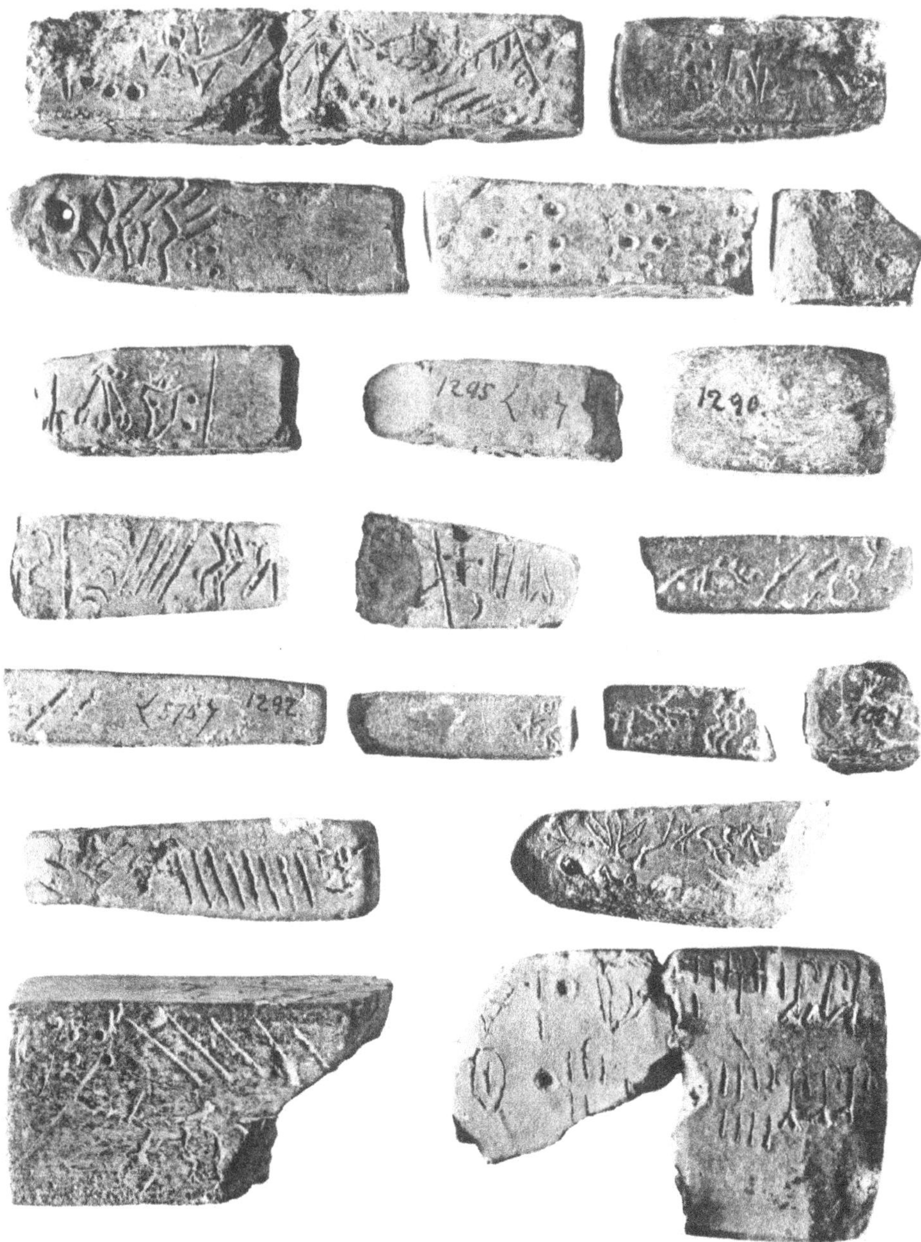

Figure 4.4 Clay bars and tablets from the palace at Knossos, including the sole Hieroglyphic tablet (bottom left) from Knossos. Olivier and Godart 1996, 122, No. 068, **KN Hi 01**; Evans 1909, 120. After Evans 1909, Plate X.

Table 4.3 Protopalatial 'administrative' documents from Knossos and elsewhere in Crete

	Nodules	Medallions	3-sided bars	4-sided bars	Tablets	Seal impressions	Seals	Other	Total
Knossos	29	18	1	20	1	32	1	1	103
Rest of Crete	1	20	0	11	3	25	137	32	229
Total	30	38	1	31	4	57	138	33	332

Source: Olivier and Godart 1996; Schoep 2007.

'archive'. This is a fragment (SF68) of a two-sided bar of MMIIA date from deposit E in the south-west houses outside the palace (Schoep 2007). The deposit it comes from is secondary (i.e., redeposited; Macdonald and Knappett 2007, 131–4). Both the script and the subject are uncertain, but it may have formed a record of sixty animal hides – hides that may have been associated with the processing of animal carcasses and the working of horn (Isaakidou 2007).

This document, therefore, does not shed much light on the earliest form of 'palatial administration'. But there is some evidence from deposit A (see above; Macdonald and Knappett 2007, 134–9; Weingarten 2007), datable to MMIB, that might do so. This takes the form of seal-based noduli (noduli with seal impressions) – all bearing the image of an *agrimi*, the Cretan wild goat. These noduli were associated with the 'cup' deposit and some miniature vases. Weingarten speculates that these miniatures – as often happened in the Near East – were used as tokens to provide counts (of the vases? Of something being eaten or drunk?). The seal-based noduli would provide a link to a particular person or office-holder – perhaps the man or woman in charge of the 'commensal' event signalled by the pyramid of cups.

Neither of these two early deposits, then, were archives. Though the finds from both deposits A and E might have something to do with administration – something is being counted out – they do not provide evidence for a system of record-keeping such as we find at major Near Eastern palace sites (such as Ebla or Mari), where records can be cross-checked and referenced for later use. These two deposits are rather small. There are, of course, larger deposits. The greatest concentration of Hieroglyphic documents in Knossos is to be found in the eponymous 'Hieroglyphic Deposit'. Is this an 'archive'?

Here, context and date are important. The Hieroglyphic Deposit was discovered early on in Evans' excavations, in a 'chamber at the North End of the Long Gallery' (Evans 1900, 25, 59–63; 1909, 19–22; 1921, 271–85) – this being the gallery that connects all the west magazines. It comprises 102 documents (noduli, medallions, bars and tablets – see Table 4.2) as well as at least fifty-seven seal impressions (Platon et al. 2002a; 2002b; Gill 2002; Müller 2002). The number of written documents could, in principle, make it possible to interpret it as an archive that could later be consulted by administrators. But there are three problems with this interpretation. The first is that, if the small chamber in which these documents were stored was an archive, it was a very awkward one for any administrator wanting to consult the material. The second problem is the date, which appears to be MMIIIA – that is, at the very end of the protopalatial period.[3] The third problem is the association of written documents with seal impressions; seal impressions, moreover, that seem to indicate that they sealed something organic, fibrous and perishable (such as papyrus letters; Müller 2002). In brief, it has the appearance, not so much of an archive as of a dump – a dump of now redundant 'administrative' material that had been tidied away into a small room.[4]

The Hieroglyphic Deposit also illustrates another perennial feature of the uses of writing in Bronze Age Crete: scripts are almost invariably associated with seals and sealings (Krzyszkowska 2005). That is to say, unlike the archives of Ebla or Mari (where cuneiform documents are stacked together; see Archi 2015 and Dalley 1984, 15–20, respectively), written documents are usually found together with seal impressions, and these seal impressions seem to be associated with seals found on (presumably) written documents written on material (papyrus?) that has now perished. Seals are often thought to have functioned in much the same way as seals did in Western Europe in medieval times (as on the numerous sealings to be found on the Declaration of Arbroath, representing the barons of Scotland in their support for Robert the Bruce): they represented the person or office of the seal-holder, and were a means therefore of authenticating a document, to make it 'official'.

In sum, then, there is no positive evidence for archives in the Near Eastern sense – that is, of rooms equipped specifically for administrative documents that were stored in such a way that they could be consulted and cross-checked. Instead, we have a great variety of relatively short documents. These documents have very few signs but mention very large numbers. Some of these documents (the medallions, perhaps the noduli) seem to have originally been attached to something else – perhaps a letter written in a material that has now perished. So, we might be dealing with documents that indicate correspondence, presumably between persons of equivalent status. Does this then constitute administration? Yes, of a kind – but again of a kind very different to that found in the Near East. Cretans, then, did not simply 'borrow' Near Eastern administrative practices – writing in Crete is not a straightforward case of diffusion.

4.4 Town and cemetery in protopalatial times

There is no doubt that the town of Knossos grew rapidly around this time. While Knossos had become much more than a village towards the end of the third millennium BC (EMIII–MMIA), its expansion continued in this period. Recent estimates (Whitelaw et al. 2019) suggest it reached a size exceeding sixty hectares. We are now dealing with a town of several thousand people rather than a village of several hundred.

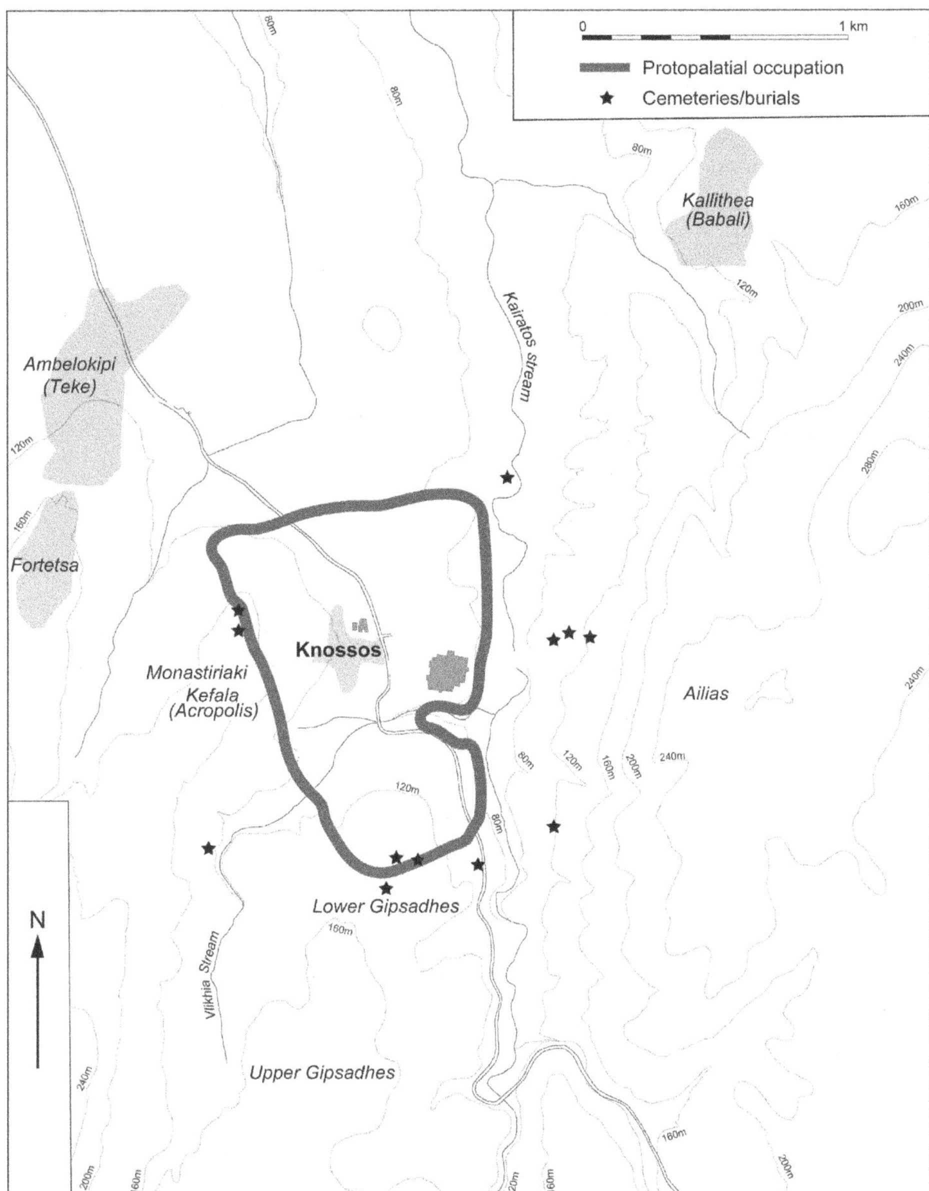

Figure 4.5 The extent of the town in protopalatial times (after Whitelaw et al. 2019, Figures 3 and 4), with the location of principal cemeteries (drawn by Kirsty Harding).

Figure 4.6 Knossos, town mosaic. AMH, 145014.jpg. Licensed under Wikimedia Commons.

We are rather less well informed, however, about houses in this phase. Hilda and J. D. S. Pendlebury had excavated some 'protopalatial' (MMI) houses cut by the kouloures in the west court (Pendlebury and Pendlebury 1930) – houses which might be pre- rather than protopalatial. Evans (1928a, 366–73) noted some small MMII–III simple structures which could be houses to the west of the palace. In the same general area, part of what looks like a house has been excavated (Popham 1974), but not completely. This held at least one cup deposit – though the cups were of poorer quality than those found within the palace. The house was built on stone foundations and seemed to have been built of mud brick; its architecture is broadly consistent with the MMII 'town mosaic' (Evans 1921, 301–14). These were houses with flat roofs having up to three storeys.

More now can be said about cemeteries. For the several centuries that preceded the 'Old Palace' of Knossos, the question of where 'Minoan' bodies were buried has remained a mystery. This is particularly curious for the latest, EMIII–MMIA phase of the 'pre-palatial' period, which remains an almost complete blank[5] when it comes to mortuary practices. How is it that the size of the settlement (and so the population) increased so dramatically, and yet bodies were not buried (or not buried in a manner that archaeologists can recover)? Elsewhere on the island there are plenty of cemeteries, and indeed distinct regional mortuary traditions in pre-palatial times (Herrero 2009; 2014). Why not in Knossos?

Something seems to change in the protopalatial times. There are at least three MMIB–MMIIB cemeteries with several collective tombs. The first of these (moving from north

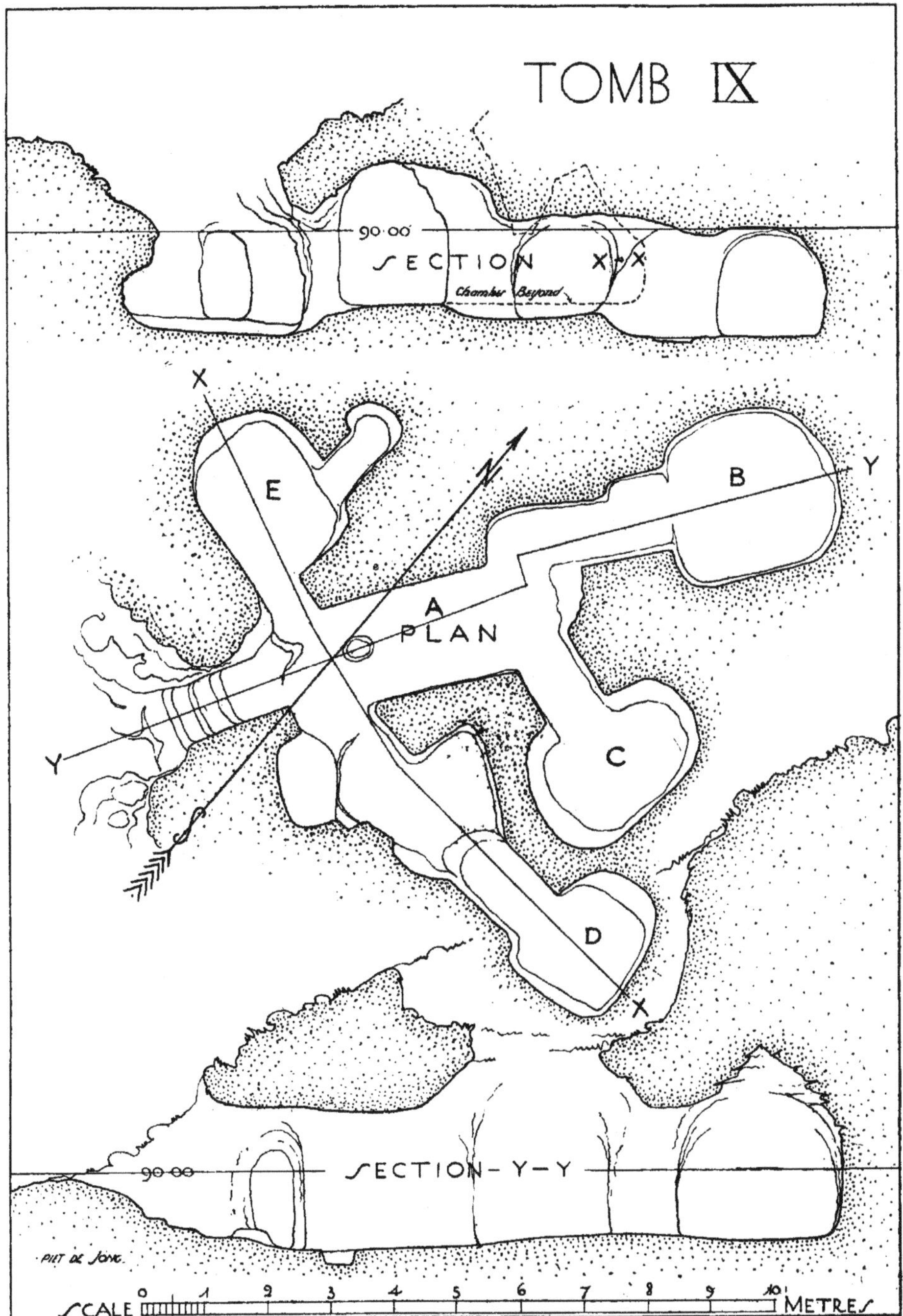

Figure 4.7 Plan and section of Tomb IX from the Mavro Spelio cemetery. After Forsdyke 1927, 265, Figure 19.

to south) is at Mavro Spelio, which lies to the north-east of the palace on the slopes of the Ilias hill. 'Mavro Spelio' means black cave, and in later times this small natural cavern was the focus of a minor spring cult (Forsdyke 1927; Herrero 2014, 234–5; see also Alberti 2013). Around the cave were a number of rock-cut tombs. Most of these are, much later, Mycenaean-style chamber tombs (with a simple chamber and dromos), but some are more complex tombs with multiple chambers. In three of these, rather cave-like, tombs (tombs VI, VII and XVII) there was found evidence of MMII activity in the forms of painted pots and seal-stones (Platon et al. 1977, 47–54). Skeletons that we can date to this earliest (MMII) phase remain very hard to identify, and the finds have clearly been disturbed by multiple periods of reuse (in some cases as late as Geometric times). Rich tombs indicating a social hierarchy are simply not to be found.

The picture is somewhat clearer in the Ailias cemetery, just to the south of Mavro Spelio (Herrero 2014, 230–2; Hood 2010; Platon et al. 1977, 55–81). The earliest interments (in tomb I, MMIB) in these seven tombs seem to be inhumations in pithoi. These are multiple interments over several generations in multiple chamber tombs, which were cleared out from time to time (a fact which allows for the possibility that burial in these tombs began slightly earlier than protopalatial times). Whether burial in the Upper Gypsadhes cemetery (tomb XVIII) to the south also begins this early is unclear (Hood et al. 1959, 220–4, 252–3; Herrero 2014, 232–4). In all these cases we have individual interments in collective tombs,[6] where the dead number at least twenty or perhaps as many as forty persons per tomb. This raises a question which in modern parlance could be said to be one of 'personhood' (Fowler 2004; Herrero 2016). Was it the single person, or was it the social group, that was most important in burial?

The practices evident in these cemeteries exemplify the oddity of Minoan social developments at the time of 'state formation'. There is a long-standing theory in archaeology which goes back to Gordon Childe (Parker Pearson 1999, 86–7; Childe 1945), which is that when early states form (and so early hierarchies are in need of legitimation) then there is a marked emphasis on funerary display, whether in the form of rich burials (as at the Shaft Graves at Mycenae) or in the forms of elaborate funerary monuments (think of the mastabas and pyramids of Egypt). Mavro Spelio does not really support this theory. Indeed, while there are numerous 'rich graves' elsewhere in pre-palatial and protopalatial Crete (at Archanes Phourni, for example; Herrero 2014, 216–24), very few of these seem to be concentrated near the earliest 'palaces' of Knossos, Malia and Phaistos (Herrero 2009; 2011; 2014; Murphy 2011b). There is almost a *negative* or inverse correlation between Early to Middle Minoan tombs and sites where palaces develop. Could it be that Knossians were, in general, burying their dead very far from where they lived?

There are possible ethnographic analogies for this kind of behaviour. The Merina of Madagascar bury their dead in large, monumental tombs near ancestral villages – villages where their forebears once lived but they do not (Bloch 1971). The Cretan pattern, however, seems to be the inverse of this. If ever there were a site which might have been a plausible 'ancestral village' for many communities on the island it is Knossos. And it is

Knossos that seems to have been shunned as a place of burial during that crucial, formative period in EMIII–MMIA. Could it be that burial was somehow incompatible with the new cosmological significance of Knossos' new 'central courtyard' structure? Might the dead have been thought of as somehow 'polluting' the new focus of a cult that these structures represented?

4.5 The palace as sanctuary: the transition to the 'new' palace period

Crete is an island subject to frequent earthquakes (Evans 1928a, 286–325). In antiquity these earthquakes would often destroy buildings, and large structures (such as the first 'palace') were particularly vulnerable. Earthquakes are the principal cause of most of the destruction that the palace experienced. The first of these (or at least the first we can document) took place at the end of MMIIB (Evans 1928a, 287), which some scholars have taken to mark the end of the Old Palace period in Knossos; another is perhaps to be associated with the 'House of the Fallen Blocks', south-east of the palace (Mathioudaki 2018).

The question of when the 'Old' Palace ends and the 'New' Palace begins is, however, far from clear. For some scholars there was not one 'new palace' but several. Colin Macdonald (2002) discerns three architectural phases: the MMIIIB 'new palace'; the LMIA 'painted palace'; and the LMIB 'ruined palace'. All these reconstructions made use of blocks with 'masons' marks' (Hood and Bendall 2020). Even if it still makes sense to distinguish an overall 'new' palace from an 'old', scholars disagree as to when this took place. Many assign the transition to some point in MMIIIA, close to the beginning of MMIIIB (MacGillivray 2007; Hatzaki 2007a); others insist that the transition (such as it was) took place at the very beginning of the MMIIIA ceramic phase (Macdonald and Knappett 2013a; Knappett et al. 2013). There is, then, despite the earthquakes, very little evidence for a clean break between the two palaces.

In any case, one person's destruction horizon is another's rebuilding opportunity. Old structures could be put to new uses. Is there any strong evidence for this during MMIII? Well, there is plenty of evidence of deposits under later neopalatial floors, which most scholars from Evans onward have interpreted as the result of cleaning-up operations after damage or destruction. One such is the Vat Room deposit in the so-called central palace sanctuary area (Panagiotaki 1999, 8–44). This comprises pottery (principally jugs) and fragments of shell, ivory, gold, ostrich egg and obsidian.

It would be difficult to interpret such deposits as 'rubbish', given that they contain material that is both exotic and valuable. Some slightly earlier deposits which seem to be associated with ritual could be interpreted as deliberately marking an 'ending' in a suitably ritual manner. Driessen (2013, 17; see also Mathioudaki 2018) has argued that the (MMIIIA) deposit in the House of the Sacrificed Oxen (Evans 1928a, 301–3), just to the south-east of the palace and just next to the 'House of the Fallen Blocks', represents just such a 'Termination Ritual' (for which parallels can be found in the archaeology of the American Southwest). Are there other such 'Termination Rituals'? This question becomes both more urgent and more intractable when we look at possibly the most enigmatic find from the 'Palace of Minos': the 'Temple Repositories'.

The Temple Repositories comprise two large stone-lined cists in a small room just behind a room with a large pithos. Ritual activity also seems to have taken place in the area around the Temple Repositories, in the so-called pillar crypts (Hallager 1987). This area of the palace, just to the south of the throne room on the west side of the palace, lying between the central court and the west magazines, has come to be referred to as the central palace sanctuary area (Panagiotaki 1999), containing as it does several deposits (such as the Vat Room deposit) most easily interpreted as 'ritual'. The Temple Repositories were excavated in 1903 (Evans 1903, 35–94). Their date is controversial – MMIIIB or LMIA (Haztaki 2007a, 173; Panagiotaki 1998). They are most famous for their faience female figurines, especially the so-called 'snake goddesses' (Evans 1921, 463–523; Figure 2.4). But they also clearly contained faience beads, a marble cross and much administrative material, including tablets and sealings (seal impressions; see Platon et al. 2002, 113–14). Panagiotaki (1999, 71–179) has collected all the data, which has led to several reappraisals (Hatzaki 2009; Simandiraki-Grimshaw and Stevens 2013; Stevens and Simandiraki-Grimshaw 2016). Below is Hatzaki's (2009, 24, Table 2.1) summary of the evidence.

Table 4.4 The contents of the Temple Repositories

Level	East Temple Repository	West Temple Repository
1st (top) level	No finds	No finds
2nd (middle) level	Storage jars, wood, fragments of gold foil	Storage jars, wood, fragments of gold foil
3rd (bottom) level	Administrative paraphernalia (tablet), clay sealings (160 or so), stone hammers, faience beads, ivory objects, marble cross, stone libation tables, antlers, weasel head, fish vertebrae, carbonized cereals	Lower body of 'snake goddess' figurine, gold foil, carbonized matter, rock crystal disk with petals, bronze
	Faience fragments (including inlays)	Roundels?
	Seashells and faience seashells	
	Faience cups	
	Figurines (articulated)	
	Skirts	
	Arms	
	Head (of snake goddess?)	

Source: Panagiotaki 1999, 71–179; Hatzaki 2009.

It appears that large numbers of finds within these deposits were deliberately and intentionally broken before deposition – particularly (and most especially) the faience 'goddesses', including the so-called snake goddess. As Hatzaki puts it, 'The circumstance makes for compelling evidence for both intentional fragmentation and the simultaneous deposition of objects within the two cists' (Hatzaki 2009, 24).

These deposits then represent ritual activity following a festival. The deposit contains one Linear A tablet (Godart and Olivier 1976a, xv, 84–5) which lists ninety of (something) on one side and 240 of (something else) on the other. One of the jars from the upper levels seems to have contained a wine offering (as its inscription indicates; Christakis 2010). The number of seashells (around 6,340) could be seen as representing the number of people who could stand in the central court. The fragmentation of what to us appear valuable objects – in particular the snake goddess – was a part (the end point) of this ritual. The documents might be seen as records of how resources were mobilized – not something to be administered so much as *enacted* or *performed*.

There is further evidence that parts of the 'palace' were becoming more temple-like. Just to the north of the Temple Repositories is the throne room (Evans 1935b, 903–48). The name may be a misnomer, at least for the neopalatial period. Though what we see today is (largely) neopalatial, evidence from Mallia suggests that this complex of rooms may go back to MMII times. This room is not one room but comprises a complex of several rooms (Niemeier 1987). First, there is a room with an off-centre 'throne' reached from the central court through a pier-and-door partition. Next to this (to the south) is a 'lustral basin', around which are several rooms which Niemeier interprets as rooms for ritual preparation. Preparation for what, one may ask? Well, the 'throne' is flanked by frescoes of griffins. The restored griffins we see today are of final palatial date (Galanakis et al. 2017; Hood 2005, 65, No. 8), though these could conceivably be modifications of earlier frescoes. Contemporary iconographic evidence (from seals and finger rings) shows a woman in special costume surrounded by griffins, and Niemeier follows Reusch (Reusch 1958; Niemeier 1987, 165) in saying that 'during the ritual performed in the throne room a priestess sitting on the throne represented or even *was* the goddess'. That this room had a ceremonial function – and that these rituals may have taken place at the equinox or solstice – is reinforced by Goodison's (2004) observations about solar alignments.

The whole area of the 'central palace sanctuary' faces onto the central court. Iconographic evidence, in particular the miniature fresco showing a central pillar shrine and a crowd of spectators looking on (Evans 1930, 46–65; Hood 2005, 63–4, No. 6; Davis 1987) – the 'Grandstand Fresco' (Figure 4.9) – supports the idea that both the central and the west courts were used for large gatherings. The ritual nature of these gatherings was emphasized by the construction of the 'tri-pillar shrine' facing the court; their seasonal nature, by the solar alignments of the throne room and elsewhere (Goodison 2004) and by the construction of painted floors around narrow entrances, some of which recall the design of the Labyrinth itself (Shaw 2012). Some have interpreted these gatherings as akin to 'Harvest Festivals' (Hallager 1987). That the central court was also used for performances – athletic ones involving bulls – was an argument forcefully

Figure 4.8 The throne room. Stock images – best image on reddit 'artefactporn', https://www.reddit. com/r/ArtefactPorn/comments/2xwhe6/the_throne_room_at_the_heart_of_the_bronze_age/; https://out.reddit.com/t3_2xwhe6?url=http%3A%2F%2Fi.imgur.com%2F0sPTTSs.jpg&token= AQAAlbz7YtCj4-4AmKhSoTxVaK6cD_QXAkBnIJeboocxYbci5t2M&app_name=web2x&web_ redirect=true.

put forward by Evans (1921, 203–32; Shapland 2013). This argument is strongly supported by the iconography of some of the frescoes (notably the taureador frescoes; Hood 2005, 79–80, No. 33; and the 'Grandstand Fresco', see Figure 4.9) as well as that of gems and finger rings (Evans 1930, 209–32). Whether 'bull leaping' was linked to such seasonal gatherings is, of course, more difficult to argue – in any case, such athletic performances were special occasions linked to the 'central palace sanctuary'. All this lends support to the supposition that the 'Palace of Minos' was, in neopalatial times, more temple than palace.

But to this it may be objected – what about the 'domestic quarter'? Knossos, unlike Mallia, seems to have a large, multi-storey complex on its eastern side (the slope of the Kephala hill), which Evans interpreted as the quarters of the king and queen of Knossos. Its architectural elaboration certainly took place from MMIIIB onwards. And what about the frescoes, now mainly datable to the 'New Palace' (Hood 2005)? Are these not the most suitable decoration for this Cretan Versailles?

The palace of Knossos on its eastern side is built into the hill of Kephala. Bronze Age architects took advantage of this gentle slope to extend the structure downwards toward the east. Though parts of this quarter may have been constructed earlier, major construction here seems to have taken place in MMIIIB (Evans 1901a, 102–17; 1902, 39–87, Figures 30–32) to produce a multi-storey complex which can find no parallel in any other Cretan Bronze Age palace (*pace* Graham 1987, 84–113). This is Evans' 'Domestic Quarter', where he located the apartments of the royal family (the King's and Queen's megara; Evans 1928a, 354–6), as well as an impressive complex of reception rooms (such as the 'Hall of the Double Axes'), galleries and a grand staircase. Some of these domestic areas are, however, also supplied with features we might consider ritual – such as lustral basins (Nordfelt 1987).

These constructions are part of what Evans and others called 'the Great Re-building'. One feature of this rebuilding was improved drainage. Though a drainage system existed in MMIIA (the Old Palace), a more complex system of drains seems to have been built in neopalatial times (MMIIIA and MMIIIB: Driessen and Macdonald 1988). Rebuilding, moreover, requires redecoration. Hood (2005, 50) argues that it is this phase – MMIIIB – that witnessed not only extensive reconstruction, which not only made elaborate use of ashlar masonry amongst others, but also heavy use of wall paintings – more particularly frescoes. A fresco is a form of wall painting where the paint is applied to wet lime plaster (as opposed to a *secco* where paint is applied when the plaster is dry). Most of the wall paintings in Knossos are true frescoes. Painting frescoes is an extremely skilled craft. That it, in part, derives from a long tradition of plastering walls and floors with lime is not in doubt – suitable sources for the right kind of lime can be found just to the south of Knossos (Jones and Photos-Jones 2005, 207, Figure 13.4). Frescoes, however, do not seem to have been a major feature of the 'Old Palace'. Only one fresco (No. 29 in Hood 2005, 76) can be securely dated to MMIIB. This is a very simple design – a dado with curving bands. The MMIIIA period sees the appearance more complex scenes, such as the 'saffron gatherers' (Hood 2005, 62, No. 5).

But the bulk of the frescoes that can be assigned to the 'New Palace' (Hood 2005, nos. 9, 10, 11, 12, 13, 20, 28 and 32) date to the 'Great Reconstruction' of MMIIIB.[7] These include the 'Ladies in Blue' (No. 32); slightly later come the Dolphin Fresco (No. 21) and the dancing lady (No. 22), which seem to decorate parts of the domestic quarter. This extensive programme of redecoration must be linked to changes in function. They find no parallel in the other major 'Minoan' palaces (Mallia and Phaistos in particular). Evans and other have seen these as 'palatial' and royal. Their appearance makes the 'Palace of Knossos' stand out from other palaces, and (in the eyes of some scholars) indicates the establishment of a kind of Knossian hegemony over most of the island.

But if MMIIIB (rather than LMIA) marks the high point of the 'Painted Palace' (*pace* Macdonald 2002), then there is something of a paradox here. For as the art of fresco-painting reached new heights, the craft of pottery plumbs new depths. While MMIIIB shapes and decoration are still much the same as those of earlier periods, the quality seems to decline. Sinclair Hood has called it 'squalid', and, while some might object to this term (see contributions to Macdonald and Knappett 2013), something has clearly

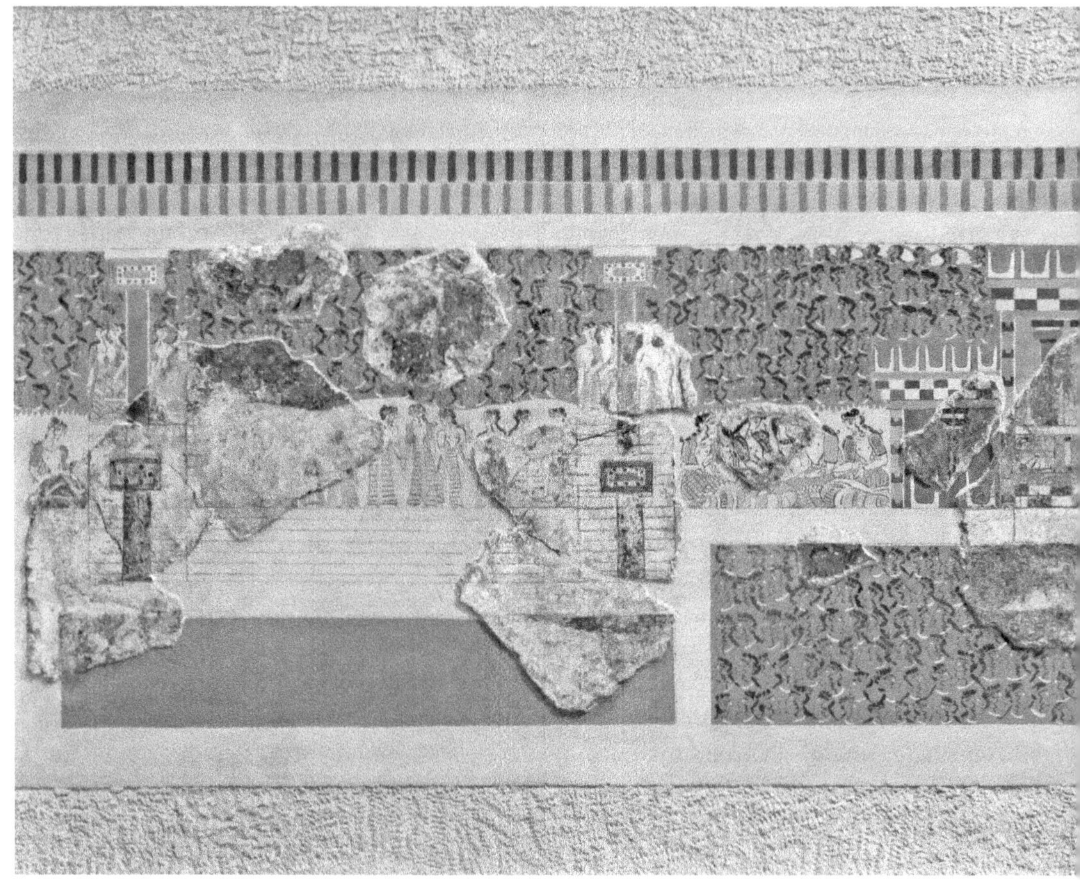

Figure 4.9 The 'Grandstand Fresco' miniature fresco with central pillar shrine and crowds. Hood 2005, 63–4, No. 6; Evans 1930, Plate XVI, facing page 47. Heraklion AM – 0.1 jpg Wikimedia Commons.

slipped. The thin-walled, fineware drinking cups of earlier periods are no more. What has happened?

4.6 Craft and industry in neopalatial Knossos

The domestic quarter is not purely domestic. One of the more unusual finds that Evans made close to the 'Hall of the Double Axes' was the MMIIIB 'Lapidary Store' (Evans 1930, 258–71). This is store of large unworked blocks of Laconian basalt (*lapis lacedaemonicus*), a mottled hardstone quarried from Mount Taygetus, near Sparta. This stone was used to make some beautiful vessels, an example of which came from the Isopata tomb. Evans inferred that this was a store for a workshop located one storey up from the store. That skilled craftsmen were also producing equivalent work in ivory is indicated by the 'Ivory

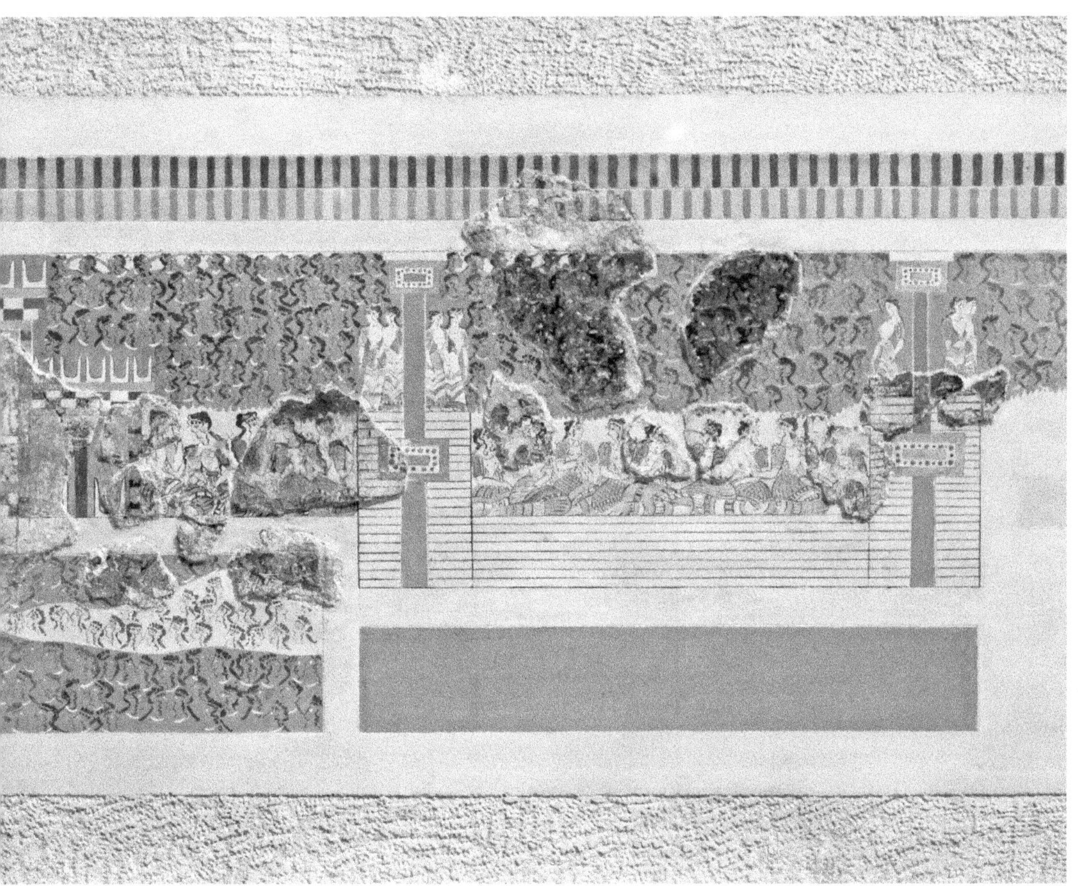

Store' in another part of the palace (Evans 1930, 399–402, 428–35). This contained finished works in imported (elephant?) ivory, including that of a leaping youth. We know that such craftsmen also worked to produce small chryselephantine (gold and ivory) sculptures, found elsewhere in Crete. The palace then was also in part a workshop, and, if not all of the skilled craftsmen in neopalatial Knossos actually worked within the palace, then there is good reason to believe that the production of engraved gems (seal-stones), gold finger rings, bronze both hammered and cast, worked stone and the materials needed for frescoes (Jones and Photos-Jones 2005) took place nearby, somewhere in the town. Partial confirmation of this is provided by the discovery of bronze hoards of neopalatial date in the area to the north-west of the palace (Evans 1928b, 623–33). Such considerations have led many scholars to talk about 'palatial control' of the production of luxury goods, goods which would then be passed on as gifts or used as trade items. Perhaps 'palatial control' is to overstate things; yet those who were in charge of the palace clearly had an interest in supervising and managing such craft production.

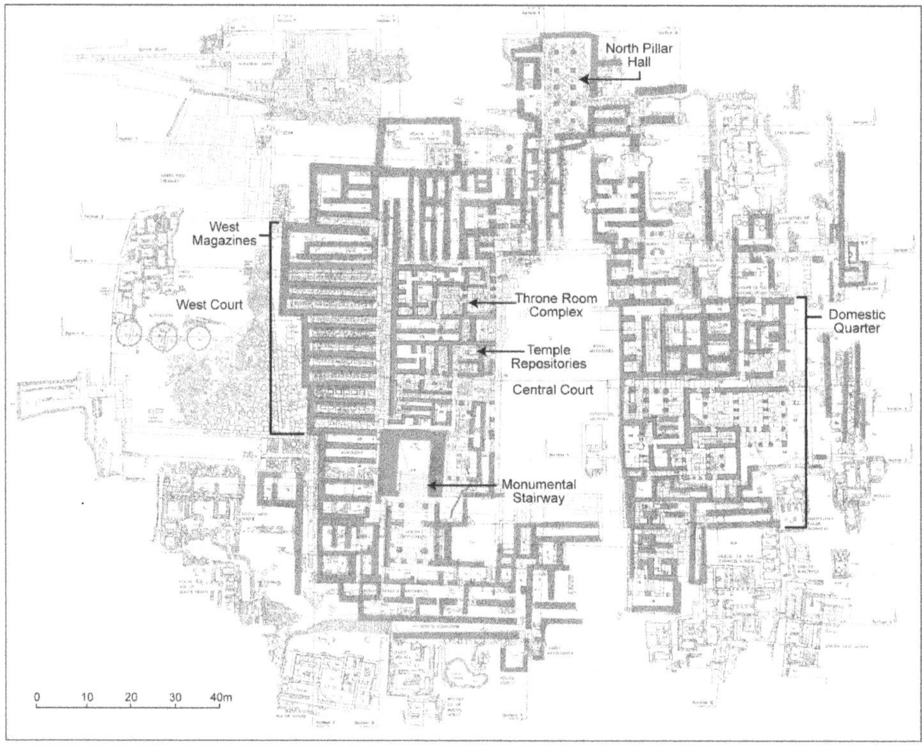

Figure 4.10 Plan of the 'neopalatial' palace with the domestic quarter. Drawn by Kirsty Harding.

The other item produced in large numbers around (but probably not in) Knossos was pottery. Fineware pots were produced using kilns – so probably they were not manufactured very close to the palace itself. Coarsewares are a different matter. We do not know what degree of skill was needed to produce kitchen pottery or cooking wares, but the production of pithoi was clearly for specialists. It requires a quite different skill set from that needed for finewares, and in modern Crete there are two villages (Thrapsano and Eleftherna) that specialize in the production of such vessels. Again, we must infer some 'palatial supervision' in the management of such specialized (and long-lasting) vessels (Christakis 2005).

This period also saw the beginnings of 'mass production' in one area: conical cups. These are more or less uniform vessels, finewares but of poor quality, produced in very large numbers from at least MMIII if not earlier. They are so numerous and so ubiquitous that archaeologists barely bothered to record them (and in the not-so-distant past were used by modern archaeologists as ash trays). What they were for is unclear, but their general uniform size suggest that they were perhaps (like Mesopotamian ledge-rim bowls) used for rations, or for doling out food at gatherings.

From a low point in the MMIIIB period, however, the quality of Knossian finewares gradually improved (Hatzaki 2007a). The LMIA period represents a change from a dark-ground to a light-ground style, where figures and motifs are painted directly on the clay; some are decorated in the so-called 'Floral Style', incorporating images of plants. LMIB is even more exuberant. Here the main style is the 'Marine Style', with motifs of octopus, sea creatures, dolphins and so forth covering whole vessels. The 'Marine Style' is no longer simply 'Minoan': it is an international, pan-Aegean style, found throughout Crete, the islands and much of the 'Mycenaean' mainland (Mountjoy 1984). It betokens a more integrated Aegean world, a fact which will have important consequences for Knossos.

4.7 Linear A: administration and literacy in neopalatial Knossos

In Evans' original view (1909, 28–37), Linear A succeeded Cretan Hieroglyphic in a straightforward evolutionary sequence. Given what we now know of the coexistence of at least three (and possibly four) scripts in protopalatial Crete – one being the Linear A of Phaistos – this view is no longer tenable. Linear A resembles Cretan Hieroglyphic in that it is largely a phonetic syllabary, though with some logograms for objects or commodities that have to be referred to frequently. Linear A must have been adopted in Knossos sometime during the MMIII period. The earliest datable finds are from the Temple Repositories; that is, in MMIIIB at the earliest (see above).

What was this script used for? Like Cretan Hieroglyphic and indeed any other Bronze Age script apart from Linear B, it remains undeciphered – we cannot determine the content of these inscriptions, though we can count the numbers. Elsewhere in Crete, large numbers of Linear A documents (tablets, roundels and nodules) are found in Hagia Triada, Phaistos and Zakro in neopalatial times (Godart and Olivier 1976a; 1976b; 1979). The largest deposit of tablets (147 in all) is from Hagia Triada near Phaistos, and at Zakro a proper archive of such tablets has been identified (Platon and Brice 1975). So Linear A was certainly used for administration in many areas of Crete. One would therefore expect that, since Knossos was the largest neopalatial 'palace', it would also have the clearest evidence of administration and so the largest archive. Here one would be disappointed. Take a look at the figures below.

Whereas the finds from Knossos in protopalatial times represented 31 per cent of known documents (predominantly administrative), in neopalatial times the finds from Knossos are less than 1 per cent of a much larger administrative corpus of Linear A documents – the most common form of document in Knossos being not the tablet (which could contain some detailed information) but the roundel (Hallager 1996, 158–74). Now of course there are ways of explaining this anomaly: other larger palaces (such as Mallia and Phaistos) have a dearth of documents; the strata from neopalatial Knossos have been subject to more interference from later episodes of rebuilding than other 'palaces', with clear destruction horizons at the end of the neopalatial period (though this in itself would not explain the large numbers of finds from Hagia Triada); and there may be archives yet to find. On the last point, if we follow the example set by Zakro (Platon and Bryce 1975), then archives of one kind or another ought to be found on the west side

Table 4.5 'Administrative' documents in Linear A from neopalatial Crete

	Tablets	Other administrative items (roundels, nodules, etc.)	Total
Knossos	5	7	12
Hagia Triada	147	885	1,032
Zakro	30	0	30
Khania	85	106	191
Other sites (including Mallia and Phaistos)	45	21	66
Total	312	1019	1331

Source: Olivier and Godart 1976a; 1976b; 1979.

of the palace. So far, they have not been discovered – and it is not as if the 'neopalatial' levels have not been fully explored (something that cannot be said of earlier levels). So there appears to be a genuine anomaly here.

The few administrative documents we do have come from two places: the Temple Repositories (Panagiotaki 1999, 106–18, 163–72), where they seem to be associated with sealings; and a 'small gallery flanking the sanctuary of the SE insula' (Evans 1921, 618–21). The numbers of documents are small – two tablets can certainly be assigned to the 'south-east insula', and only one tablet from the Temple Repositories. Clearly these are not 'archives' – they are not available for checking or cross-referencing. Like the 'Hieroglyphic deposit', they are deposits which seem to be associated with the ending and 'sealing' of some kind of ritual. The large numbers (ninety on one side, 240 on the other) from the tablet in the Temple Repositories may indicate that the ritual might have been associated with the provisioning of the event (again, a ritual or ceremony, perhaps involving over 6,000 people) that these 'repositories' represent.

We should not then be talking about administration so much as mobilization. Such mobilization may relate to what Evans (1921, 612–46) called the 'sacred usage' of Linear A. In Knossos at least, Linear A does not seem to have been primarily *administrative* – there are signs that writing was put to other ends. Finds from Knossos include graffiti on coarseware jars and 'two cups exhibiting around the inner surface ink written inscriptions … apparently executed by a reed pen before the final firing of the clay' (Evans 1909, 29); a Linear A inscription on an engraved gem (*CMS* II, 3.23 = Platon and Pini 1984, 26); and an MMIII gold ring with a Linear A inscription on the bezel from Tomb IX, E1 in the Mavro Spelio cemetery (Forsdyke 1927, 269, 284, Figure 37; Evans 1928b, 557 = *CMS* II, 3.38, p.48). These last three inscriptions are written as spirals, recalling to some degree the manner of the Phaistos disk. They indicate a kind of Linear A literacy that cannot be explained by, nor need to have been linked to, administration. That Linear A inscriptions are also found in sanctuaries indicates the broad range of uses to which ancient Cretans put this script.

4.8 House and town in neopalatial Knossos

In this period the town of Knossos reaches its maximum extent (more than 90ha; Whitelaw 2001; 2004; Whitelaw et al. 2019, Figures 4 and 5; Figure 4.11). The city was never to be as large again. Not only is the town larger but the houses are also more substantial. This is the era of the villas, large houses with elaborate 'Minoan' halls,

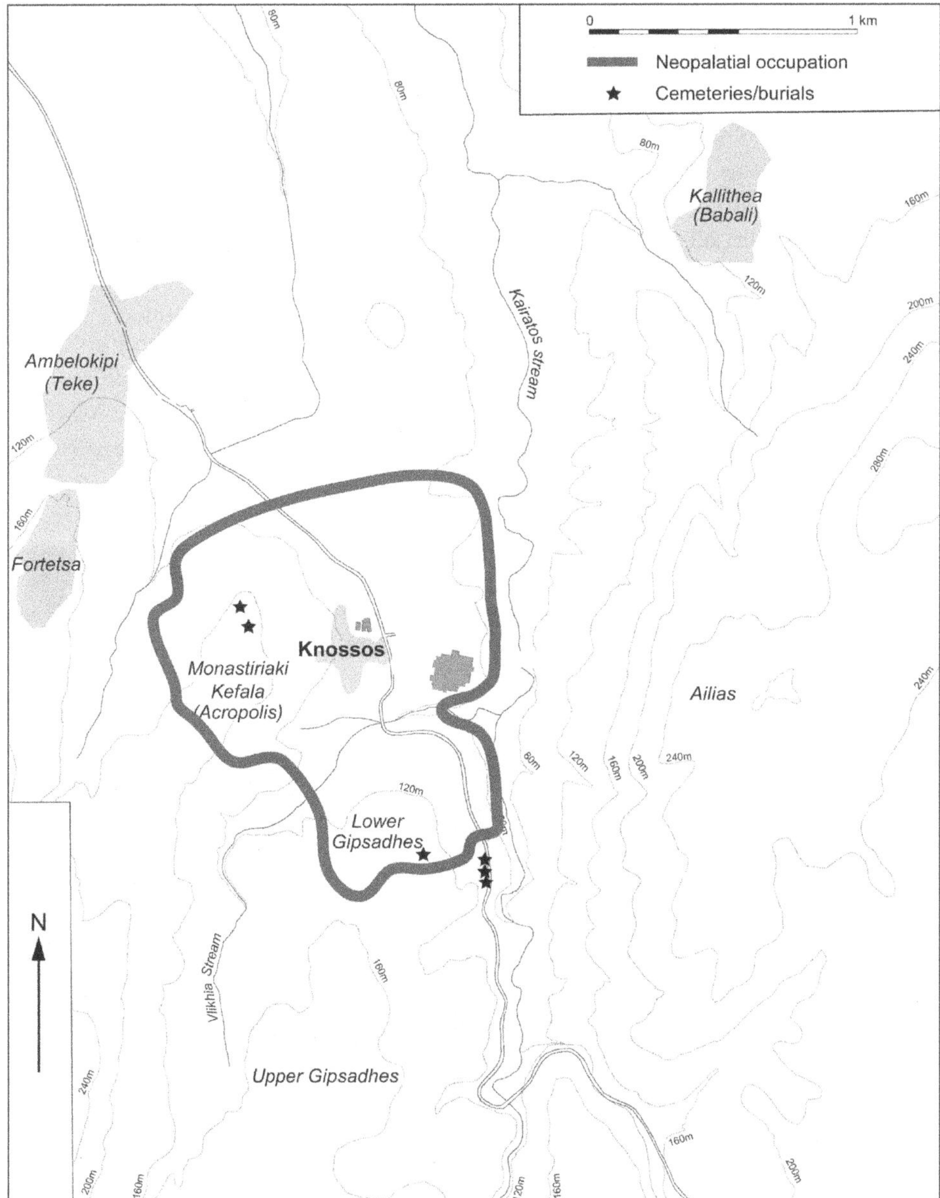

Figure 4.11 The size of neopalatial Knossos. Redrawn by Kirsty Harding, from information provided by Whitelaw et al. 2019.

constructed (at least in part) of ashlar limestone blocks and sometimes decorated with frescoes (Driessen and Macdonald 1997, 148–68). Nothing of such architectural sophistication was to be found again in Knossos until Roman times. Indeed, the foundations of Roman villas in Knossos are frequently to be found resting on the foundations of Minoan ones. Why did this period witness such architectural and decorative elaboration?

The beginnings were not promising. Protopalatial houses were relatively simple, and this remained true of some MMIII houses found near the Acropolis (Catling et al. 1979). But gradually, during MMIII, these houses became larger and more complex (Macdonald 2013; Rethemiotakis and Warren 2014). Evans, Hogarth and others had of course found numerous large houses which they dubbed villas which seem to be of slightly later date than MMIIIA. Some of these villas were connected by a complex of paved streets, of which the 'Royal Road' is the best surviving example (Evans 1928b, 572–87; Warren 1994). I will not list all these villas, but just deal with examples that demonstrate the range of house types in neopalatial Knossos: the 'House of the Frescoes'; the Little Palace; the Unexplored Mansion; the South House; and the so-called Caravanserai.

The 'House of the Frescoes' (Figure 4.12) is a relatively small, two-storey structure found by Evans in 1923 (Evans 1928a, 431–67); it was thoroughly reappraised both by Cameron (1968) and now Chapin and Shaw (2006).[8] Its construction began in MMIIIB. It does not have large rooms, but it does have impressive frescoes. Cameron reconstructed

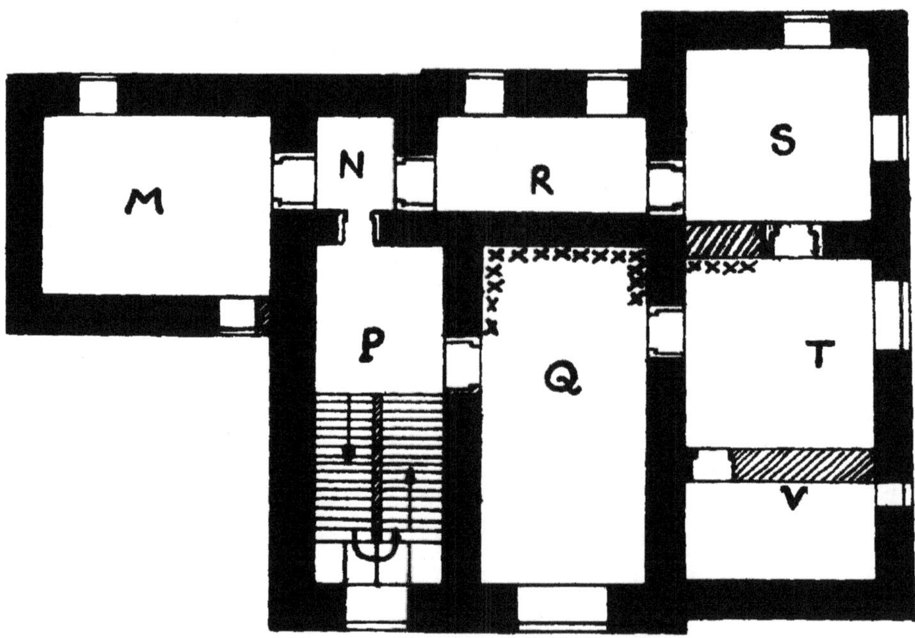

Figure 4.12 Plan of the House of the Frescoes. Redrawn by Kirsty Harding after Cameron 1968, 17, Figure 9. Courtesy British School at Athens.

these as one frieze, with blue monkeys, birds, spring flowers (including crocuses) and a waterfall; and another panel with two agrimi flanking an olive tree surrounded by crocuses. Crocuses flower in Crete in both spring and autumn, so that on its own this does not pin down the season. The first frieze, however, must represent a kind of *primavera*, a spring scene (March–April) after the heavy rains of winter – even if it is no more realistic than Botticelli's famous painting of that title. The other panel would, I suggest, represent the opposite. Olives are harvested in November, and the hunting season in Crete takes place during late September–October, when autumn crocuses flower.

Above the House of the Frescoes, to the west and along the 'Royal Road', is the Little Palace (Evans 1928a, 513–44; Hatzaki 2005; Figure 4.13), which seems to have formed a

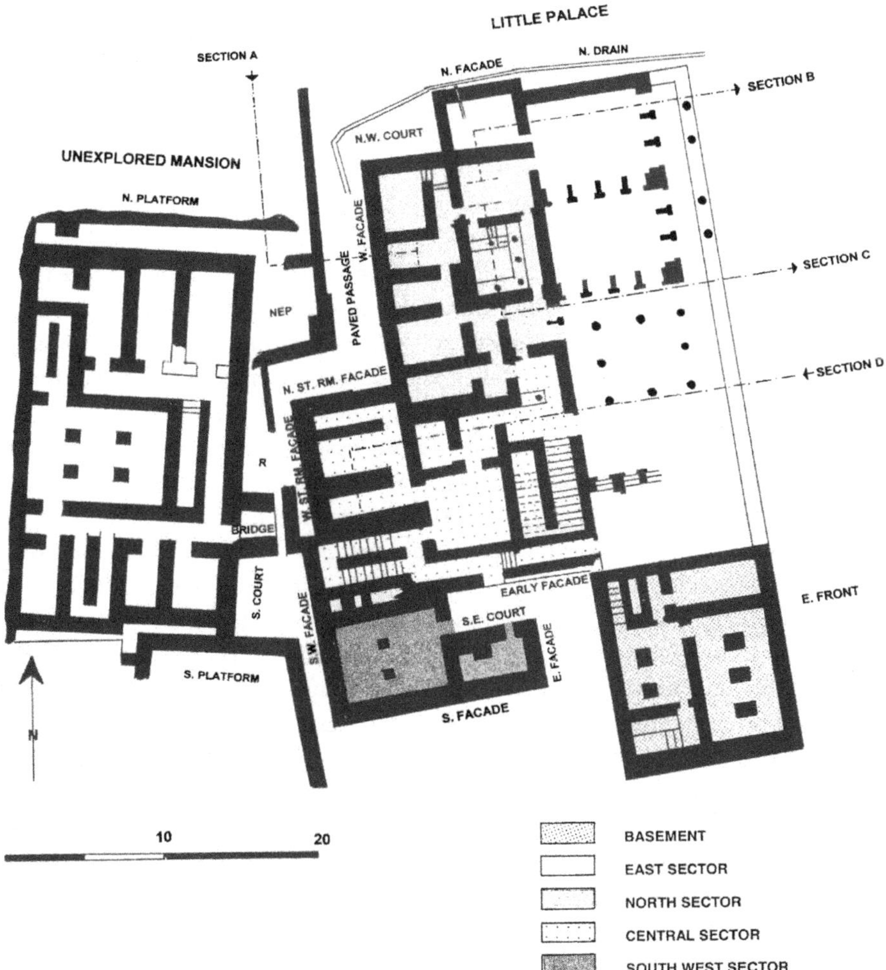

Figure 4.13 Plan of the Little Palace and the Unexplored Mansion. After Hatzaki 2005, Plan 3. Courtesy British School at Athens.

complex with the Unexplored Mansion (Evans 1928a, 545–6; Popham 1984–5). The Little Palace is by far the largest villa (about 30 x 30m), built on three storeys (basement, ground floor and upper floor) and containing architectural features that distinguish it from much smaller houses and link it to the palace itself (or the 'Greater Palace'). These include the use of gypsum, an internal 'peristyle hall', with eight internal columns, and what Evans called a 'Minoan megaron'. Both the Unexplored Mansion and the Little Palace have frescoes, though these are difficult to reconstruct. While construction of the Unexplored Mansion, including its impressive ashlar façade, seems to have begun in neopalatial times, it was not completed before the end of LMIB.

Other houses in neopalatial Knossos (e.g., the South House; Mountjoy 2003; Driessen 2003) were neither as architecturally elaborate, nor as well decorated as these examples. This house did, however, have 'ritual' features – a pillar crypt and a lustral basin – that links its function to the palace itself. Such features do not accord well with our notions of what is 'domestic' – that is, of the house as a centre of family life. This architectural oddity is even more marked in our last example. To the very south of the town of Knossos there are some constructions it is difficult to interpret as a house – that is, as clearly a domestic dwelling for a family unit. Directly south of the palace is the 'viaduct' (Evans 1928a, 96–102) over the Vlychia stream, which connects with an architecturally impressive pavilion which Evans dubbed the 'Caravanserai' (Evans 1928a, 103–23). This does not seem to take the form of a house, and Evans interpreted it as a staging post for travellers who had come from the south of the island to stay in Knossos – hence the term Caravanserai. This 'hostel' had a ritual dimension in Evans' eyes – there was a stone bath supplied with water from the Vlychia stream, which Evans interpreted to be for washing feet (as a form of ritual cleansing, as takes place before one enters a mosque in Istanbul). This pavilion was also highly decorated with frescoes. There are at least two friezes just below the ceiling, one clearly decorated with images of partridges and hoopoes, birds whose arrival is again associated with spring (Shaw 2005).

It is difficult then to generalize about these structures, or even to be sure if the majority were houses as we understand the term. There is no obvious correlation between size, architectural elaboration and the complexity (or quality) of their decoration. Many – if not all – of these structures seem to have had frescoes, and taphonomic factors (that is, the hazards of recovery and survival) have undoubtedly skewed the picture. Frescoes may have adorned structures which were not houses in our understanding of the term, as in the area to the west of the Stratigraphical Museum (Warren 2005). Evans' picture of a city of wealthy burghers living in elaborate houses is only one of several possible interpretations of how the town of Knossos might have looked and felt.

A larger issue is the relation of these structures to the 'palace' itself. Many of these houses (such as the South House) have ritual features we would normally associate with the palace (Nordfelt 1987). Much modern scholarship has moved in the direction of treating the palace as less of a residence and more of a ritual centre. There is another school of thought that sees the palace primarily as a very large house, albeit one with a primarily communal focus. Against the view that the palace is a scaled-up house is the fact that large, solidly constructed houses of the kind I have been describing only appear from MMIIIB onwards. If the earliest palace was an enlarged house, we do not yet have a model (that is, an example of an earlier house from which it was 'scaled up') on which to base this. It is easier to see the villas of neopalatial Knossos as scaled-down versions of the palace itself.

4.9 Religion, iconography and narrative in neopalatial Knossos

One of the many crafts practised in and around Knossos was that of gem engraving. The iconography of engraved gems has always intrigued scholars, and from Evans onwards has often been interpreted in religious terms. The rich iconography of people and animals in both landscapes and seascapes invites all kinds of interpretation. A frequent theme in the Knossos frescoes is the antithesis of spring (birds) and autumn (*agrimia*); and, while the seal-stones have a full range of images both of land and of sea, there seems to be a slight turn towards the inland, towards the rocky heart of Crete, in this period (Haysom 2011; Goodison 2009). The temptation has often been to infer some general 'Minoan' religion from later periods. So the 'double axe' has been taken to be as religious in neopalatial times as it undoubtedly was in the final- and post-palatial periods. But this is a mistake. Religious symbols evolve, and the symbolism of the double axe is less exclusively religious and more practical in our period – an axe is mainly just an axe (see Haysom 2010). Similarly, the 'horns of consecration' have largely been interpreted as ritual symbols – in which case the 'religious' is more or less ubiquitous. Whether indeed we should call them 'horns of consecration' (as Evans did), or, as J. A. MacGillivray has suggested (MacGillivrary 2004), see them as symbolizing the rising or setting sun is also open to question. Either interpretation is possible.

Can the iconography of glyptic provide more precise information on the nature of neopalatial ritual? Distinct imagery is found not only on frescoes and engraved gems but also on finger rings. The largest of these, in gold (Younger's (1984) type 4), have some extraordinarily elaborate scenes engraved on their bezels. Three are known from the Knossos area: the Oxford ring (*CMS* VI, 2.280 = Hughes-Brock and Boardman 2009b; Oxford Ashmolean 1938.1129); the gold ring from the Isopata cemetery (*CMS* II, 3.51 = Platon and Pini 1984, 61–2; see Preston 2007); and the 'Ring of Minos' (Krzyszkowska 2005, 335–7, No. 625 a and b; Evans 1935b, 947–56). The imagery on the last two is of particular interest.

The Isopata ring seems to show several women apparently in a grove, who appear to be dancing. That this image conveys an image of a ceremony seems inescapable; its iconography has good parallels from within the palace itself and from elsewhere in Crete (Evans 1930, 66–80). Whether or not the scene itself may be part of a larger story is unclear. The larger 'Ring of Minos' is even more striking. Its mysterious appearance, disappearance and reappearance have led some to doubt its authenticity, but this is no longer in question. It shows (from right to left) a woman seated on a building with 'horns of consecration', top-centre a woman (on an island?) grasping a branch of a tree set within an enclosure, to the left a woman (?) simply grasping a branch and in the centre below a woman on a ship. Ritual in groves seems to be part of the story, but this cannot simply be (as the Isopata ring can) a depiction of a ritual. The individual elements must be connected by a story. In other words, we are dealing with art which is as much narrative as ritual. On both the Oxford ring and the Ring of Minos these narratives seem to involve travelling across the sea by ship (Alexiou 1958a; Haysom 2011).

As for the rituals, they seem to be taking place 'outside' – that is, not within the structure we call the palace. Precisely what kind of location these rituals are taking place in cannot be inferred from this imagery alone – they do not appear to be related to peak sanctuaries but to groves of trees (and no such shrines have definitively been identified). That rituals were taking place within the palace is demonstrated by the Temple Repositories, and possibly by the lustral basins and 'pillar shrines' which form part of the palace as temple complex (if we follow Evans 1901b).

Whatever the location of these rituals, they were clearly significant to the elites of neopalatial Crete. Most scholars agree that the use of seals and finger rings relates to the exercise of authority: impressions of seals and finger rings are found associated with correspondence. If the finger rings were associated with the most important officials, then secular authority is linked very strongly to religious authority, and to an iconography that largely focuses on women rather than men. Such gynocentric imagery has often reinforced the picture of 'peaceful' Minoans as opposed to 'warlike' Mycenaeans (as in

Figure 4.14 The Ring of Minos. Wikimedia Commons, archmus Heraklion.jpg.

Hawkes 1968). It is not, however, quite true to say that there is a total absence of any iconography relating to warfare or hunting (Evans 1930, 107–91; Molloy 2012). The iconography of seals and sealings refer to both.

Categories such as warfare or hunting are, of course, our categories. The 'ontological turn' in the human sciences (Descola 2013) has made many sceptical of our 'etic' terminology, as they presume (ultimately) that it is a matter of how humans (culture) relate to the natural world (nature). Human–animal relations in Bronze Age Crete might be quite different from our understanding of such things (Shapland 2010; 2022); bull-leaping (if it really existed) might not be a 'sport' as we understand the term (Shapland 2013). These are deep waters. We can at least infer that neither warfare nor hunting was as celebrated in the iconography of neopalatial Crete as it was to be either on the Mycenaean mainland or in the final palatial period at Knossos. This fact has important implications.

4.10 Burial practices in neopalatial Knossos

MMIII burial practices are still rather elusive. Multiple (but far from architecturally uniform) chamber tombs continue from protopalatial times. Preston (2013a; 2013b) points out that there are only fourteen tombs with clearly defined MMIII use, largely to be found in well-established cemeteries. Though this represents an increase over the previous period, there are still too few tombs for the population of a town as large and dense as palatial Knossos. The use of the Mavro Spelio continues (Alberti 2013): tomb IX contains the gold ring with a Linear A inscription. In general, MMIII and neopalatial tombs are slightly richer in grave goods than in MMII times, as indicated by the numerous engraved seal-stones (Platon and Pini 1984, 31–88). Though tombs continue to be collective, two trends become more evident later in this period: an increase in the quantity and quality of grave goods; and an increase in monumentality in grave architecture.

There can be nothing more monumental than the 'Temple Tomb' (Evans 1935b, 964–83, 989–1001) at the south edge of the town (and south of the palace). This is a structure whose date and meaning remain controversial. But it is a controversy very much worth investigating. I start with Evans' account, and then go on to some possible criticisms.

The tomb itself was discovered accidentally, as a result of the finding of the Ring of Minos (Evans 1935b, 947–56). Myths about Minos, in particular a story told by Diodoros (4.79.4) about Minos' 'double tomb' (διπλόυν τάφον) on Sicily, seem to have very much influenced Evans' interpretation. The tomb, crowned with a 'horn of consecration' at the top, was reached by a stair going down. You then passed into the pavilion, a paved court, an inner hall and then a pillar crypt with two pillars which supported beams of cypress wood. Construction of this seems to have begun in MMIIIB – the tomb being destroyed in LMIA (according to Evans, by an earthquake), an interpretation largely confirmed by the extensive use of masons' marks (Hood and Bendall 2020, 254–61). Within the crypt was found a 'rock chamber' with MMIIIB vessels and finds, which Evans associated with 'scores of individuals' found within. The tomb itself had a door (with a key), that could be opened from the inside. It was thus a reusable sepulchre – hence the term 'Temple Tomb'.

The tomb was clearly also reused both in LMII and in LMIIIA1. Evans interpreted the latter (an assemblage of amphoroid kraters and 'Ephyraean' goblets) as a form of memorial cult rather than burials. But other interpretations are possible. What if the 'rock chamber' was nothing more than a disturbed MMIII multiple chamber tomb, rather than the first phase of use of the ostentatiously monumental Temple Tomb? What if the main phase of funerary use is to be associated with the LMII to LMIII finds?[9] If so, this tomb (along with the Isopata Royal Tomb and the Kephala Tholos tomb) would be associated, not with the floruit of 'King Minos' in neopalatial Crete, but with the 'coming of the Mycenaeans' – that is, with not the neopalatial but the Final Palatial?

4.11 The 'final palatial' (LMII–LMIIIA1): the coming of the Mycenaeans? The view from the grave

During both the Old Palace and the New, the bodies of dead Knossians are few and far between. The emphasis in burial seems to have been on the collective rather than the individual. If we except the Temple Tomb (if it is indeed neopalatial), there is no monumental architecture and little in the way of grave goods. All this was to change dramatically during the final phase of the palace of Knossos (a period defined in ceramic terms as LMII to LMIIIA2; Hatzaki 2007b, 197–223).

Burials now become a highly visible feature of the landscape around Knossos. New areas for cemeteries appear. Moving from north to south, these are to be found at the end of the Isopata ridge (Preston 2007; Evans 1914, 1–59); at the Kephala (Hutchinson 1956; Preston 2005); at least one tomb at Ayios Ioannis (Hood and Coldstream 1968); and at Zafer Papoura (the largest cemetery, Evans 1905b). To the east, near Ailias, the Mavro Spelio cemetery continues, while a new cemetery area is to be found at Sellopoulo (Popham and Catling 1974). To the south, at Gypsades, the cemetery expands (Hood et al. 1959). With new cemeteries come new forms of cemetery architecture. Evans (1905b, 391–411) identified three types: chamber tombs, shaft graves and 'pit caves' at Zafer Papoura (see Figure 5.3 for a later example). It now appears that we can add the tholos tomb (at Kephala; Preston 2005; 1999) to this list. Three of these types (tholos, chamber tomb and shaft grave) have clear antecedents in the Mycenaean mainland.

Table 4.6 Types of final palatial grave architecture from Zafer Papoura

	All graves	*Well-preserved graves*
Chamber tombs	49	18
Shaft graves	33	25
Pit Caves	18	17
Total	100	60

Source: Evans 1905b, 493–4.

What then is the significance of these changes? Let us start with Evans' figures for Zafer Papoura in the table below.

These new forms of interment (all for inhumations) changed the relationship between a person buried and the objects interred with that person. Bodies are now buried in an 'individualizing' manner that seems to emphasize the relationship between a person and his/her role in life (or at least how the buriers imagined this to have been). Unfortunately, no osteological study was made of these graves, and so interpretation has been based on grave goods. What struck Evans was the general increase in these goods, and in particular the appearance of weapons with bodies. An example is the 'chieftain's grave' (No. 36, Evans 1905b, 441–9), an extended inhumation of a man at the bottom of a shaft grave. With the body were two long swords, and on the cover of the shaft was placed a bronze ewer, a spear and some other valuable objects. Other 'warrior graves' were to be found in other shaft graves (Nos. 42 and 44) but were not confined to this burial type. Burials with weapons appear in pit caves (Nos. 43, 51 and 55) and in chamber tombs (Nos. 95 and 98).

To infer what someone did and suffered in life from what that someone was buried with may appear a natural inference. Burials with weapons have thus been called warrior graves, a term popularized by Sinclair Hood (Hood et al. 1959). But it is also an unwarranted one, based on the assumption that grave goods provide a material biography of a person's role in life (Whitley 2002). Burials are not autobiographies but represent, ultimately, what the buriers chose to emphasize in death about a particular person mediated by practical, ideological and religious considerations. As has often been said, the dead do not bury themselves. Burial assemblages cannot be taken 'literally'.

To illustrate this point, let us think of what we actually find in these Knossian graves. What happens when a person is buried with not just one but two swords? Or when the person so buried appears to be too young to be a warrior, in any practical sense? Burials with weapons are, however, a common feature of Bronze Age, Iron Age and post-Roman (barbarian) Europe. A study of pagan Anglo-Saxon burials (Härke 1990), however, revealed that weapons are not buried with men with war wounds but are often interred with adolescents or children too young to fight. Instead of 'warrior graves', Härke (1990) talks of a 'weapon burial ritual'. Interment with weapons was not a quasi-biographical description of what someone did or suffered, but a symbolic means of indicating a certain kind of masculine status. Something similar seems to be happening in both early Mycenaean Greece and Late Minoan Crete (LMII–IIIA), where burials with weapons are common. Here too, as in the Sellopoulo tombs (Popham and Catling 1974; Whitley 2002, 221–3), there are too many weapons interred with persons too young to wield them.

But something has clearly shifted in the symbolic universe around Knossos. For with 'warrior graves' also appear boar's tusk helmets (Borchardt 1974, 18–37), a form of headgear with unambiguously Homeric associations (Homer *Iliad* 10.260–71). A new iconography of performative masculinity associated with drinking, hunting and fighting, an iconography more at home at Mycenae, Pylos and Tiryns than in 'Minoan' Knossos, has entered the stage. Does this change in burial customs and imagery indicate the coming of Homer's Achaeans (that is, the Mycenaeans)? Do the new cemeteries indicate a wholesale takeover of one group by another?

Some scholars think not (Preston 2004). Let us take another look at the funerary architecture. The Royal Tomb at Isopata, far to the north of both the town and the palace of Knossos at the end of the Isopata ridge, is perhaps the most monumental of the new tombs that become established in this period (Evans 1905b, 526–62; 1935b, 771–6). This 'Royal Tomb' is set apart from the nearest cemetery, further down the Isopata ridge (Evans 1914; Preston 2007). The Royal Tomb's dromos and use of ashlar masonry certainly represent a major departure from the mortuary traditions we glimpse in neopalatial times, and its grave goods (palace-style three-handled jars) proclaim the new era. But its architecture, being rectilinear, does not so much mimic as comment upon Mycenaean antecedents such as the famous tholos tombs (of Clytemnestra and Aegisthus) near Mycenae. Similar points can be made about the 'Tomb of the Double Axes' (Evans 1914, 33–49), whose design has no parallel anywhere else; and, more generally, the 'pit caves', where antecedents can be found more easily in earlier tombs from Mavro Spelio than anything to be found near Mycenae.

4.12 The final palace (and the first?)

The transition between neo- and final-palatial is most easily seen in the burials. It is less easy to discern in the architectural history of the palace. This may have been damaged to some degree by the Thera eruption, whose date remains controversial. Reappraisals of some of the tephra deposits from east Crete (Bruins et al. 2008), and a further analysis of some short-lived samples from Akrotiri itself (Manning et al. 2014; Manning 2018), favour an earlier date (around 1620 BC) for this event. In ceramic terms, this eruption must have taken place somewhere in LMIA. There is some indication that parts of the town may have been damaged. Some villas, such as the House of the Frescoes, seem to fall out of use during LMIA (Whitelaw 2022, 36; Driessen and Macdonald 1997, 148–66). But there is no wholesale destruction of the palace in LMIB – it does not form part of the general destruction horizon. For these reasons, scholars such as Whitelaw (2022) emphasize that the transition was a slow process rather than a sharp break, even if the palace itself had to undergo major architectural reconstruction (Whitelaw 2022, 43–8).

Other changes seem both more abrupt and more profound. One is changes in the shapes, and to a lesser extent the style, of fineware pottery (in LMII and LMIIIA; Hatzaki 2007b, 197–223). While chemical analysis indicates that all wares used in Knossos continue to have been produced in north-central Crete in a predominantly 'light ground' (Late Bronze Age) style and while there are few changes in storage or cooking vessels, there is a marked change in the fineware assemblage. Most noticeable are changes in drinking vessels, particularly the introduction (in LMIII) of the large two-handled kylix or goblet (sometimes referred to as the Ephyraean goblet; Evans 1935a, 359–71; Hatzaki 2007b, 197–222; Figure 4.15) and the appearance of the highly decorated, large vessels in what Mackenzie and Evans called the 'Palace Style' (Evans 1935a, 297–358; Niemeier 1985). Palace style vessels are concentrated in particular locations (Niemeier 1985, 139–69), notably the Royal Villa (Evans 1928a, 396–413), a structure whose architectural layout is strikingly different from those of neopalatial times.

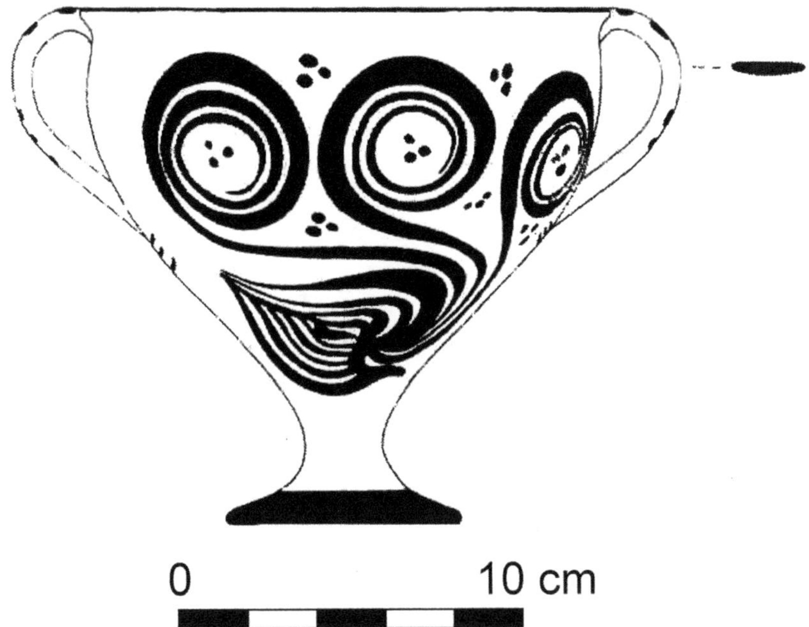

Figure 4.15 An Ephyraean goblet. After Momgiliano 2007b, 203, Fig. 6.3, No. 1. Courtesy British School at Athens.

These changes did not come about entirely peacefully. Much of the town of Knossos was severely damaged at the end of Late Minoan IB (Driessen and Macdonald 1997). Many neopalatial houses – including the Little Palace – were reoccupied and reused (Hatzaki 2005) and the structure of the neopalatial town (including the road systems) seems to have been retained for the most part. Recent survey has, however, suggested that the size of the community shrank, from about 90ha in neopalatial times to less than 50ha in this period (Whitelaw et al. 2019, Figures 6 and 7). We are dealing with a smaller Knossos.

The palace itself seems to have escaped destruction – or at least major destruction by fire. This may, of course, be because it was still a ruin (Macdonald 2002) – it was in the process of being rebuilt when the damage to other structures occurred in LMIB. In any case the structure was soon redecorated and repurposed. Hood (2005, 50) assigns ten new frescoes to the LMII phase (Nos. 2d, 8, 15, 16, 19, 23, 24, 25, 26 and 33). These include frescoes with a procession and cup bearers (15 and 16) and palanquins and charioteers (19). Most marked are the changes to the decoration of the throne room (Figure 4.8). Here this space was redecorated at some point in LMII–IIIA. The new frescoes combine features of 'neopalatial' iconography such as the (clearly female) palm fronds while also introducing features which are more clearly 'final palatial' (Galanakis et al. 2017). The griffins that flank the throne itself (Hood 2005, No. 8) have clear parallels in contemporary Near Eastern palaces such as Tell Achana/Alalakh. Another innovation in this period are the relief frescoes, such as the bull fresco by the north Entrance and the 'Priest King' decorating the narrow south entrance (Hood 2005, nos. 2 and 18 respectively; Evans

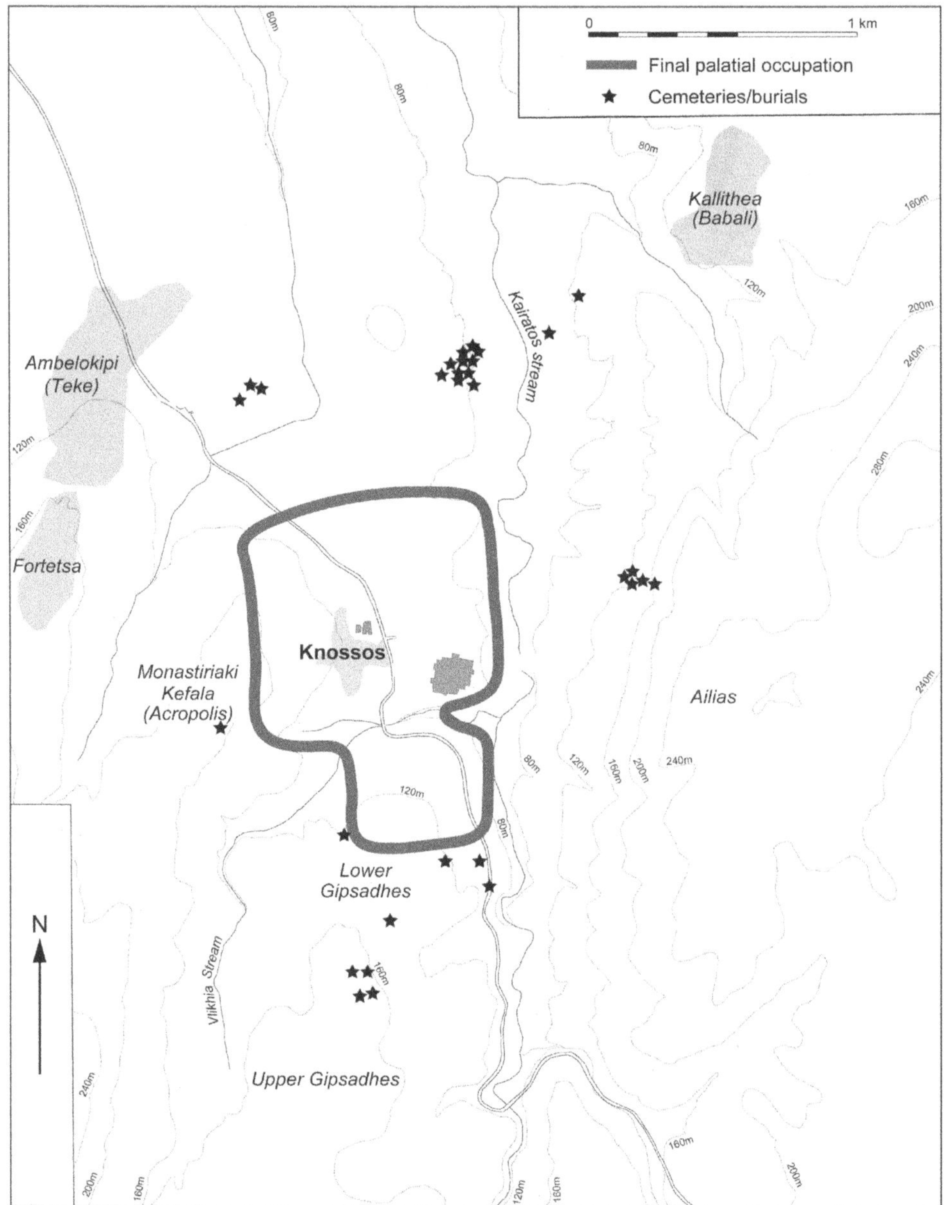

Figure 4.16 The size of final palatial Knossos. After Whitelaw et al. 2019. Redrawn by Kirsty Harding.

1928a, 774–85; Haysom 2018a). The 'Priest King' has caused much controversy. Evans' reconstruction was a pastiche, parts of which may have depicted a boxer (Coulomb 1979). There was probably no actual 'Priest King'.

Much later than these relief frescoes comes the 'Camp Stool' Fresco (end of LMIIIA2; Hood 2005, No. 4, Plate 61; *contra* Evans 1935b, 381–96; Figure 4.17), which shows women

Figure 4.17 The 'Camp Stool' Fresco, Heraklion Museum. AMH, 145731.jpg, Wikimedia Commons.

using large cups – Ephyraean goblets– a shape which belongs more happily in the Mycenaean (mainland) rather than the Cretan sequence. It is material facts such as these that led many scholars to conclude that these changes represent the 'coming of the Mycenaeans'.

Who do we mean by 'Mycenaeans'? Well, for one thing, we are referring to Greek speakers. That the ruling stratum in final palatial Knossos used and almost certainly spoke a form of Greek has been clear since the decipherment of Linear B, a script used exclusively to write down an early form of the Greek language. This form of Greek has many similarities to the language – that is, principally to the vocabulary – of the Homeric poems. But in almost every other respect there is nothing remotely poetic about Linear B. Linear B was primarily a tool of administration, and its study can tell us much about the political structure of Mycenaean Knossos.

4.13 The kingdom of Idomeneus? Hierarchy, politics and administration in final palatial Knossos

Knossos holds the largest concentration of written documents in the Late Bronze Age Aegean world. At least 2,444 Linear B tablets are known to have been found in Knossos. Most come from various locations within the palace itself (Ventris and Chadwick 1973, 114–5), though there are some examples from outside the 'palace' proper, such as the small cache of finds from the 'Little Palace' (Hatzaki 2005, 177–8). Evans noticed (Evans

1909, 38–55) that these tablets had been burnt, that they were probably stored in boxes of lead or gypsum and were grouped by subject (such as the 'Chariot Tablets'). Most seemed to have fallen from various places, either above the west magazines or above parts of the domestic quarter, in the final destruction (or destructions) of the palace.

Linear B is a 'mixed' script like Cretan Hieroglyphic and Linear A. That is to say, it has around 200 signs not all of which are phonetic (Ventris and Chadwick 1973, 28–66). Around ninety of these (at least eighty-seven) are phonograms, vowel–consonant combinations or syllables. The phonograms seem to represent the phonetic values of an early form of Greek (Ventris and Chadwick 1973, 67–91) – one similar to the language of the Homeric poems but also distinct in both vocabulary and grammar. As well as phonograms there are also signs for numerals and logograms (or ideograms, over 100 of these). The latter represent abbreviated pictures of common commodities or objects of interest to the Knossian administration. These can include swords, chariots and sheep (of both sexes). So when we say that the script 'represents an early form of Greek', that is only partially true. The vowel/consonant grid is a very imperfect mechanism for representing the phonetic values of Greek speech when compared with either the Cypriot Syllabary (clearly derived from Linear B, and much improved) or the early Greek alphabets (Jeffery 1990). This is only in part because it was adapted from Linear A (a script used to write a non-Greek language). It is also because phonetic values were not the primary concern for the users of the script – as they would be if its purpose were (say) to transcribe the sounds of Greek epic verse. Its principal purpose was not poetic but administrative – with some minor exceptions (such as the inscribed stirrup jars), all documents and inscriptions in Linear B take the form of clay tablets, and they are found close to the centres of Mycenaean kingdoms. Linear B literacy, as far as we know it, was entirely geared to the running of the kingdom of Knossos. This is clear if we look at how the script functioned.

Linear B tablets come in two forms: the larger page-shaped tablet, and the smaller leaf-shaped variety (Figure 4.18). The latter is easier to hold and more common; the former holds more information. There is indeed much more writing – much more content – on each Linear B tablet than there ever was on any document written in Linear A or Cretan Hieroglyphic. A greater variety of things are mentioned, and there is more detail about the things that are (judging simply by the combination of signs used). Strangely though, the numbers of things are, if anything, smaller than the numbers mentioned on documents in these earlier scripts. Linear B seems to be linked to annual accounting and record keeping. So the Chariot Tablets tell us how many chariots were available for use by the small military force kept by the ruler of Knossos. Driessen and MacDonald (1984) link these tablets to the new mortuary practice of burying weapons with individuals – the warrior graves. Their argument is that there is a new, warrior elite in Knossos, reflected not only in burial practices but in the interest many of the Linear B tablets have in maintaining bronze arms, armour and chariots (Ventris and Chadwick 1973, 359–72, 379–81). That this new elite also probably spoke Greek is reflected in the many Greek personal names listed in the tablets from Knossos (Ventris and Chadwick 1973, 171–2, No. 38 = As1516).

The tablets – at least when combined with the information from other Mycenaean sites – tell us quite a lot about the hierarchical political structure of Knossos. At its apex was the *wanax*. This name, attested at least once at Knossos (Ventris and Chadwick 1973, 589), is clearly related to the Homeric *anax*, the title of the supreme leader of the expedition against Troy (ἄναξ ἀνδρῶν Ἀγαμέμνων (*Iliad* 2.612), 'Agamemnon King of Men'). Below the *wanax* (and it seems to have been a 'he') was the rather more mysterious *lawagetas*, and then, below him, the *hequetai* and the *telestai* (Ventris and Chadwick 1973; Chadwick 1976, 69–77). This then is a hierarchical pyramid with the ruler (king) on top.

We seem to be dealing with a patriarchal and hierarchical political structure, where power flows from the top – in other words, a kingdom. The Linear B tablets tell us quite a lot about the extent of this unitary state. John Bennet (1985; 1990; 1992) has looked at the place name evidence for the second-order administrative centres. Many have identifiable names – A-MI-NI-SO seems to be Amnisos (Hiller 1992); and KO-NO-SI-JA (or KO-NO-SO), Knossos itself (Ventris and Chadwick 1973, 171–2, No. 38). When grouped together, most names seem to relate to central Crete – an area extending from the Lasithi plateau, covering the Mesara and with a western outlier in Kydonia (modern Khania). Kydonia may have been a subordinate kingdom, as this is the only other place in Crete where Linear B tablets have been found (Figure 0.2). Notable by its absence is eastern Crete, especially the far east of the Siteia peninsula, which Bennet (1987b) has dubbed the 'Wild Country East of Dikte'.

The kingdom of Knossos did not then extend over the whole of the island but only its central part (Driessen 2001). The geographical coincidence of this with the extent of the Kingdom of Idomeneus in book II of the *Iliad* is striking. Idomeneus (*Iliad* 2.645–50) ruled over Knossos, Gortyn, Lykastos, Lyktos, Milatos, Phaistos and Rhytion – that is, a territory stretching from Dikte to Ida in the north and extending over the Mesara. This area (by which I mean the area indicated by Linear B) is, on the one hand, much larger than any plausible reconstruction of earlier Minoan states based on Malia, Knossos or Phaistos, but also much smaller than anything to be found in the Near East. Whereas Knossos has over 2,000 tablets, Mari has 20,000 (Dalley 1984, 15–20); the tablets from Mari again provide much more detail and are thus a much more effective tool for administration.

Knossos in the final palatial period was nonetheless demonstrably the administrative and political centre of a unitary state. The administration had at least two tiers, with local elites in the western and southern parts of the island acting as agents for the central administration (Bennet 1992). Knossos (with Amnisos), moreover, seems to have become better known within the East Mediterranean world. *Amnisa* with *Kanusa* are mentioned on an inscription at the base of one of the colossi of Amenhotep III (1391–1353 BC) at Kom-el Hetan in Upper Egypt (Cline 2015, 43–51; Helck 1992), an inscription which seems to be an itinerary. But while Knossos was now a much better-known kingdom, it was not in comparative terms a very powerful one. It could field a small army of professional warriors numbering several hundred and administered no more than the centre of the island. And it did not last long.

This picture is at variance with an earlier view of the Mycenaean state as redistributive – that is, controlling all the ingoings and outgoings of the economy. Chadwick (1976) seems sometimes to imply that Knossos was (with Pylos) a kind of Soviet-style economic system located in the Bronze Age. Is this picture an accurate one?

4.14 Linear B and the Mycenaean economy

When the tablets were first deciphered, it often seemed to scholars that the Mycenaean bureaucracy had almost total control over the economy. This view was reinforced by Renfrew's (1972) insistence that Late Bronze Age states were essentially redistributive – they collected agricultural produce, stored it centrally and then redistributed it to households. This vision of a highly centralized Bronze Age economy did not survive the collapse of the highly centralized command economies in the Soviet Union and Eastern Europe between 1989 and 1991 (Murray 2017). Halstead (1993; 2001) has made a useful distinction between the public and private sectors in Late Bronze Age socio-political structures, arguing that there were certain sectors (most agricultural production, almost all ceramic production, production of perfumed olive oil used in stirrup jars) in which the palace seemed to take absolutely no interest. Halstead estimates that the palace controlled no more than 10 per cent of the Late Bronze Age economy – of which the tablets in any case give us only a partial view. There was a lively trade in stone vessels and faience with Egypt (Cline 1999). Specialized crafts that had flourished in neopalatial times, such as the production of stone vases within the palace itself (Warren 1967) seem to have continued – though this is not something you could have inferred from the tablets. The range of the palace of Knossos' interests (Driessen 2001b) were then much narrower than those of the later palace at Pylos.

It is easy enough to list the economic interests of the palace as given in the tablets. The palace oversees the management of miscellaneous livestock (sheep, goats, horses, oxen, sows; Ventris and Chadwick 1973, 208–13); the distribution of grain consignments and rations (Ventris and Chadwick 1973, 213–15); the consignments of olive oil (Ventris and Chadwick 1973, 217); of mixed rations (Ventris and Chadwick 1973, 218–19); and even of spices (Ventris and Chadwick 1973, 221–3). Beyond the inference that the palace managed agricultural estates (and did so partly in order to feed men and women whom the palace retained for various services), it is more difficult to state what these interests amounted to. There is much less information on land tenure in Knossos than at Pylos (Ventris and Chadwick 1973, 269–72), though Knossos seems to have had a particular interest in

Figure 4.18 One of the 'sheep tablets' from Knossos, now in the Ashmolean Museum in Oxford. The text can be translated as, 'Of Wewesios 58 rams 2 ewes; [herded by] Artemos/Anthemos [at/near] Kutato. 50 rams [wethers] are missing.' Courtesy Ashmolean Museum, Oxford, AN 1938.850.

orchards (Ventris and Chadwick 1973, 272–4) – that is, in the growing of apples and figs. More puzzling still is the focus on flocks of sheep and their wool (Ventris and Chadwick 1973, 201–5, Figure 5.24). The large numbers of rams as opposed to ewes seemed difficult to explain, as did the reasons for maintaining so many sheep. Enlightenment only came when John Killen (1964) made an explicit historical comparison to the way in which flocks were managed in late medieval Eastern England. These medieval flocks were managed by monasteries with a view to their 'secondary products' – that is, their wool. Wool is usually produced from wethers – castrated rams. Flocks of wethers are (for obvious reasons) not self–sustaining. This fact both explains the skewed distribution of rams and ewes in the tablets and gives us a major insight into the palatial economy.

This economy was geared to producing particular surpluses both for export and to maintain the palace. The 60,000 or so sheep indicated by the sheep tablets were primarily managed for their wool. This wool production was primarily related to the palace's interest in the production of textiles. Tablets note flax and wool, and processes of dying fabrics (Ventris and Chadwick 1973, 313–21), often undertaken by female workers.

Where did these textiles go? Probably for export. For the other major palatial interest noted in the tablets lies in the production and distribution of bronze – something that required an Aegean-wide weight standard, evidence of which has been found in the palace (Michailidou 1999). Tablets provide inventories of vessels (Ventris and Chadwick 1973, 329–31), weapons, corselets and chariots (Ventris and Chadwick 1973, 359–72, 379–81), all of bronze. Tomb assemblages from this time – particularly the assemblage of bronze vessels from the tomb of the tripod hearth in the Zafer Papoura cemetery (Ventris and Chadwick 1973, 323–9; Evans 1905b, 424–35) and the Sellopoulo tombs (Popham and Catling 1974; Catling and Catling 1974) – show that Cretan metalworking had reached heights of sophistication not seen in the Middle Bronze Age. Clearly, Knossos was an important centre of for the manufacture of bronze weapons, vessels and other equipment. But there are no significant natural sources for either copper or tin in Crete – all such raw materials would have had to be imported. The copper may have come from Cyprus or Sardinia, the tin possibly from as far away as Cornwall. But the palace had to exchange something for these vital metal resources; and that something was (almost certainly) textiles, the finished products of flax or wool.

Skilled workers in bronze (men) and textiles (women) still had to be fed – and fed from the palace's farms and fields. Halstead (1993; 2001) has characterized the style of agricultural management in the palatial sector of Knossos as 'extensive' – involving large fields geared to producing surpluses (rather than in buffering risk). The palatial agricultural sector had also more specialized functions – not only in producing spices, but also products relating to religious practices in 'Mycenaean' Knossos.

4.15 Religion in final palatial Knossos

If the religion of neopalatial Crete (with its mysterious Temple Repositories, lustral basins and pillar crypts) remains something of a mystery, the Linear B tablets present us with something much more familiar: the names of a pantheon of recognizably Greek divinities (Chadwick 1976, 84–101). Names found in both Knossos and Pylos include Zeus (in the dative), Poseidon, Athena, Potnia and Eileithyia (the goddess of childbirth). The tablets provide details of offerings of grain, oil and honey – though not very large amounts – to these deities, and sometimes other things such as the quotas of horns from *agrimia* for ritual purposes (Ventris and Chadwick 1973, 301–3), given in the Knossos Mc tablets.

Offerings to divinities at Knossos (Ventris and Chadwick 1973, 303–12) include No. 203 F 953 + 955 various substances (but chiefly oil) to gods at Amnisos (a harbour site to the north-east of Knossos on the coast). Amnisos is the site of a cave sanctuary to Eileithyia. Both the cave and the poor harbour are mentioned in the *Odyssey* (19.188–90) as the site where Odysseus mendaciously claims to have landed in Crete. Strabo (10.4.7–8) notes that the cave was still known in his day, and that 'Minos' had used the harbour. Both the cave and the Archaic to Classical sanctuary of Zeus at Amnisos, partially built over the neopalatial villa, were excavated by S. Marinatos. In 1932, Marinatos found a neopalatial 'villa' decorated with frescoes (S. Marinatos 1932; Stürmer 1992a). In the cave itself, Marinatos found evidence of use from Neolithic times down until the Geometric (S. Marinatos 1929; 1930; Prent 2005, 336–7). It is then significant that Eileithyia (here spelt Eleuthia) is also the recipient of jars of honey on another Knossos tablet (No 206 Gg 705)?

In later Greek religion we usually associate one divinity with one sanctuary, but in these documents we sometimes have indications of many divinities being listed. Tablet 208 V52 lists Athena (or Athena Potnia), Enyalios (Ares?), Paian (Apollo) and Poseidon. Amnisos aside, it is often difficult to determine where these sanctuaries are located. Tablet 200 Fp1 lists gifts of olive oil for Dictaean Zeus. If this epithet indicates a location, it is one far from Knossos, either in the mountain of Dikte or even further east at Palaikastro (at the furthest extremity of the island). The 'wild country East of Dikte' is generally thought to be beyond the control of palatial Knossos (Bennet 1987b).

With the possible exception of the cave of Eileithyia at Amnisos, therefore, we cannot locate any of the shrines to which these offerings were made. We have in any case very little archaeological evidence for 'shrines' in this period – that is, it is difficult to determine the architectural expression of sacred places. Nor are the offerings large – the largest is perhaps the 36 litres (or so) of oil given 'to all the gods' on 200 Fp1. All offerings are of grain, olive oil or honey (which presumably the god consumed). There is no suggestion of animal sacrifice, nor that the gods were recipients of elaborate metalwork or 'works of art' (votives); and in this respect, 'Mycenaean' religion differed markedly from that of Archaic and Classical Greece. There is also no suggestion that the location of sanctuaries at the extremities of the palace's territory was linked to annual rituals which might have had an 'integrative' function (as has been suggested for later Greek religion by De Polignac (1984)). Whatever Mycenaean palatial states were, they were not 'covenants between gods and men' (in Josine Blok's sense (2014; 2017)). Religious practices such as these were peripheral to the function of the palace in its final phase.

4.16 The end (or ends) of the palace

At some point in the fourteenth century BC the whole of the palace at Knossos was destroyed in a violent conflagration (Evans 1900). This conflagration preserved as much as it destroyed – that we have the Linear B tablets at all is because all were baked hard (so most scholars think) in this single event (see Figure 2.5). Most scholars would date this in ceramic terms to the LMIIIA2 stylistic phase – though the latest sealings (Popham and Gill 1995) suggest, if anything, a slightly earlier date. Inconsistencies such as these suggest that there may not have been one destruction but several: the conflagrations may not represent a single event. Jan Driessen (Driessen 1990, 112–16; 1997) has argued that the Chariot tablets may date to an earlier destruction in LMII; Whitelaw (2022, 40–3) has gone further, and argued for at least three destruction events taking place between the end of LMII and LMIIIA. He thereby argues for a later 'final destruction' than most scholars – LMIIIA2 final or even early LMIIIB early. While I agree that several destruction horizons are possible (indeed likely), I find it hard to reconcile this with the very strong evidence for the shrinkage in size of the town of Knossos in LMIIIB that Hatzaki (2007b) has documented in detail by looking at the surviving pottery deposits. The final destruction of the palace of Knossos cannot be contemporary with the major horizon of destructions of the Mycenaean palaces on the mainland. It must be earlier by several decades if not a century.

The single most important fact about the final act of destruction in LMIIIA2 is that it did not lead to any subsequent programme of reconstruction. If Peter Tomkins (2016) is right (that the first 'palace' dates to around 2700 BC), then, at the time of its destruction, a monumental structure – whether palace or 'central courtyard structure' – had been on this site for over a thousand years. Evans had noted several reconstructions after earthquakes, one in MMIIB, one possibly a little later, and noted damage done to the structure in LMIA (damage possibly caused by the indirect effects of the volcanic eruption of Santorini). The 'palace' had been rebuilt and repurposed on several occasions. Why not on this one?

This is probably the biggest enigma in Aegean prehistory. Looking for outside agents for the destruction of the palaces – whether these be invaders, or civil strife, or climate change – misses the point. Invasion or civil strife might have been the immediate cause of the destruction, and climate stress may well have been an underlying factor. The 'collapse of complex societies' (Tainter 1988) usually has multiple causes. Institutions, however, which are regarded as central to a particular society are, in general, usually maintained by that society. Moreover, in neighbouring societies such as Egypt and the Near East, while a political structure might collapse and a period of disunity follow, there is often an attempt at reconstruction: Middle Kingdom Egypt tries to emulate the glories of the Old Kingdom; Neo-Babylonian Babylon emulates the glories of Hammurabi; and, further afield, in Mexico, Mayapan is a kind of reconstruction of Maya Tikal. In all these cases the later structures reference the older ones – which makes them easier for us to understand. But in the Aegean world the end of the Bronze Age palaces does not lead to their emulation after the end of the 'Dark Ages'. When palaces appear again in the Aegean (in Macedon in Late Classical and Hellenistic times), they bear absolutely no relation to the 'palaces' of the Bronze Age.

Whatever the palace stood for in its final phase it must have lost that ideological hold on the Cretan population which had led to its continual renewal or reinvention in the past. That the destruction left obvious traces of burning (Evans 1900) – which are very much in contrast to many of the elusive traces of destructions of cities of historical date which often require microstratigraphy and micromorphology in order to detect them (Karkanas 2021) – is also a significant fact. The final destruction was not simply an *act* but also a *spectacle* of destruction. Susan Sherratt's phrase 'Potemkin Palaces' (Sherratt 2001), which she uses for all the Mycenaean palace states, is surely apt. These were, in Near Eastern terms, pretend palaces – façades hiding an empty shell behind, no more substantial than a Hollywood set of Ancient Rome.

4.17 The evolution of the Knossos 'palace': a new model

The final palace of Knossos was then also the first. That is to say, it is only in the Late Bronze Age (ceramically LMII–IIIA2 early) that Knossos became the seat of a hierarchically organized, unitary state where the palace was both a centre of authority (and administration) and the residence of a king. Before that the 'palace' had been something else entirely. This essentially Mycenaean kingdom was, of all the polities that the 'palace' had been associated with, also the least resilient. The palace functioned as a palace for less than 150 years; when it was burnt down it was not rebuilt. This, I would argue, is in large part due to the imposition of a pyramidal hierarchy, or the Mycenaean system of a quasi-chiefdom trying to imitate the structure and authority of Near Eastern palace states (such as Mari or Ebla) – and failing.

What purpose had this structure served then before it became a palace? The basic sequence is from gathering place ('henge') to courtyard complex to temple to palace. If we follow Tomkins (2016), then the levelling of the tell to form a platform for the 'gathering place' occurred before 2000 BC. Here then is the proposed sequence.

Phase 1: The gathering place (pre-palatial). The tell was levelled to create a platform perhaps as early as 2700 BC. Slightly later (in EMIII), some structures (e.g., the keep) were built around this, and some granaries (the hypogaeum) built. The open space may already have been aligned on a north–south axis. The levelled space was used for seasonal gatherings.

Phase 2: The courtyard complex (protopalatial). The central court was laid out, and more buildings were established around it. Major storage facilities such as the west magazines were built. Cup deposits seem to indicate hierarchically organized gatherings centred on drinking from fine 'Kamares' ware cups (Hatzimichael and Whitley 2012). Writing (Hieroglyphic) was used to help mobilize resources for seasonal festivals centred on the central court. The west court was set up, and the west façade is was decorated with gypsum blocks.

Phase 3: The temple (neopalatial). After a number of earthquake destructions in MMII and MMIIIA (MMIIIA being a kind of intermediate phase), the palace was both rebuilt and redecorated. There seemed to be less emphasis on communal drinking, and perhaps more on rations for festivals (conical cups) – that is, there may have been less hierarchy during this phase. The structure was redecorated with frescoes, and the domestic quarter was built up (perhaps to accommodate priests and other office holders). Communal rituals were commemorated and incorporated into the fabric of the structure through deposits (such as the Temple Repositories) in which ritual artefacts were ceremonially broken. The central court was used for events with spectators – some of which we would call sports. Linear A was adopted for very limited purposes – more to mobilize resources rather than to administer territory.

Phase 4: The palace (final Palatial). The palace finally became a palace – that is, the residence of a monarch and the centre of administration for a unitary state. The past was not entirely forgotten – there was an attempt (at its clearest in the decoration of the throne room) to devise a new iconography that accommodated both the new significance of the structure as a palace, and its older role as a gathering place or temple. Writing (Linear B) was used to administer and control a large territory in central Crete (the 'kingdom of Idomeneus'). More specifically, it was used to manage flocks of sheep for wool, to ensure that the military was properly supplied and that the gods (now a clearly Greek pantheon) were properly honoured. The palace was rebuilt and redecorated to reflect a new, more frankly pyramidal social and political order, and to accommodate new communal drinking practices focused on large cups (the Ephyraean goblet) and the krater.

The final palatial period – the Mycenaean palace – was also possibly the shortest phase of 'the palace'. It is not to me a coincidence that the shortest phase of this architectural complex coincides with a period when the social and political structure was at its most hierarchical. Top-down managerialism is rarely a recipe for resilience, whether in Eastern Europe in the late twentieth century or in British universities in the twenty-first.

What then of King Minos? If we have to link the final phase of the palace to a legendary king, then that king must have been Idomeneus rather than Minos. 'Minos' seems to relate to an earlier period, perhaps the neopalatial. 'King Minos' is a contradictory figure. On the one hand, we have his reputation as a cruel tyrant – cruel to both his family, to his subjects and to the Athenians. On the other hand, there is his reputation as a lawgiver, the very embodiment of a just ruler. It is difficult to see how these distinct reputations could be embodied in a single man. But if 'Minos' were a title – if there were several persons who, successively, held the position of 'the Minos' – then this problem disappears. It is for this reason that I prefer to interpret the name 'Minos' as that of an office holder, rather than either a single person or a single dynasty.

All this, of course, is speculation. Any chance of looking at the textual record to investigate this further disappears with the end of Linear B literacy. Linear B was not a script that was widely used – it had a weak hold on Late Bronze Age culture. When this script falls from use, we enter a true Dark Age – that is, a period where we have to rely entirely on the archaeological rather than the written record for constructing a history of Knossos.

CHAPTER 5
AFTER THE PALACE: FROM THE IRON AGE TO LATE ANTIQUITY (AND BEYOND)

Chapter abstract

This chapter provides a period-by-period account which begins with the rapid shrinking of the settlement in the immediate aftermath of the final destruction of the palace, and the steady recovery and development of the settlement through the Early Iron Age and the Orientalizing and Archaic periods. It will discuss the emergence of a new form of social and political organization, the *polis* or citizen-state, that was demonstrably more resilient than the top-down pyramid of the final palace. It will outline the city's development in Classical and Hellenistic times and how it fared as a Roman *colonia* and early Christian bishopric.

5.1 After the palace

When the Bronze Age palace at Knossos was destroyed in the years before 1300 BC it was not rebuilt. In Crete an administrative centre making use of Linear B continued to function for a few more years at Chania (Kydonia) in western Crete (Hallager 1997a; 1997b), but it too was destroyed at some point in LMIIIB. In this respect both the 'palace' at Khania and the palace at Knossos resemble other Late Bronze Age (Mycenaean) palaces in the Aegean, most of which (at Mycenae, Tiryns and Pylos) were brought to an end at least one hundred years after the final destruction of Knossos. The experiment in replicating (in the Aegean) the pyramidal hierarchies of Near Eastern states can, I think, be judged to have been a failure.

This fact has several implications. The town of Knossos survived the fall of the palace; Knossos after the palace remained a community within a Late Bronze Age eastern Mediterranean world whose economy remained highly integrated. Indeed, in the thirteenth century BC (before the final end of the Mycenaean palaces) the Mediterranean world became even more connected – and its various regions more interdependent – than it had ever been before (Broodbank 2013, 386–460). Mycenaean pottery was reaching Italy, Cypriot bronze and copper enriched Nuraghic Sardinia, and trade flourished between Syria, the Aegean, the central Mediterranean and Egypt. This was a world still dominated by the great powers of the Hittite and Egyptian empires (Cline 2015).

Knossos at the very end of the Bronze Age now cut a poor figure. The town had ceased to be the centre of a substantial kingdom and the settlement shrank to little more than 10ha (Whitelaw et al. 2019). This shrinkage, in some ways, anticipates the long recession in Greece that we used to call the 'Dark Age', where population diminished, literacy was lost and the material standard of life was reduced (Snodgrass 1971; Murray 2017). What kind of community this reduced Knossos was, and how this community subsequently found another form of political existence first as a *polis* in a largely Greek-speaking Mediterranean world and then as a flourishing town within the Roman Empire, are the principal themes of this penultimate chapter.

5.2 Taking leave of the Minoans: the end of the Bronze Age and the coming of the Age of Iron (Late Minoan IIIB, Late Minoan IIIC and Sub-Minoan)

How does a community cohere when it loses its principal institution? A structure with a central courtyard had been the centre of both the religious and political life of the town of Knossos for over 600 years. Now it was no more. What could replace it? Well, there seems to have been some reoccupation (Hatzaki 2007b, 233–48). Pottery in a style now called LMIIIB has been found in part of the palace, in Makryteichos, around the Unexplored Mansion and in the area of the Stratigraphical Museum extension excavations. Much of this pottery seems domestic, as it includes characteristic cooking shapes such as the tripod cooking vessel.

Domestic reoccupation is, however, only part of the story. Clearly much of the town of Knossos (as well as the palace) in this period was a ruin – if some neopalatial and final palatial structures were reoccupied, others were not. Parts of the Little Palace (Hatzaki 2005, 165) were reused, but this was on a much smaller scale than previously. Indeed, 'occupation' seems to be the wrong word – squatting seems more appropriate for the reuse of such buildings.

Knossos was a community in shock, and communities in shock often look more to the past than the future. This is reflected in local attitudes to the dead. Signs of fundamental continuity can be seen in the continued use of final palatial cemetery areas on the Gypsades Hill (Hood et al. 1959), at Zafer Papoura and at Mavro Spelio. Mortuary practices that by now must have seemed very traditional – interments in pit caves, tholos and chamber tombs – did not change much (Perna 2011, 141–2). The reuse and reappropriation of the Kephala tholos tomb (Preston 2005) testifies to the fundamental continuity in funerary customs in the immediately post-palatial period.

Nor did the production and use of pottery break with earlier practice. Workshops based in north-central Crete (if not Knossos itself) continued to produce wheel-made, kiln-fired painted pottery in a style still recognizably late Minoan throughout the Late Minoan IIIB and IIIC phases (Hatzaki 2007b, 233–51). The shapes remain much the same as in LMIIIA – that is, the 'final palatial' period. The latest Bronze Age (that is LMIIIB and LMIIIC) assemblages continue to be dominated by drinking cups and kraters of Mycenaean (mainland) type; and other distinctive Late Bronze Age shapes (the stirrup vase, for perfumed oil) simply carry on (Figure 5.1). This essentially 'Mycenaean' pattern was to persist for quite some time.

What of the palace itself? This structure, though certainly now a ruin, had not yet fully lost its religious significance. In the south-east part of the ruined palace, a new, if very

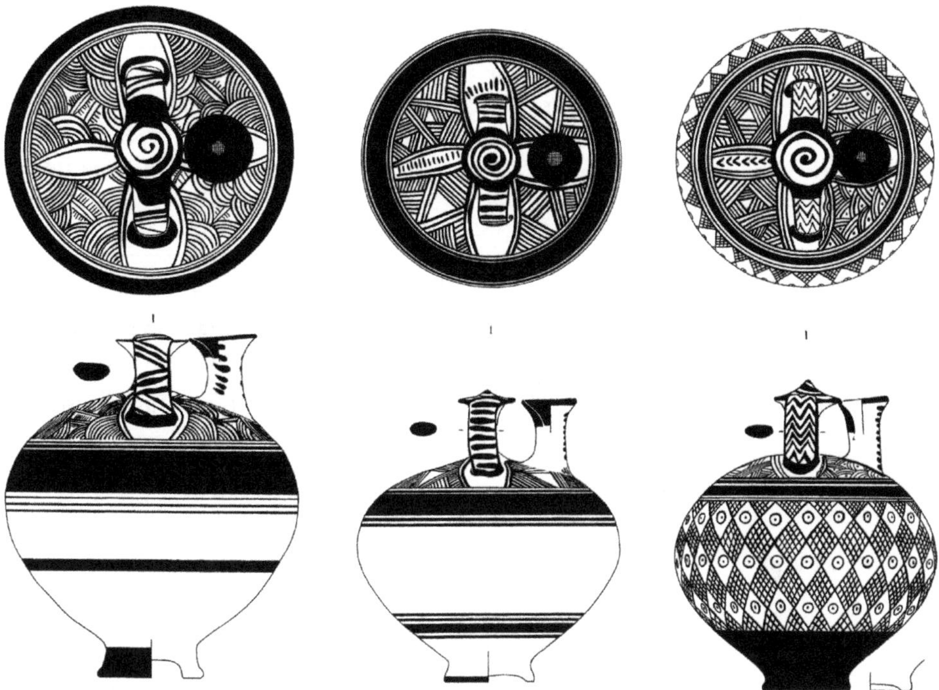

Figure 5.1 Drawing of three LMIIIC/Sub-Minoan stirrup jars from the 200–202 tomb complex. After Coldstream and Catling 1996, Vol. III, Figure 123 = KNC 200.1, 2 & 3). Courtesy British School at Athens.

small, shrine (1.5 x 1.5m) – the 'Shrine of the Double Axes' – was built (Evans 1928a, 332–44; Prent 2004, 412–14). This shrine was located close to an earlier, MMIII shrine and continued to use 'Minoan' religious symbols, such as the double axe itself and 'horns of consecration'. In this respect it looks back on the past. But its basic design anticipates the 'bench shrines' which were to become common in Crete during the earliest part of the Early Iron Age (Prent 2005, 188–200). Some of the terracotta figurines – in particular a (female?) figurine 'with upraised arms' – look forward to the religious symbolism of the Iron Age (Alexiou 1958b).

Marked change has to wait until the next phase, the so-called Sub-Minoan (the term is Evans'). Where LMIIIC ends and 'Sub-Minoan' begins has been much discussed, but it does seem that these labels do represent distinct ceramic phases and assemblages (Coldstream and Catling 1996, 295–318; Catling 1996a; Popham 1992; D'Agata 2011). We now enter the 'Early Iron Age' or 'the Dark Age' (these terms too are disputed: Kotsonas 2016a; Murray 2018), a period which some would still see as 'Dorian' rather than 'Minoan'. The ceramic and chronological terms used for this period (down to around 600 BC) reflect this.

The first major deposit from the Sub-Minoan phase is from the Spring Chamber shrine, south of the palace and found within the Caravanserai (Evans 1928a, 123–39;

Table 5.1 The chronological scheme for Iron Age Knossos, down to the 'Archaic gap'

	Approximate calendar dates BC according to Brock (1957)	*Approximate calendar dates BC according to Coldstream (2001)*	*Corresponding mainland phase (Athens), principally after Coldstream 1968, Cook 1935 and Lemos 2002.*
Sub-Minoan (SM)	1020–970	1050–970	Early Protogeometric
Early Protogeometric (EPG)	970–920	970–920	Middle to Late Protogeometric
Middle Protogeometric (MPG)	920–870	920–875	Late Protogeometric to Early Geometric I
Late Protogeometric (LPG)	870–850	875–840	Early Geometric II
Protogeometric B (PGB)	850–820	840–810	Middle Geometric I
Early Geometric (EG)	820–800	810–790	Middle Geometric II
Mature Geometric (MG)	800–770	790–745	Middle Geometric II
Late Geometric (LG)	770–735	745–700	Late Geometric I
Early Orientalizing (EO)	735–680	700–670	Late Geometric II to earliest Protoattic
Late Orientalizing (LO)	680–630	670–630 (in cemeteries, some LO on other deposits later)	Middle Protoattic (black and white style)

Source: Brock 1957; Coldstream 2001.

Prent 2004, 414–16; 2005, 135–6). This too contains a figurine 'with upraised arms' (Alexiou 1958b) and numerous wide-mouthed bowls (the so-called kalathoi) containing the remains of olives. Cult both here and at the 'Shrine of the Double Axes' was short-lived. Neither cult practice can be said to prefigure anything that was to happen in the future.

Neither does what we know of the town, which simply persists as a small settlement no larger than 10ha (with occupation persisting over the 'Unexplored Mansion' (Popham 1992)). While this may not have seemed large (in international terms) during the end of the palatial Bronze Age (LMIIIB and LHIIIB on the mainland), by Sub-Minoan times the wider picture had changed dramatically. LMIIIC and Sub-Minoan represent the heyday of the 'refuge settlement' in Crete – many Cretans had taken to the hills and established large settlements on mountain peaks. Karphi is the largest and best known of

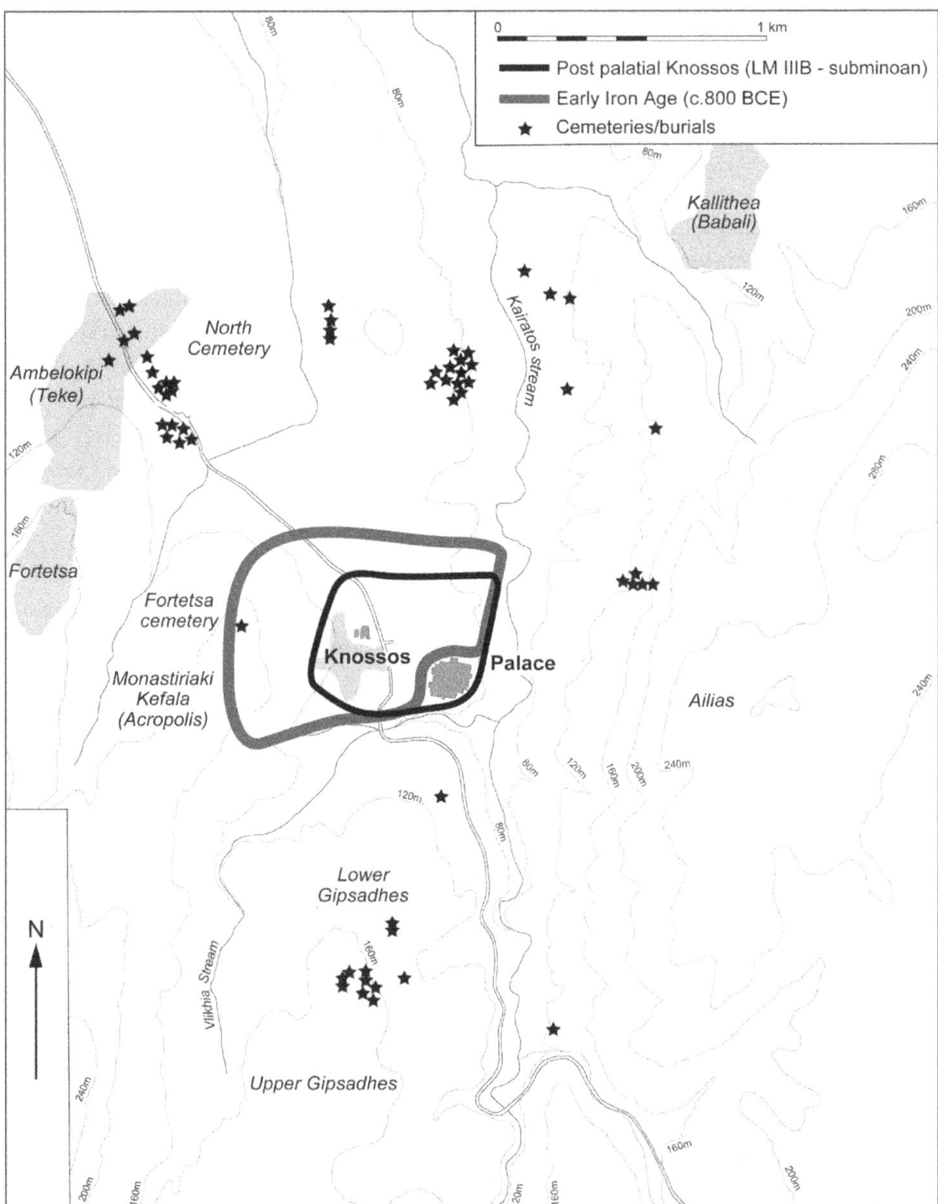

Figure 5.2 The extent of the settlement of Knossos in the immediate post-palatial and later Iron Age periods, showing the position of major Iron Age cemeteries. Kirsty Harding after Whitelaw et al. 2019, Figure 8, and Kotsonas 2019b, Figures 5–6.

these (Pendlebury et al. 1938). But in comparative terms these settlements were not large – few exceeded 6ha (Nowicki 2000). So, just by staying the same, Knossos at the beginning of the Iron Age became a (relatively) large Cretan community.

Sub-Minoan, moreover, is generally taken to mark the beginning of the Iron Age. Small iron objects (pins) appear in some of the tombs in the North Cemetery associated with 'Sub-Minoan' pottery such as that from tomb Π (Brock 1957, 8–10). Iron dirks, knives and pins turn up in other tombs of the same date (Catling 1996b, 528–30). As a new technology, iron-working was probably imported from Cyprus – something that the shapes of early iron objects seem to confirm (Snodgrass 1996). Such objects often take forms already established in the Late Bronze Age – the flange-hilted, leaf-shaped Naue II sword being a perfect example of this transition. But they were not made in the same way. Iron-working rarely makes use of moulds – making objects requires hot and cold hammering, heating, carburization and quenching (quite different processes from casting, say, an axe). The raw material for iron – iron ore – is also much more common than the ores of either copper or tin – viable iron deposits can be found throughout the Aegean. Iron, like clay, can almost always be 'locally sourced'.

Childe (1964, 190–2, 199–200; see Whitley 2001, 80–4) was the first to argue that this transition was more than technological; it also had a social and political significance. In his Marxist view, it had two long-term effects: one economic and one political. First, its introduction changed the mode of production – leading to more and better tools and an increase in the productive forces of the society. Second, its mode of production dispersed and decentralized political power. Whereas the social and political order of the palaces depended on controlling the flow and distribution of relatively rare metals (copper, tin), iron-working democratized metallurgy.

This view has been much criticized. For one thing, the introduction of iron did not, in the first instance, bring about a new range of tools that increased the 'productive forces' of society. We have to go a very long way into the Iron Age to encounter any iron tools – most of the objects in iron we find in Knossos are weapons or ornaments, and continue forms established in the Late Bronze Age (Morris 1989; 2000, 208–18). Nonetheless, when we do have a glimpse of the social order of the Cretan *polis*, it is, if not exactly democratic, much less of a social pyramid than that of the Mycenaean palaces.

The gradual formation of this social order can be traced in the new cemeteries established at this time – the North Cemetery and the Fortetsa cemetery. Both are located at some distance from the town of Knossos itself and so mark something of a break with what had gone before. Establishing new cemetery areas is in itself a sign of social change. The break with the Bronze Age is at its most marked in the case of the tomb complex 200–202 in the North Cemetery (Coldstream and Catling 1996, 191–5). The tomb architecture itself looks back to the Bronze Age – it is a 'pit cave' (Figure 5.4), a type common in the LMII–IIIA Zafer Papoura cemetery (Evans 1905b). But the manner in which both the persons interred and the goods that accompanied them were treated in the burial ceremony represents a major change (Whitley 2016; Kotsonas 2018b). For one thing, the bodies were burnt. Cremation is itself an innovation, and one that seems to have spread from eastern Crete (Perna 2011). Interments in earlier Bronze Age tombs

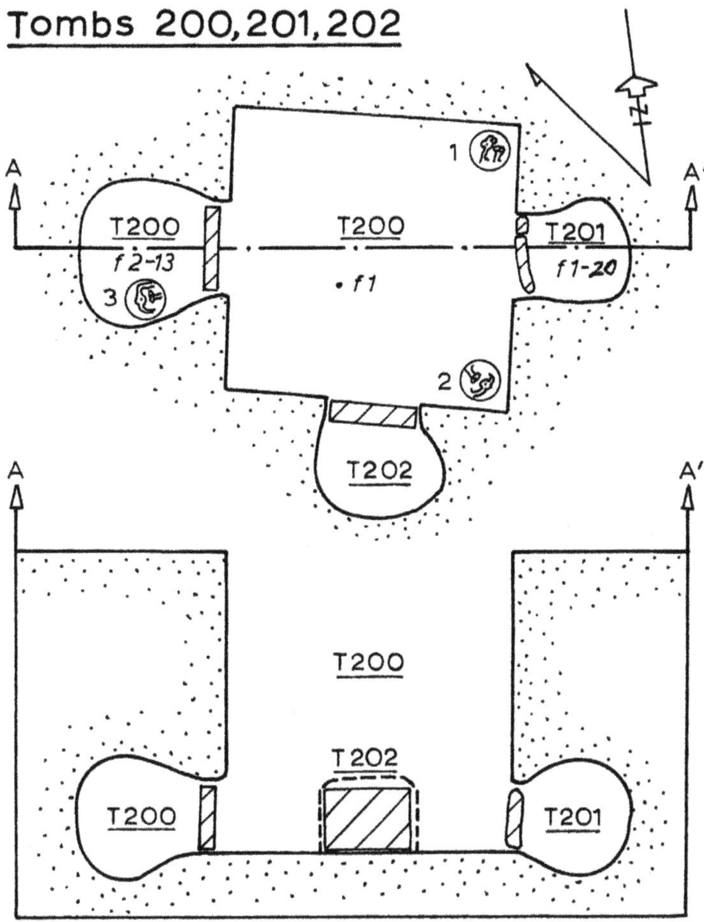

Figure 5.3 North Cemetery plan and section of 200–202 complex. After Coldstream and Catling 1996, Vol. III, Figure 43, lower right. Courtesy British School at Athens.

had invariably been inhumations; cremation is introduced during the Sub-Minoan period. From now on, distinctions between who is buried whole and who burnt will have social significance (Cavanagh 1996, 651–2; Musgrave 1996, 691–2). Just as the bodies were burnt, so the weapons, armour and other valuables that accompanied the principal, male grave of this complex were broken as well as burnt. These included a bronze Naue II sword (the flange-hilted sword that now becomes common across the whole of Late Bronze Age and Early Iron Age Europe), fragments of a boar's tusk helmet and an antique Cypriot Late Bronze Age four-sided stand that must have been over 100 years old at the time of its deposition (Papasavvas 2001, 82–5; 2017; Figure 5.4).

Such practices recall the burials of the heroes Patroklos and Hector at the end of the *Iliad* (*Iliad* 23.161–257; 24.782–804). Hector Catling (1995) inferred from this that these burials represent 'heroes returned'; Kotsonas (2018b) speculates (none too seriously)

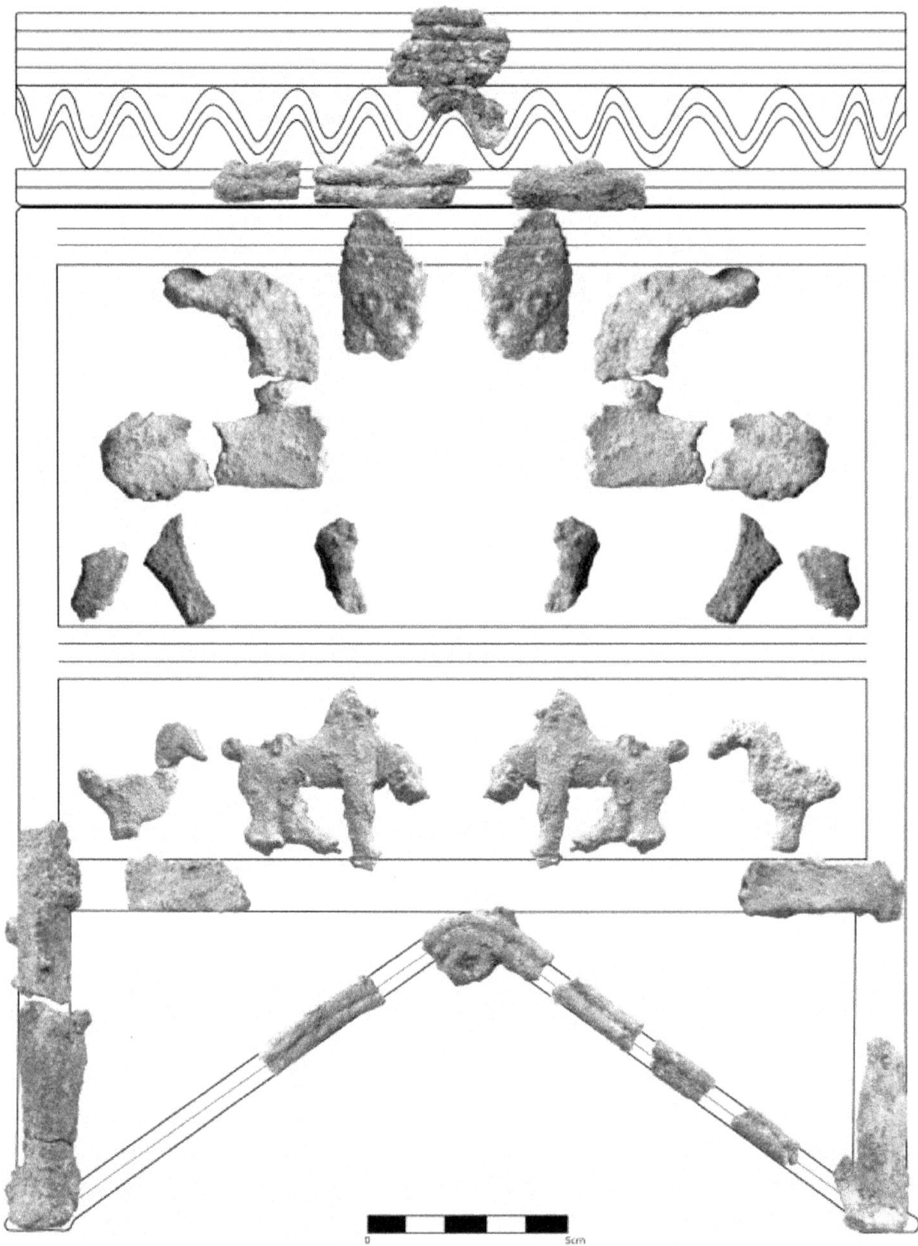

Figure 5.4 Reconstruction (by Georgios Papasavvas) of the burnt Cypriot bronze stand (KNC 201.f1) from this tomb complex. Courtesy G. Papasavvas.

that this tomb might be the 'tomb of Meriones', a Knossian hero whose tomb later Greek and Roman writers associated with Knossos. Whatever the truth behind this suggestion, the study of mortuary practices – that is, the tombs and their contents – has dominated the social archaeology of the Early Iron Age in Knossos. Very much in contrast to the study of the Bronze Age, the close analysis of Iron Age tombs has become the prism through which archaeologists have attempted to trace the changing social order that leads from the 'Dark Ages' to the 'rise of the polis'.

Somewhere in this transition the Minoans disappear. The term Sub-Minoan suggests that 'Minoan-ness' has somehow reached an end, and the next phase (describing a ceramic style), 'Proto-Geometric', suggests that something new is being born. Coldstream (2001) sometimes describes these phases as 'Greek', sometimes as Dorian. How we get from pots to people is, of course, a perennial question in archaeology; readers should nonetheless be aware that these kinds of terms carry with them their own subliminal set of expectations about the ethnic and linguistic character of the people of Knossos. We know from the Linear B evidence that some Knossians made use of (and so spoke) a dialect of Greek in the last phase of the palace. Early Iron Age Knossos must have had many Greek speakers. Did that make it Greek? Here we encounter once more Homer's (*Odyssey* 19.175–7) description of the island as having five peoples – Achaeans, Dorians, Eteocretans, Kydonians and Pelasgians. The first two of these undoubtedly spoke some form of Greek (though Homer does not use the term – Achaeans is used for everyone on the 'Greek' side in the Trojan War). The dialect of the Linear B tablets – Arkado-Cypriot – is closer to some notion of Achaeans; but by the time we have public inscriptions from Knossos the dialect appears to be Dorian. Can archaeology shed any light on this question? Perhaps – but if so, only indirectly. But we need to start with some basic facts about the settlement of Knossos in this time of transition.

5.3 The Early Iron Age settlement

That the settlement of Knossos grew between the eleventh (Sub-Minoan) and the seventh (Orientalizing) century BC is hardly in doubt. But how much it grew remains controversial. One view (Coldstream 2000) is that it hardly grew at all – that it was confined to an area of little more than 10ha, barely encroaching on the ruins of the palace to the south and extending no further north than the area of the Taverna (see again Figure 5.2). Coldstream based this conclusion on what had, up until then, been excavated and identified (mainly painted pottery). Such 'Geometrical' pottery and the deposits from which it came had not been of great interest to Evans, who often treated anything after the Bronze Age as an encumbrance to the 'Minoan' palace and town. These deposits were, moreover, hardly ideal for understanding the nature of the Early Iron Age settlement. Parts of house floors and some fill were to be found in levels by the Royal Road (Coldstream 1972; 1973a) and from levels above the Unexplored Mansion (Sackett et al. 1992a; Coldstream 1992).

Elsewhere, knowledge of the settlement is derived indirectly – from deposits in wells that had been filled in after they had fallen into disuse (e.g., Coldstream 1960; Coldstream and Sackett 1978); and from some reoccupation of Minoan structures in the area of the south-west houses (Coldstream and Macdonald 1997). Such information tells us little about the shape of the settlement – that is, its structure. For there were no complete houses, nor any information about such things as street plans. For the internal structure of the settlement we have to turn to analogies from elsewhere – and there are no direct analogies from any Cretan *polis* site whose topography is similar to Knossos. One thing is almost certain, however: Cretan Early Iron Age houses were, in general, smaller and meaner than Bronze Age ones (Westgate 2015). It is likely then that the houses of Early Iron Age Knossos consisted of two- or three-room structures no larger than 10m by 5m. We are very far from the 'villas' of the Late Bronze Age.

This picture has changed a little since the turn of the millennium. For one thing, preliminary results from the Knossos survey seem to suggest that the town was much larger than this – reaching 50ha or so by the end of the Iron Age (around 500 BC; Whitelaw et al. 2019; Kotsonas 2019b; see Figure 5.11). There are also hints that the town might have expanded to the north-west in Protogeometric times. Excavation under the Villa Dionysus revealed floor levels of this date – the only direct evidence of Early Iron Age houses (Coldstream and Hatzaki 2003). Crops used included 'glume wheat, barley, a variety of pulses and all the common fruits locally available, including fig, grape and olive' (Livarda 2012, 203). In its use of crops, Knossos was not then much different from other contemporary settlements.

What about faunal remains? One Geometric animal bone assemblage from Well 12 from the Unexplored Mansion possibly contained evidence of elite feasting (Dibble 2012, 22). The well contained a very high proportion of cattle remains (43.5 per cent of Minimum Number of Anatomical Units), deriving from at least five cattle, which contrasts with other Early Iron Age deposits from the Royal Road and Unexplored Mansion that typically had around 20 per cent cattle remains in the assemblages (Dibble 2012, Table 6.1). There do then seem to be differences in consumption or feasting practices, not all of which relate to the household.

Another way of looking at the household is to view the pottery as household assemblages – that is, shapes with a specific purpose. Many of the shapes simply continue from those known in the Late Bronze Age with little modification – Crete and Knossos continue to make use of stirrup jars for perfumed olive oil down into Late Protogeometric times (Brock 1957, 152–3; Coldstream 1996, 338–40; Desborough 1952, 236–50; see Figure 5.1). Many shapes relate to drinking (see 'commensality' below), but also to storage of grain (pithoi) and to food preparation – cooking. When it comes to the function of pottery, it is sometimes best to look at fabric as well as shape. Here we have to turn to petrology; different kinds of petrological analyses are suitable for different kinds of pottery. When it comes to finewares, chemical analysis seems to confirm a picture of fundamental continuity in pottery production from the Bronze Age onwards. A study of semi-fine to coarsewares from Knossos (Boileau and Whitley 2010) found that most fabrics are local (83.3 per cent from north-central Crete) and that few are used exclusively for any one purpose. Of the seven major local fabrics defined, only one (fabric 7) is used *exclusively* for cooking and another (fabric 5) *exclusively* for storage (pithoi). Other fabrics are used for both purposes, including the mysterious fabric 4. This seems to be the same as Coldstream's (2001) 'Gritty Red Micaceous Ware'. It starts out as a multi-purpose fabric in the late ninth century but ends up as the favoured fabric for cooking by the end of our period (Boileau and Whitley 2015). Intriguingly it appears to be non-local, raising the possibility of specialized production and trade in cooking wares from elsewhere in the Aegean. But if so, the potters continued to make cooking pots in the local shape inherited from the Bronze Age, the 'Minoan' tripod cooking vessel. This shape is particularly appropriate for stews and lasts well into the Geometric period.

Needless to say, this shape is not found in tombs whose pottery tends to be grander. Mortuary practices rarely mirror the world of the living but rather tell us something about, not what the dead had done and suffered in life, but what they ought to have done (given their age, sex and social standing). That the shifting representations in the manner in which Knossians buried their dead in the Early Iron Age has become our chief guide to social and political change in this period is a proposition we need to examine more closely.

5.4 Early Iron Age society: the view from the graves

Throughout the Early Iron Age, Knossians buried their dead in collective tombs. These tombs were grouped into cemeteries: principally the North Cemetery (Coldstream and Catling 1996; Coldstream 1963); the Fortetsa cemetery to the west of the Acropolis (Brock 1957); and tombs on the Gypsadhes hill to the south (Coldstream et al. 1981). Whether or not cemeteries located further afield (such as at Ayios Ioannis; Boardman 1960) form part of the burial grounds of the community of Knossos is unclear – though they certainly shared the same range of burial architecture. This took the form of either chamber tombs with dromos (as in Figure 5.5) and chamber cut out of the rock or built tholos tombs (Cavanagh 1996) – pit-caves seem to disappear. Given the variety of forms of burial architecture in Early Iron Age Crete (Eaby 2011), this concentration on two forms seems rather restrictive. It does, nonetheless, underline Knossos' emphasis on the collective over the individual when it comes to burial practices.

Sometimes (not often) earlier Bronze Age tombs were cleared out and reused. This is not too surprising given that both forms of tomb architecture derive from a Late Bronze Age 'Mycenaean' rather than an earlier 'Minoan' tradition. Each tomb contained at least two interments, both inhumation and cremation being attested in this period. The osteological data we have from these tombs is rather scrappy (Musgrave 1996) – a testament to the efficiency with which cremation was practised. We cannot then be sure which practices relate to which gender. The little data we do have indicate that inhumation was preferred for infants and very young children. Cremation (now almost invariably in urns) was practised for some persons as young as nine to ten years (Musgrave 1996, 680,) for adolescents and for adults of both sexes.

Cremated remains were placed in urns, which become the 'visible face' of burials for adults throughout this period. Urns come in many shapes and sizes, and in several fabrics, both fine and coarse. In the earlier periods, both kraters and amphoras may have been used to hold human remains (Cavanagh 1996, 659–60), an example being the assemblage from Teke tomb E (Figure 5.6; Sackett 1976). From Late Protogeometric times onwards, however, the principal shape was the funerary pithos.[1] This shape – or rather range of related shapes, since there are several varieties (necked pithos, straight-sided pithos, two-handled pithos, four-handled pithos and so forth; see Coldstream 1996, 311–24; Moignard 1996, 421–7) – is the one whose decoration is most sensitive to changing fashions in style.

And these styles do change rapidly, beginning with necked pithoi in Protogeometric times and moving on to the straight-sided pithos in the mysterious 'Protogeometric B' phase of the late ninth century BC (Figure 5.7). This change in shape is accompanied by a change in the style of the decoration of the urns, a style which many have taken as the first, precociously 'Orientalizing' style in Greek vase painting, one in which we can identify our first 'artistic personality', the Tree Painter (Coldstream 1996, 315–16). At the same time as this Orientalizing style flourished, so did an 'Atticizing' Early Geometric style (sometimes both styles are seen on the same vase; Whitley 2013); and just as some of the new straight-sided pithoi are in these distinct painted styles, so there are some unpainted produced in various coarse fabrics (in particular the 'Gritty Red Micaceous Ware'). This alternation between 'Orientalizing' polychrome styles and 'Atticizing' Sub-Geometric ones reappears in the seventh century BC (Moignard 1996; 1998), after a century when most urns were decorated in a distinctly Geometric style. If we look at the individual interments, we might think that the more important persons were buried in the fanciest pots – that there would be a correlation between the wealth of each interment in one urn and the more elaborate, or florid forms of external decoration of that urn (e.g. the urn in Figure 2.6). There is, however, nothing of the kind. There are rich interments in plain vessels, and poor in elaborately decorated examples (Whitley 2004); and vice versa. When I use the words 'rich' and 'poor', these terms are relative – the differences between the 'wealth' of the individual interments are slight. By the seventh century BC there is a move towards greater uniformity in the grave goods deposited – most cremations inside even the most elaborately decorated polychrome urn are accompanied by nothing more than a simple perfume flask (aryballos) and some bronze depilatory tweezers – even if some of these aryballoi are decorated in a startlingly distinctive manner (Moignard 1998).

But if there is perhaps greater uniformity in burial practices at the level of the individual as we approach the end of the seventh century BC, then there are also marked differences when we compare the tombs as a whole. Differences in the wealth of tombs can be detected if we measure this by the number of metal objects present, whether these be bronze (Catling 1996c) or iron (Snodgrass 1996). A clear hierarchy of tombs becomes apparent. That these are collective tombs has also led to the widespread belief that they are family tombs, and that kinship was somehow the underlying organizing principle of EIA Knossian society and its social groups. Certainly collective burial underplays individual interment and emphasizes the collective. But were these really family tombs? There is some slight osteological evidence for consanguinity between three individuals

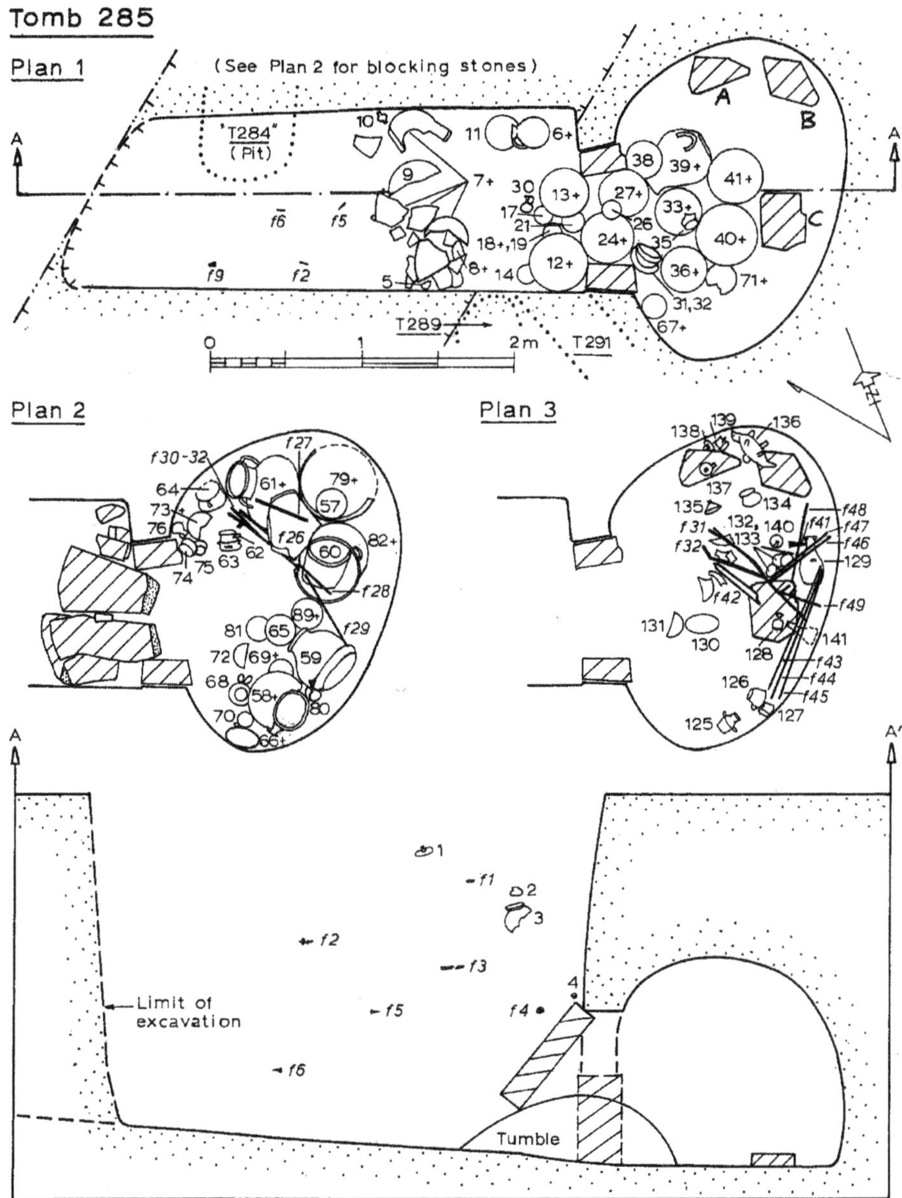

Figure 5.5 Plan and section of chamber Tomb 285 from the North Cemetery of Knossos. After Coldstream and Catling 1996, Vol. III, Figure 50. Courtesy British School at Athens.

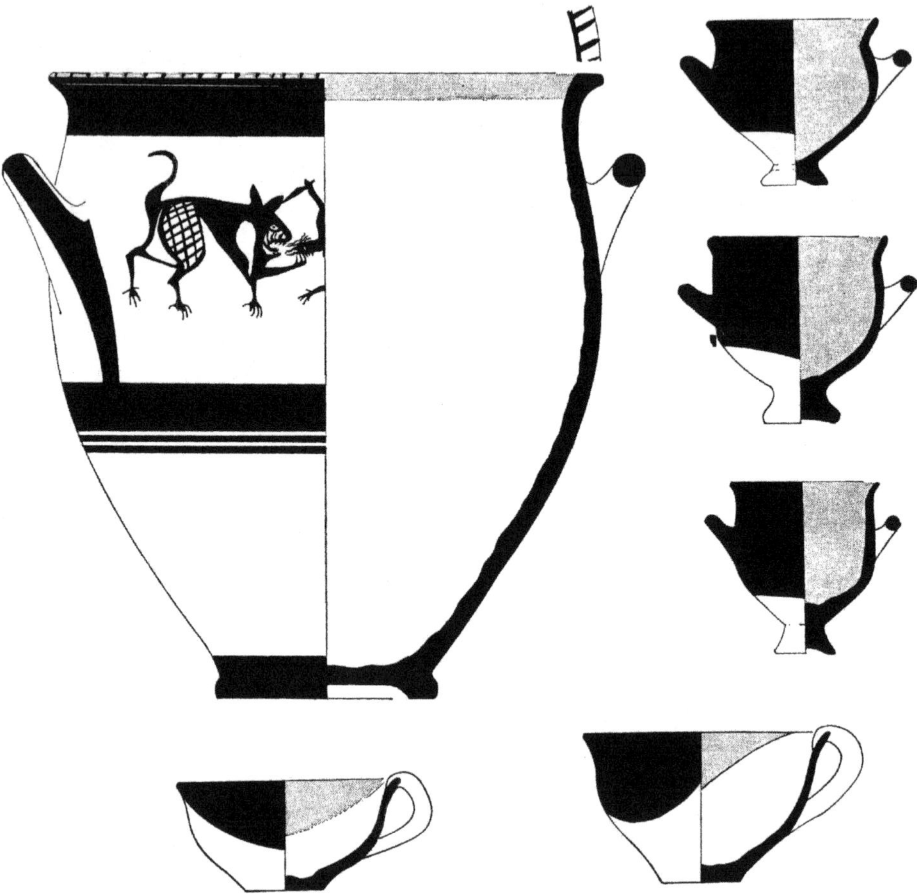

Figure 5.6 Assemblage of krater (used for interment) and cups (bell-skyphoi) from Teke tomb E (Sackett 1976, 121, Figure 4). Courtesy British School at Athens.

in the case of tomb 285 (Musgrave 1996, 681). There are, however, many senses of the term family. Are we talking of a nuclear family? Or a kin-group that is in fact a lineage, one that lasts several generations?

Some simple statistics might help here. Following Cavanagh (1996; cf. Pollard 2021), if we assume that one urn represents one person buried, then we can estimate the number of persons per tomb and see if this changes through time. My counts are given in the table below.

These patterns hold good for all Knossian cemeteries but are particularly marked in the Fortetsa tombs and the Lower Gypsadhes tomb (Coldstream et al. 1981), the one from which we have the best osteological data.

At first sight these figures seem to confirm the view that it was the eighth century that witnessed the major transformation of Knossos (as argued by Cavanagh 1996). Certainly the later eighth century witnessed a huge increase in the number of urns

Figure 5.7 Straight-sided Protogeometric B pithos with lid from the North Cemetery (KNC 292.144 + 61). From Coldstream and Catling 1996, Vol. III, Figure 150, left. Courtesy British School at Athens.

(Pollard 2021, 9, Figure 6). If we take the number of urns as an index of the number of people alive in the immediately preceding period (a dubious proposition at the best of times), then population 'peaks' around 700 BC – a pattern evident in other regions of Greece, such as Attica and the Argolid (Snodgrass 1980, 15–48). There are two odd features, however: one is that there is an earlier peak in the years before 800 BC (Pollard 2021); the second, that after a 'peak' in the Early Orientalizing period, the number tails off in Late Orientalizing times. This too is consistent with a pattern we find elsewhere in Greece (Morris 1987), particularly in Attica. Whereas in Attica the number of interments recovers in the sixth century after a trough in the seventh, in Knossos, burials simply disappear after 630 BC.

Another difference with mainland patterns is that the major percentage increase in the number of interments seems to occur in the middle of the ninth century BC (between Late Protogeometric and Protogeometric B) rather than in the eighth (see also Wallace

Table 5.2 Number of interments per tomb and ratio of interments per tomb in Early Iron Age cemeteries at Knossos

Period	Minimum number of interments	Number of tombs in which these interments were found	Ratio of interments per tomb
LMIIIC/Sub-Minoan (1150–950 BC)	21	15	1.4
Protogeometric (EPG-LPG) (950–850 BC)	61	34	1.79
PGB/EG (Protogeometric B and Early Geometric) (850 –790 BC)	102	43	2.37
MG (Mature Geometric) (790–750 BC)	93	39	2.38
LG (Late Geometric) (750–700 BC)	163	65	2.51
EO (Early Orientalizing) (700–660)	156	42	3.71
LO (Late Orientalizing) (660–630)	100	31	3.22

Source: Brock 1957; Coldstream and Catling 1996; Coldstream et al. 1981.

2010, 304–11; Pollard 2021). Now of course Knossos is not the only site in Greece where the number of burials does not mirror demography – this case has been made most strongly for Athens. But the dearth of child burials does not allow us to construct arguments analogous to those of Morris (1987) for Knossos. We cannot argue that the same principles of inclusion/exclusion were operating here that were operating in Attica.

The only clear trend seems to be a steady increase in the number of interments per tomb. If these were family tombs then these families were getting both fewer in number and larger in size. Moreover, just as the arrival of the Protogeometric B style sees an increase in population, so it also witnesses the founding of tombs which persist over many generations. Whereas a Protogeometric tomb such as Teke tomb E (Sackett 1976; see Figure 5.6) is a single period tomb, many (if not all) of the tombs which flourished at the end of the period (KMF tombs 218, 219 and 292 (Coldstream and Catling 1996); Fortetsa tombs II, Rho and Rho 2; Brock 1957; see again Figure 5.5.) are precisely those founded in the ninth century BC. These are also the tombs where the increase in the number of interments per tomb is at its most dramatic.

These are also, for the most part, the richest tombs, as measured by the number of bronze and iron objects. Many of these iron objects consist of obeloi (spits) and fire-dogs, leading some scholars to emphasize the role of funerary feasting in the transformation of Knossian society (Rabinowitz 2014; Small 2018). These items are certainly appropriate for the ostentatious cooking and eating of meat, but this is not the only form of commensality we can detect here. In earlier tombs we often find assemblages that resemble to some degree both the later Greek symposium and the earlier Mycenaean practice of krater-centred drinking (that is, an assemblage of kraters associated with large drinking vessels). Let us look at the Late Protogeometric tomb, Teke tomb E (Sackett 1976; Figure 5.6). Here we have a single krater with a rather mysterious figured scene of a man being devoured by two animals or monsters, an amphora (for storing liquids), two one-handled cups and five so-called bell-skyphoi (Coldstream 1996, 378–380). Similar assemblages are found in many Geometric graves, and these patterns persist in the Orientalizing tombs KMF 34 and 56 (dinos sets; Whitley 2004; Moignard 1996, 451). In brief, the thesis (put forward by David Small 2018) that there was more feasting around 700 BC than in earlier times (and so that Knossos fits in with a model of a transegalitarian society) is not proven.

Both the symposium (Wecowski 2014) and the krater represent social practices that have come to Knossos from elsewhere in the Aegean. They are signs of Knossos' external relations which must have a bearing on how Knossian society developed.

5.5 Iron Age Knossos and the wider Mediterranean

The Early Iron Age is sometimes seen as a period of relative isolation, when the Aegean was cut off from the Near East. If this is true of other regions of Greece, it is certainly not true of north-central Crete. Bronzes and faience from the shrine at Amnisos (Stürmer 1992b, 248–52) and the stand from Tomb 200–202 (see above, Figure 5.4) is evidence of connectons to Cyprus as indeed is iron-working itself, connections which were maintained throughout the Iron Age. According to Papasavvas (2001, 190–205), bronze workers possibly from Cyprus established a workshop for the manufacture of tripods and four-sided stands at some point in the tenth century BC. At about the same time (*c.* 950 BC), Knossos started to receive imports of Athenian painted pottery, first in the Protogeometric and then the Geometric style. It is this range of outside connections that are held partly responsible for the spectacular changes we witness after 850 BC – the appearance of the so-called Protogeometric B (PGB) style (whose inspiration lay in part in Oriental metalwork) and soon after the 'atticizing' Early Geometric style (Whitley 2013). Boardman (1961; 1967) thought that these changes were due to something more than 'Oriental influence'. He argued, based largely on the finds from the Khaniale Tekke tomb (Hutchinson and Boardman 1954), that this period saw the arrival of a Near Eastern, specifically north Syrian, guild or family of craftsmen who worked not only in bronze (producing such singular pieces as the Fortetsa quiver; Brock 1957, 197–9) but also a range of objects in gold manufactured using imported techniques such as granulation and filigree. The style of their metalwork certainly incorporates figured scenes (such as a 'hero' set within two antithetical lions; see Figure 5.8) as well as classic 'metalworking' motifs such as the cable and guilloche (motifs also found on

Figure 5.8 Gold sheet showing a hero set between two antithetical lions, from the Khaniale Tekke tombs. After Boardman and Hutchinson 1954; Boardman 1967, Plate 12.3. Courtesy British School at Athens.

PGB painted pottery; see Figure 5.7). Boardman speculates that this guild of craftsmen may also have been responsible for the famous Cretan shields (Kunze 1931) found in the Idaean cave, shields probably manufactured in the eighth century BC.

This period also witnessed signs of links to the West. A Sardinian askos turns up in the Khaniale Tekke tombs (Vagnetti 1989), perhaps a by-product of Knossos' role in Cypriot and Phoencian trade. North Syrian and Cypriot connections were to be maintained throughout the next century, principally in the shape of Cypriot Black-on-red lekythoi (perfume flasks; Coldstream 1984). Indeed from the late ninth century BC until the 'Archaic gap' finds of imports from Euboea, Attica, the Argolid, the Corinthia, the Cyclades (Naxos) as well as from Cyprus and Phoenicia proper are to be found in the North Cemetery – a stylistic inference (Coldstream 1996, 393–409; Moignard 1996) confirmed by chemical analysis of the clay (Liddy 1996).

Throughout all this time, Knossian potters and painters continued to produce their own painted wares – some using a kiln located at the south side of the palace (Coldstream and Macdonald 1997). What effect did these connections have on local manufacture? Well, a very great one. Knossian potters and painters rarely encountered an exotic style they did not wish to imitate; they seem torn by a desire to copy the austere beauty of Attic wares and at the same time incorporate motifs from Near Eastern metalworking. There is no Knossian style that is not, in some sense, eclectic. But they were not slavish imitators, and certainly did not use imports for the purposes they were originally intended. Take the example of the Attic belly-handled amphora, a shape which in Athens is used to contain the ashes of dead women. Attic imports are never used for this purpose in Knossos, though both the shape and the decoration are imitated (with varying degrees of fidelity) and then adapted to curious Knossian purposes (Whitley 2015). By the Orientalizing period these differing sources of inspiration had settled down into two main styles: one an elaborate polychrome style, employing standard Orientalizing motifs such as the palmette; the other a plainer, almost SubGeometric style (Whitley 2004; 2013).

So far we have looked at the Orientalizing entirely from the viewpoint of metalworking and pottery styles (and their interrelations). But there is of course one major innovation of the Early Iron Age that falls into neither category – the adoption of the alphabet. The Greeks in general borrowed their letter forms from the Phoenicians (a fact of which Herodotus was in no doubt; Hdt. 5.58; see Jeffery 1990, 1–5; Rollston 2010, 20–41). The principal Greek innovation was to introduce vowels for some of these Phoenician letters. Some have argued (Powell 1991) that the alphabet was invented specifically to write down epic verse – an hypothesis supported by a number of early (that is late eighth century) inscriptions written in hexameters. Recent scholarship (e.g., Janko 2015) has tended to suggest that this borrowing of the letters and subsequent invention of the Greek alphabet took place around 800 BC. Following a suggestion by the Cretan Hellenistic historian Dosiadas (*FrGrHist* IIIB, No. 458, F6 = Jacoby 1950, 396, No. 6) that the alphabet originated in Crete, many scholars (e.g., Janko 2015; Jeffery 1990, 9, 425–6) have also been struck by the similarity between the letter forms of the earliest Cretan alphabetic inscriptions and those to be found on Phoenician inscriptions. Might the Greek alphabet have originated in Crete? Might a Cretan term for 'scribe' (*poinikastas* – 'phoinicianizer'; see Jeffery and Morpugo Davis 1970; Gagarin and Perlman 2016, 181–96, Da1) provide support for this contention?

Well, Knossos does have evidence for early contact with Phoenicians. A bronze hemispherical bowl from tomb J in the Teke cemetery bears an inscription in Phoenician letters (Coldstream and Catling 1996, 30, No. f1; Sznycer 1979; Rollston 2010, 36–7). The latest finds from this tomb date to the Late Protogeometric period (the early ninth century BC; Figure 5.9), as must this bowl. This is the earliest, firmly dated Phoenician

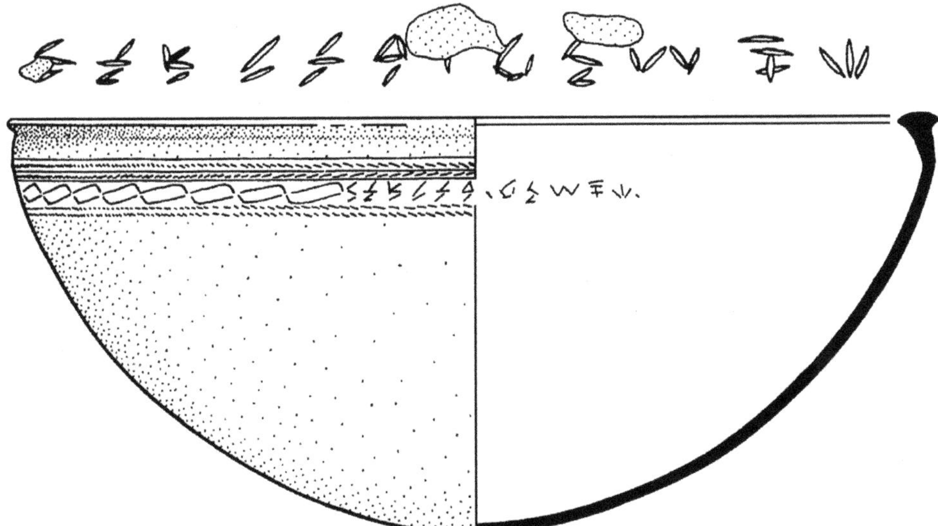

Figure 5.9 Plain hemispherical bowl from Teke tomb J in the North Cemetery of Knossos, datable to just after 900 BC, inscribed with Phoenician letters (Sznycer 1979). The inscription reads (phonetically) N ?'KLNB??SSSK – and may indicate two names (father and son?). Image after Coldstream and Catling 1996, Vol III, Figure 157. Redrawn by Kirsty Harding. Courtesy British School at Athens.

inscription found in the Greek world, and might at first sight seem to provide support for the idea that Crete was the original home of the Greek alphabet. If contact in and of itself leads to diffusion – to the adoption of ideas and technologies – we might then expect that Knossos would be the place where the earliest examples of Greek alphabetic writing might be found.

And here we would be disappointed. The earliest Greek inscriptions (including recent finds from Methoni in Macedonia and Eretria itself; Janko 2015) are generally found in areas where Euboeans had been active or in the Cyclades (Naxos). Early Greek inscriptions are generally to be found on cups (Kotsonas 2022). Crete seems to come late to this party. The earliest Cretan alphabetic inscription, datable to around 700 BC, is one that is etched into the surface of a Geometric pithos from Phaistos (Levi 1969). The earliest inscription in the Greek alphabet from Knossos is a small graffito incised onto the lip of a Late Orientalizing aryballos (perfume flask) from tomb 107 in the North Cemetery (Johnston 1996; Coldstream and Catling 1996, 154, No. 107.84). It reads (retrograde, that is, right to left), περατας καλ<λ >ιστο π[... *peratias kal isto p* – which may be a name. It is in other respects an unremarkable inscription and (being dated no earlier than 650 BC) much later than those found in most of the Greek world.

There are then few signs of early writing in Knossos and little indication of the highly personal dimension of early Greek literacy we find in Euboea, the Cyclades or Attica (Whitley 1997; 2017a; Kotsonas 2022). The new form of writing was just not much used – indeed we have fewer informal uses of writing in the new alphabet than we had for 'informal' uses of Linear A during neopalatial times. If the new form of writing was to 'democratize' literacy in the rest of the Greek world – to remove it from being the monopoly of a scribal class – then again Crete seems to be going in a different direction from the rest of the Aegean.

Writing was, eventually, put to use in the service of the political community – the *polis*. But there are few early signs of this. To detect the *polis* we have to look at another category of evidence – cult.

5.6 Cult and the early *polis*

Since the 1980s, the rise of the *polis* – that is, the appearance of a political community based on the principle of citizenship – has been linked to changes that took place in the Aegean in the eighth century BC (Snodgrass 1977; 1980). Chief amongst these is the appearance of major sanctuary sites associated with political communities, often positioned in locations that enabled a political community to make claims to territory (De Polignac 1984). Since that time the notion of the 'bi-polar city' (with a town at one end and a state sanctuary at the other) has come in for much criticism. There are still reasons, however, for associating citizen-states (*sensu*; Runciman 1990) with sanctuaries. Most forms of Greek political community were 'communities of cult' (Morgan 2003). Josine Blok's (2014; 2017) concept of the *polis* as a 'covenant between gods and men' crucially depends on there being, not only sanctuaries, but sanctuaries where communal feasting took place that cemented bonds between citizens. On the mainland of Greece these feasts took place during major festivals where participants in the cult cooked and then ate the flesh of sacrificed animals. Dibble (2021) reports similar communal feasting deposits from middens in the Communal Dining Buildings at Azoria in eastern Crete. In Late Archaic Azoria, animal remains that were ritually burned seem to be predominantly associated with abandonment or transitional rituals. The large feasting deposits are typically similar to deposits from residential contexts except that they are larger and the animals were butchered differently (with cleavers) from those found in houses (butchered with knives). If we follow Blok's logic, then we need to look not for cult but for communal feasting, and for large deposits of the bones of sacrificed animals (particularly domesticates such as pigs, sheep, goats or cattle).

The small offerings found at the Spring Sanctuary do not conform to this expectation, and in any case cult here did not last beyond the Early Protogeometric period. During the Iron Age there appear to be three substantial sanctuary sites within the territory of Knossos. Within Knossos itself there was the 'Cult of Rhea' within the ruins of the palace, and the cult of Demeter on the slopes of the Gypsades hill. Outside of Knossos, but probably within its territory judging by later epigraphic evidence (Davaras and Masson 1983), was the Sanctuary of Zeus Thenatas at Amnisos (Prent 2005, 332–6). We also know from later sources (*IC* I.8.8, lines 9–13; *IC* I.8.10, lines 6–8; *IC* I.8.12, lines 44–6) that there also existed a sanctuary of Apollo Delphidios in Hellenistic times. No archaeological trace of an early sanctuary, however, has been found for the earlier phases.

Cult at the so-called 'Sanctuary of Rhea' is hard to characterize (Prent 2004, 416–18; 2005, 261; see also Evans 1928a, 5–7; Hartley 1931, 92–3). There seems to have been a small temple, 10.5m x 7m in extent, visible between the Propylaeum and the central court. The attribution of the cult to Rhea (Evans 1928a, 7, n. 1) is based on a single passage in Diodorus (5.66.1) and is not supported by any inscription. The earliest Protogeometric phases of cult seem to have been associated with drinking vessels (Hartley 1931, 92–3). The only other evidence is a hoard of Aeginetan silver staters, probably to be dated to the early fifth century BC. Of course, if there were major deposits of animal bones they would probably have been disturbed or moved. But there is nothing to suggest that this was anything other than a site of modest 'drinking with the gods' (Van den Eijnde 2018), rather than more elaborate 'giving to the gods' or 'feasting with the gods'.

The Sanctuary of Demeter is different. That this is a shrine to Demeter is attested epigraphically – the name is found on a silver ring datable to the second half of the fifth century BC (Coldstream 1973b, 131–3; Prent 2005, 262–3; Figure 5.10). Though the architecture is modest, the votive finds (which appear to begin at some point in the eighth century BC) are substantial, consisting for the most part of terracotta figurines (only a small proportion of which were ever published). Higgins (1973) gives us a good idea of the types but not the quantities of votives, which number in the many hundreds (Whitelaw, personal communication). More significant is the huge volume of animal bones recovered, which testifies both to the practice of sacrifice and to feasting. In the

Figure 5.10 Silver ring from sanctuary of Demeter with dedicatory inscription to Demeter on the bezel. After Coldstream 1973b, 132. Figure 29. Courtesy British School at Athens.

earlier periods many species are represented – it is only later that our expectation that only pigs were fit for Demeter is adequately fulfilled (Jarman 1973).

At Amnisos the presence of at least two sanctuaries has been confirmed by excavation. The cave sanctuary of Eileithyia (Prent 2005, 366–7; Marinatos 1929; 1930) continued in a small way. The sanctuary of Zeus Thenatas at Amnisos was more substantial (Schäfer 1992a; Stürmer 1992b, 226–39). Though there is no architecture to speak of, there was certainly an ash altar – and so probably evidence of feasting that accompanies animal sacrifice. The sequence of votives begins around 900 BC and includes fragments of Cypriot bronzes and Egyptian and Egyptianizing faience figurines.

This sanctuary is a fitting candidate for one of De Polignac's 'extra urban sanctuaries' – the outer pole of the one focused on Knossos and the sanctuary of Demeter. But if we ask Ehrenberg's (1937) question – when did the Knossian *polis* rise? – the answer does not appear to place this rise in the eighth century BC. The sanctuary of Demeter may begin then, but cult at both sanctuaries at Amnisos starts earlier. If we combine this evidence with our earlier review of the material from the cemeteries, then a very different picture emerges from the one that either Snodgrass (1980) or De Polignac (1984) would have put forward for most mainland *poleis*. Instead of the eighth century, the key period of major transformation appears to be the ninth century BC. This period has been known chiefly for the strange, early Orientalizing style the Protogeometric B (Brock 1957; Coldstream 2001; Whitley 2013), but this is also a period when Knossos' horizons across the Mediterranean broaden quite dramatically. We await the results of the Knossos Urban Landscape project to tell us whether this corresponds to any increase in the size of the settlement.

These observations provide indirect support for hypotheses put forward by Saro Wallace (2010, esp. 233–62) and Anna Lucia D'Agata (2012) to the effect that identifiable political communities emerged far earlier in Crete (around 900 BC) than they did in mainland Greece. On the other hand, these observations do not disprove the ideas put forward by Haggis (2014) and Small (2018) – that the transformation of Cretan political communities into *poleis* (citizen-states) was only really underway by 600 BC.

Both hypotheses, however, may be true. That is, in Crete the *polis* rose twice – or rather there were two principal phases to its rise. The mid-ninth century witnessed a major form of community reorganization, where the burying groups (if they were indeed kinship groups) became fewer and larger. Community values – and the essential equality of persons – are signalled by the emphasis on collective tombs and the universal adoption of inurned cremation. But at this stage, while there was funerary feasting, there was no *andreion* (that is, no communal feasting in the service of the creation of citizens – see Whitley 2018) and no use of that new technology (the alphabet) to write down and impose a community's laws. This kind of *polis* only emerged in Knossos after the 'Archaic gap' around 525 BC.

5.7 After the gap: Late Archaic and Classical Knossos

After 630 BC the impressive series of Early Iron Age tomb groups we find in the Fortetsa and North Cemeteries comes to an abrupt end. Soon after this it also becomes very hard to trace domestic deposits; the sequence of votives at the Demeter sanctuary seems to come to a sudden halt. This is the mysterious Archaic gap in the Knossian sequence (Coldstream and Huxley 1999) which lasts until around 525 BC. The Archaic gap was once thought to cover the whole of Crete (apart from the far eastern part) – it was widely believed that the flourishing culture of 'daedalic' Crete suffered a wholesale catastrophe. Recent work by Brice Erickson (2010; 2014) combined with excavations at Azoria (Haggis 2014) have demonstrated that this is not so. It is rather that Cretan material culture in the sixth century is both austere and conservative – and so harder for archaeologists, trained to search for decoration and iconography, to identify. Kraters come in the form of the Laconian stirrup krater (both Spartan imports and local imitations) which, while they have a high gloss to their paint, have no figured decoration; cups become much plainer than before; and where objects continue to be decorated, seventh-century styles seem to continue. In this respect Crete is very much out of step with a Greek-speaking Mediterranean bound together, in part, by the shared visual imagery of the epic cycles and the 'aristocratic' institution of the *symposion* (Wecowski 2014).

For the time being at least nothing has appeared to fill the gap in the Knossian sequence. We are faced with the possibility that the site might have been temporarily abandoned. What then might have brought about such an abandonment? Several causes have been adduced – one is civil strife (*stasis*), alluded to in Pindar's twelfth Olympian ode (Pind *Olympian* 12.16); another, an island-wide drought alluded to in Herodotus (Coldstream and Huxley 1999).

Just as abruptly as it began the gap ends with the resumption of datable domestic deposits in the area of the Unexplored Mansion (Callaghan 1992, 90–3) and the Royal Road (Coldstream 1973a; 1999; see also Coldstream and Eiring 2001); votives in sanctuaries reappear, as do finds of identifiably Late Archaic metalwork (Boardman 1962). The sanctuary of Zeus at Amnisos acquires two eagles sculpted from limestone

(Brize 1992). The city of Knossos is now quite large, extending over 50ha or more (see Figure 5.11). What we have not found, however, are tombs. Saro Wallace (2010, 286–311) has speculated that the chamber and tholos tombs of the Iron Age have now been replaced by urnfields – that is, large cremation cemeteries where bodies were placed in undecorated vessels which archaeologists have not recognized. This is possible, but there is little evidence to support it.

Is this gap in Knossos then a real one? Not all archaeologists think so – Antonis Kotsonas (personal communication; see Kotsonas 2019), who has been working on Iron Age and Archaic pottery picked up by the Knossos Urban Landscape project, thinks it is a 'mirage'. The gap remains entirely archaeological – and as such it is not clear whether it results from our failure to recognize deposits or represents a genuine gap in the occupation of the site. And it does not really fit in well with what our rather scattered literary sources suggest – which is a political community whose citizens were engaged in the affairs of the wider Greek world. For there is one possibly historical personality whose lifespan really ought to correspond to the gap. This is the rather shadowy Epimenides, whom some sources (Diogenes Laertius 1.109) suggest might have been from Knossos. Epimenides is sometimes seen as a philosopher (the author of the Cretan Liar paradox, which has plagued philosophy ever since; Diels-Kranz 1934, 32), sometimes as one of the Seven Sages, whose tomb was said to be either in Sparta (Pausanias 3.11.11) or Argos, and author of an epic on Minos and Rhadymanthus (Diogenes Laertius 1.112). Sources differ as to his date – Ps-Aristotle (*Athenian Constitution* 1) places him at the time of the Kylonian conspiracy in Athens (where he was asked to come in to purify the city) in the late seventh century BC; Plato (*Laws* 642d) places him just before the Persian Wars (Jacoby 1950, 384–94). The Cretans, as Herodotus (7.170–1) notes, decided against involving themselves in these wars, though a very late source (Pausanias 3.12.11) suggests that Sparta might have gone to war with Knossos at the time of Epimenides.

These stories are, of course, more legend than history. But there must have been an Epimenides and he may well have come from Knossos. And whatever he did, it had some impact on the Greek world. Knossos was by now clearly one of the larger of the forty-nine *poleis* (Perlman 2004) we know from Archaic and Classical Crete. Survey data (Whitelaw et al. 2019; Trainor 2019) suggests that the Late Archaic town had now grown to almost the same size as that of protopalatial Knossos – though the urban area seems to have shifted a little to the north (Figure 5.11). And while we have domestic deposits from floors and filled-in wells, we have little architecture – apart from some evidence of reuse of earlier buildings in the area of the south-west houses (Coldstream and Macdonald 1997, 240–2). It is safest to infer that houses in Knossos were like houses elsewhere in Crete – small, two- or three-roomed structures constructed along a single long axis (Westgate 2007; 2015). The absence of houses means that, while we can estimate the rough size of the urban area of this *polis* (at 50–60ha at the larger end of urban communities on Crete), we have little idea of either its density or its urban structure – except that it appears to have had some (Classical) paved streets (Coldstream and Macdonald 1997, 199–202). Estimates of Knossos' population would vary from as low

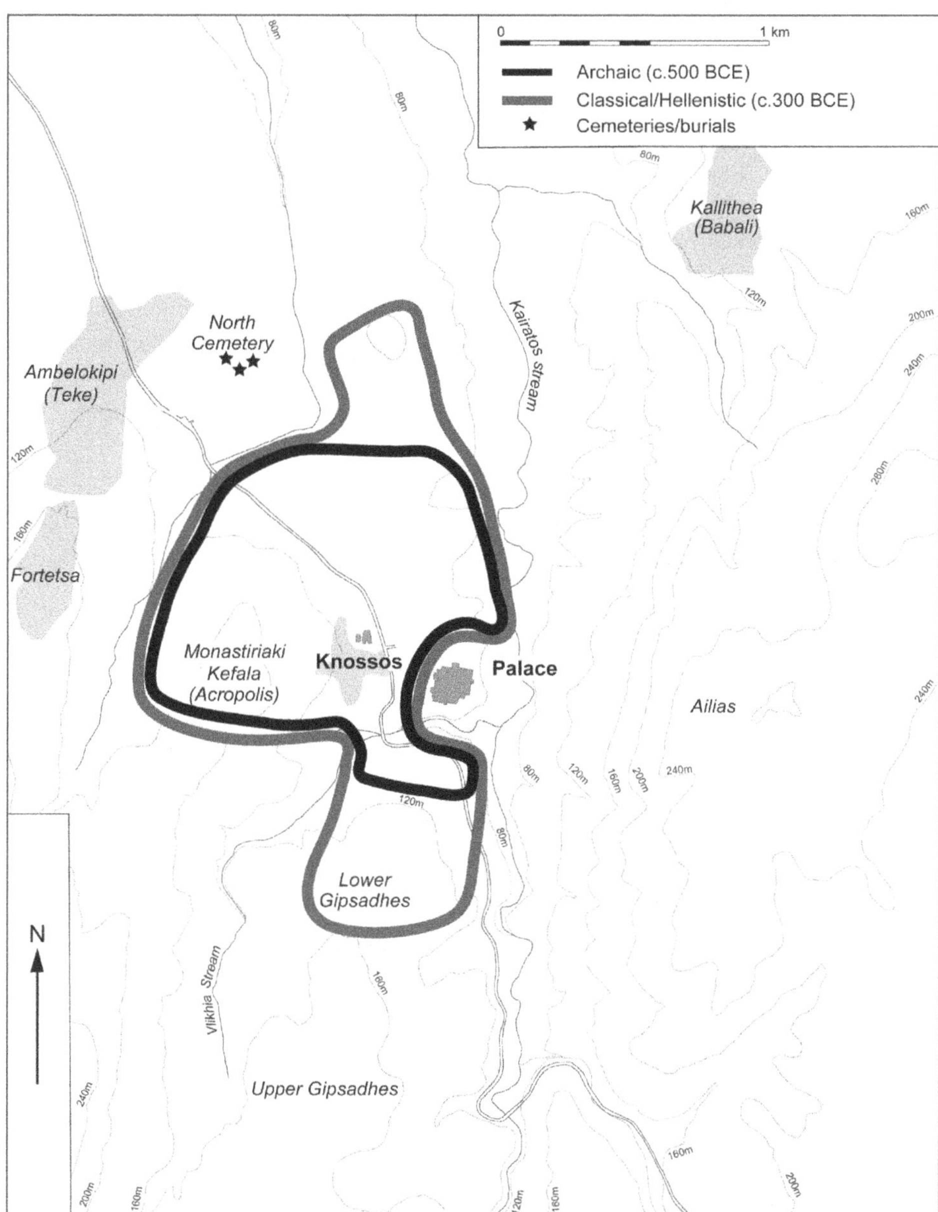

Figure 5.11 The extent of the Late Archaic to Classical/Hellenistic settlements. After information from KULP (Whitelaw et al. 2019; Trainor 2019). Redrawn by Kirsty Harding.

as 5,000 to as many as 15,000, depending on how dense we think the settlement might have been.

In these and other respects Knossos seems to be in step with other Archaic to Classical Cretan *poleis*. The imported Laconian stirrup kraters and their local imitations that we find in some deposits are plain – without visual imagery (Coldstream 1973a) – something we find in many other *poleis* in central Crete. The main drinking cups are now the Cretan high- and low-necked varieties – again undecorated. The largest concentration of these vessels is to be found in the Shrine of Glaukos (Callaghan 1978), a deposit that seems to represent a communal drinking event (Figure 5.12). Just as wine was drunk in this shrine, so animals were eaten – and many of the species consumed (such as hare) seem to have been hunted (Jones 1978). If the plainness of the vessels emphasizes equality, the presence of hunted species hints at a particular form of 'performative masculinity'. Literary and

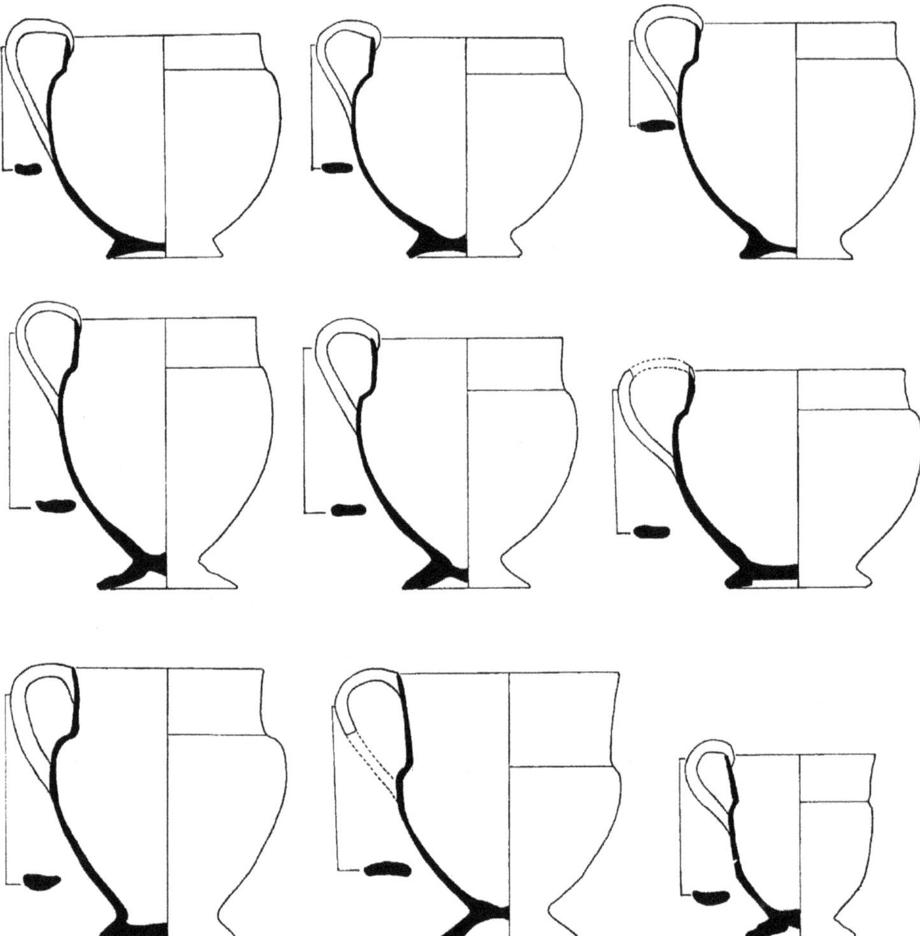

Figure 5.12 Fifth-century cups (both high- and low-necked varieties) from the Shrine of Glaukos. After Callaghan 1978, 7, Figure 5. Courtesy British School at Athens.

other evidence hints that this deposit may represent a Cretan *andreion* or men's club, an institution by which the civic community of male citizens reproduced itself (Whitley 2018; Whitley and Madgwick 2018). The presence of an *andreion* makes it likely that Knossos shared many of the institutions characteristic of other Cretan cities in this period (Seelentag 2015; Gagarin and Perlman 2016). Chief amongst these is the chief magistrate or *kosmos* (regulator), attested in later inscriptions at Amnisos (Olivier and Masson 1983; Chaniotis 1992c, 288–313). This is not to say that Knossos did not have its own laws – or legal inscriptions. Three fragments are known, datable to around 500 BC (e.g., Guarducci 1935, 56 = *IC* I.8.1–3; Gagarin and Perlman 2016, 472–3). While in themselves they tell us very little about the workings of this particular *polis*, they do demonstrate that Knossos, like other Cretan cities, shared the habit of inscribing numerous laws on stone. Whether such laws were principally for others to see and so read (Gagarin and Perlman 2016, 53–4) – thus 'democratizing' the rule of law – or whether the monumentality (rather than the legibility) of these inscriptions was their chief point in a society where there are few signs of informal literacy (Whitley 1997) remains a highly contested issue.

There remains a sharp difference between the seventh-century picture and the late sixth-/early fifth-century one. This I think supports the notion that in Crete, it seems, states (if *poleis* are states) did not emerge with one giant leap, but in a series of smaller steps. The 'rise of the *polis*' was a process, not an event. And of course we are not simply talking about one *polis* but one *polis* among many. Knossos was only one – albeit a large one – of forty-nine identifiable political communities on the island (Perlman 2004). Its neighbours were Lyktos to the east, Eltyna or Eltynia to the north-east, Tylissos to the west and Apollonia/Apellonia to the north-west; its territory probably extended north as far as modern Archanes (Huxley 1994). Within its territory were not only Amnisos but Herakleion, which served as its port (Strabo 10.4.7–8).

And this Cretan *polis* now looks thoroughly un-Minoan, as can be seen if we look at some of the details of domestic material culture. Up until around 800 BC the chief cooking vessel in Knossos remained the tripod cooking pot. This shape did not survive the transition to the Archaic *polis*. The cooking shapes we now find in Classical domestic deposits – the *chytra* and the *lopas* – are now more or less identical with shapes we find on the Greek mainland (Boileau and Whitley 2015). Cooking is culture at its most basic and this had changed profoundly by the beginning of our period.

These changes in cooking wares (and so, cooking practices) illustrate, in microcosm, what might be called the dilemma of the Late Archaic/Classical Cretan city. On the one hand, Crete as a whole – and central Crete in particular – had gone in a political and cultural direction quite opposite to most of the Greek-speaking world. On the other hand, many Cretan cities – again particularly in central Crete – at this time thought of themselves as Dorian, that is, as part not only of a Greek world but a particular 'ethnic' part of it. While the letter forms of inscriptions often remained resolutely and idiosyncratically Cretan (Jeffery 1990, 308–16), the dialect they are written in appears to many scholars to be Doric. Being Dorian was part of the identity of these communities, and this was expressed in mythical terms as having ancestors in great Dorian cities such as Argos or Sparta. Various (later) inscriptions indicate that Knossos had now adopted Dorian names for its 'tribes' (Chaniotis 1992c). The most explicit expression of this relationship was to be found in two related inscriptions of the mid-fifth century BC, one found in Argos (*IC* I.8.4), the other in Tylissos, neighbour to Knossos (*IC* I.30.1). These seem to form part of a treaty between these two neighbours, where Argos has been brought in as an arbiter since Argos was (by implication) accepted as the Dorian 'mother city' of both communities (Osborne and Rhodes 2017, 146–55, No. 126).

The desire to emulate the 'Classical' as it was now being expressed on the Greek mainland – and so to align Knossos more closely with other parts of the Greek world – can be seen in other areas. One is the adoption of coinage. Knossos started minting coins soon after 470 BC (Stefanakis 1999) – one of only five Cretan cities (the others being Kydonia, Gortyn, Phaistos and Lyttos/Lyktos) to do so. The first issue is a silver stater (Figure 1.4), showing on the obverse a Minotaur running, holding an object in his hand, accompanied by an inscription that reads ΚΝΟΣΙΟΝ (of the Knossians); on the reverse is a labyrinth with a star at its centre. At first these coins (silver staters) followed an Aeginetan weight standard – though this was soon replaced by a slightly smaller (at 11.10 grammes) 'Cretan' one.

Another trend that could be seen as 'Hellenizing' can be seen in Knossos' sanctuaries. That of Zeus Thenatas at Amnisos was graced with two fine sculptures of eagles in limestone around 500 BC (Brize 1992). And other changes in practice within sanctuaries now seem to bring Knossos closer to ideas and practices current in the wider Greek world: the increasingly classical look of the terracottas (Higgins 1973) and the new emphasis on pigs in the bone assemblages in the shrine of Demeter (Jarman 1973) form unambiguous evidence of this trend. Perhaps more striking is a marble metope found reused in a later Roman drain. It depicts Herakles carrying the (Erymanthian) boar – just before he is about to throw it over Eurystheus (Benton 1937). This image, which shows one of Herakles' twelve labours, has parallels in the temple of Zeus at Olympia and the temple of Hephaistos and Athena (the 'Theseion' or Hephaisteion) in Athens. Though Benton considers the work 'Archaic' (*c.* 520 BC), its overall style is better characterized as Severe, giving it a date in the middle of the fifth century BC. Benton argues – quite plausibly – that this metope must have come from a mainland-style Doric temple, and that the most likely candidate would be the temple of Apollo Delphidios, a temple which later held the city's laws and treaties (*IC* I.8.8, lines 9–13; *IC* I.8.10, lines 6–8; *IC* I.8.12, lines 44–6). There are suggestions that Knossos was now producing sculptors who could produce elaborate works in the Severe style: one Amphion from Knossos is recorded to be the creator of a (bronze) chariot group dedicated by the Cyrenians at Delphi, commemorating the founding of Cyrene by Battos (Pausanias 10.15.6–7).

This 'Hellenizing' trend accelerates in the fourth century BC. The connection with Cyrene is shown in Knossos' grateful receipt of grain from that city after the famines and shortages of the 330–326 BC (*SEG* 9.1.2, lines 30 and 37 = Hondius et al. 1938, 4–5). Crete in general seems to adopt mainland – specifically Athenian- forms of tomb sculpture, some examples of which have been found in Heraklion (Sporn 2014). Towards the end of this century, graves in the North Cemetery area reappear (though they have yet to be published): these take the form of extended inhumations in cists, accompanied by a small perfume flask (a practice which perhaps has its best parallel in the North Cemetery of Corinth). But the most striking testimony of how Knossos was becoming more integrated into the wider Greek world during this period is not archaeological but literary. Philosophers based in Athens suddenly acquire a great interest in Crete. Plato's *Laws* is a discussion of the relative merits of the Athenian, Spartan (Lacedaimonian) and Cretan constitutions. The debate takes place between an Athenian stranger, the Spartan Megillos and the Cretan (specifically Knossian; see *Laws* 629c) Kleinias on a long walk between Knossos itself and the Cave of Zeus on Mount Ida (*Laws* 625b). A concern with the 'Cretan constitution' (and the supposedly unchanging 'laws of Minos') is also evident in Aristotle's *Politics*. Though Perlman (1992) has argued that Aristotle's 'Cretan' constitution is essentially that of Lyktos, in the *Laws* (636e) the Cretan legislation discussed is stated to be explicitly that of Knossos. What impressed these writers was the apparent stability of Cretan constitutions; what Plato sought in Crete was a panacea for the very instability he saw in his native Athens.

Crete (and Knossos), of course, had not been entirely ignored by earlier writers – the island figures in the tales of Homer and Hesiod and the histories Herodotus and Thucydides. But the interest shown by these authors in the island was always peripheral to their main concerns. What changes in these fourth-century writers is that Crete – and Knossos – is now centre-stage in the long Greek conversation about what is good, beautiful, honourable and just. The idea that Cretan *poleis* in general – and Knossos in particular – were particularly stable (and therefore disinclined towards warfare and destruction) is not, however, borne out by the historical narratives that have come down to us from late Classical and Hellenistic times. Already there are signs of a very aggressive stance Knossos held towards its neighbour and rival, Lyktos. Diodorus (16.62.3) notes an attempt by Knossos – unsuccessful, as it turns out – to destroy this city in the late fourth century. This was a taste of things to come.

5.8 Knossos in Hellenistic times: the resilience of the Cretan citizen-state

Historians and archaeologists love periods. Periods allow one to specialize and develop as a scholar (particularly when young). In Ancient History and Classical Archaeology, we have perhaps become too used to working within the framework of the Archaic, Classical and Hellenistic. Insofar as this periodization make sense, it is determined by a sequence of events that work for mainland Greece: the Persian Wars at the end of the Archaic and beginning of the Classical periods (with their clear break in destruction horizons); for the Classical and Hellenistic periods, the career of Alexander the Great who, before dying in 323 BC, had extended the horizons of the Greek world to India and Central Asia (Whitley 2001, 60–74). Historians have also traditionally seen the Hellenistic world of Alexander's successors as marking a great shift not only in the political geography but also the institutional frame of Greek history. The *polis* or citizen-state (Runciman 1990) becomes increasingly irrelevant, and high politics is dominated by kingdoms and dynasties. Cities are pawns in the power struggles of great kings – especially so after the Battle of Ipsos (301 BC), when the eastern Mediterranean world was divided between the three great powers of Macedon (Cassander and subsequently the Antigonids), the Seleucids of Syria (Antioch) and the Ptolemies in Egypt.

But this traditional scheme does not really work for Crete. This is not only because we lack clear destruction horizons that would separate these periods (and allow us to link up the archaeological with the historical record), but because Cretan history was always at one remove from Greek history in general. Apart from a small Ptolemaic garrison in the far east of Crete (at Itanos), no Cretan city was incorporated into any Hellenistic kingdom. Historians, moreover, interested in institutional developments (Seelentag 2015; Gagarin and Perlman 2016), prefer to lump Archaic with early Classical Crete, treating the fourth century as a kind of prelude to the Hellenistic (a practice shared by some archaeologists; Erickson 2010).

Figure 5.13 An example of a 'Hadra hydria' attributed to the Dromeus painter, now in the British Museum (GR 1995, 1003.1). The inscription reads 'of Dorotheos'. Its findspot is not clear, but probably from Egypt near Alexandria. Courtesy British Museum.

All this is not to say that Hellenistic kingdoms had no interest at all in Crete. Hellenistic rulers liked to portray themselves not only as powerful kings, but as benevolent patrons and friends of the free Greek cities (a trend that became more apparent with the rise of Pergamon in the late third and second century BC). The Hellenistic world created new cultural centres in Antioch, Pergamon and Alexandria, and poets from these cities took a new interest in Crete. That Knossos is now part of this wider world is reflected in the literary record. Poetry (with epigraphy) now sheds more light on the cults of Knossos. We know, for example, that at Amnisos there were cults of Artemis and 'the nymphs' (Amnisides) as well as those of Eileithyia and Zeus Thenatas (Callimachus, *Hymn to Artemis* 3, 15–17, 162–7; Callimachus, *Iambus* 12; Apollonius of Rhodes, *Argonautica* 3.876–86; Diodorus 5.70.2–4). Copies or versions of the decrees of the *kosmoi* of Knossos are now to be found in the cities of Teos, Magnesia on the Maeander and the sanctuary of Delos (*IC* I.8.8; *IC* I.8.10; *IC* I.8.12). Hellenistic kingdoms, moreover, realigned trade and cultural relations. This can be seen most clearly in a Cretan vessel exported to Alexandria – the Hadra hydria. Chemical and stylistic analysis (Callaghan and Jones 1985) has shown that these vessels were manufactured in two centres in Crete – in the Mesara plain (near Gortyn) and in north-central Crete (that is, somewhere near Knossos). In Alexandria they are used as cremation urns – indeed they seem to be the principal vessel for the disposal of the dead in what became the Hellenistic world's newest and greatest metropolis.

There are lots and lots of these vessels, and they are now decorated in a clearly figurative style. So many are there, indeed, that it becomes possible (for the first time since the Orientalizing period; Moignard 1996) to talk about workshops, hands and painters. Unsurprisingly, these 'artistic personalities' are given some odd names ('the Dromeus painter', 'the Fussy Painter', 'the El Manara painter') that reflect more on their Alexandrian funerary context than their Cretan origins. Their iconography, however, remains resolutely Cretan, particularly in their emphasis on hunted animals. The Cretan *agrimi*, often paired with dogs, is a common theme (Eiring 2004). Dogs paired with hares (another hunted species) also now appear on Knossian painted pottery (Coldstream 1999, 338, No. S3; Plate 32.3; see Figure 5.14); and the hunt continues to figure prominently in the iconography of Knossos' probable *andreion*, the Shrine of Glaukos (Eiring 2004, 447, Figure 39.9). The fundamental continuity in the drinking practices associated with this form of Cretan commensality is also reflected in the development of that distinctively Cretan shape, the one-handled cup. In the Hellenistic period the plain high-necked and low-necked varieties gradually develop into the cylindrical cup (Callaghan 1981, 37–8) and finally become the tall 'tulip cup' (Eiring 2001, 95–6; Figure 5.15). Drinking cups feature prominently in the Hellenistic phase of the 'Temple of Rhea' (Prent 2004, 418; Popham 1978, 186–7, Plate 27). Unusual ritual activity is also evident in some animal bone assemblages. For example, in Well 1 from the Unexplored Mansion (dating to the Early Hellenistic period) there are the remains of a complete equid (a small horse or donkey), three complete dogs and the left half of a female, pregnant pig with many fetal piglet bones (Dibble 2012, 23–4). Butchery marks on the equid indicates it had been skinned, and those on the sow indicate it had been consumed. Knossian drinking

Figure 5.14 Dog and hare (facing away from each other) on a fragment of an Hellenistic drinking cup from Knossos. After Coldstream 1999, 338, No. S3; Plate 32.3. Redrawn by Kirsty Harding after a drawing by Peter Callaghan.

Figure 5.15 An example of Late Hellenistic 'tulip cups'. After Eiring 2001, 94, Figure 3.1, No. a. Courtesy British School at Athens.

practices, ceramic production and forms of ritual consumption (*agrimi*, hares) continue then to reflect particular Cretan institutions – institutions about which our literary sources now have quite a lot to say (see discussion in Whitley and Madgwick 2018).

In these respects, the production and consumption of painted pottery reflects both fundamental continuities and new realities. The continuity lies in Cretan political institutions such as the *andreion*, which seem to remain much the same as in Classical times. This is reflected in inscriptions: the Knossian *kosmoi* continued to exercise authority over all of the Knossian territory, including Amnisos (Olivier and Picard 1983; Chaniotis 1992c, 288–313). Houses probably remained small, as they did in the rest of Crete (Westgate 2007), and the dead continued to be buried in the form of extended inhumations in the area of the North Cemetery. The size and density of settlement remains much the same – as does the quality of our evidence, which continues to be in the form of deposits rather than complete house plans (Coldstream 1999; Callaghan 1992).

These deposits nonetheless also exhibit some opposite tendencies – the 'Hellenizing' trends mentioned earlier. Knossian painted pottery is now more figured and more florid – much less austere than the Cretan pottery from Classical times. We have some almost complete kraters, decorated in a way that no longer sets them clearly apart from ceramic traditions in other parts of the Greek world (Callaghan 1992, H28, No. 34). The plain drinking cup of this period – the tulip cup – is not found in nearly the same numbers as the earlier Archaic and Classical necked cup, and there are no cup deposits on quite the same scale. These trends come to the fore in perhaps the most informative pottery deposit from Hellenistic Knossos, the Little Palace well (Callaghan 1981). This filled-in well contains a variety of drinking cups (cylindrical one-handled varieties as well as a 'baggy' two-handled kantharos), the 'tulip jug' (cousin to the tulip cup), an elaborately decorated bell-krater and a variety of cooking vessels. At the bottom of the well was an Archaic pithos – a find that is far from unusual for its date, the middle of the second century BC.

Crete changed profoundly during the second century. This is partly reflected in the material record. There are some fresco fragments (presumably from nearby houses) from the Little Palace well (Callaghan 1981, 57–8), and elsewhere indications that some Knossians were now making use of imported glassware (J. Price 1992, 416). Politics too was changing. Whereas the older Hellenistic kingdoms (Macedon, the Seleucids, the Ptolemies) had little interest in Crete, this was not so true of the rising powers of Pergamon and Rome. In 183 BC, Pergamon made a treaty of friendship with thirty Cretan cities, including Knossos (*IC* 4. 179, from Gortyn). Just as Pergamon and Rome show a greater interest in Crete so the chroniclers of the rise of Rome – Livy, Polybius and Strabo – now show a greater interest in the island. And what they come to describe for much of the second century BC is grim: continuous warfare and the destruction of cities (Callaghan 1994). Our sources do not tell us much about how this warfare was conducted – they give us no real details of either battles or sieges. Indeed, there seem to be no sieges, as few if any Cretan cities were surrounded by city walls (in contrast to the Greek mainland). This is not quite to say that there were no fortifications at all – there seems to be a small Hellenistic fort in the north-east corner of Knossos (Coutsinas 2013, 65–6, 421–2, No.25; Hood and Boardman 1957; Kotsonas 2016b, 305–7; KS86) and some Cretan cities seem to have created small garrisons at the borders of their territories (this is how I would interpret the Hellenistic fort at Prinias). Similarly, from what we can tell from archaeology, there was more emphasis on archers and slingers (Kelly 2012) than on heavily armed infantry.

In these wars Knossos was often the aggressor. In 220–219 BC, Knossos attempted the complete destruction of its great rival, Lyktos (Polybius 4.53–4; Chaniotis 1996, 36–8). It failed – the city of Lyktos (or Lyttos) was badly damaged, but the political community

Table 5.3 Destruction horizons in Hellenistic Crete (with sources)

City	Date	Ancient source
Lyktos/Lyttos	220/221 BC	Polybius 4.53–4
Apellonia/Apollonia	171/170 BC	Polybius 28.14
Rhaukos	Between 171 and 150.	Polybius 30.23.1
Phaistos	*Circa* 150 BC	Strabo 10.4.14
Praisos	145–140 BC	Strabo 10.4.12 (and *IC* III.4.9 and 10)

persisted (Kotsonas 2019a). For political communities were hard to destroy – damaging or burning a settlement wholly or in part was not usually sufficient; one had to remove and enslave the women and children and slaughter all the citizen males. In the case of Lyktos, the Knossians damaged the city and managed to enslave part of the population, but a significant proportion of the male citizens survived, and these citizens succeeded in refounding the city soon after (Chaniotis et al. 2015, 220–2).

The moral of this failure seemed clear. The destruction of cities had to become more efficient, their would-be destroyers more ruthless. Destruction (κατασκαφή) also became more 'ritualized' (Gaignerot-Driessen 2013). There followed in the second century a whole series of more effective destructions where citizen-states that had been in existence for hundreds of years were brought to their final end. In succession, Dreros, Apollonia, Rhaukos, Phaistos and Praisos were all eradicated.

By the end of the Hellenistic period only twenty-six out of the original forty-nine Cretan cities were still there. Knossos was among the survivors.

The later part of the Hellenistic period – which for Crete I take to be from the destruction of Praisos before 140 BC to the Roman conquest of 67 BC – is a curious time (Chaniotis 1996, 44–60). We do not know much about Late Hellenistic Knossos archaeologically: there appear to be some late Hellenistic walls beneath the Villa Dionysos (Paton 1998), and evidence for the production of wine in the form of a wine press (Carrington-Smith 1994; Trainor 2021) – but that is it. Knossos firmly maintained its identity – its coins show a Head of Zeus and a Labyrinth down to at least 68 BC (Jackson 1973, 108, Plate 79). Its politics were nonetheless affected by the rise of Rome, whose dominance in the eastern Mediterranean had been established after the sack of Corinth in 146 BC. The Romans had begun to take an interest in Crete from as early as 189 BC; Romans had acted as arbiters in many of the quarrels of Cretan cities, including one between Knossos and Gortyn (De Souza 1998, 112–13). For a while the Romans were content to interfere in Crete from a distance. The wars against Mithridates of Pontus, however, were to bring Roman legions as far east as Syria. By the first century BC, Cretan independence was something of an anomaly in an eastern Mediterranean full of Roman provinces and Roman client states. The Roman impact on the island was to be far greater and more permanent than that of any Hellenistic kingdom.

5.9 Roman Knossos: the *Colonia Julia Nobilis Cnossus*

The substantial architectural remains we see in Knossos today date principally from two periods – the neopalatial (in the Bronze Age) and the Roman (in the first two centuries AD). In both periods we have villas – large buildings constructed in part of dressed stone and having elaborate forms of domestic decoration. Both periods have frescoes; the Roman also has mosaics. This fact – this apparent similarity– undoubtedly coloured Evans' view of Minoan Knossos as a paradise for a cultivated and leisured aristocracy. And in modern times the idea that both the 'Minoans' and the Romans were ordered and civilized – that they represent two different paradigms of ordered civilization – persists.

Roman Knossos did not begin in order, however. The Roman conquest of Crete brought the independence of the Cretan *poleis* to an end. It entailed destruction and disorder. Opinion is divided as to why the Romans invaded. Most literary sources suggest that the Romans wished to eliminate potential allies of their implacable enemy Mithridates, king of Pontus; they would thereby also rid the eastern Mediterranean of pirates (Diodorus 40.1; Appian *Sicelica* 6.1). De Souza (1998) disagrees, arguing that the Romans were primarily motivated more by the prospect of rich pickings – that is, plunder. In any case, Crete was not an easy conquest for the Romans. All the Cretan cities (save Gortyn) firmly resisted the Roman incursion. Knossos was at the heart of this resistance – the Cretan allies were led by one Lasthenes, who for a time held the post of *protokosmos* ('first regulator') of Knossos (Chaniotis 1992c, 300–3). The attempt in 72–1 BC by M. Antonius Creticus to conquer the island was decisively rebuffed. When the Romans returned in 69 BC – led by Q. Caecilius Metellus Creticus – they came with greater force (three legions) and a firm determination to get the job done. Metellus' conquest ended with the capture of Knossos in 67 BC[2] (Diodorus 40.1a; Appian *Sicelica* 6.1–2).

What happened in the following decades is unclear. That part of the town continued to be occupied by the original inhabitants (whatever the legal status of the community) is confirmed by Late Hellenistic deposits from the area of the Unexplored Mansion (Callaghan 1992, 124–7; deposits H35–7). At least one small house may have been both built and abandoned in this intermediate period between 68 and 30 BC, when the Romans were moreover preoccupied with their own civil wars (Catling et al. 1981, 82–101). It was only after these had ended and Octavian (later Augustus) had established his unchallenged rule over what was now clearly a Roman Empire that the status of Knossos itself was resolved. In or around 27 BC, Augustus established a *colonia* at Knossos (Strabo 10.4.9); Knossos the Greek *polis* became the *Colonia Julia Nobilis Cnossus* (Paton 1994; 2004, 451–2). The name itself is significant, as Augustus did not claim the 'colony' as his but as his 'father's' – Julius Caesar. The likely inference is that this had originally been planned by Caesar himself – but never executed.

What do we mean by 'colony'? For the Romans, the term *colonia* had a very specific meaning. It was a settlement of veterans – Roman soldiers who had fought under a specific general were given land for their service, land which they were to cultivate. So Knossos received a number of Roman ex-soldiers and other Roman citizens. At the same time, part of the territory of the Greek city (perhaps as much as half) was given to the Italian town of Capua (Rigsby 1976; España-Chamorro 2021) – Knossos was being punished for having been the centre of the resistance to Roman rule. It seems unlikely, however, that all the previous inhabitants of Knossos simply left. Knossos remained a self-governing municipality, autonomous if not independent. Its relative status within Crete had, however, declined – the provincial capital of the combined province of Crete and Cyrene was henceforth to be Gortyn in the south of the island.

What emerged then was a mixed community of both Greek- and Latin-speakers, clearly attested in the epigraphy; Greek inscriptions continue alongside Latin ones (that is, inscriptions both in the Latin language and in Latin script). What is not entirely clear, however, is the status of all the inhabitants. Roman veterans would be Roman citizens – citizens of Rome, with rights that most Roman subjects did not possess. A recent study notes that Knossos possessed fewer inscriptions (in either language or script – fifty-nine Latin as against thirty Greek) than other Aegean *coloniae* (Corinth, Philippi and Patras);[3] the proportion of Latin to Greek epigraphy is about 63 per cent, in line with Patras but far lower than Corinth. The first Latin inscription (around the turn of BC to AD) is a tombstone of one Licinius Rufus (Baldwin Bowsky 2006, 420, A1); in the first century of the Roman *colonia* the local magistracies of Knossos were held by people with Latin names and Italian connections (Sanders 1982, 14–15).

Just as the magistracies were dominated by people with Latin names, so too were the priesthoods. In the Roman as in the Greek world, holding a priesthood was as much a civic as a religious duty – both magistracies and priesthoods were held by the major families in any community. The basic structure of Graeco-Roman polytheism (and the embeddedness of cult in politics, and politics in cult) remained much as before. There are, however, some signs of religious change. Some earlier cults – such as the cults of Eileithyia and Zeus and Amnisos (Marinatos 1929; Stürmer 1992b) and the well-established cult of Demeter (Coldstream 1973) – continued as before; some new cults (such as one to Castor) are attested in the epigraphy (Baldwin Bowsky 2006, 396–403). Cults which had helped to maintain the civic functions of the Greek *polis*, however (such as the cult of Glaukos), simply ceased. As a *colonia*, Knossos (unsurprisingly) also had an imperial cult – a cult of the emperor himself, the divine Augustus (Divus Augustus). This is attested both in literature (Tacitus *Annals* 3.63) and in the survival of several marble portraits of Augustus, Gaius Caligula and later Hadrian (Lagogianni-Georgokarakos 2004).

Mixed populations, however, also encourage a degree of cosmopolitanism, particularly in religion. In this respect Knossos was to resemble (if on a much smaller scale) some of the other, larger 'mixed' *coloniae* of the Aegean world, such as Corinth and Philippi. Foreign cults – to Isis – now begin to appear (Paton 1994, 147; Baldwin Bowsky 2006, 403–7). That Crete was now both more multicultural and multi-confessional than before is indicated in the Acts of the Apostles (2.10–12) – who are the 'Cretans' visiting Jerusalem at Pentecost if not Greek-speaking Jews from Crete? It was in these mixed communities, these *coloniae*, where early Christian preachers – or at least Paul of Tarsus – seemed to have had most success. And one of Paul's disciples, Titus, seems to have been responsible for establishing Christian presbyters (elders) in 'every town' on the island (Letter to Titus,

5–6). In the later second century AD we know that there was a Christian community at Knossos led by its bishop (ἐπίσκοπος) Pinytos (Eusebius, *Ecclesiastical History* 4.23.7–8).

These long-term cultural changes are not, however, much evident in the material record, at least initially. The earliest clearly Roman deposits (from a number of filled-in wells) show that the basic elements of material culture, from finewares to cooking wares, were becoming more Roman (Hayes 1971). Early deposits elsewhere give us a picture of a prosperous and well-connected community. The Roman levels above the Unexplored Mansion indicate different forms of economic activity. The animal bone assemblages from the Roman phases indicate it functioned as a bone workshop in the second to third centuries AD, processing the limb bones of mostly cattle and equids (Dibble 2012, 2; Sackett 1992c). The ceramic assemblages (Sackett 1992b, 147–256; Sackett and Grace 1992) demonstrate Knossos' economic contacts with most of the major production centres of mould-made fineware pottery (sigillata) in the eastern Mediterranean. Sigillata produced in Cyprus, Italy, around the Black Sea and other (as yet unidentified) parts of the eastern Mediterranean is all attested (see Forster 2001, 139–43). Imported transport amphoras include examples from Spain, Italy, Cyprus, North Africa, Asia Minor and regions of the Aegean (Forster 2001, 161–4; Sackett and Grace 1992). Glass, probably manufactured elsewhere, comes into widespread use for drinking shapes and perfume flasks (J. Price 1992).

Yet more dramatic changes can be seen in the architecture. In the area of the Unexplored Mansion we now have the remains of at least four houses: the Southeast House, the Southwest House, the 'House of the Diamond Frescoes' and the North House (Sackett 1992a, 17–58). Though they may incorporate some Hellenistic walls, all these are much more substantial structures – with solid stone foundations and tiled roofs – than anything we have seen since neopalatial times. As in neopalatial times, there is evidence for a paved street. The earliest phases of both the North and Southwest Houses seem to date to the earliest phase of the Roman colony (all have complicated architectural histories). Public architecture too became more sophisticated, perhaps concentrated around the civic basilica (the centre of the city had now moved north by north-west to some degree). At least one very fine possibly public structure – a Corinthian portico made of imported marble – has survived, even though we do not know exactly where it was set up (Paton 1991; see Figure 5.16). Elsewhere, the most dramatic change lies in the way floors were made and decorated.

Knossos contains some of the best Roman mosaics in Crete (and some would say in the eastern Mediterranean). Mosaic floors, built with *tesserae* and not pebbles, begin to be made in the first century AD and continue down to the third century. Nineteen mosaics are known from the 'Knossos valley' (Sweetman 2003; 2013, 157–84). Some of these may be associated with civic buildings (such as 'Hutchinson's mosaic' near the civic basilica; Sweetman 2003, 532; 2013, 178–9). The most elaborate of such mosaics are, however, to be found in the Villa Dionysus (Sweetman 2003, 521–7; 2013, 158–69; Figure 5.17), which appears to be a private house with a very complex history of construction and occupation (Paton 1998; Hayes 1983). These exceptional mosaics depict themes (Dionysus, the Four Seasons) found across the Roman world – there are few allusions to the specific mythology of Knossos. The most elaborate mosaics seem to be the products of a local workshop, active mainly in the second century AD – the century of Hadrian and Antoninus Pius. We know the (Greek) name of one of the craftsmen – Apollinaris (ΑΠΟΛΛΙΝΑΡΙΣ ΕΠΟΙΕΙ; Sweetman 2003, 527–8; 2013, 169–73).

Mosaics then give us the impression of Romanization – and indeed 'globalization', within at least a Mediterranean setting (Sweetman 2013, 16–17). Mosaics may have been produced locally – and for local, if largely Greek-speaking patrons (Baldwin Bowsky 2006) – but were made for a culture that was increasingly wealthy and cosmopolitan. Cosmopolitanism had a Roman tinge to it, of course – a similar accommodation between the 'global and the local' can be seen in the production and iconography of the over 2,000 terracotta lamps (Catling and Catling 1992). These too were made (largely in moulds) by a local workshop and with some local idiosyncrasies – but to an overall Roman template (Figure 5.18). Material culture does not provide a direct index of identity, but it is interesting that a particular 'Knossian' iconography does not entirely disappear: the

Figure 5.16 Restored elevation of Roman public building with Corinthian columns. After Paton 1991, 315, Figure 13. Courtesy British School at Athens.

Labyrinth appears both on a Roman coin of Augustus (M. J. Price 1992, 328, No. 128, Plate 276) and on a tile stamp (Sackett 1992b, Plate 222 F/J 70) from near Fortetsa.

If material culture is concerned with identity, it is also concerned with hierarchy. Both may be reflected in burial practices. The Roman cemeteries of Knossos are extensive, and the variation in the types of tombs (and wealth of graves) is much greater than in Hellenistic times. At the poor end of the scale are the tile graves – a type ubiquitous in the Mediterranean. Some such (highly damaged) were found south-east of the Acropolis (Catling et al. 1981, 101–4). Close by were some rock-cut tombs (Wardle 1972, 270–83), where more survives partly because they were meant to. Rock-cut tombs – some of

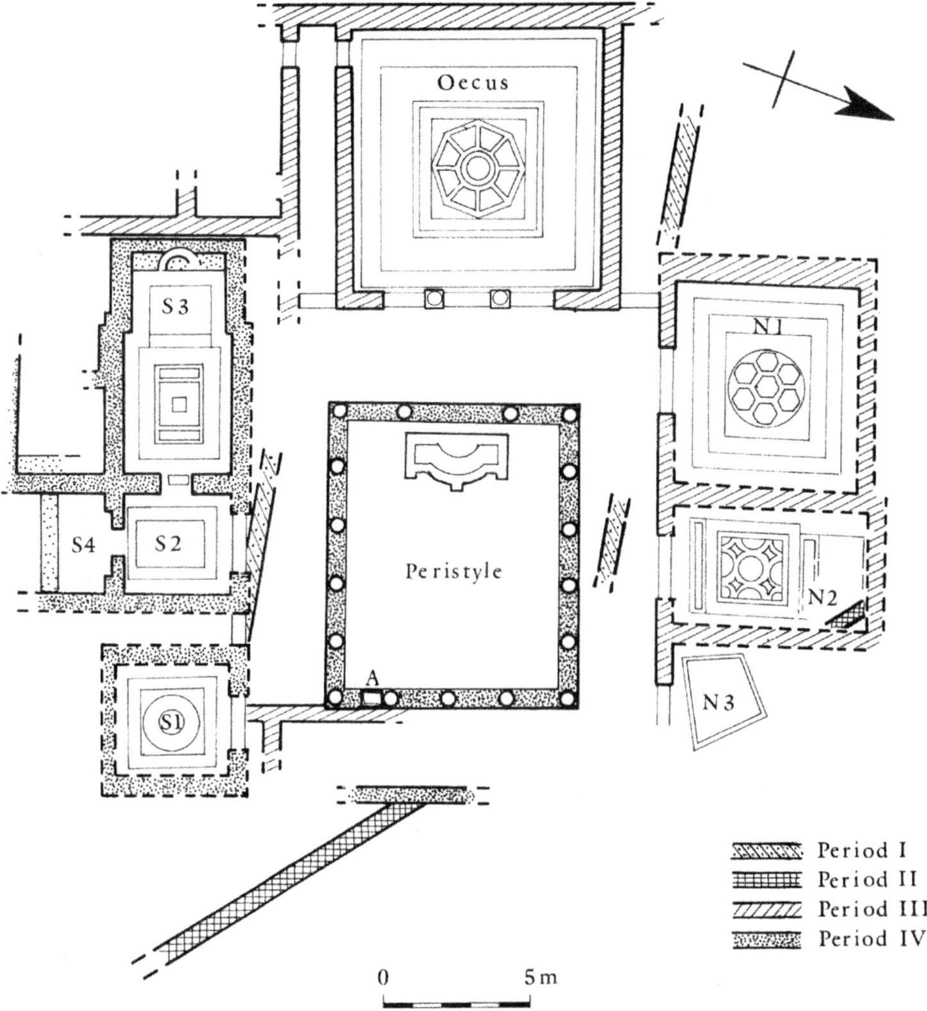

Figure 5.17 Plan of the Villa Dionysus. After Paton 1998, 125, Figure 15.1. Courtesy British School at Athens.

which could be effectively locked and reused (Wardle and Wardle 2004) – are probably best interpreted as those of the 'middling sort' in Roman Knossos. The richest graves are stone-built monuments possessing a degree of architectural elaboration not found in Knossos since the time of the Temple Tomb (Gramatikaki 2004). These are mainly found to the north of the city. The hierarchy of graves then reflects a social (and spatial) hierarchy already evident in houses and mosaics: that of a provincial elite keen to show off their 'Roman-ness'.

In one sense, Roman-ness was becoming less important as we move into the later periods. In 212 AD the Emperor Caracalla issued a decree which abolished the distinction between Roman citizens and all the other free inhabitants of the Roman Empire. The privileges associated with being a citizen in a *colonia* now disappeared. These distinctions were in any case on the wane – the use of Latin for official purposes had been in decline since the time of Trajan (Baldwin Bowsky 2006), and informal inscriptions had always been much more Greek than Latin. Still it is a remarkable coincidence that Caracalla's decree seems to be concurrent with a decline in at least the visibility of Roman Knossos. There are few mosaics in the third century, and fewer still in the fourth. Occupation in the area of the Unexplored Mansion can no longer be detected after the final architectural phase (in 170–190 AD) of the North House there (Sackett 1992a, 51–4; 1992b, 246–56). Evidence of cult practice at the Sanctuary of Demeter peters out by the end of the second

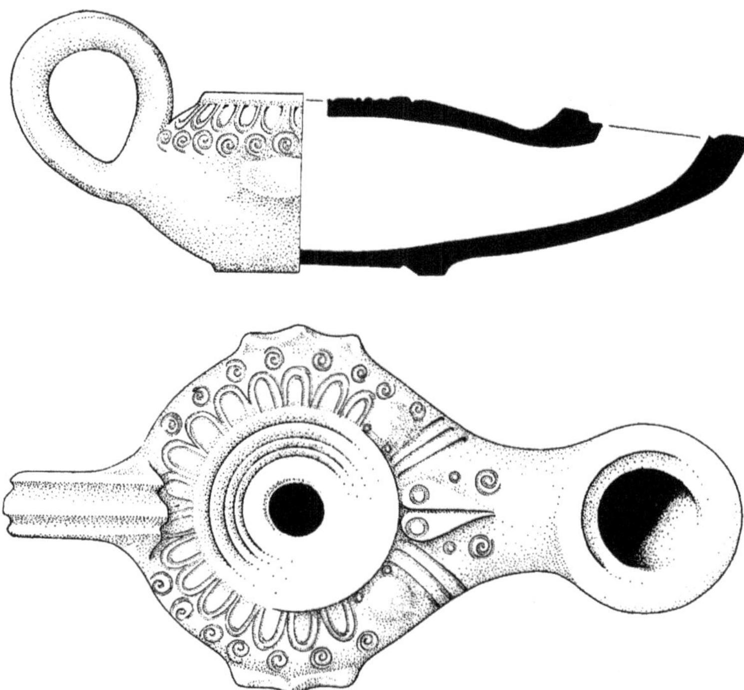

Figure 5.18 Roman lamp from the area of the Unexplored Mansion. After Sackett 1992a, Plate 231, No. 209). Courtesy British School at Athens.

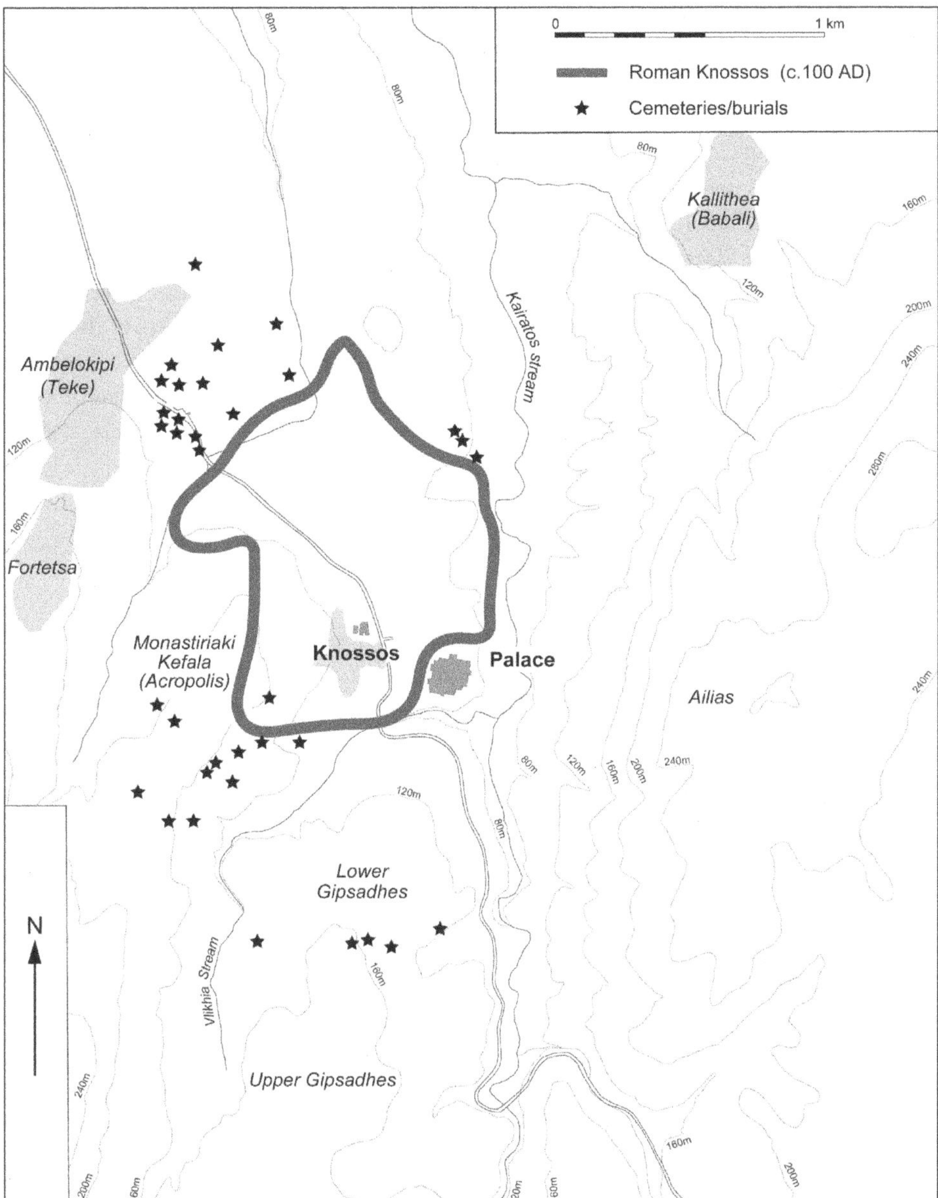

Figure 5.19 Roman Knossos. Drawn by Kirsty Harding, after information in Whitelaw et al. 2019; Trainor 2019.

century (Coldstream 1973b). This apparent absence of third- and fourth-century material has led to various theories that the city might have been 'abandoned' during this time – perhaps not once but twice (Sweetman 2004a, 483–5). But as Sweetman has shown, these arguments have little merit. That we continue to find coins of the fourth century (in particular issues of Constantine I and his sons; M. J. Price 1992, 330; Jackson 1973, 106–7) probably indicates that we are dealing with issues of archaeological visibility rather than a gap in occupation. Late Roman red-slipped wares remain fairly ubiquitous over the whole of the site (Forster 2001, 145–9; 2004). But the fact remains that, in purely architectural terms, these last two centuries are far less impressive than the first two after Christ.

The Roman period also witnessed a gradual northward shift in the centre of the town. Survey and other evidence (Whitelaw et al. 2019; Trainor 2019; Sweetman 2010; Fig 5.20) indicates that the size and density of the settlement remained around its mean of 40ha – perhaps slightly smaller than it was in Late Archaic and Classical times. This scale of occupation was not, however, to be maintained.

5.10 Late Antique Knossos: the end of the city?

Debate has long raged about the length of occupation of Roman Knossos. Whilst it is clear that the settlement lasted into 'Late Antiquity' (that is, the late fourth, fifth, sixth and early seventh centuries AD), quite when it was finally abandoned has remained controversial. Recent survey evidence (Trainor 2019; see also Sweetman 2013, 303–4) has clarified matters. This demonstrates the general northward drift of the city during Roman times – we are now very far away from the hill of Kephala which had been the focus of the original Neolithic settlement and Bronze Age 'palace'. While its size remained constant throughout Early and Middle Roman times, in Late Antiquity the settlement shrinks to little more than 20ha.

The focus of the settlement (and of the city) had now changed. For we are now dealing with a Christian city. While a Christian community had been known in Knossos since the second century AD, it was not until first Constantine and then Theodosius made Christianity the established religion of the empire that this new religion could find architectural expression. Two (perhaps three) substantial basilicas were constructed: the KMF basilica and the Sanatorium basilica (now underneath the University of Crete Medical Faculty and the Venizeleion hospital respectively) are reasonably well known and understood (Sweetman 2004b; 2013, 210–13); the probable basilica underneath the modern church of Ayia Sophia at Makryteichos, much less so.

Two of these basilicas (the KMF and the Sanatorium) were built in the early fifth century AD. They are quite elaborate, with three aisles, and are thought to have slightly different liturgical emphases. Whatever their exact function (and together they could accommodate a considerable number of people), they provided a new focus for the community at some distance from the old civic centre to the south. Both were decorated with mosaics; those on the KMF basilica extended to its walls (which makes this one of the earliest examples of wall mosaics known anywhere). The KMF basilica also became

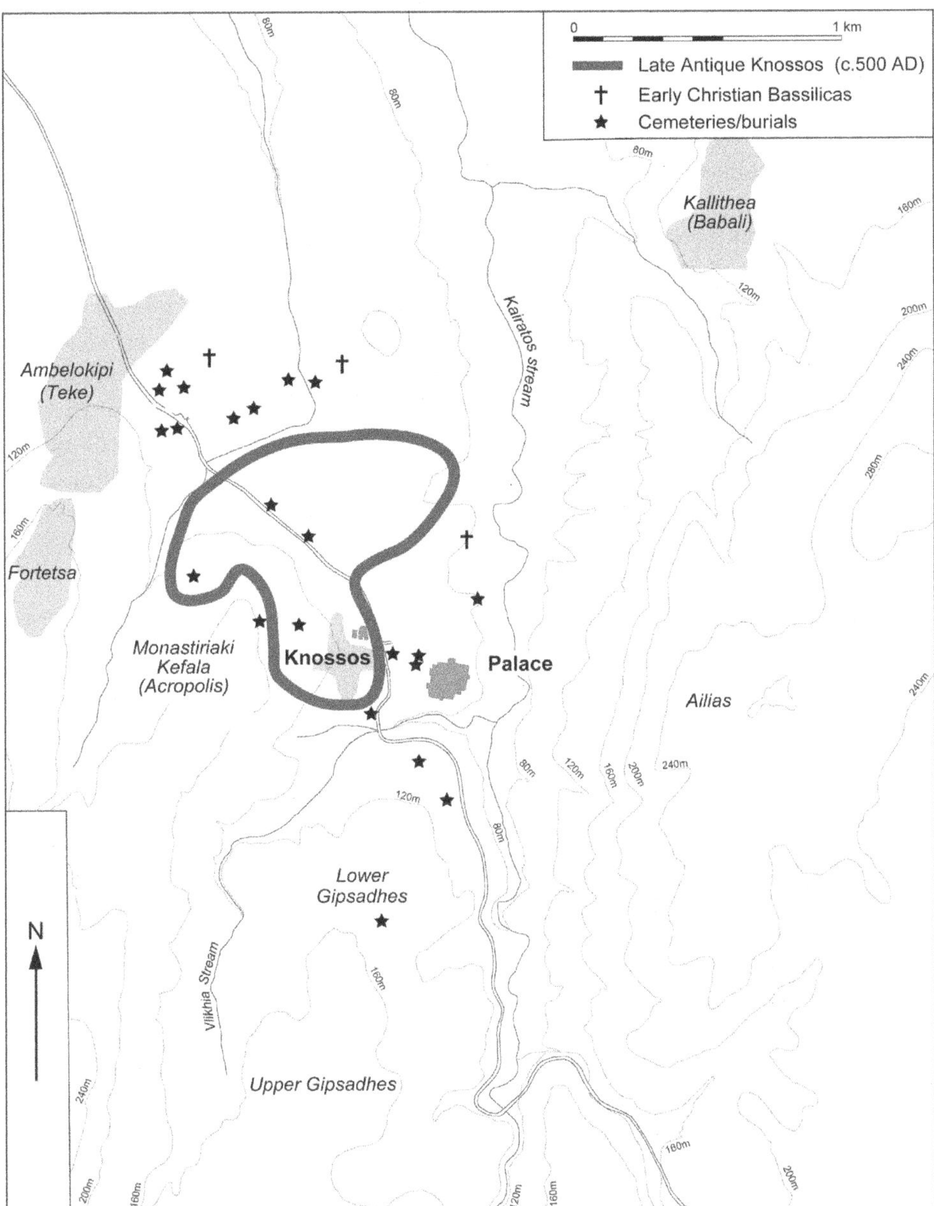

Figure 5.20 Location and estimated size of the Late Antique town, showing the position of the basilicas. After Trainor 2019; Whitelaw et al. 2019.

the focus of a graveyard (Sweetman 2005) – churchyards now became graveyards in a way that is familiar to anyone who has visited an English country church, and many tombs were marked by inscriptions (all now in Greek). One very elaborate tomb was constructed from the *disiecta membra* of an earlier Roman building (Paton 1991). All burials were now inhumations, though modified by a new process of secondary burial. For this, *osteothekai* (bone houses) were needed (Catling and Smyth 1976). This pattern of tombs around a church marks a sharp break with previous practice – throughout most of Graeco-Roman antiquity, most cities located their cemeteries outside the walls, or if (as in Knossos) there were no walls, far away from areas of habitation. In Late Antiquity this all changed: the dead were now placed *apud sanctos* ('amongst the holy ones') – the closer to the church the grave, the more pious (or the richer) the deceased (Ariès 1982). Habitation now spread out between the spaces occupied by the churches (Hayes 2001). Though we have no houses, we do have clear signs of domestic debris in the area of the earlier North Cemetery (Hayes 2001). Knossos remained a substantial settlement – a city whose most prominent public figure was now its bishop. Bishops from Knossos are known to have attended the Ecumenical councils of Ephesus (431), Chalcedon (451) and the Second Council of Nicaea (787).[4] This would imply occupation down to the time of the Arab invasion.

Here our literary sources are at variance with the material evidence. The last domestic deposit we know of from Late Antique Knossos (from the KMF area) is a cistern whose fill dates to between 620 and 640 AD (Hayes 2001, 443–53). Hayes interprets this filling-in as a deliberate act of abandonment – of clearing up before leaving for good. That this cistern contained cooking and other wares of recognizably Late Roman types, including red-slipped wares imported from North Africa, and that some vessels containing lengthy (Greek) inscriptions, all indicate that the community remained a full and active member of the wider Late Antique world until its very end.

After this deposit, though there may have been activity in the Knossos area (witness the coins of Maurice and Heraclius from the area of the Sanctuary of Demeter; Jackson 1973, 107, nos. 160 and 161), there is no evidence that Knossos remained either a city or a community in any meaningful sense. One or more of the basilicas may have remained in use (how else would Knossos still have a bishop?), but by 650 AD at the latest most of the population had moved elsewhere.

Did this mean the end of Knossos? Not quite. It does, however, mean an end to our archaeological history of the Iron Age and later city and political community of Knossos. It is time to sum up.

5.11 Summary: political communities and 'gaps in the record'

At some point after 900 BC a political community emerged in Knossos whose organizing principles were quite different from those of the latest Bronze Age palace. Judging from the burial record, it seems to have been organized by clans represented in the substantial collective tombs established around 850 BC that last until the seventh century. These groups seem to have become fewer and larger through time. The relative modesty and uniformity of the grave goods (belied by the variety and ostentation of the burial urns) suggest a society of equals – some form of polity close to the citizen-state of later times.

This emergence around 850 BC does not conform to a model of the *polis* 'rising' just after 700 BC (Ehrenberg 1937) nor with the central role of sanctuaries, as put forward by Snodgrass (1980) and De Polignac (1984). Sanctuaries in Knossos seemed to have performed a lesser role than those on the mainland. A political community where notions of citizenship were created and maintained through ritualized feasting – Blok's 'covenant between gods and men' – only clearly emerges after the 'gap', that is after 525 BC. Its focus in Crete was not the sanctuary so much as the *andreion* – a role served in Knossos most probably by the Shrine of Glaukos (Callaghan 1978; Whitley 2018). Written laws and coins confirm that this Cretan variety of the citizen-state had fully developed by 450 BC.

The 'rise of the *polis*' was not then an event but a process with at least two distinct stages (ninth century and sixth century). Knossos remained one of the more important of the forty-nine *poleis* of Crete from the Archaic to the end of the Hellenistic period. A question remains about the status of this political community. For there are many (e.g., Berent 2000) who wonder whether any Greek *polis* – and especially the numerous and small *poleis* of Crete – could have been states in a sense that makes sense to anthropologists or political scientists (e.g., Yoffee 2005). If we, crudely, apply 'Yoffee's Rule', 'if you can argue whether a society is a state or isn't then it isn't' (Yoffee 1993, 69; cf Broodbank 2013, 269), then Knossos was not a state, and neither was any other political community in the Archaic and Classical Aegean. Either there is something deficient in the anthropological theory, or something very unusual about Greek states (Anderson 2009).

Both may be true. That is, Greek *poleis* are certainly very unusual when we compare them to other 'pristine states' (Whitley 2019). They lack – and sometimes eschew – the hierarchy we associate with a stratified social order and have little administrative complexity. If we follow Blok (2014; 2017), they were states which made up through participation what they lacked in administration and did so through forms of ritualized feasting (see Van den Eijnde et al. 2018). In Crete these forms of ritualized commensality were as likely to take place in the *andreion* as in the sanctuary proper (Whitley 2018; Madgwick and Whitley 2018).

The Cretan *polis* is distinct from the mainland one; but it is beginning to look a lot like earlier forms of Cretan polity. The proto-palatial phase in the central courtyard structure at Knossos was characterized by a form of ritualized feasting – albeit not one focused on the consumption of animal flesh (Knappett and Macdonald 2007). Ritualized feasting may have been the social glue that kept both Middle Bronze Age and Archaic forms of polity together (Hatzimichael and Whitley 2012).

Some of the features of the *polis* continued into Roman times. If citizens ceased to be defined by warfare and feasting, local magistracies and a strong sense of local identity continued down to the third century AD. It is then that we have our second 'gap' – in the fourth century. This gap, like the earlier Archaic one, is more apparent than real. Neither is likely to represent an abandonment of the site. They represent gaps, not in occupation, but in our understanding.

Still the fact that, for both gaps, our understanding is poor must indicate something. Of course, one cannot rule out taphonomic factors – factors, that is, relating to how the archaeological record is created. But I don't think that it is a coincidence that both gaps occur just after major phases in the political reorganization of the community of Knossos: the first between the Early Iron Age and then Archaic/Classical polis, when public feasting becomes more austere and more likely to be located within *andreia*; the second between a traditional Roman order based on magistrates and polytheism and a new Late Antique Christian community based as much on ecclesiastical as on social principles. These profound changes in the underlying principles of community structure may well form a large part of the explanation for our 'gaps in the record'.

5.12 Postscript: the Knossos area after Knossos

After Late Antique Knossos was finally abandoned, where did the people go? Well, Gortyn remained a substantial Roman settlement throughout this Early Byzantime period (down to 828 AD at least), while Crete remained a province of the East Roman Empire and at some point Heraklion supplanted Knossos to become the principal city of north-central Crete. When Muslims from Spain conquered Crete after 827 AD they made Heraklion their capital (renaming it Chandax).

Some of the population may not have gone far at all. The modern village of Ambelokipi (vine gardens) is quite old. Ambelokipi is the very recent name for the former Muslim village of Teke, which lies close to the latest Late Antique manifestation of Knossos. If Teke's origins lie in the medieval period, then some Knossians may only have moved a few hundred metres from the Late Antique town.

And of course let us not forget the two historical hamlets of Knossos: Bougada Metochi and Makry Teichos. These too must have medieval roots. The modern church at Makryteichos overlies the Early Christian basilica of Ayia Sophia. Here there is an intriguing coda to the history of the city. Near the modern church are the remains of a small 'Arab' building – that is, one that can be dated to this otherwise poorly documented period (828–961). This was 'no amir's palace' (Warren and Miles 1972), but it did contain some coins of a succession of the island's Islamic rulers. This is one of the few early medieval structures to have been properly excavated and shows that what was once the city of Knossos had now become the hamlet (at best) of medieval Makryteichos.

Makryteichos was one part of the settlement that Evans saw when he first visited the site. No one has shown very much interest in investigating the medieval origins of either of these two hamlets, nor of the village of Teke. There is archaeological evidence of activity in the Knossos region of course – the Venetians constructed an aqueduct over the Vlychia stream, and the Egyptians (that is Ibrahim Pasha, son of Mehmet Ali of Egypt) constructed the 'Egyptian' aqueduct over the Kairatos to the south of Knossos in the years after the uprising of 1821 (Mazower 2021). Both were built to supply Herakleion with water – not to help the inhabitants of Knossos.

By the time of both aqueducts the local inhabitant had little notion that they might be Knossians. The name Knossos had of course survived: bishops of Knossos reappear in the Second Byzantine period (961–1204 AD): a Nicephoros around 1050, a Paul around 1192 and a Constantine just before 1200 (Tsougarakis 1988, 353–9, nos. 30, 109 and 127), though the seat of these bishops had by this time moved to Ayios Myron (D'Agata 2010, 62).

It was travellers and antiquaries in search of the Labyrinth who were to reunite the name of Knossos with the remains of the ancient city. These travellers and antiquaries were the products of an early modern world that was increasingly connected – increasingly globalized. This too can be glimpsed in the material record of Knossos. Ottoman pipes from the area of the North Cemetery (Evely 1988) demonstrate that Muslims (or Turks) had taken up the vile habit of smoking tobacco, so roundly condemned by James VI (of Scotland) and I (of England). That the ordinary (largely Muslim) inhabitants of Teke had taken up using a plant imported from the Americas is an indication, as much as anything else, of this emerging connectedness.

Globalization and the modern world eventually brought Classical scholarship and archaeology to birth, and so brought Western travellers, antiquarians and archaeologists to Knossos. We have come full circle. It is time to review our subject.

CHAPTER 6
KNOSSOS YESTERDAY AND TODAY

Chapter abstract

This chapter looks at how interpretations of Knossos have changed over the past few decades, partly through recent work on the site and how interpretation is changing. It looks in particular at the relationship between language, script and identity. It assesses Knossos' place in the modern imagination (whether for Cretans, scholars or visitors) and the prospects for work in the future.

6.1 On languages, scripts and peoples

We have come full circle. Let us return to the image we started with – the inscribed marble gravestones from the Muslim village of Teke (Figure 1.1), close to Knossos. These are written in a script and a language which few could read today – Ottoman Turkish. Even modern-day Turks would struggle to read them, as modern Turkish is now written using a version of the Latin script. There are a few Greek scholars who study such inscriptions; far fewer, I would imagine, than those studying inscriptions in any of the other scripts and languages that have been used in Knossos over the millennia. These scripts are as much a part of the 'stratigraphy' of Knossos as the levels uncovered in the recent 'Little Palace North' excavations (an exercise which revealed the depth and complexity of occupation at Knossos; Hatzaki et al. 2008). Let us lay out this stratigraphy in the following table, with the latest levels highest and the earliest lowest.

In sum, then, at least eight, and possibly nine, scripts have been in use in Knossos since 1950 BC. There is no obvious correlation between either the predominant language/script and the political order – or if there is, it would require a more nuanced and quantitative analysis than the one given here. The principal script in use from around 700 BC has been varieties of the Greek alphabet (starting with the local Cretan version, moving through Ionic and later manifestations). Greek has probably been the predominant language of Knossos since the Late Bronze Age (that is, from 1400 BC) – but has been written in at least two different scripts (Linear B and the Greek alphabet). Languages probably in use include the 'Minoan' languages of the earliest scripts (whatever their affinities), Greek, Phoenician (and possibly other Semitic languages), Latin, Arabic, Ottoman Turkish and (from the twentieth century onwards) English (and other European tongues).

How Greek then is or was Knossos, or indeed Crete? Knossos, from the visitor's point of view, now looks thoroughly 'Minoan' – 'Minoan-ness' and 'Cretan-ness' are linked in the minds of both. The Minoan heritage remains a strong element in modern Cretan

Table 6.1 Scripts and languages attested in Knossos (in reverse chronological order)

Period	Approximate dates	Languages in use	Scripts in use (attested epigraphically)	Political structure (hierarchical/ communal)
Modern	AD 1896 to present	Modern Greek; other European, principally English	Greek; Latin (for road signs)	Communal (Greek democracy for the most part)
Ottoman	AD 1649–1896	Ottoman Turkish; Greek	Ottoman Turkish; some Greek	Hierarchical (Ottoman Empire)
Venetian	AD 1204–1649	Italian; Greek	None attested at Knossos	Hierarchical (Empire of Venetian Republic)
Late Byzantine	AD 961–1204	Greek	None attested at Knossos	Hierarchical (East Roman/Byzantine Empire)
Arab	AD 823/7–961	Greek; Arabic	Arabic inscriptions on coins from Knossos	Hierarchical (Emirate of Crete)
Late Antique	AD 400–823/7	Greek	Greek (on ceramics etc)	Hierarchical (East Roman Empire)
Roman	67 BC–AD 400	Greek; Latin	Greek (Ionic derived script); Latin	Hierarchical (Roman Empire)
Archaic, Classical, Hellenistic	700–67 BC	Greek (Dorian)	Greek (local Cretan script, then Greek Ionic script)	Communal (Citizen-state)
Iron Age/ post-Minoan	1300–700 BC	Greek (Dorian, possibly also Achaean/ Arkado-Cypriot); Phoenician/N. Syrian possibly	One Phoenician inscription from North Cemetery	Probably communal (kinship based)
Final Palatial	1450–1300 BC	Greek (Mycenaean/ Arkado-Cypriot); possibly some earlier 'Minoan' languages (no positive evidence)	Linear B (several hundred inscriptions)	Hierarchical (Mycenaean-style kingdom with *wanaks* at the apex of the pyramid)

Period	Approximate dates	Languages in use	Scripts in use (attested epigraphically)	Political structure (hierarchical/communal)
Neopalatial	1750–1450 BC	'Minoan' (pre-Greek) language(s) –affinities unknown	Linear A; residual Cretan Hieroglyphic	Communal with some hierarchy – unclear
Protopalatial	1950–1750 BC	'Minoan' (pre-Greek) language(s) – affinities unknown	Cretan Hieroglyphic; possibility of some use of 'Archanes Script'	Communal with some hierarchy (evidenced in feasting) – unclear
Early Minoan	3100–1950 BC	'Minoan' (pre-Greek) language(s) – affinities unknown	None attested	Communal
Neolithic	7000–3100 BC	Anatolian languages?	None attested	Communal

identity – including their identity as Greeks. A few years ago, a member of the Cretan public put what might seem to be a straightforward question to two distinguished Greek scholars: were the Minoans Greek (Momigliano 2017, 6)? I myself would not know how to answer this question. For if you answer 'no' – on the grounds that Cretans in proto- and neopalatial times probably did not speak Greek – you also suggest that present-day Cretans are somehow not the descendants of 'the Minoans'. If, on the other hand, you answer 'yes', you imply that the people of Crete spoke Greek before the final palatial period – which implication is, at the very least, misleading.

Any honest answer to the question would require a qualification to either a 'yes' or a 'no' – neither answer can be straightforward. And this is what the two Greek archaeologists tried to do – to answer this question with a qualification. The answers did not satisfy the audience. A rather unpleasant online spat, with markedly anti-Semitic overtones, took place. For the Minoans can only be one thing or another – Greek (and so European) or non-Greek (and so Oriental). This is the kind of impossible question that can spark a culture war. Culture wars demand a 'yes' or a 'no' without qualification. They ask you to decide, in Lilliputian fashion (Swift 1939, 45) on which side of the boiled egg you should break ('and they shall break their eggs at the convenient end'). They force you to be either a 'Big-Ender' or a 'Little-Ender'. You cannot qualify; you have to choose a side.

It is perhaps for this reason that 'the Minoans' remain a perennial subject of controversy – both within academia and within the wider politics of identity (Momigliano 2020; Momigliano and Farnoux 2017). Knossos in turn remains central to our notion of 'Minoan Crete'. How has this idea fared since the turn of the millennium?

6.2 Knossos after 2000

The year 2000 was not only the turn of the millennium – it also marked 100 years since Evans first broke ground on the hill of Kephala. It was clearly time for a reappraisal. Several subsequently appeared. The British School at Athens and the Greek Archaeological Service organized a commemorative (and prospective) volume on Knossos in that year, whose proceedings appeared soon after (Cadogan et al. 2004). Other volumes came out: one focused on architecture and the function of those buildings conventionally called 'palaces' (Driessen et al. 2002); the other two explicitly concentrating on 'the Minoans' – considered, as it were, in inverted commas or 'scare quotes' (Hamilakis 2002; Hamilakis and Momigliano 2006). The label had clearly become problematic (at least to academic audiences), and this was a problem that both volumes sought to explore. The papers in the earlier volume were more explicitly 'theoretical', looking at new ways to approach Bronze Age Crete making use of the conceptual and methodological tools now available to processual and post-processual archaeologists. The later volume (Hamilakis and Momigliano 2006) was more historiographic, concentrating mainly on the role that 'the Minoans' played in the Cretan, Greek and European imagination during the twentieth century – a theme that Nicoletta Momigliano has since followed up in spectacular fashion (Momigliano 2020; Momigliano and Farnoux 2017). These reappraisals were accompanied by critical biographies of the men (and they were all men) who shaped our notion of 'the Minoans' in the twentieth century: Duncan Mackenzie (Momigliano 1999), Arthur Evans (MacGillivray 2000) and John Pendlebury (Grundon 2007).

Such reflexivity has not proven a bar to further empirical research. Palatial Crete (the Crete of the Minoans) continues to be a vigorous field of study (Christakis 2020). Active field projects include the palace of Petras (near Sitia), led by Metaxia Tsipopoulou; a whole host of American projects in the Ierapetra isthmus, now supported by the INSTAP study centre in eastern Crete; continued study excavation at Phaistos and Mallia; and, in central Crete, ongoing projects at Archanes and Galatas by members of the Greek Archaeological service (principally Giorgios Rethemiotakis); and the American/Canadian work at Kommos. Knossos too has had its 'Minoan' excavations – principally those exploring neopalatial houses on the Gypsadhes hill and Minoan deposits in the Anetaki hill, undertaken by Eleni Hatzaki (Christakis 2020, 95–8). Athanasia Kanta has undertaken further explorations of the area around the palace. Research into Bronze Age Knossos is now as likely to take the form of reappraisals of older excavations (e.g., Hatzaki 2005) as new empirical research in the form of excavations. Knossos is then not as central to 'Minoan' studies as it was in Evans' time. Nor are 'Minoan' studies quite as central to research at Knossos, where there is increasing interest in the Roman period.

This loss of centrality was reflected in the centenary volume (Cadogan et al. 2004). Though the bulk of the papers in the volume were on 'Minoan' topics, there was a greater emphasis on both earlier and later periods, particularly the Roman, than we had seen before (an emphasis that has been reflected in recent British research at Knossos in the area immediately around the Villa Dionysos). This bilingual volume also shed light on the differing priorities of British and Greek scholars. Alexandra Karetsou (2004) was explicitly concerned with issues of heritage management – that is, how effectively to present and maintain the fabric of the palace and present it in a reasonably accurate and up-to-date manner to the horde of visitors who come there every year.

These issues were very much on my mind when I took over as director of the British School at Athens in 2002. The research facilities at Knossos (the Taverna and Stratigraphical Museum) needed to be both maintained and expanded. More storage space was needed for finds from new excavations, and to meet the more demanding requirements of archaeological conservation. The museum itself was full and fully used by researchers of all nationalities, and yet it was built on very shallow foundations over Evans' tennis courts. The Stratigraphical Museum Extension excavations of Peter Warren had revealed (as early as the 1980s) just how difficult it would be to extend the museum – too difficult, so the project was temporarily dropped. Test excavations by Don Evely (who had taken over from Eleni Hatzaki as Knossos curator) had revealed how close the Roman levels were to the surface. The need for longer-term solutions was clear – but the means for such a solution were simply not to hand.

The School also had to demonstrate to its principal funder (the British Academy) that it had a viable research agenda for Knossos – the largest and most complex site that British archaeologists had investigated in Greece. Excavation that focused on research problems of primary interest to specialists in particular periods were singularly hard to plan for because of the complexity of Knossos' stratigraphy. Most of the Bronze Age town lay under many metres of overlay, and the periods of occupation we knew least about archaeologically (anything from the Iron Age to the Hellenistic) were architecturally elusive. We were unlikely to find any Iron Age to Hellenistic houses (such that we could place objects in a clear domestic context), and further excavation offered diminishing returns when it came to better understanding of the material (chiefly ceramic) sequence.

One possible solution presented itself in the form of the Knossos Urban Landscape Project (KULP). This was dreamt up by Todd Whitelaw and John Bennet and was originally conceived as a multi-period, diachronic survey project (Whitelaw et al. 2019). It would build upon David Smyth's and Sinclair Hood's Knossos Survey (Hood and Smyth 1981) and cover the same area while taking advantage of the fact that Knossos now possessed one of the best ceramic sequences from Neolithic to Late Antique in the whole Mediterranean world. This raised the possibility that the extent of the urban area could be precisely mapped by the recovery of datable surface finds. Such information would also be essential to any long-term heritage management plan that did not simply focus on the palace but treated the Knossos survey area as a totality: as an important archaeological landscape and a precious part of Greece's archaeological heritage. The project began in 2005 as a *synergasia* (joint project) between the British School at Athens and the Greek Archaeological Service under the general direction of Todd Whitelaw, John Bennet and Antonis Vasilakis. It was, by any measure, very successful – yielding a vast number of datable surface material from all periods. I joined the project for one day in 2005. The area was difficult to survey because it consisted of small fields, often difficult to enter. Much of the area was inaccessible – it had been (illegally) fenced off by people building houses on land that ought to have remained agricultural. And it shed other light on contemporary Heraklion.

A diachronic project picks up material from all periods. Some of the teams found some very recent finds – 'shooting galleries', deposits of discarded syringes for injecting heroin. For Heraklion – a city that has grown quickly and haphazardly since the 1960s – has a very serious drugs problem.

The survey also helped with another apparent enigma. Greece has numerous UNESCO World Heritage sites, most of which are to be found on the mainland. At the time of writing, none are to be found on Crete. That the second-most visited archaeological site in Greece was not as highly regarded as a sanctuary such as Delphi has struck the present Greek prime minister (Kyriakos Mitsotakis, whose family is Cretan) as odd. From the perspective of politicians in Athens, KULP looks like a very good idea. Whether or not this gains the support of the local population (many of whom have encroached on the survey area) is another matter.

Nonetheless, the KULP project has yielded a steady stream of publications which have managed to track changes in the size of the urban occupation through time (Kotsonas 2019b; Trainor 2019; Whitelaw et al. 2019). These show some quite striking variations – the maximum size being in neopalatial times when the town was between 90 and 120 hectares in extent (Christakis 2020, 96–7; Whitelaw et al. 2019). The project makes it much easier to draw comparisons between periods. I have drawn on many of the KULP's publications in this book because, in large part, I share its diachronic and comparative objectives. Perhaps it is time to draw some conclusions.

6.3 The political community: an interpretive synthesis

Knossos is the earliest inhabited agricultural community we know of on Crete. It is difficult to gain any real understanding of how the community functioned before Early Minoan times. The latest KULP data (Christakis 2020, 97, Figure 123; Whitelaw et al. 2019, 14–15) indicate that a step change in community size (from less than 10ha to around 35ha) took place between EMII and EMIII, at the very end of the third millennium BC. The reasons for this remain controversial. I am persuaded by Peter Tomkins' (2016) thesis that the major reorganization of the site (the levelling of the tell and the establishment of the first 'gathering place' – or, if you insist, the 'palace') took place around 2500 BC (in the middle of EMII) and that the expansion of the settlement was a secondary effect of this.

In any case, even if we follow the more traditional model, and believe that the 'first palace' was laid out after 1950 BC (MMIB–MMII and possibly MMIIIA), then the structure cannot have been a 'palace' as we normally understand the term. It was rather a 'court complex' (*sensu*, Driessen 2002) used for seasonal gatherings and occasional ritual functions, laid out with some regard to cosmological principles. The written records (largely in Cretan Hieroglyphic) were not used so much for 'administration' (again, as we would normally understand the term) but for the mobilization of resources for these seasonal gatherings. Though the word feast has been much used to describe what these gatherings might have involved, there is no positive evidence for the large-scale consumption of meat from slaughtered domestic animals. These are not sanctuaries on the model of those to be found on the Greek mainland in historical times. Rather, the commensality seems to have focused on drinking practices (MacDonald and Knappett 2007, 57–68, 161–5) with a clearly hierarchical structure (Hatzimichael and Whitley 2012).

Hierarchy is, however, much less evident in contemporary mortuary practices (Herrero 2014), where we have far fewer burials than one might expect for what was now a community of considerable size. This relative paucity of burials relative to the size of the settlement persists into neopalatial times (MMIIIB–LMIB). The town (or city) now reaches its maximum size. The 'palace' was elaborated and now decorated with frescoes, particularly in the domestic quarter. Architectural and decorative elaboration is also evident in the numerous villas, built with ashlar masonry and set alongside paved roads (Adams 2017). Evidence of an established hierarchy is, however, as elusive as it had been in the earlier period. The large number of conical cups if anything speak more of a communal ethos than of a social pyramid, and the iconography indicates that the structures of power were much more 'gynocentric' than in most cultures we know of. The sparse finds of Linear A documents do not support the notion that this structure was principally administrative. In short, everything points to a modification of the palace's previous role as a gathering place and occasional temple.

It is this 'neopalatial' period that best represents 'the Minoans' in the popular imagination. It is also the one that most puzzles those who look for general patterns in human social and cultural evolution (e.g., Flannery and Marcus 2012). It just does not fit any general model (Graeber and Wengrow 2021, 434–9). Some have seen in neopalatial Crete something akin to the 'theatre state' of nineteenth-century Bali (Geertz 1980) – a state which is not a state (in the sense of a power structure) but where performance is all.

The next period (the final palatial, LMII–LMIIIA) is far easier to understand and to fit into broad evolutionary models. It is a kingdom. The settlement shrinks in size and the palace is modified to become, probably for the only time in its history, a palace in the proper sense – that is, the residence of a ruler and the centre of administration for a unitary state that extended over most of central Crete. Signs of hierarchy are evident both in mortuary practices (where warrior graves and other tombs appear with marked differences in the quantity of grave goods between 'rich' and 'poor') and in the Linear B tablets. These, the first signs of the Greek language in Crete, indicate that the social order of Knossos was now a pyramid, with the 'wanaks' (king) at its apex.

To my mind it is no coincidence that Knossos was destroyed soon after this more hierarchical (and less resilient) political order was established. Once destroyed it was not rebuilt and the size of the settlement in the immediately post-palatial period (LMIIIB–LMIIIC) shrank dramatically; post-palatial Knossos was only slightly larger than that of the final Neolithic/Early Minoan settlement. Throughout the Early Iron Age the settlement expanded, reaching a size not far short of the Bronze Age maximum by around 500 BC.

For evidence of social hierarchy in the Early Iron Age we have to turn to the burial record. Richly furnished and distinctive single interments are more a feature of the earlier rather than the later periods in the Iron Age. Burial in collective tombs became the norm, and in general fewer and fewer tombs accommodated larger and larger numbers of interments as we reach the eighth and seventh centuries BC. Distinctions between richer and poorer tomb groups are easier to discern than those between individual interments within larger tombs. Evidence of social stratification (as opposed to social ranking) is lacking.

By 500 BC we are dealing with a citizen-state of some considerable size. Citizen-states, like the earlier polities based around courtyard complexes (and unlike the brief period when Knossos was a palatial state, in the final palatial period) were political communities of great resilience – they were difficult to destroy. I have argued (following Wallace 2010) that there were two stages in the reorganization of the community: one, after 850 BC, when the cemeteries were reorganized and tombs became fewer, larger and longer-lived; and another that coincided with the 'Archaic gap', when institutions such as the *andreion* were established. While not a democracy in the normal Greek sense, these Cretan republics did emphasize 'equality between citizens'. They also functioned as 'covenant states' in Blok's (2017) sense, where commensality, both within the *andreion* and the sanctuary, was probably now geared to the maintenance of this political community, which continued to flourish and expand down to the end of the Hellenistic period. With the Roman conquest of 67 BC and the establishment of the *colonia* soon afterwards, Knossos ceases to be an independent political community – it becomes just another Roman town. For most of the Roman period, at least down to the time of the emperor Caracalla, it maintains its own amongst the other Roman towns of Crete. But gradually it shrinks and settlement drifts northward away from the earliest centre on the Kephala hill. By Late Antique times the new ritual and civic centres were the large basilicas in the area of the former North Cemetery; civic leadership had fallen to the bishops. It was in this ghostly form of a bishopric that the name of Knossos persisted after the town was abandoned sometime after 650 AD.

This is a summary from the perspective of political developments. That is one perspective. From the point of view of a contemporary Cretan, however (see above), what matters is not so much political and social evolution as issues of identity.

6.4 The question of identity: Minoans, Cretans and Greeks

Today's Cretans are very proud both of being Cretan and of being Greek. They are also conscious of their archaeological heritage in a past that goes back to prehistory and to myth. 'The Archaeology of Identity' has been much discussed – recently it has overlapped with a concern with 'ontologies' (Descola 2013). This notion suggests a radical difference between cultures like us (modernity) and those in most times and places elsewhere. Were I to follow the pattern of the previous section, I would be moving forward in time from the Neolithic to the present day. But in prehistory, issues of identity are very hard to grasp. I propose therefore to start from the present and then go back into the past.

Before the twentieth century (in Ottoman and Venetian times) the Minoans did not really exist. Myths surrounding Minos and the Minotaur were known, and locals would be quite willing to show distinguished foreign visitors where the Labyrinth might be found. But this is hardly a compelling reason to believe that these myths played any role in local identities. The Balkan pattern (Mazower 2000, 50–85) in Ottoman times was for identity to have a primarily religious basis – people thought of themselves as Christians, Muslims or Jews (and were classified as such for purposes of taxation and administration). Such a pattern is likely to have held in earlier times – in the Venetian, Late Byzantine, Arab – even as far back as Late Antiquity.

The Romans – that is Roman-era inhabitants of Knossos – were more involved with the myths surrounding King Minos. The Labyrinth appears on local Roman coins; Knossos was known to be both the location of the 'Tomb of Meriones' and the alleged findspot of the poems of Dictys of Crete. The Romans, it must be remembered, were comfortable with 'nested' identities – one could be Roman (that is, a Roman citizen), Greek, Cretan and a member of a local community such as Knossos all at the same time. Other distinctions had harder boundaries – particularly those between slave and free, citizen and non-citizen.

Nested identities existed in earlier (Hellenistic, Classical and Archaic) times in Knossos. Coin evidence suggests that the primary identity was the political one – Knossos was the community of the ΚΝΩΣΙΟΝ (the Knossians). The iconography of these coins implies that local Knossian identity was linked to legends of the Labyrinth and the Minotaur. A passage in Herodotus (7.169–71) suggests that there existed some kind of 'Cretan' identity in Late Archaic/Early Classical times; an Early Classical inscription from the neighbouring city of Tylissos implies that the cities of north-central Crete also thought of themselves as 'Dorian' (tracing their ancestry to well-known Dorian cities such as Argos and Sparta). To what degree they also thought of themselves as 'Greek' (that is, as Hellenes) is harder to determine – though the passage in Herodotus seems to suggest this.

Questions of identity are in any case fraught even when we have good literary and epigraphic evidence. Jonathan Hall (1997; 2002) has argued that ethnic identities such as 'Dorian' only emerged in the Late Archaic period. A consciousness of being Hellenes (Greeks) emerged even later. At first this was an ethnic identity; that is, one supported by an origin myth (that is, descent from a mythical ancestor). It was only by the late fourth century, the time of Aristotle, that it became what Hall (2000) calls a 'cultural' identity. That is, being a Hellene was no longer simply a matter of descent from a mythical ancestor; one could acquire 'Greekness' by following behaviours or practices that were deemed 'Greek' (principally by learning Greek and participating in a Greek political community). Cultural identities of this kind are, however, very much the exception. For most people in most periods the principal vectors of identity were politics (locality), language, ethnicity (descent), kinship, gender and religion. At times these vectors intersected with what we might call personhood (Fowler 2004). Where religion intersects with personhood, as has recently been argued was the case for Classical Athens (Anderson 2018), then we appear to be dealing not with 'people like us' but people quite unlike 'us' (modern Europeans or Americans) – in other words, people with a quite different 'ontology'.

It is harder to discern what identity (and, *a fortiori*, 'ontology') might have been in the Early Iron Age and final palatial periods. For the Early Iron Age, it is likely that some kind of collective 'Knossian' identity had emerged possibly as early at 850 BC; it is also likely that Knossos accommodated a number of ethnic (Semitic-speaking) minorities in a population that largely spoke Greek. For the final palatial period we know that at least the upper stratum of society used a dialect of Greek (Mycenaean or Arkado-Cypriot) and knew the name Knossos. Whether they thought of themselves as 'Knossians' or had a collective noun for 'Mycenaean Greeks' is unknown; it is possible they might have thought of themselves as 'Achaeans' (see Homer, *Odyssey* 19.175–7).

For the neopalatial and protopalatial periods we are entirely dependent on the material record; written documents exist but we cannot read them to gain any insights about identity. Archaeologists generally agree that the material culture of Crete was becoming both more homogeneous (within Crete) and more distinctive (from other areas of the Aegean) as the Bronze Age wore on. Cretan material culture was at its most distinctive in the neopalatial period (MMIII–LMIB). Many have taken this material distinctiveness as being an expression of a common identity (Adams 2017). Archaeologists have also noticed that other areas of the Aegean world (the Cyclades, Kythera and Ionia) were increasingly (if also selectively) adopting features of Cretan (so, 'Minoan') material culture – a process dubbed 'Minoanization' (Broodbank 2004). This has led some to talk of 'Minoan cultural identity' (Adams 2017, 209–29). Bronze Age Cretans (Minoans) identified with their distinctive material culture (their distinctiveness is an expression of their identity). This identification of a people ('the Minoans') with their 'Minoan' material culture was so strong and so well understood that we can infer that when the peoples Kythera, the Cyclades or Ionia begin to adopt these 'Minoan' cultural traits, they too were identifying with Cretans (by a process of acculturation analogous to Hellenization in the Hellenistic world and Romanization in the Roman).

I think these arguments are mistaken, for several reasons (Whitley 2006). First, because the concept of 'cultural identity' is a tautology. All identity is cultural (as it cannot be natural) – identity is a dimension of culture. Of course, Hall (2002) uses 'cultural identity' in a rather different sense – as something that could be consciously emulated or adopted. For such a form of cultural identity to exist, however, there must first be an Aristotle or an Isocrates to formulate what (for example) Greek cultural identity might mean. Nothing like this seems possible in the Bronze Age. The second reason for regarding the arguments noted as mistaken is that the term 'cultural identity' when applied to a term like 'Minoan' creates a confusion between the emic with the etic. Identity, by definition, must be emic – that is, it is something that relates to a people's view of themselves (e.g., the Ukrainians). 'Minoan' is a label that archaeologists have used to classify the Bronze Age of Crete. It is not an 'emic' term – one, like 'the Knossians', that was used by the peoples themselves. In Hall's view, all forms of identity (political, ethnic, etc.) have first and foremost to be emic – that is, forms of self-identity using terms that those people could have used. 'Minoan' is what I would call a pseudo-emic term – one that looks like it might have been used by Bronze Age Cretans but simply cannot have been. My third reason for dismissing the arguments above is that culture and cultures are, by and large, polythetic entities. Cultures are not blocks where language, ethnicity, political boundaries and material culture exactly coincide. We cannot assume – as cultural nationalists generally do – an isomorphism between ethnic groups, political groups and material culture groups (Clarke 1978, 263–6, 311–15, 363–408). This makes it extremely difficult to infer identities from differing degrees of homogeneity in material culture. Or to put it another way, the idea that the more Cretan material culture in the Bronze Age begins to resemble that of Knossos (and central Crete) the more justification we have in calling it Minoan is simply not a valid inference. In the Cretan case the term 'Minoan' seems less applicable to the Early Minoan period when there is a high degree of regional diversity within the island (Herrero 2009). There is no archaeological case for there being a primordial period of 'Minoan' homogeneity later broken up by successive waves of Achaeans and Dorians.

Strangely, we may be on firmer ground when it comes to ontology. The very strangeness of the rich iconography of neopalatial Knossos hints at very different forms of human-animal relations to those found in the modern world. A combination of contextual and iconographic study may yield insights into Bronze Age 'ontologies' that a straightforward concern with identity may not (Shapland 2013; 2022). In that it indicates the strangeness of this lost lifeworld – which generations of scholars have tried to understand – there may be life in the 'Minoans' yet.

That a people ('the Minoans') could appear with the coming of copper (and bronze) and disappear with the introduction of iron remains nonetheless an absurdity. This is not to say that there were not changes in identity between the Bronze and Iron Ages. Some of us (Whitley 2016; Kotsonas 2018b) have detected a change in 'personhood' at the very end of the Bronze Age and the beginning of the Iron Age. This marks a sharp cultural break when what we call the 'palace' ceased to be understood.

What do I mean by this? The palace had changed as an institution several times between 2000 and 1300 BC – so what was remembered perhaps became confused. Its original function – that of a gathering place– was obscured when it became the residence of a ruler. Its architectural layout is not obviously legible as a ruler's residence – much less so than the megaron-centred structures of the Mycenaean mainland. As a ruin it became even harder to understand.

Cultural (that is oral) memory is also selective – there are things we want to remember and things we would rather forget. We often think of the Heroic Age in Greece as something glorious, and in so doing we equate the Heroic Age with the Bronze Age. Yet the recollection of Bronze Age of Greece in general, and Crete in particular, could equally be seen as a memory that contained more than a hint of trauma. The legacy of a 'complex society' for later generations in many parts of the world may not always have been a positive one. Graeber and Wengrove (2021, 463–92) see the memory of the large settlement at Cahokia in the American Midwest in the eyes of later Native Americans as being largely painful: 'complexity' for later Woodland peoples meant overlords, and overlords must never return. The legacy of the palace at Knossos was undoubtedly more ambiguous, partly because it held different memories of different kinds of institutions. The recollection of 'the palace' mixed trauma with glory. The ruined structure became a jumble of a building around which stories of kings with seemingly schizophrenic personalities (Minos as a tyrant; Minos as wise ruler), and families as dysfunctional as any other in Greek mythology, grew up. The palace became the Labyrinth, a place of wonder, horror and continued fascination.

NOTES

Chapter 1

1. There are several minotaurs on sealings (seal impressions) and on seals (engraved gems) – e.g. *CMS* II.3.67 = Platon and Pini 1984, 78, No. 67 from Sellopoulo grave 1.

2. Bacchylides, *Ode* 16 (dithyramb 4); see Maehler 2004, 57–62 and 172–89. Knossos and Minos are both mentioned.

3. GR 1877, 0728.3.

4. *CMS* II,3.67 = Platon and Pini 1984, 78, No. 67.

5. Evans 1901a, 18–19, Figures 7a, 7b, 7c.

6. Carpenter 1991, 163; Schefold 1966, 39, Figure 7. A *Schildband* is exactly what it sounds like – a shield band, the interior bronze strap of a shield which in Archaic times is frequently decorated with figure scenes.

7. Beazley 1956, 109, No. 29; old BM catalogue B148; current catalogue BM GR 1848, 0619.5.

8. London example by the Codrus painter: BM old catalogue E84, now GR 1850, 0302.3; Beazley 1963, 1269, No. 4.

9. Basel relief pithos (or amphora), Basel Antikenmuseum Kappeli collection 601 (see Brommer 1982, Plate 26; Schefold 1966, Plate 25a); François vase (Florence 4209 from Chiusi; Beazley 1956, 76, No. 1).

10. Paris, Cabinet des Médailles 1066; Beazley 1947, 54–5 & Plate X, 3; Papadopoulos 1994, J.25.

11. First attested in one of the Linear B tablets: Ventris and Chadwick 1973, 171–2, No. 38 = As1516 line 2 KO-NO-SI-JA. For the stele of Amenhotep III, see Helck 1992.

12. https://www.metmuseum.org/art/collection/search/245585?ao=on&ft=minotaur&offset=0&rpp=20&pos=17.

13. https://www.khm.at/objektdb/detail/52079/.

14. Of course, we do not see this story of the finding of the manuscript in an ancient tomb as being deliberately fraudulent today – as a 'literary imposture' in Evans' words – but rather as a 'frame story' to lend Dictys' account a degree of plausibility (see discussion by Gainsford 2012).

Chapter 2

1. This is Ashmolean 1889.998 (*CMS* VI, 1, No. 104 = Hughes Brock and Boardman 2009a, 242–3, No. 104); see Evans 1894, 294, Figure 32; 1909, 8–10.

2. Furtwängler 1900a, Plates II and III; 1900b, 7–17; 1900c, 12–56. See also Hughes Brock and Boardman 2009a, 4–12.

3. Marinatos 1929; 1930; 1932; 1933.

4. This is a different location from the hill of Kephala, where the Palace lies.

5. That is, Britain, India, Australia, South Africa, Canada and New Zealand, with their various colonies and dependencies. France had surrendered before Greece joined the war.

6. The exact circumstances are disputed, particularly whether the Germans who shot Pendlebury knew who he was; see Grundon 2007, 310–18.

Chapter 3

1. Contributors to Isaakidou and Tomkins (2008) now seem to prefer the term 'Initial Neolithic' to 'Aceramic'. For the actual evidence from Stratum X, see Evans 1964, 138–42.

2. The terminology here is that of Tomkins (2007), which is slightly different from that of J. D. Evans (1994).

3. I am not endorsing this insular attitude, which few (if any) scholars now explicitly support. In any case, the overall 'discursive frame' is now changing. See Broodbank 2013, esp. 257–432; papers in Cadogan et al. 2012.

4. This is not Evans' 'North West Bailey'. The term is used by Wilson (1994, 33–5, Figure 3), based on Catling (1988, 69). Its character only really became clear in 1987.

Chapter 4

1. Dickinson (1994) uses a slightly different terminology: First, Second and Third Palaces (corresponding to Old, New and Final respectively).

2. A suggestion first made at the TAG (Theoretical Archaeology Group) conference in Cardiff in 1999 by G. Vavouranakis and D. Catapoti.

3. Evans himself changed his mind about the date of this deposit (Evans 1921, 272, n. 2), here assigning it to MMIIB. Most scholars now prefer an MMIIIA date. In any case, it is clear it dates to the very end of the protopalatial period.

4. This may have been a clearing-out operation in advance of major architectural reconstruction in MMIIIB.

5. Not a complete blank, however. There is some scanty evidence gathered together by Herrero (2014, 234, nos. 226 and 227) and Preston (2013b).

6. There has unfortunately been no osteological study of any of these tombs, so numbers of interments are 'guestimates'.

7. The exact date of the Great Reconstruction remains controversial. See the different views expressed in Macdonald and Knappett (2013a).

8. Chapin and Shaw (2006) disagree with Cameron's interpretation, finding no firm evidence of *agrimia* nor for there being a second floor.

9. Eleni Hatzaki is currently restudying this material, and this discussion owes much to a joint visit to the tomb in 2003.

Chapter 5

1. This use of the term pithos for a shape not used for storage might be a potential cause for confusion, so I use the term 'funerary pithos' throughout.

2. Though some have suggested that the house of Lasthenes was burnt as a punishment, our sources (in particular Appian) say that Lasthenes burnt his own house – to prevent the Romans from gaining the money (Χρηματα) therein (Appian *Sicelica* 6.2). So there is no suggestion of a destruction by fire of the town as a whole.

3. Baldwin Bowsky 2006, 411–19; see now Baldwin Bowsky 2012. I have combined the figures.

4. The bishops concerned were Zenobius (Ephesus, 431), Gennadius (Chalcedon, 451) and Anastasios (2nd Nicaea, 787). See Tsoungarakis 1988, 351–61, nos. 5, 52 and 157; Sweetman 2004b, 323.

BIBLIOGRAPHY

Adams, E. 2017. *Cultural Identity in Minoan Crete: Social Dynamics in the Neopalatial Period.* Cambridge: Cambridge University Press.

Alberti, L. 2013. 'Middle Minoan III burial customs at Knossos: a *pianissimo intermezzo?*' In Macdonald and Knappett 2013a, *Intermezzo*, 47–55.

Alcock, S. E. 2002. *Archaeologies of the Greek Past: Landscape, Monuments and Memories.* Cambridge: Cambridge University Press.

Alcock, S. E., Cherry, J. F. and Elsner, J. (eds), 2001. *Pausanias: Travel and Memory in Roman Greece.* Oxford and New York: Oxford University Press, 207–23.

Alexiou, S. 1958a. Ὁ δακτύλιος τῆς Ὀξφόρδης. In E. Grumach (ed.), *Minoica: Festschrift zum 80 Geburtstag von Johannes Sundwall,* 1–5. Berlin: Akademie Verlag.

Alexiou, S. 1958b. Ἡ μινωϊκὴ θεὰ μεθ' υψωμένων χειρῶν. *Kretika Chronika* 12: 179–299.

Anderson, G. 2009. 'The personality of the Greek state'. *JHS* 129: 1–22.

Anderson, G. 2018. *The Realness of Things Past: Ancient Greece and Ontological History.* Oxford: Oxford University Press.

Antoniadis, V. 2017. *Knossos and the Near East: A Contextual Approach to Imports and Imitations in Early Iron Age Tombs.* Oxford: Archaeopress.

Antoniadis, V. 2021. 'Heirloom or antique? Import or imitation? Objects with fictive "biographies" in Early Iron Age Knossos'. *Tekmeria* 15: 73–107. doi: https://doi.org/10.12681/tekmeria.26161.

Archi, A. 2015. *Ebla and Its Archives: Text, History and Society* (Studies in Ancient Near Eastern Records 7). Berlin and Boston: De Gruyter.

Ariès, P. 1982. *The Hour of our Death.* Translated from the French by Helen Weaver. New York: Vintage.

Badal, E. and Ntinou, M. 2013. 'Wood charcoal analysis: the local vegetation'. In Efstratiou et al. 2013, *Neolithic Knossos,* 95–118.

Baldwin Bowsky, M. W. 2006. 'From capital to colony: five new inscriptions from Roman Crete'. *BSA* 101: 385–426.

Baldwin Bowsky, M. W. 2012. 'Four inscriptions from Greater Knossos and the road to its port at Heraklion (Crete)'. *BSA* 107: 313–39.

Bar-Gal, G. K., Smith, P., Tchernov, E., Greenblatt, C., Ducos, P., Gardeisen, A. and Horwitz, L. K. 2002. 'Genetic evidence for the origin of the agrimi goat (*Capra aegagrus cretica*)'. *Journal of the Zoological Society of London* 256: 369–77.

Barrett, J. C. and Halstead, P. (eds), 2004. *The Emergence of Civilisation Revisited* (Sheffield Studies in Aegean Archaeology 6). Oxford: Oxbow.

Bažant, J. 1992. 'Minos'. *Lexikon Iconographicum Mythologiae Classicae* VI, 1. Munich and Zürich: Artemis, 570–4.

Beaton, R. 2019. *Greece: Biography of a Modern Nation.* London: Penguin.

Beazley, J. D. 1947. *Etruscan Vase Painting.* Oxford: Clarendon.

Beazley, J. D. 1956. *Attic Black-Figure Vase-Painters.* Oxford: Clarendon.

Beazley, J. D. 1963. *Attic Red-Figure Vase-Painters,* 2nd edition. Oxford: Clarendon.

Beazley, J. D. 1986. *The Development of Attic Black Figure,* revised edition. Edited by D. von Bothmer and M. B. Moore. Berkeley and Los Angeles: University of California Press.

Beevor, A. 1991. *Crete: The Battle and the Resistance.* London: John Murray.

Bibliography

Bennet, J. 1985. 'The structure of the Linear B administration at Knossos'. *AJA* 86: 231–49.

Bennet, J. 1987a. 'Knossos and LM III Crete: A post-palatial palace?' In Marinatos and Hägg 1987, *Function of Palaces*, 307–12.

Bennet, J. 1987b. 'The Wild Country East of Dikte: The Problem of East Crete in the LMIII Period'. *Minos* 20–22: 77–88.

Bennet, J. 1990. 'Knossos in context: comparative perspectives on the Linear B administration of LMII–IIIA Crete'. *AJA* 94: 193–212.

Bennet, J. 1992. '"Collectors" or "owners"? An examination of their possible functions within the palatial economy of LMIII Crete'. In J. P. Olivier (ed.), *Mykenaïka: Actes du IXe Colloque international sur les textes mycéniens et égéens organisé par le Centre de l'Antiquité Grecque et Romaine de la Fondation Hellénique des Recherches Scientifiques et l'École française d'Athènes (Athènes 2–6 octobre 1990)* (*BCH* Suppl. XXV), 65–101. Paris: De Boccard.

Benton, S. 1937. 'Herakles and Eurystheus at Knossos'. *JHS* 57, no. 1: 38–43.

Berent, M. 2000. 'Anthropology and the Classics: War, violence and the stateless *polis*'. *Classical Quarterly* 50: 257–89.

Betancourt, P. B. 2006. *The Chrysokamino Metallurgy Workshop and its Territory* (*Hesperia* Suppl. 36). Princeton, NJ: American School of Classical Studies at Athens.

Bevan, A. 2004. 'Emerging civilized values? The consumption and imitation of Egyptian stone vessels in EMIII–MMI Crete and its wider Eastern Mediterranean context'. In Barrett and Halstead 2004, *Emergence Revisited*, 107–26.

Blakolmer, F. 2010. 'Small is beautiful: The significance of Aegean glyptic for the study of wall paintings, relief frescoes and minor relief arts'. In Müller 2010, *Glyptik*, 91–108.

Blegen, C. W. 1966. *The Palace of Nestor at Pylos in Western Messenia, Volume I: The Buildings and Their Contents* (2 parts, text and plates). Princeton, NJ: Princeton University Press.

Bloch, M. 1971. *Placing the Dead: Tombs, Ancestral Villages and Kinship Organization in Madagascar*. London: Seminar Press.

Blok, J. 2014. 'A "covenant" between gods and men: *hiera kai hosia* and the Greek polis'. In C. Rapp and H. A. Drake (eds), *The City in the Classical and Post-Classical World: Changing Contexts of Power and Identity*, 14–37. Cambridge: Cambridge University Press.

Blok, J. 2017. *Citizenship in Classical Athens*. Cambridge: Cambridge University Press.

Boardman, J. 1960. 'Protogeometric graves at Ayios Ioannis near Knossos'. *BSA* 55: 128–48.

Boardman, J. 1961. *The Cretan Collection at Oxford: The Dictaean Cave and Iron Age Crete*. Oxford: Clarendon.

Boardman, J. 1962. 'Archaic finds at Knossos'. *BSA* 57: 28–34.

Boardman, J. 1963. 'The date of the Knossos tablets'. In Palmer and Boardman 1963, *On the Knossos Tablets*, 167–76.

Boardman, J. 1967. 'The Khaniale Tekke tombs II'. *BSA* 62: 57–75.

Boileau, M. and Whitley, J. 2010. 'Patterns of production and consumption of coarse to semi-fine pottery at Early Iron Age Knossos'. *BSA* 105: 225–68.

Boileau, M. C. and Whitley, J. 2015. 'True grit: production and exchange of cooking wares in the 9th century BC Aegean'. In M. Spataro and A. Villing (eds), *Ceramics, Cuisine and Culture: The Archaeology and Science of Kitchen Pottery in the Ancient Mediterranean*, 75–90. Oxford and Philadelphia: Oxbow.

Borchhardt, J. 1972. *Homerische Helme: Helmformen der Ägaïs in ihren Beziehungen zu orientalischen und europäischen Helmen in der Bronze- und frühen Eisenzeit* (Römisch–Germanisches Zentralmuseum Mainz). Mainz: Philipp von Zabern.

Bradley, R. 2000. *An Archaeology of Natural Places*. London and New York: Routledge.

Branigan, K. 1967. 'The Early Bronze Age daggers of Crete'. *BSA* 62: 211–39.

Branigan, K. 1968. 'A transitional phase in Minoan metallurgy'. *BSA* 63: 185–203.

Branigan, K. 1992. 'The Early Keep, Knossos: a reappraisal'. *BSA* 87: 153–63.

Branigan, K. (ed.), 1998a. *Cemetery and Society in the Aegean Bronze Age* (Sheffield Studies in Aegean Archaeology 1). Sheffield: Sheffield Academic Press.

Branigan, K. 1998b. 'The nearness to you: proximity and distance in Early Minoan funerary landscapes'. In Branigan 1998a, *Cemetery and Society*, 13–26.

Branigan, K. (ed.), 2001. *Urbanism in the Aegean Bronze Age* (Sheffield Studies in Aegean Archaeology 4). London: Sheffield Academic Press.

Brize, Ph. 1992. 'Amnisos: Die Funde: Die Adler des Zeus Thenatas'. In Schäfer, *Amnisos*, 254–73.

Brock, J. K. 1957. *Fortetsa: Early Greek Tombs near Knossos* (*BSA* Suppl. 2). Cambridge: Cambridge University Press.

Brommer, F. 1982. *Theseus: Die Taten des griechischen Helden in der antiken Kunst und Literatur*. Darmstadt: Wissenschaftliche Buchgesellschaft.

Broodbank, C. 1992. 'The Neolithic Labyrinth: social change at Knossos before the Bronze Age'. *Journal of Mediterranean Archaeology* 5: 39–75.

Broodbank, C. 2004. 'Minoanisation'. *Proceedings of the Cambridge Philological Society* 50: 46–91.

Broodbank, C. 2008. 'Long after hippos, well before palaces: A commentary on the cultures and contexts of Neolithic Crete'. In Isaakidou and Tomkins 2008, *Escaping the Labyrinth*, 273–90.

Broodbank, C. 2013. *The Making of the Middle Sea: A History of the Mediterranean from the Beginning to the Emergence of the Classical World*. London: Thames and Hudson.

Brown, A. 1983. *Arthur Evans and the Palace of Minos*. Oxford: Ashmolean Museum.

Brown, A. and Bennet, K. 2001. *Arthur Evans' Travels in Crete, 1894–99* (BAR IS 1000). Oxford: Archaeopress.

Bruins et al. 2008. 'Geoarchaeological deposits at Palaikastro (Crete) and the Late Minoan Ia eruption of Santorini'. *Journal of Archaeological Science* 35: 191–212.

Cadogan, G., Hatzaki, E. and Vasilakis, A. (eds), 2004. *Knossos: Palace, City, State: Proceedings of a Conference Organised by the British School at Athens and the 23rd Ephoreia of Prehistoric and Classical Antiquities at Heraklion in November 2000, for the Centenary of Sir Arthur Evans' Excavations at Knossos* (*BSA* Studies 12). London: British School at Athens.

Cadogan, G., Kopacka, K., Iacovou, M. and Whitley, J. (eds), 2012. *Parallel Lives: Ancient Island Societies in Crete and Cyprus* (*BSA* Studies 20). London: British School at Athens.

Callaghan, P. J. 1978. 'KRS 1976: excavations at a shrine of Glaukos at Knossos'. *BSA* 73: 1–30.

Callaghan, P. J. 1981. 'The Little Palace Well and Knossian pottery of the later third and second centuries BC'. *BSA* 76: 34–58.

Callaghan, P. J. 1992. 'Archaic to Hellenistic pottery'. In Sackett 1992a, *Greek City to Roman Colony*, 89–136.

Callaghan, P. J. 1994. 'Chapter 9: Archaic, Classical and Hellenistic Knossos – a historical summary'. In Evely et al. 1994, *Labyrinth of History*, 135–40.

Callaghan, P. J. and Jones, R. E. 1985. 'Hadra hydriae and Central Crete'. *BSA* 80: 1–17.

Cameron, M. A. S. 1968. 'Unpublished paintings from the "House of the Frescoes" at Knossos'. *BSA* 63: 1–31.

Carpenter, T. H. 1991. *Art and Myth in Ancient Greece*. London: Thames and Hudson.

Carrington Smith, J. 1994. 'A late Hellenistic wine press at Knossos'. *BSA* 89: 358–76.

Catling, E. A. and Catling, H. W. 1974. 'Sellopoulo tombs 3 and 4: The Bronzes'. *BSA* 69: 225–54.

Catling, E. A., Catling, H. W. and Smyth, D. 1979. 'Knossos 1975: Middle Minoan III and Late Minoan I houses by the Acropolis'. *BSA* 74: 1–80.

Catling, H. W. 1988. 'Archaeology in Greece, 1987–88'. *AR* 34 [1987–8]: 3–85.

Catling, H. W. 1995. 'Heroes returned? Subminoan burials from Crete'. In J. B. Carter and S. P. Morris (eds), *The Ages of Homer: A Tribute to Emily Townsend Vermeule*, 123–36. Austin: University of Texas Press.

Catling, H. W. 1996a. 'The Subminoan pottery'. In Coldstream and Catling 1996, *Knossos North Cemetery*, 295–310.

Bibliography

Catling, H. W. 1996b. 'The objects other than pottery in the Subminoan tombs'. In Coldstream and Catling 1996, *Knossos North Cemetery*, 517–42.

Catling, H. W. 1996c. 'The Dark Age and later bronzes'. In Coldstream and Catling 1996, *Knossos North Cemetery*, 543–74.

Catling, H. W. 1996d. 'The Subminoan phase in the North Cemetery at Knossos'. In Coldstream and Catling 1996, *Knossos North Cemetery*, 639–49.

Catling, H. W. and Catling, E. A. 1992. 'The lamps'. In Sackett 1992a, *Greek City to Roman Colony*, 257–322.

Catling, H. W., Catling, E. A., Callaghan, P., Smyth, D. and Spawforth, A. 1981. 'Knossos 1975: Minoan *paralipomena* and post-Minoan remains'. *BSA* 76: 83–107.

Catling, H. W. and Smyth, D. 1976. 'An early Christian osteotheke at Knossos'. *BSA* 71: 25–47.

Cavanagh, W. G. 1996. 'The burial customs'. In Coldstream and Catling 1996, *Knossos North Cemetery*, 651–75.

Cavanagh, W. G., Curtis, M., Coldstream, J. N. and Johnston, A. W. (eds), 1998. *Post-Minoan Crete: Proceedings of the First Colloquium* (*BSA* Studies 2). London: British School at Athens, 112–16.

Chadwick, J. 1967. *The Decipherment of Linear B*, 2nd edition. Cambridge: Cambridge University Press.

Chadwick, J. 1976. *The Mycenaean World*. Cambridge: Cambridge University Press.

Chaniotis, A. 1992a. 'Amnisos: Direkte und Indirikte Zeugnisse von Homer bis zur Eroberung Kretas durch die Türken'. In Schäfer 1992b, *Amnisos*, 51–73.

Chaniotis, A. 1992b. 'Die Geschichte von Amnisos von Homer bis zur Eroberung Kretas durch die Türken'. In Schäfer 1992b, *Amnisos*, 73–104.

Chaniotis, A. 1992c. 'Die Inschriften von Amnisos'. In Schäfer 1992b, *Amnisos*, 287–322.

Chaniotis, A. 1996. *Die Verträge zwischen kretischen Poleis in der hellenistischen Zeit* (Heidelberger Älthistorische Beiträge und Epigraphischen Studien 24). Stuttgart: Franz Steiner Verlag.

Chaniotis, A., Corsten, T., Papazarkadas, N. and Tybout, R. A. 2015. *Supplementum Epigraphicum Graecum LXI (2011)*. Leiden and Boston: Brill.

Chaniotis, A. (ed.), 1999. *From Minoan Farmers to Roman Traders: Sidelights on the Economy of Ancient Crete*. Stuttgart: Franz Steiner Verlag.

Chapin, A. P. and Shaw, M. C. 2006. 'The frescoes from the House of the Frescoes at Knossos: A reconsideration of their architectural context and a new reconstruction of the crocus panel'. *BSA* 101: 57–88.

Charalambidou, X. and Morgan, C. (eds), 2017. *Interpreting the Seventh Century BC: Tradition and Innovation*. Oxford: Archaeopress.

Cherry, J. 1981. 'Pattern and process in the earliest colonization of the Mediterranean islands'. *Proceedings of the Prehistoric Society* 47: 41–68.

Cherry, J. 1983. 'Evolution, revolution and the origins of complex society'. In O. Krzyszkowska and L. Nixon (eds), *Minoan Society*, 33–45. Bristol: Bristol Classical Press.

Cherry, J. 1986. 'Polities and palaces: some problems in Minoan state formation'. In C. Renfrew and J. F. Cherry (eds), *Peer Polity Interaction and Socio-Political Change*, 19–45. Cambridge: Cambridge University Press.

Cherry, J. 1990. 'The first colonization of Mediterranean islands: a review of recent research'. *Journal of Mediterranean Archaeology* 3: 158–9.

Childe, V. G. 1925. *The Dawn of European Civilisation*. London: Routledge and Kegan Paul.

Childe, V. G. 1954 (1928). *New Light on the Most Ancient East*, 4th edition (1st 1928). London: Routledge and Kegan Paul.

Childe, V. G. 1945. 'Directional change in funerary practice during 50,000 years'. *Man* 45: 13–19.

Childe, V. G. 1964. *What Happened in History*, 3rd edition. Foreword and notes by G. Clark. Harmondsworth: Penguin.

Christakis, K. S. 2005. *Cretan Bronze Age Pithoi: Traditions and Trends in the Production and Consumption of Storage Containers in Bronze Age Crete* (Prehistory Monographs 18). Philadelphia: INSTAP Academic Press.

Christakis, K. S. 2010. 'A wine offering to the Central Palace Sanctuary at Knossos: the evidence from KNZb27'. In O. Kryzyszkowska 2010, *Cretan Offerings*, 49–55.

Christakis, K. S. 2020. 'Palatial Crete: recent discoveries and research'. *AR* 66: 83–115.

Clarke, D. L. 1978. *Analytical Archaeology*, 2nd edition. London: Methuen.

Cline, E. 1999. 'The nature of economic relations of Crete with Egypt and the Near East during the Late Bronze Age'. In Chaniotis 1999, *Minoan Farmers to Roman Traders*, 115–44.

Cline, E. 2015. *1177 B.C.: The Year Civilization Collapsed*, revised edition. Princeton, NJ, and Oxford: Princeton University Press.

Clogg, R. 2009. 'Academics at war: the British School at Athens during the First World War'. In M. Llewellyn Smith, P. M. Kitromilides, and E. Calligas (eds), *Scholars, Travels, Archives: Greek History and Culture Through the British School at Athens: Proceedings of a Conference held at the National Hellenic Research Foundation, Athens, 6–7 October 2006* (*BSA* Studies 17), 163–77. London: British School at Athens.

Coldstream, J. N. 1960. 'A Geometric well at Knossos'. *BSA* 55: 159–71.

Coldstream, J. N. 1963. 'Five tombs at Knossos'. *BSA* 58: 30–43.

Coldstream, J. N. 1972. 'Knossos 1951–61: Protogeometric and Geometric pottery from the town'. *BSA* 67: 63–98.

Coldstream, J. N. 1973a. 'Knossos 1951–61: Orientalizing and Archaic pottery from the town'. *BSA* 68: 33–64.

Coldstream, J. N. 1973b. *Knossos: The Sanctuary of Demeter* (*BSA* Suppl. 8). London: Thames and Hudson.

Coldstream, J. N. 1984. 'Cypriaca and Cretocypriaca from the North Cemetery at Knossos'. *Report of the Department of Antiquities, Cyprus*, 69–91.

Coldstream, J. N. 1992. 'Early Hellenic pottery'. In Sackett 1992a, *Greek City to Roman Colony*, 67–87.

Coldstream, J. N. 1996. 'The Protogeometric and Geometric pottery'. In Coldstream and Catling 1996, *Knossos North Cemetery*, 18–420.

Coldstream, J. N. 1999. 'Knossos 1951–61: Classical and Hellenistic pottery from the town'. *BSA* 94: 321–51.

Coldstream, J. N. 2000. 'Evans's Greek finds: the early Greek town of Knossos, and its encroachment on the borders of the Minoan palace'. *BSA* 95: 259–99.

Coldstream, J. N. 2001. 'The Early Greek period: Subminoan to late Orientalising'. In Coldstream et al. 2001, *Greek Pottery Handbook*, 21–76.

Coldstream, J. N. 2002. 'Knossos: "Geometric" tombs excavated by D.G. Hogarth'. *BSA* 97: 201–16.

Coldstream, J. N., Callaghan, P. J. and Musgrave, J. H. 1981. 'Knossos: an early Greek tomb on the Lower Gypsadhes hill'. *BSA* 76: 141–65.

Coldstream, J. N. and Catling, H. W. (eds), 1996. *Knossos North Cemetery: Early Greek Tombs*. 4 volumes (*BSA* Suppl. 28). London: British School at Athens.

Coldstream, J. N. and Eiring, L. J. 2001. 'The Late Archaic and Classical periods'. In Coldstream et al. 2001, *Greek Pottery Handbook*, 77–89.

Coldstream, J. N., Eiring, L. J. and Forster, G. (eds), 2001. *Knossos Pottery Handbook: Greek and Roman* (*BSA* Studies 7). London: British School at Athens.

Coldstream, J. N. and Hatzaki, E. M. 2003. 'Knossos: early Greek occupation under the Roman villa'. *BSA* 98: 279–306.

Coldstream, J. N. and Huxley, G. L. 1999. 'Knossos: The Archaic gap'. *BSA* 94: 289–307.

Coldstream, J. N. and Macdonald, C. F. 1997. 'Knossos: area of south-west houses: Early Hellenic occupation'. *BSA* 92: 191–245.

Bibliography

Coldstream, J. N. and Sackett, L. H. 1978. 'Knossos: two deposits of Orientalizing pottery'. *BSA* 73: 45–60.

Connolly, J. 2008. 'The knapped stone technology of the first occupants at Knossos'. In Isaakidou and Tomkins 2008, *Escaping the Labyrinth*, 73–89.

Coulomb, J. 1979. 'Le "prince aux lis" de Knossos reconsideré'. *BCH* 103: 29–50

Coutsinas, N. 2013. *Défenses Crétoises: Fortifications Urbaines et Défense du Territoire en Crète aux Époques Classique et Hellénistique* (Cahiers archéologique de Paris 1, no. 3, Université de Paris 1 Panthéon-Sorbonne). Paris: Publications de la Sorbonne.

Crowley, J.C. 2010. 'The composition of complex scenes in Aegean glyptic'. In Müller 2010, *Glyptik*, 131–47.

D'Agata, A. L. 2010. 'The many lives of a ruin: history and metahistory of the Palace of Minos at Knossos'. In Kryzyszkowska 2010, *Cretan Offerings*, 57–69.

D'Agata, A. L. 2011. 'Subminoan: A neglected phase of the Cretan pottery sequence'. In W. Gauss, M. Lindblom, R. A. K. Smith and J. C. Wright (eds), *Our Cups are Full: Pottery and Society in the Aegean Bronze Age: Papers Presented to Jeremy B. Rutter on the Occasion of his 65th Birthday* (BAR IS 2227), 51–64. Oxford: Archaeopress.

D'Agata, A. L. 2012. 'The power of images: a figured krater from Thronos Kephala (ancient Sybrita) and the process of *polis* formation in Early Iron Age Crete'. *Studi Micenei ed Egeo-Anatolici* 54: 207–47.

D'Agata, A. L. and Van de Moortel, A. (eds), 2009. *Archaeologies of Cult: Essays on Ritual and Cult in Crete in Honor of Geraldine C. Gesell* (*Hesperia* Suppl. 42). Princeton, NJ: American School of Classical Studies at Athens.

Dalley, S. 1984. *Mari and Karana: Two Old Babylonian Cities*. London and New York: Longman.

Davaras, K. and Masson, O. 1983. 'Cretica: Amnisos et ses inscriptions'. *BCH* 107: 383–403.

Davis, E. N. 1987. 'The Knossos miniature frescoes and the function of central courts'. In Hägg and Marinatos 1987, *Function of Palaces*, 157–61.

Day, P. M. and Wilson, D. E. 1998. 'Consuming power: Kamares ware in protopalatial Knossos'. *Antiquity* 72: 350–8.

Day, P. M. and Wilson, D. E. 2002. 'Landscapes of memory, craft and power in pre-palatial and proto-palatial Knossos'. In Hamilakis 2002, *Labyrinth Revisited*, 143–66.

Day, P. M., Wilson, D. E. and Kiriatzi, E. 1998. 'Pots, labels and people: burying ethnicity in the cemetery at Aghia Photia, Siteia'. In Branigan 1998a, *Cemetery and Society*, 133–49.

Decorte, R. P. J. E. 2018. 'The first "European" writing: re-defining the Archanes script'. *Oxford Journal of Archaeology* 37: 341–72.

De Polignac, F. 1984. *La Naissance de la Cité Grecque: Cultes, Éspace, Société*. Paris: Éditions la Decouverte.

Desborough, V. R. d'A. 1952. *Protogeometric Pottery*. Oxford: Clarendon.

Descola, P. 2013. *Beyond Nature and Culture*. Translated from the French by Janet Lloyd. Chicago and London: Chicago University Press.

De Souza, P. 1998. 'Late Hellenistic Crete and the Roman conquest'. In Cavanagh et al. 1998, *Post-Minoan Crete*, 112–16.

Dibble, F. 2012. 'Diachronic Changes in Animal Use at Iron Age through Early Roman Knossos: Lifestyle and Economic Choices in a Changing Environment.' MSc dissertation, University of Sheffield.

Dibble, F. 2021. 'Bones around town: Taphonomic patterns from civic feasting and residential dining contexts at Late Archaic Azoria, Crete'. *Journal of Archaeological Science: Reports* 36: 102771. https://doi.org/10.1016/j.jasrep.2020.102771.

Dickinson, O. T. P. K. 1994. *The Aegean Bronze Age*. Cambridge: Cambridge University Press.

Diels, H. and Kranz, W. 1934. *Die Fragmente der Vorsokratiker (Griechisch und Deutsch): Fünfte Auflage: Erster Band*. Berlin: Weidmannsche Buchhandlung = Diels-Kranz.

Dietler, M. 1996. 'Feasts and Commensal Politics in the Political Economy: Food, Power, and Status in Prehistoric Europe'. In P. Wiessner and W. Schiefenhovel (eds), *Food and The Status Quest: An Interdisciplinary Perspective*, 87–125. Oxford and Providence, RI: Berg.

Dietler, M. 2001. 'Theorizing the feast: rituals of consumption, commensal politics and the power in African contexts'. In M. Dietler and B. Hayden (eds), *Feasts: Archaeological and Ethnographic Perspectives on Food, Politics and Power*, 65–114 (Smithsonian Series in Archaeological Enquiry). Washington, DC: Smithsonian Institute.

Driessen, J. 1990. *An Early Destruction in the Mycenaean Palace at Knossos: A New Interpretation of the Excavation Field Notes of the South-East Area of the West Wing* (Acta Archaeologica Lovaniensia Monographiae 2). Leuven: University of Leuven.

Driessen, J. 1997. 'Le palais de Cnossos au MR II–III: Combien de destructions?' In Driessen and Farnoux 1997, *La Crète Mycénienne*, 113–34.

Driessen, J. 2001a. 'History and hierarchy: preliminary observations on the settlement pattern of Minoan Crete'. In Branigan 2001, *Urbanism*, 51–71.

Driessen, J. 2001b. 'Centre and periphery: some observations on the administration of the kingdom of Knossos'. In Voutsaki and Killen 2001, *Economy and Politics in the Mycenaean Palace States*, 96–112.

Driessen, J. 2002. 'The king must die: some observations on the use of Minoan court compounds'. In Driessen et al. 2002, *Monuments of Minos*, 1–14.

Driessen, J. 2003. 'An architectural overview'. In Mountjoy 2003, *The South House*, 27–36.

Driessen, J. 2004. 'The Central Court of the Palace at Knossos'. In Cadogan et al. 2004, *Knossos: Palace, City, State*, 75–82.

Driessen, J. 2013a 'Time capsules? Destructions as archaeological phenomena'. In Driessen 2013b, *Destruction*, 9–26.

Driessen, J. (ed.), 2013b. *Destruction: Archaeological, Philological and Historical Perspectives*. Louvain-la-Neuve: Presses Universitaires de Louvain.

Driessen, J. and Farnoux, A. (eds), 1997. *La Crète Mycénienne: Actes du Table Ronde Internationale Organisée par l'École Française d'Athènes 26–28 Mars 1991* (*BCH* Suppl. 30). Paris: De Boccard.

Driessen, J. and MacDonald, C. 1984. 'Some military aspects of the Aegean in the late fifteenth and early fourteenth century B.C.' *BSA* 79: 49–74.

Driessen, J. and MacDonald, C. 1997. *The Troubled Island: Minoan Crete Before and After the Santorini Eruption* (Aegaeum 17). Liège and Austin, TX: Université de Liège/Program in Aegean Scripts and Prehistory.

Driessen, J., Schoep, I. and Laffineur, R. (eds), 2002. *Monuments of Minos: Rethinking the Minoan Palaces* (Aegaeum 23). Liège and Austin, TX: Université de Liège/Program in Aegean Scripts and Prehistory.

Eaby, M. 2011. 'Regionalism in Early Iron Age Cretan burials'. In Murphy 2011, *Prehistoric Crete*, 165–202.

Efstratiou, N. 2013. 'The stratigraphy and cultural phases'. In Efstratiou et al. 2013, *Neolithic Knossos*, 25–46.

Efstratiou, N., Karetsou, A., Banou, E. S. and Margomenou, D. 2004. 'The Neolithic settlement of Knossos: New light on an old picture'. In Cadogan et al. 2004, *Knossos: Palace, City, State*, 39–49.

Efstratiou, N., Karetsou, A. and Ntinou, M. 2013. *The Neolithic Settlement of Knossos in Crete: New Evidence for the Early Occupation of Crete and the Aegean Islands* (INSTAP Prehistory Monographs 42). Philadelphia: INSTAP Academic Press.

Ehrenberg, V. 1937. 'When did the polis rise?' *JHS* 57: 147–59.

Eiring, J. L. 2001. 'The Hellenistic period'. In Coldstream et al. 2001, *Greek Pottery Handbook*, 90–135.

Bibliography

Eiring, J. 2004. 'The "Knossos Hunt" and wild goats in Ancient Crete'. In Cadogan et al. 2004, *Knossos: Palace, City, State*, 443–50.

Englezou, M. 2005. *Ελληνιστική Κεραμεική Κρήτης: Κεντρική Κρήτη /Ellenistiki Kerameiki Kritis: Kentriki Kriti* (Supplement to Archaiologikon Deltion 89). Athens: Tameio Archaiologikon Poron kai Apallotrioseon.

Erickson, B. L. 2010. *Crete in Transition: Pottery Styles and Island History in the Archaic and Classical Periods* (*Hesperia* Suppl. 45). Princeton, NJ: American School of Classical Studies at Athens.

Erickson, B. 2014. 'Mind the gap: Knossos and Cretan archaeology of the 6th century'. In Pilz and Seelentag 2014, *Cultural Practices*, 67–90.

España-Chamorro, S. 2021. 'The *Procurator Campaniae* and the "lands of Capua" on Crete'. *BSA* 116: 377–97.

Evans, A. J. 1890. 'On a late Celtic Urn-Field at Aylesford, Kent, and on the Gaulish, Illyro-Italic and Classical connexions of the forms of pottery and bronze-work there discovered'. *Archaeologia* 52, no. 2: 315–88.

Evans, A. J. 1894. 'Primitive pictographs and a prae-phoenician script from Crete and the Peloponnese'. *JHS* 14: 270–380.

Evans, A. J. 1897. 'Further discoveries of Cretan and Aegean scripts with Libyan and Proto-Egyptian comparisons'. *JHS* 17: 327–95.

Evans, A. J. 1900. 'Knossos: summary report of the excavations in 1900 I: the palace'. *BSA* 6: 3–70.

Evans, A. J. 1901a. 'The palace of Knossos: provisional report of the excavations for the year 1901'. *BSA* 7: 1–120.

Evans, A. J. 1901b. 'Mycenaean tree and pillar cult and its Mediterranean relations'. *JHS* 21: 99–204.

Evans, A. J. 1901c. 'The Neolithic settlement of Knossos and its place in the history of early Aegean culture'. *Man: Journal of the Royal Anthropological Institute* 1: 184–6.

Evans, A. J. 1902. 'The palace of Knossos: provisional report for the year 1902'. *BSA* 8: 1–124.

Evans, A. J. 1903. 'The palace of Knossos: provisional report for the year 1903'. *BSA* 9: 1–153.

Evans, A. J. 1904. 'The palace of Knossos'. *BSA* 10: 1–63.

Evans, A. J. 1905a. 'The palace of Knossos and its dependencies'. *BSA* 11: 1–26.

Evans, A. J. 1905b. 'The prehistoric tombs of Knossos'. *Archaeologia* 59: 391–562.

Evans, A. J. 1906. *Essai de Classification des Époques de la Civilisation Minoenne*. London: B. Quaritch.

Evans, A. J. 1909. *Scripta Minoa: The Written Documents of Minoan Crete with Special Reference to the Archives of Knossos, Volume I: The Hieroglyphic and Primitive Linear Classes*. Oxford: Clarendon.

Evans, A. J. 1912. 'The Minoan and Mycenaean element in Hellenic life'. *JHS* 32: 277–97.

Evans, A. J. 1914. 'The "Tomb of the Double Axes", and associated group, and the pillar rooms and ritual vessels of the Little Palace at Knossos'. *Archaeologia* 65 [1913–14]: 1–94.

Evans, A. J. 1921. *The Palace of Minos: A Comparative Account of the Successive Stages of the Early Cretan Civilization as Illustrated by the Discoveries at Knossos, Volume I: The Neolithic and Early and Middle Minoan Age*. London: Macmillan.

Evans, A. J. 1928a. *The Palace of Minos: A Comparative Account of the Successive Stages of the Early Cretan Civilization as Illustrated by the Discoveries at Knossos, Volume II.1*. London: Macmillan.

Evans, A. J. 1928b. *The Palace of Minos: A Comparative Account of the Successive Stages of the Early Cretan Civilization as Illustrated by the Discoveries at Knossos, Volume II.2*. London: Macmillan.

Evans, A. J. 1930. *The Palace of Minos: A Comparative Account of the Successive Stages of the Early Cretan Civilization as Illustrated by the Discoveries at Knossos, Volume III*. London: Macmillan.

Evans, A. J. 1935a. *The Palace of Minos: A Comparative Account of the Successive Stages of the Early Cretan Civilization as Illustrated by the Discoveries at Knossos, Volume IV.1*. London: Macmillan.

Evans, A. J. 1935b. *The Palace of Minos: A Comparative Account of the Successive Stages of the Early Cretan Civilization as Illustrated by the Discoveries at Knossos, Volume IV.2*. London: Macmillan.

Evans, A. J. 1952. *Scripta Minoa: The Written Documents of Minoan Crete with Special Reference to the Archives of Knossos, Volume II: The Archives of Knossos: Clay Tablets Inscribed with Linear Script B* (edited from notes and supplemented by J. L. Myres). Oxford: Clarendon.

Evans, J. D. 1964. 'Excavations in the Neolithic settlement of Knossos, 1957–60. Part I'. *BSA* 59: 132–240.

Evans, J. D. 1971. 'Neolithic Knossos: the growth of a settlement'. *Proceedings of the Prehistoric Society* 37, no. 2: 95–117.

Evans, J. D. 1972. 'The Early Minoan occupation of Knossos: a note on some new evidence'. *Anatolian Studies* 22: 115–28.

Evans, J. D. 1994. 'The early millennia: continuity and change in a farming settlement'. In D. Evely, H. Hughes-Brock and N. Momigliano (eds), *Knossos: A Labyrinth of History: Papers Presented in Honour of Sinclair Hood*, 1–19. London: British School at Athens.

Evely, D. 1988. 'Clay tobacco pipes from the University of Crete medical faculty'. *BSA* 83: 135–42.

Evely, D., Hughes-Brock, H. and Momigliano, N. (eds), 1994. *Knossos: A Labyrinth of History: Papers in Honour of Sinclair Hood*. Oxford: British School at Athens/Oxbow.

Fabricius, F. 1886. 'Alterthümer auf Kreta IV: Funde der mykenaïschen Epoche in Knossos'. *Mitteilungen des deutschen archäologischen Instituts, athenische Abteilung* 11: 135–49.

Facorellis, Y and Maniatis, Y. 2013. 'Radiocarbon dates from the Neolithic settlement at Knossos: an overview'. In Efstratiou et al. 2013, *Neolithic Knossos*, 193–200.

Farnoux, A. 1996. *Knossos: Unearthing a Legend*. Translated from the French by Harry N. Abrams. London: Thames and Hudson.

Ferrara, S., Montecchi, B. and Valério, M. 2021. 'What is the "Archanes Formula"? Deconstructing and reconstructing the earliest attestations of writing in the Aegean'. *BSA* 116: 43–62.

Fitton, J. L. 1995. *The Discovery of the Greek Bronze Age*. London: British Museum Press.

Flannery, K. and Marcus, J. 2012. *The Creation of Inequality: How our Prehistoric Ancestors Set the Stage for Monarchy, Slavery and Empire*. Cambridge, MA: Harvard University Press.

Flouda, G. 2017. 'Archaeology in the war zone: August Schörgendorfer and the *Kunstschutz* on Crete during World War II'. *BSA* 112: 341–77.

Forsdyke, E. J. 1927. 'The Mavro Spelio cemetery at Knossos'. *BSA* 28: 243–96.

Forster, G. 2001. 'The Roman period'. In Coldstream et al., *Greek Pottery Handbook*, 137–67.

Forster, G. 2004. 'Shadow of a city? A review of Late Roman Knossos'. In Cadogan et al. 2004, *Knossos: Palace, City, State*, 489–91.

Fowler, C. 2004. *The Archaeology of Personhood: An Anthropological Approach*. London and New York: Routledge.

Furtwängler, A. 1900a. *Die Antiken Gemmen: Geschichte der Steinschneidekunst im klassischen Altertum: Erster Band: Tafeln*. Leipzig and Berlin: Giesecke & Devrient.

Furtwängler, A. 1900b. *Die Antiken Gemmen: Geschichte der Steinschneidekunst im klassischen Altertum: Zweiter Band: Beschreibung und Erklärung def Tafeln*. Leipzig and Berlin: Giesecke & Devrient.

Furtwängler, A. 1900c. *Die Antiken Gemmen: Geschichte der Steinschneidekunst im klassischen Altertum: Dritte Band*. Leipzig and Berlin: Giesecke & Devrient.

Gagarin, M. and Perlman, P. 2016. *The Laws of Ancient Crete 650–400 BCE*. Oxford: Oxford University Press.

Gaignerot-Driessen, F. 2013. 'The "killing" of a city: destruction by enforced abandonment'. In Driessen 2013b, *Destruction*, 285–97.

Bibliography

Gaignerot-Driessen, F. 2014. 'Goddesses refusing to appear? Reconsidering the Late Minoan III figures with upraised arms'. *AJA* 118: 489–520.

Gaignerot-Driessen, F. and Driessen, J. (eds), 2014. *Cretan Cities: Formation and Transformation* (Aegis 7). Louvain: Presses Universitaires de Louvain.

Gainsford, P. 2012. 'Diktys of Crete'. *Cambridge Classical Journal* 58: 58–87.

Galanakis, Y. 2013. *The Aegean World: A Guide to the Cycladic, Minoan and Mycenaean Antiquities in the Ashmolean Museum*. Athens and Oxford: Kapon.

Galanakis, Y., Tsitsa, E. and Günkel-Maschek, U. 2017. 'The power of images: re-examining the wall paintings from the Throne Room at Knossos'. *BSA* 112: 47–98.

Galanidou, N. and Manteli, K. 2008. 'Neolithic Katsambas revisited'. In Isaakidou and Tomkins 2008, *Escaping the Labyrinth*, 165–76.

Geertz, C. 1980. *Negara: The Theatre State in Nineteenth-Century Bali*. Princeton, NJ: Princeton University Press.

Gehrke, H. J. 2009. 'States'. In K. A. Raaflaub and H. van Wees (eds), *A Companion to Archaic Greece* (Blackwell Companions to the Ancient World), 395–410. Malden, MA, Oxford and Chichester: Wiley-Blackwell.

Gill, M. A. V. 2002. 'The find-spots of the sealings'. In Platon et al. 2002a, *CMS* II 8, no. 1, 101–36.

Godart, L. and Olivier, J. P. 1976a. *Recueil des Inscriptions en Linéaire A, Volume 1: Tablettes Éditées avant 1970* (Études Crétoises XXI, 1). Paris: École Française d'Athènes.

Godart, L. and Olivier, J. P. 1976b. *Recueil des Inscriptions en Linéaire A, Volume 3: Tablettes, Nodules et Rondelles Édités en 1975 et 1976* (Études Crétoises XXI, 3). Paris: École Française d'Athènes.

Godart, L. and Olivier, J. P. 1979. *Recueil des Inscriptions en Linéaire A, Volume 2: Nodules, Scellés et Rondelles Édités avant 1970* (Études Crétoises XXI, 2). Paris: École Française d'Athènes.

Goodison, L. 2004. 'From tholos tomb to throne room: some considerations of dawn light and directionality in Minoan buildings'. In Cadogan et al. 2004, *Knossos: Palace, City, State*, 339–50.

Goodison, L. 2009. '"Why all this about oak and stone?" Trees and boulders in Minoan religion'. In D'Agata and Van de Moortel 2009, *Archaeologies of Cult*, 51–7.

Graeber, D. and Wengrow, D. 2021. *The Dawn of Everything: A New History of Humanity*. London: Allen Lane.

Graham, J. W. 1987. *The Palaces of Crete*, revised edition. Princeton, NJ: Princeton University Press.

Grammatikaki, E. 2004. 'Ταφικά μνημεία Κνωσού'. In Cadogan et al. 2004, *Knossos: Palace, City, State*, 465–72.

Grote, G. 1849a. *History of Greece: Legendary Greece, Volume I*, 2nd edition. London: John Murray.

Grote, G. 1849b. *History of Greece: Legendary Greece – Grecian History to the Reign of Peisistratus of Athens, Volume II*, 2nd edition. London: John Murray.

Grundon, I. 2007. *The Rash Adventurer: A Life of John Pendlebury*. London: Libri.

Guarducci, M. 1935. *Inscriptiones Creticae Opera et Consilio Friderici Halbherr Collectae I: Tituli Cretae Mediae Praeter Gortynios*. Rome: Libreria dello Stato = *IC* I.

Guarducci, M. 1950. *Inscriptiones Creticae Opera et Consilio Frederici Halbherr Collectae IV: Tituli Gortynii*. Rome: Librería dello Stato = *IC* IV.

Hägg, R. and Marinatos, N. (eds), 1987. *The Function of the Minoan Palaces: Proceedings of the Fourth International Symposium at the Swedish Institute in Athens, 10–16 June 1984*. Stockholm: Paul Åströms Förlag.

Haggis, D. C. 2002. 'Integration and complexity in the late pre-palatial period: A view from the countryside in Eastern Crete'. In Hamilakis 2002, *Labyrinth Revisited*, 120–42.

Haggis, D. C. 2014. 'Azoria and Archaic urbanization'. In F. Gaignerot-Driessen and J. Driessen (eds), *Cretan Cities: Formation and Transformation* (Aegis 7), 12–39. Louvain: Presses Universitaires de Louvain.

Hall, J. M. 1997. *Ethnic Identity in Greek Antiquity*. Cambridge: Cambridge University Press.

Hall, J. M. 2002. *Hellenicity: Between Ethnicity and Culture*. Chicago: University of Chicago Press.

Hallager, E. 1987. 'A "harvest festival room" in the Minoan palaces? An architectural study of the Pillar Crypt area at Knossos'. In Hägg and Marinatos 1987, *Function of Palaces*, 169–77.

Hallager, E. 1996. *The Minoan Roundel and Other Sealed Documents of the Neopalatial Linear A Administration, Volume II: Catalogue, Lists, Concordance* (Aegaeum 14). Liège: Université de Liège.

Hallager, E. 1997a. 'New Linear B tablets from Khania'. In Driessen and Farnoux 1997, *La Crète Mycénienne*, 169–74.

Hallager, E. 1997b. 'Architecture of the LMII/III settlement in Chania'. In Driessen and Farnoux 1997, *La Crète Mycénienne*, 113–34.

Halstead, P. 1989. 'The economy has a normal surplus'. In P. Halstead and J. O'Shea (eds), *Bad Year Economics*, 68–80. Cambridge: Cambridge University Press.

Halstead, P. 1993. 'The Mycenaean palatial economy: making the most of the gaps in the evidence'. *Proceedings of the Cambridge Philological Society* 38: 57–86.

Halstead, P. 2001. 'Mycenaean wheat, flax and sheep: palatial intervention in farming and its implications for rural society'. In Voutsaki and Killen 2001, *Economy and Politics in the Mycenaean Palace States*, 38–50.

Halstead, P. 2008. 'Between a rock and a hard place: coping with marginal colonization in the later Neolithic and Early Bronze Age of Crete and the Aegean'. In Isaakidou and Tomkins 2008, *Escaping the Labyrinth*, 229–57.

Hamilakis, Y. 1998. 'Eating the dead: mortuary feasting and the politics of memory in the Aegean Bronze Age societies'. In Branigan 1998a, *Cemetery and Society*, 115–32.

Hamilakis, Y. 2007. *The Nation and Its Ruins: Antiquity, Archaeology, and National Imagination in Greece*. Oxford: Oxford University Press.

Hamilakis, Y. (ed.), 2002. *Labyrinth Revisited: Rethinking 'Minoan' Archaeology*. Oxford: Oxbow.

Hamilakis, Y. and Momigliano, N. (eds), 2006. *Archaeology and European Modernity: Producing and Consuming the 'Minoans'* (Creta Antica 7). Padua: Bottega d'Erasmo.

Hansen, M. H. and Nielsen, T. H. (eds), 2004. *An Inventory of Archaic and Classical Poleis: An Investigation Conducted by the Copenhagen Polis Centre for the Danish National Research Foundation*. Oxford: Oxford University Press.

Härke, H. 1990. '"Warrior graves"? The background to the Anglo-Saxon weapon burial ritual'. *Past and Present* 126: 22–43.

Hartley, M. 1931. 'Early Greek vases from Crete'. *BSA* 31: 56–114.

Hassoullier, B. 1880. 'Vases peints archaiques découverts à Knossos (Crète)'. *BCH* 4: 124–7.

Hatzaki, E. 2005. *Knossos: The Little Palace* (*BSA* Suppl. 38). London: British School at Athens.

Hatzaki, E. 2007a. 'Chapter 5: Neopalatial (MMIIIB–LMIB): KS 178, Gypsades Well (Upper Deposit) and SEX North House groups'. In Momgliano 2007b, *Minoan Pottery Handbook*, 151–96.

Hatzaki, E. 2007b. 'Chapter 6: Final palatial (LMII–LMIIIA2) and Postpalatial (LMIIIB– LMIIIC Early): the MUM South Sector, Long Corridor Cists, MUM pits, Makritikhos "Kitchen", MUM North Platform pits and SEX Southern half groups'. In Momigliano 2007b, *Minoan Pottery Handbook*, 197–251.

Hatzaki, E. 2009. 'Structured deposition and ritual action at Knossos'. In D'Agata and Van de Moortel 2009, *Archaeologies of Cult*, 19–30.

Hatzaki, E. 2013. 'The end of an *intermezzo* at Knossos: ceramic wares, deposits and architecture in a social context'. In Macdonald and Knappett 2013a, *Intermezzo*, 37–45.

Hatzaki, E. M., Prent, M., Coldstream, J. N., Evely, D. E. and Livarda, A. 2008. 'Knossos: The Little Palace North Project part 1: the Early Greek periods'. *BSA* 103: 223–73.

Hatzimichael, C. and Whitley, J. 2012. 'Differential complexities: political evolution, devolution and re-evolution in Crete 3000–300 BC'. In Cadogan et al. 2012, *Parallel Lives*, 331–43.

Hawkes, J. 1968. *Dawn of the Gods*. London: Chatto and Windus.

Hayes, J. W. 1971. 'Four Early Roman Groups from Knossos'. *BSA* 66: 249–76.

Hayes, J. W. 1983. 'The Villa Dionysos excavations, Knossos: The pottery'. *BSA* 79: 97–169.

Hayes, J. W. 2001. 'The early Christian pottery from Knossos: the 1978–81 finds from the Knossos Medical Faculty site'. *BSA* 96: 431–54.

Haysom, M. 2010. 'The double axe: a contextual approach to the understanding of a Cretan symbol in the neopalatial period'. *Oxford Journal of Archaeology* 29: 35–55.

Haysom, M. 2011. 'Fish and ships: neopalatial seascapes in context'. In G. Vavouranakis (ed.), *The Seascape in Aegean Prehistory* (Monographs of the Danish Institute in Athens 14), 77–98. Aarhus: Aarhus University Press.

Haysom, M. 2018a. 'The find contexts of Knossian relief wall paintings: some ramifications'. In J. Becker, J. Jungfleisch and C. von Rüden (eds), *Tracing Technoscapes: The Production of Bronze Age Wall Paintings in the Eastern Mediterranean*, 253–78. Leiden: Sidestone Press.

Haysom, M. 2018b. 'Mass and elite in Minoan peak sanctuaries'. In G. Vavouranakis, K. Kopanias and Chr. Kanellopoulos (eds), *Popular Religion and Ritual in Prehistoric and Ancient Greece and the Eastern Mediterranean*, 19–28. Oxford: Archaeopress.

Helck, W. 1992. 'Amnisos in einem ägyptischen Text'. In Schäfer 1992b, *Amnisos*, 13–18.

Herrero, B. L. 2009. 'The Minoan fallacy: cultural diversity and mortuary behaviour on Crete at the beginning of the Bronze Age'. *Oxford Journal of Archaeology* 28: 29–57.

Herrero, B. L. 2011. 'The secret lives of the Early and Middle Minoan tholos cemeteries: Koumasa and Platanos'. In Murphy 2011a, *Prehistoric Crete*, 49–84.

Herrero, B. L. 2014. *Mortuary Behavior and Social Trajectories in Pre- and Protopalatial Crete* (Prehistory Monographs 44). Philadelphia: INSTAP Academic Press.

Herrero, B. L. 2016. 'Bones in a pickle: burial jars, individualism and group identities in Middle Minoan Crete'. In Mina et al. 2016, *Embodied Identities*, 180–8.

Higgins, R. A. 1973. 'The terracottas'. In Coldstream 1973b, *Sanctuary of Demeter*, 56–92.

Hiller, S. 1992. 'Amnisos in der Tontafelarchiven von Knosos'. In Schäfer 1992b, *Amnisos*, 18–50.

Hodder, I. 2006. *Çatalhöyük: The Leopard's Tale – Revealing the Mysteries of Turkey's Ancient Town*. London: Thames and Hudson.

Hoeck, K. 1823. *Kreta: Ein Versuch zur Aufhellung der Mythologie und Geschichte, der Religion und Verfassung dieser Insel, von der ältesten Zeiten bis auf der Römer-Herrschaft: Erster Band*. Göttingen: Carl Eduard Rosenbusch.

Hoeck, K. 1828a. *Kreta: Ein Versuch zur Aufhellung der Mythologie und Geschichte, der Religion und Verfassung dieser Insel, von der ältesten Zeiten bis auf der Römer-Herrschaft: Zweiter Band: Das Minoische Kreta*. Göttingen: Carl Eduard Rosenbusch.

Hoeck, K. 1828b. *Kreta: Ein Versuch zur Aufhellung der Mythologie und Geschichte, der Religion und Verfassung dieser Insel, von der ältesten Zeiten bis auf der Römer-Herrschaft: Dritte Band: das Dorische Kreta*. Göttingen: Carl Eduard Rosenbusch.

Hogarth, D. G. 1900. 'Knossos: summary report of the excavations in 1900 II: Early town and cemeteries'. *BSA* 6: 70–85.

Hondius, J. J. E., Klaffenbach, G., Robert, L. and Tod, M. N. 1938. *Supplementum Epigraphicum Graecum IX Fasc. 1*. Leiden: A.W. Sijthoff = *SEG* 9.1.

Hood, M. S. F. 1987. 'An early British interest in Knossos'. *BSA* 82: 85–94.

Hood, S. 2005. 'Dating the Knossos frescoes'. In Morgan 2005, *Aegean Wall Painting*, 45–81.

Hood, S. 2010. 'The Middle Minoan cemetery on Ailias at Knossos'. In Kryzyszkowska 2010, *Cretan Offerings*, 160–8.

Hood, M. S. F. and Bendall, L. M. 2020. *The Masons' Marks of Minoan Knossos* (*BSA* Suppl. 49). London: British School at Athens.

Hood, M. S. F. and Boardman, J. 1957. 'A Hellenic fortification tower on the Kefala ridge at Knossos'. *BSA* 52: 224–30.

Hood, M. S. F. and Boardman, J. 1961. 'Early Iron Age tombs at Knossos'. *BSA* 56: 68–80.

Hood, S. and Cadogan, G. 2011. *Knossos Excavations 1957–1961: Early Minoan* (*BSA* Suppl. 46). London: British School at Athens.

Hood, S. and Coldstream, J. N. 1968. 'A late Minoan tomb at Ayios Ioannis near Knossos'. *BSA* 63: 205–18.

Hood, M. S. F., Huxley, G. and Sandars, N. K. 1959. 'A Minoan cemetery on Upper Gypsadhes'. *BSA* 53–4: 194–262.

Hood, M. S. F. and Smyth, D. 1981. *Archaeological Survey of the Knossos Area* (*BSA* Suppl. 14). London: Thames and Hudson.

Hood, M. S. F. and Taylor, W. 1981. *The Bronze Age Palace at Knossos: Plan and Sections* (*BSA* Suppl. 13). London: British School at Athens.

Horwitz, L. K. and Bar-Gal, G. K. 2006. 'The Origin and Genetic Status of Insular Caprines in the Eastern Mediterranean: A Case Study of Free-Ranging Goats (*Capra aegagrus cretica*) on Crete'. *Human Evolution* 21: 123–38.

Hughes-Brock, H. and Boardman, J. 2009a. *Corpus der minoischen und mykenischen Siegel VI: Oxford: The Ashmolean Museum: Part 1*. Mainz: Philipp von Zabern = *CMS* VI, 1.

Hughes-Brock, H. and Boardman, J. 2009b. *Corpus der minoischen und mykenischen Siegel VI: Oxford: The Ashmolean Museum: Part 2*. Mainz: Philipp von Zabern = *CMS* VI: 2.

Hutchinson, R. W. 1956. 'A tholos tomb on the Kephala'. *BSA* 51: 74–80.

Hutchinson, R. W. and Boardman, J. 1954. 'The Khaniale Tekke tombs'. *BSA* 49: 215–28.

Huxley, D. (ed.), 2000. *Cretan Quests: British Explorers, Excavators and Historians*. London: British School at Athens.

Huxley, G. 1994. 'Chapter 8: On Knossos and her neighbours (7th to mid–4th century BC)'. In Evely et al. 1994, *Labyrinth of History*, 123–33.

Isaakidou, V. 2007. 'Bioarchaeological analysis'. In Macdonald and Knappett 2007, *Protopalatial Deposits*, 139–43.

Isaakidou, V. 2008. 'The fauna and economy of Neolithic Knossos revisited'. In Isaakidou and Tomkins 2008, *Escaping the Labyrinth*, 90–114.

Isaakidou, V. and Tomkins, P. (eds), 2008. *Escaping the Labyrinth: New Perspectives on the Neolithic of Crete* (Sheffield Studies in Aegean Archaeology 8). Oxford: Oxbow.

Jackson, A. 1973. 'The coins'. In Coldstream 1973b, *Sanctuary of Demeter*, 99–113.

Jacoby, F. 1950. *Die Fragmente der Griechischen Historiker: Dritter Teil: Geschichte von Staedten und Voelkern (Horographie und Ethnographie): B Autoren ueber einzelne Staedte (Laender) Nr 297–607*. Leiden: E.J. Brill = *FrGrHist* III B, 297–607.

Janko, R. 2015. 'From Gabii and Gordion to Eretria and Methone: the rise of the Greek alphabet'. *Bulletin of the Institute of Classical Studies* 58, no. 1: 1–32.

Jarman, M. R. 1973. 'Preliminary report on the animal bones'. In Coldstream 1973b, *Sanctuary of Demeter*, 177–9.

Jeffery, L. H. 1990. *The Local Scripts of Archaic Greece*, 2 volumes. Revised by A. Johnston. Oxford Monographs in Classical Archaeology. Oxford: Clarendon.

Jeffery, L. H. and Morpurgo-Davies, A. 1970. 'ΠΟΙΝΙΚΑΣΤΑΣ and ΠΟΙΝΙΚΑΖΕΝ: BM 1969.42.1: A New Archaic Inscription from Crete'. *Kadmos* 9: 118–54.

Johnston, A. W. 1996. 'The graffito on the aryballos 107.84: a note'. In Coldstream and Catling 1996, *Knossos North Cemetery*, 463–4.

Johnston, A. W. 2013. 'Writing in and around Archaic Crete'. In Niemeier et al., *Kreta in der geometrischen und archaischen Zeit*, 427–36.

Johnston, A. W. 2017. 'Chapter 32: Frontiers in seventh-century epigraphy: aspects of diffusion and consolidation'. In Charalambidou and Morgan 2017, *Seventh Century*, 375–81.

Jones, G. 1978. 'Appendix: Bone report (KRS 1976: Excavations at a Shrine of Glaukos, Knossos)'. *BSA* 73: 29–30.

Jones, R. E. and Photos Jones, E. 2005. 'Technical studies of Aegean Bronze Age wall painting: methods, results and future prospects'. In Morgan 2005, *Aegean Wall Painting*, 199–228.

Bibliography

Karadimas, N. and Momigliano, N. 2004. 'On the term "Minoan" before Evans' work in Crete'. *Studi Micenei ed Egeo Anatolici* 46, no. 2: 243–58.

Karetsou, A. 2004. 'Knossos after Evans: past interventions, present state and future solutions'. In Cadogan et al. 2004, *Knossos: Palace, City, State*, 547–55.

Karkanas, P. 2021. 'Destruction, abandonment, reoccupation: what microstratigraphy and micromorphology tell us'. In S. Fachard and E. M. Harris (eds), *The Destruction of Cities in the Ancient Greek World*, 34–49. Cambridge: Cambridge University Press.

Kelly, A. 2012. 'The Cretan slinger at war – a weighty exchange'. *BSA* 107: 273–311.

Killen, J. T. 1964. 'The wool industry of Crete in the Late Bronze Age'. *BSA* 59: 1–15.

Knappett, C. 1999. 'Tradition and innovation in pottery forming technology: wheel throwing at Middle Minoan Knossos'. *BSA* 94: 101–30.

Knappett, C. 2004. 'Technological innovation and social diversity at Middle Minoan Knossos'. In Cadogan et al. 2004, *Knossos: Palace, City, State*, 257–65.

Knappett, C., Mathoudiaki, I. and Macdonald, C. F. 2013. 'Stratigraphy and ceramic typology in the Middle Minoan III palace at Knossos'. In Macdonald and Knappett 2013a, *Intermezzo*, 9–19.

Kopaka, K. 1993. 'New evidence on the pottery from the early excavations at the Palace at Knossos'. *BSA* 88: 93–102.

Kopaka, K. 2004. 'Η Κνωσός πριν τον Καλοκαιρινό: μια λησμονημένη μητροπόλη των πηγών;'. In Cadogan et al. 2004, *Knossos: Palace, City, State*, 497–511.

Kotsonas, A. 2016a. 'Politics of periodization and the archaeology of Early Greece'. *AJA* 120: 239–70.

Kotsonas, A. 2016b. 'Greek and Roman Knossos: the pioneering investigations of Minos Kalokairinos'. *BSA* 111: 299–324.

Kotsonas, A. 2018a. 'A cultural history of the Cretan Labyrinth: monument and memory from prehistory to the present'. *AJA* 122: 367–96.

Kotsonas, A. 2018b. 'Homer, the archaeology of Crete, and the "Tomb of Meriones" at Knossos'. *JHS* 138: 1–35.

Kotsonas, A. 2019a. 'Politics, research agendas and abortive fieldwork plans over Lyktos, Crete: a history of archaeological research'. *BSA* 114: 399–443.

Kotsonas, A. 2019b. 'Early Iron Age Knossos and the development of the city of the historical period'. In C. Mitsotaki, L. Tzedaki-Apostolaki and S. Giannadaki (eds), *Proceedings of the 12th International Congress of Cretan Studies Heraklio 21–25.9.2016*. Heraklion: International Congress of Cretan Studies. https://12iccs.proceedings.gr/en/proceedings/category/39/35/811.

Kotsonas, A. 2022. 'Early Greek alphabetic writing: Text, context, material properties and socialization'. *AJA* 126, no. 2: 167–200.

Kryzyszkowska, O. 2005. *Aegean Seals: An Introduction* (*Bulletin of the Institute for Classical Studies* Suppl. 85). London: Institute of Classical Studies.

Kryzyszkowska, O. (ed.), 2010. *Cretan Offerings: Studies in Honour of Peter Warren* (*BSA* Studies 18). London: British School at Athens.

Kunze, E. 1931. *Kretische Bronzereliefs*. Stuttgart: W. Kohlhammer.

Lagogianni-Georgakarakos, M. 2004. 'Divus Augustus – νέα στοιχεία αυτοκρατορικής λατρείας στη ρωμαϊκή Κνωσό'. In Cadogan et al. 2004, *Knossos: Palace, City, State*, 457–63.

Lapatin, K. 2006. 'Forging the Minoan past'. In Hamilakis and Momigliano 2006, *Archaeology and European Modernity*, 89–105.

Lebessi, A. 1985. *Το Ιερό του Ερμή και της Αφροδίτης στη Σύμη Βιάννου I: Χάλκινα Κρητικά Τορεύματα*. Βιβλιοθήκη της εν Αθήναις Αρχαιολογικής Εταιρείας 102. Athens: Archaeological Society of Athens.

Lemos, I. S. 2002. *The Protogeometric Aegean: The Archaeology of the Late Eleventh and Tenth Centuries BC* (Oxford Monographs on Classical Archaeology). Oxford: Oxford University Press.

Levi, D. 1969. 'Un pithos iscritto da Festòs'. *Kretika Chronika* 21: 153–76.

Liddy, D. 1996. 'A chemical study of decorated Iron Age pottery from the Knossos North Cemetery'. In Coldstream and Catling 1996, *Knossos North Cemetery*, 465–514.

Livarda, A. 2012. 'The archaeobotanical evidence of the late Bronze Age and Protogeometric occupation under the Roman Villa Dionysus, Crete, and an overview of the Protogeometric data of Greece'. *BSA* 107: 189–209.

Loy, M. 2019. 'Early modern travellers in the Aegean: routes and networks'. *BSA* 114: 369–98.

Macdonald, C. F. 2002. 'The neopalatial palaces of Knossos'. In Driessen et al. 2002, *Monuments of Minos*, 35–54.

Macdonald, C. F. 2013. 'Between Protopalatial houses and Neopalatial mansions: an "*intermezzo*" southwest of the palace at Knossos'. In Macdonald and Knappett 2013, *Intermezzo*, 21–30.

Macdonald, C. and Driessen, J. 1988. 'The drainage system of the domestic quarter in the Palace at Knossos'. *BSA* 83: 235–56.

Macdonald, C. F. and Knappett, C. 2007. *Knossos: Protopalatial Deposits in Early Magazine A and the South West Houses (BSA* Suppl. 41). London: British School at Athens.

Macdonald, C. F. and Knappett, C. (eds), 2013a. *Intermezzo: Intermediacy and Regeneration in Middle Minoan III Palatial Crete (BSA* Studies 21). London: British School at Athens.

Macdonald, C. F. and Knappett, C. 2013b. 'Introduction'. In Macdonald and Knappett 2013a, *Intermezzo*, 1–7.

MacGillivray, J. A. 1994. 'The early history of the palace of Knossos'. In Evely et al. 1994, *Labyrinth of History*, 45–55.

MacGillivray, J. A. 1998. *Knossos: Pottery Groups from the Old Palace Period (BSA* Studies 5). London: British School at Athens.

MacGillivray, J. A. 2000. *Minotaur: Sir Arthur Evans and the Archaeology of the Minoan Myth*. London: Jonathan Cape.

MacGillivray, J. A. 2004. 'The astral labyrinth at Knossos'. In Cadogan et al. 2004, *Knossos: Palace, City, State*, 329–38.

MacGillivray, J. A. 2007. 'Protopalatial (MMIB–MMIIIA): Early chamber beneath the West Court, the trial KV, and the West and South polychrome deposit groups'. In Momigliano 2007b, *Minoan Pottery Handbook*, 105–49.

Mackenzie, D. 1903. 'The pottery of Knossos'. *JHS* 23: 157–205.

Mackenzie, D. 1906. 'The Middle Minoan pottery of Knossos'. *JHS* 26: 243–67.

Maehler, H. (ed.), 2004. *Bacchylides: A Selection* (Cambridge Greek and Latin Classics). Cambridge: Cambridge University Press.

Manning, S. W. 2018. 'Events, episodes and history: Chronology and the resolution of historical processes'. In Nevett and Whitley 2018, *An Age of Experiment*, 119–37.

Manning, S. W. et al. 2014. 'Dating the Thera (Santorini) eruption: archaeological and scientific evidence supporting a high chronology'. *Antiquity* 88: 1164–79.

Manteli, K. and Evely, D. 1995. 'The Neolithic levels from the Throne Room system, Knossos'. *BSA* 90: 1–16.

Marcus, J. 1998. 'The peaks and valleys of ancient states: An extension of the dynamic model'. In G. M. Feinman and J. Marcus (eds), *Archaic States* (School of American Research Advanced Seminar Series), 59–94. Santa Fe, NM: School of American Research Press.

Marinatos, N. 1987. 'Public festivals in the West Courts of the Palaces'. In Hägg and Marinatos 1987, *Function of Palaces*, 135–43.

Marinatos, S. 1929. 'Ἀνασκαφαὶ ἐν Κρήτῃ'. *Praktika tis en Athenais Archaiologikis Etaireias*: 94–104.

Marinatos, S. 1930. 'Ἀνασκαφαὶ ἐν Κρήτῃ'. *Praktika tis en Athenais Archaiologikis Etaireias*: 91–9.

Marinatos, S. 1932. 'Ἀνασκαφὴ Ἀμνισοῦ Κρήτης'. *Praktika tis en Athenais Archaiologikis Etaireias*: 76–94.

Bibliography

Marinatos, S. 1933. Ἀνασκαφὴ Ἀμνισοῦ Κρήτης'. *Praktika tis en Athenais Archaiologikis Etaireias*: 93–100.

Mathioudaki, I. 2018. 'The pottery deposit from the houses of the Fallen Blocks and the Sacrificed Oxen at the Southeastern corner of the Palace of Knossos'. *BSA* 113: 19–73.

Matz, F. 1951. *Forschungen auf Kreta 1942*. Berlin: Walter de Gruyter.

Mazower, M. 2000. *The Balkans: From the End of Byzantium to the Present Day*. London: Phoenix.

Mazower, M. 2021. *The Greek Revolution: 1821 and the Making of Modern Europe*. London: Allen Lane.

Michailidou, A. 1999. 'Systems of weight and social relations of "private" production in the Late Bronze Age Aegean'. In Chaniotis 1999, *Minoan Farmers to Roman Traders*, 87–113.

Mielczaruk, M. 2013. 'More on the Labyrinth on the coins of Knossos'. *Studies in Ancient Art and Civilization* (Krakow) 17: 127–36.

Mina, M. 2008. 'Figurin' out Cretan Neolithic society: anthropomorphic figurines, symbolism and gender dialectics'. In Isaakidou and Tomkins 2008, *Escaping the Labyrinth*, 115–35.

Mina, M., Triandaphyllou, S. and Papadatos, Y. (eds), 2016. *An Archaeology of Prehistoric Bodies and Embodied Identities in the Eastern Mediterranean*. Oxford: Oxbow.

Moignard, E. 1996. 'The Orientalizing pottery'. In Coldstream and Catling 1996, *Knossos North Cemetery*, 421–64.

Moignard, E. 1998. 'Native wit: some Orientalising pottery from the Knossos North Cemetery'. In Cavanagh et al. 1998, *Post-Minoan Crete*, 80–6.

Molloy, Barry P. C. 2012. 'Martial Minoans? War as social process, practice and event in Bronze Age Crete'. *BSA* 107: 87–142.

Momigliano, N. 1991. 'MMIA pottery from Evans' excavations at Knossos: a reassessment'. *BSA* 86: 149–271.

Momigliano, N. 1992. 'The "proto-palatial façade" at Knossos'. *BSA* 87: 165–75.

Momigliano, N. 1999. *Duncan Mackenzie: A Cautious, Canny Highlander and the Palace at Minos at Knossos* (*Bulletin of the Institute of Classical Studies* Suppl. 72). London: Institute of Classical Studies.

Momigliano, N. 2000. 'Knossos 1902, 1905: the prepalatial and protopalatial deposits from the Room of the Jars in the Royal Pottery Stores'. *BSA* 95: 65–105.

Momigliano, N. 2007a. 'Late prepalatial (EMIII–MMIA): South Front house foundation trench, Upper East well and House C/Royal Road South fill groups'. In Momigliano 2007b, *Minoan Pottery Handbook*, 79–103.

Momigliano, N. (ed.), 2007b. *Knossos Pottery Handbook: Neolithic and Bronze Age (Minoan)*. (*BSA* Studies 14). London: British School at Athens.

Momigliano, N. 2017. 'Introduction – desiring the Minoan past in the present'. In Momigliano and Farnoux 2017, *Cretomania*, 1–13.

Momigliano, N. 2020. *In Search of the Labyrinth: The Cultural Legacy of Minoan Crete*. London: Bloomsbury.

Momigliano, N. and Wilson, D. E. 1996. 'Knossos 1993: excavations outside of the south front of the palace'. *BSA* 91: 1–57.

Momigliano, N. and Farnoux, A. (eds), 2017. *Cretomania: Modern Desires for the Minoan Past*. (British School at Athens – Modern Greek and Byzantine Studies 3). London: Routledge.

Moody, J. 1987. 'The Minoan palace as a prestige artefact'. In Hägg and Marinatos 1987, *Function of Palaces*, 235–41.

Moody, J. 2012. 'Hinterlands and hinterseas: Resources and production zones in Bronze Age and Iron Age Crete'. In Cadogan et al. 2012, *Parallel Lives*, 233–71.

Morgan, C. 2003. *Early Greek States Beyond the Polis*. London: Routledge.

Morgan, C. 2009. 'Federico Halbherr and Knossos'. *Annuario della Scuola Archeologica di Atene e delle Missioni Italiane in Oriente* 87: 43–67.

Morgan, L (ed.), 2005. *Aegean Wall Painting: A Tribute to Mark Cameron* (*BSA* Studies 13). London: British School at Athens.

Morris, I. 1987. *Burial and Ancient Society*. Cambridge: Cambridge University Press.

Morris, I. 1989. 'Circulation, deposition and the formation of the Greek Iron Age'. *Man* (n.s.) 24: 505–19.

Morris, I. 2000. *Archaeology as Cultural History: Words and Things in Early Iron Age Greece*. Oxford: Blackwell.

Morris, S. P. 1992. *Daidalos and the Origins of Greek Art*. Princeton, NJ: Princeton University Press.

Mountjoy, P. A. 1984. 'The Marine style pottery of LMIB/LHIIA: towards a corpus'. *BSA* 79: 161–219.

Mountjoy, P. A. 2003. *Knossos: The South House* (*BSA* Suppl. 34). London: British School at Athens.

Muhly, J. D. 2006. 'Chrysokamino in the history of early metallurgy'. In Betancourt 2006, *Chrysokamino*, 155–77.

Müller, W. 2002. 'Untersuchungen zu Typologie, Funktion und Verbreitung der Tonplomben von Knossos'. In Platon et al. 2002a, *CMS* II 8, 1, 24–83.

Müller, W. (ed.), 2010. *Die Bedeutung der minoischen und mykenischen Glyptik* (*CMS* Beiheft 8). Mainz: Philipp von Zabern.

Murphy, J. M. A. 1998. 'Ideologies, rites and rituals: a view of prepalatial Minoan tholoi'. In Branigan 1998a, *Cemetery and Society*, 27–30.

Murphy, J. M. A. (ed.), 2011a. *Prehistoric Crete: Regional and Diachronic Studies on Mortuary Systems*. Philadelphia: INSTAP Academic Press.

Murphy, J. M. A. 2011b. 'Landscape and social narratives: a study of regional social structures in pre-palatial Crete'. In Murphy 2011a, *Prehistoric Crete*, 23–47.

Murray, S. C. 2017. *The Collapse of the Mycenaean Economy: Imports, Trade and Institutions 1300–700 BCE*. Cambridge: Cambridge University Press.

Murray, S. C. 2018. 'Lights and darks: data, labelling and language in the history of scholarship on Early Greece'. *Hesperia* 87: 17–54.

Musgrave, J. H. 1996. 'The human bones'. In Coldstream and Catling 1996, *Knossos North Cemetery*, 677–702.

Nagy, G. 2020. 'From song to text'. In C. O. Pache (ed.), *The Cambridge Guide to Homer*, 80–95. Cambridge and New York: Cambridge University Press.

Nevett, L. and Whitley, J. (eds), 2018. *An Age of Experiment: Classical Archaeology Transformed 1976–2014*. Cambridge: McDonald Institute, 119–37.

Niemeier, W. D. 1985. *Die Palaststilkeramik von Knossos: Stil, Chronologie und historischer Kontext*. (*Archäologischer Forschungen* 13). Berlin: Gebr. Mann.

Niemeier, W. D. 1987. 'On the function of the "Throne Room" in the palace at Knossos'. In Hägg and Marinatos 1987, *Function of Palaces*, 163–8.

Niemeier, W. D., Pilz, O. and Kaiser, I. (eds), 2013. *Kreta in der geometrischen und archaischen Zeit: Akten des Internationalen Kolloquiums am Deutschen Archäologischen Instituts, Abteilung Athen, 27–29 Januar 2006* (Athenaia 2). Munich: Hirmer Verlag.

Nordfelt, A. C. 1987. 'Residential quarters and lustral basins'. In Hägg and Marinatos 1987, *Function of Palaces*, 187–94.

Nowicki, K. 2000. *Defensible Sites in Crete c. 1200–800 B.C. (LMIIIB through Early Geometric)* (Aegaeum 21). Liege and Austin, TX: Université de Liège.

Nowicki, K. 2002. 'The end of the Neolithic in Crete'. *Aegean Archaeology* 6: 7–72.

Nowicki, K. 2008. 'The Final Neolithic (Late Chalcolithic) to Early Bronze Age transition in Crete and the Southeast Aegean islands: Changes in settlement patterns and pottery'. In Isaakidou and Tomkins 2008, *Escaping the Labyrinth*, 201–28.

Nowicki, K. 2014. *Final Neolithic Crete and the Southeast Aegean*. Berlin and Boston: de Gruyter.

Bibliography

Olivier, J. P. 1990. 'Les grandes nombres dans les archives crétoises du deuxième milléniaire'. In *Πεπραγμένα του ΣΤ' Διεθνούς Κρητολογικού Συνεδρίου*, 69–76. Chania: A2.

Olivier, J. P. and Godart, L. 1996. *Corpus Hieroglyphicarum Inscriptionum Cretae* (Études Crétoises 31). Paris: Écoles Françaises d'Athènes et de Rome.

Osborne, R. and Rhodes, P. J. 2017. *Greek Historical Inscriptions 478–404 BC*. Oxford: Oxford University Press.

Palmer, L. R. 1963. 'The find places of the Knossos tablets'. In Palmer and Boardman 1963, *On the Knossos Tablets*.

Palmer, L. R. 1969. *The Penultimate Palace of Knossos*. Rome: Edizioni dell' Ateneo.

Palmer, L. R. and Boardman, J. 1963. *On the Knossos Tablets*. Oxford: Clarendon.

Palyvou, C. 2002. 'Central courts: the supremacy of the void'. In Driessen et al. 2002, *Monuments of Minos*, 167–76.

Palyvou, C. 2005. 'Architecture in Aegean Bronze Age art: Façades with no interiors'. In Morgan 2005, *Aegean Wall Painting*, 185–97.

Panagiotaki, M. 1998. 'Dating the Temple Repositories vases'. *BSA* 93: 185–98.

Panagiotaki, M. 1999. *The Central Palace Sanctuary at Knossos* (*BSA* Suppl. 31). London: British School at Athens.

Panagiotaki, M. 2004. 'Knossos and Evans: Buying Kephala'. In Cadogan et al. 2004, *Knossos: Palace, City, State*, 513–30.

Papadopoulos, J. K. 1994. 'Pasiphaë'. *Lexikon Iconographicum Mythologiae Classicae* VII, no. 1: 193–200. Zurich and Munich: Artemis.

Papasavvas, G. 2001. *Χαλκινοι Υποστατες απο την Κυπρο και την Κρητη: Τριποδικοι και Τετραπλευροι Υποστατες απο την Υστερη Εποχη του Χαλκου εως την Πρωιμη Εποχη του Σιδηρου/ Chalkinoi Ypostates apo tin Kypro kai tin Kriti: Tripodikoi kai Tetraplevroi Ypostastes apo tin Ysteri Epochi tou Chalkou eos tin Proimi Epochi tou Siderou*. Nicosia: A.G. Leventis Foundation.

Papasavvas, G. 2017. 'Breaking and burning the Sphinx'. In V. Vlachou and A. Gadolou (eds), *ΤΕΡΨΙΣ: Studies in Mediterranean Archaeology in Honour of Nota Kourou* (Études d'Archéologie 10), 481–99. Brussels: CReA-Patrimoine.

Parker Pearson, M. 1999. *The Archaeology of Death and Burial*. Stroud: Sutton.

Parker Pearson, M. 2012. *Stonehenge: Exploring the Greatest Stone Age Mystery*. London: Simon and Schuster.

Pashley, R. 1837a. *Travels in Crete*, Vol. 1. London: John Murray.

Pashley, R. 1837b. *Travels in Crete*, Vol. 2. London: John Murray.

Paton, S. 1991. 'A Roman Corinthian building at Knossos'. *BSA* 86: 297–318.

Paton, S. 1994. 'Chapter 10: Roman Knossos and the *Colonia Julia Nobilis Cnossus*'. In Evely et al. 1994, *Labyrinth of History*, 141–53.

Paton, S. 1998. 'The Villa Dionysos at Knossos and its predecessors'. In Cavanagh et al. 1998, *Post-Minoan Crete*, 123–8.

Paton, S. 2004. 'Knossos: an imperial renaissance'. In Cadogan et al. 2004, *Knossos: Palace, City, State*, 451–5.

Payne, H. G. G. 1928. 'Early Greek vases from Knossos'. *BSA* 29: 224–98.

Payne, H. 1931. *Necrocorinthia: A Study of Corinthian Art in the Archaic Period*. Oxford: Clarendon.

Pendlebury, H. W. and Pendlebury, J. D. S. 1930. 'Two protopalatial houses at Knossos'. *BSA* 30: 53–73.

Pendlebury, J. D. S. 1939. *The Archaeology of Crete: An Introduction*. London: Methuen.

Pendlebury, J. D. S. 1954 (1932). *A Handbook of the Palace of Minos, Knossos, with its Dependencies*. London: Max Parrish.

Pendlebury, J. D. S., Pendlebury, H. W. and Money-Coutts, M. B. 1938. 'Excavations in the plain of Lasithi III: Karphi: a city of refuge of the Early Iron Age of Crete'. *BSA* 38 (1937–8): 57–145.

Perez Ripoll, M. 2013. 'The Knossos fauna and the beginning of the Neolithic in the Mediterranean island'. In Efstratiou et al. 2013, *Neolithic Knossos*, 133–69.

Perlman, P. 1992. 'One hundred-citied Crete and the Cretan *politeia*'. *Classical Philology* 87: 193–205.

Perlman, P. 2004. 'Crete'. In M. H. Hansen and T. H. Nielsen (eds), *An Inventory of Archaic and Classical Poleis*, 1144–95. Oxford: Oxford University Press.

Perna, K. 2011. 'The LMIIIC burial culture in Crete: A socio-economic perspective'. In Murphy 2011a, *Prehistoric Crete*, 119–64.

Pilz, O. and Seelentag, G. (eds), 2014. *Cultural Practices and Material Culture in Archaic and Classical Crete*. Berlin and Boston: Walter de Gruyter.

Pini, I. 2010. 'A short history of the *Corpus der minoischen und mykenischen Siegel*'. In Müller 2010, *Glyptik*, 3–10. Mainz: Philipp von Zabern.

Platon, N. and Brice, W. C. 1975. *Ενεπιγραφοί Πίνακες καί Πιθοι Γραμμικού Συστημαός Α εκ Ζακρόυ / Inscribed Tablets and Pithos of Linear A System from Zakro (Βιβλιοθήκη της εν Αθήναις Αρχαιολογικής Εταιρείας* 85). Athens: Archaeological Society of Athens.

Platon, N., Gill, M. A. V., Müller, W. and Pini, I. 2002a. *Corpus der minoischen und mykensichen Siegel II: Iraklion, archäologischen Museum: Teil 8,1: Die Siegelabdrücke von Knossos*. Mainz: Philipp von Zabern = *CMS* II: 8.1.

Platon, N., Gill, M. A. V., Müller, W. and Pini, I. 2002b. *Corpus der minoischen und mykensichen Siegel II: Iraklion, archäologischen Museum: Teil 8,2: Die Siegelabdrücke von Knossos*. Mainz: Philipp von Zabern = *CMS* II: 8.2.

Platon, N. and Pini, I. 1984. *Corpus der minoischen und mykensichen Siegel II: Iraklion, archäologischen Museum: Teil 3: Die Siegel der Neupalastzeit*. Berlin: Gebr Mann = *CMS* II: 3.

Platon, N., Pini, I. and Salies, G. 1977. *Corpus der minoischen und mykensichen Siegel II: Iraklion, archäologischen Museum: Teil 2: Die Siegel der Altpalastzeit*. Berlin: Gebr Mann = *CMS* II: 2.

Pollard, D. 2021. 'All equal in the presence of death? A quantitative analysis of the Early Iron Age cemeteries of Knossos, Crete'. *Journal of Anthropological Archaeology* 63: 101320. https://doi.org.10.1016/j.jaa.2021.101320.

Popham, M. R. 1964. *The Last Days of the Palace of Knossos: Complete Vases of the LMIIIB Period* (Studies in Mediterranean Archaeology 5). Lund: Paul Åstroms Förlag.

Popham, M. R. 1970. *The Destruction of the Palace at Knossos: Pottery of the LMIIIA Period* (Studies in Mediterranean Archaeology 12). Göteberg: Paul Åstroms Förlag.

Popham, M. R. 1973. 'The Unexplored Mansion at Knossos: a preliminary report on the excavations from 1967 to 1972'. *AR* 19: 50–9.

Popham, M. R. 1974. 'Trial KV (1969): A Middle Minoan building at Knossos'. *BSA* 69: 181–94.

Popham, M. R. 1978. 'Notes from Knossos, part II'. *BSA* 73: 179–87.

Popham, M. R. 1992. 'The Sub-Minoan pottery'. In Sackett 1992a, *Greek City to Roman Colony*, 59–66.

Popham, M. R. (ed.), 1984–5. *The Unexplored Mansion at Knossos*, 2 volumes, text and plates (*BSA* Suppl. 17). London: British School at Athens.

Popham, M. R. and Catling, H. W. 1974. 'Sellopoulo tombs 3 and 4: two Late Minoan graves near Knossos'. *BSA* 69: 195–257.

Popham, M. R. and Gill, M. A. V. 1995. *The Latest Sealings from the Palace and Houses at Knossos* (*BSA* Studies 1). London: British School at Athens.

Postgate, J. N. 2001. 'System and style in three Near Eastern bureaucracies'. In S. Voutsaki and J. Killen (eds), *Economy and Politics in the Mycenaean Palace States: Proceedings of a Conference held on the 1–3 July 1999 in the Faculty of Classics, Cambridge* (Cambridge Philological Society Supplementary Volume no. 27), 181–94. Cambridge: Cambridge Philological Society.

Powell, Barry B. 1991. *Homer and the Origin of the Greek Alphabet*. Cambridge: Cambridge University Press.

Powell, D. 2003. *The Villa Ariadne*. Athens: Efstathiades Group.

Bibliography

Prent, M. 2004. 'Cult activities at the Palace of Knossos from the end of the Bronze Age: continuity and change'. In Cadogan et al. 2004, *Knossos: Palace, City, State*, 411–20.

Prent, M. 2005. *Cretan Sanctuaries and Cults: Continuity and Change from Late Minoan IIIC to the Archaic Period* (Religions in the Graeco-Roman World 154). Leiden: Brill.

Preston, L. 1999. 'Mortuary practices and the negotiation of social identities at LMII Knossos'. *BSA* 94: 131–43.

Preston, L. 2004. 'A Mortuary Perspective on Political Changes in Late Minoan II–IIIB Crete'. *AJA* 108: 321–48

Preston, L. 2005. 'The Kephala tholos tomb at Knossos: a study in the re-use of the past'. *BSA* 102: 61–123.

Preston, L. 2007. 'The Isopata cemetery at Knossos'. *BSA* 104: 257–314.

Preston, L. 2013a. 'The Middle Minoan III funerary landscape at Knossos'. In Macdonald and Knappett 2013a, *Intermezzo*, 57–70.

Preston, L. 2013b. *Knossos: Monastiriako Kephali Tomb and 'Deposit'* (*BSA* Studies 22). London: British School at Athens.

Price, J. 1992. 'Hellenistic and Roman glass'. In Sackett 1992a, *Greek City to Roman Colony*, 415–62.

Price, M. J. 1992. 'The coins'. In Sackett 1992a, *Greek City to Roman Colony*, 323–31.

Rabinowitz, A. 2014. 'Drinkers, hosts or fighters? Masculine identities in pre-Classical Crete'. In Pilz and Seelentag 2014, *Cultural Practices*, 91–119.

Rackham, O. and Moody, J. 1996. *The Making of the Cretan Landscape*. Manchester: Manchester University Press.

Renfrew, C. 1972. *The Emergence of Civilisation*. London: Methuen.

Rethemiotakis, G. and Warren, P. M. 2014. *Knossos: A Middle Minoan III Building at Bougada Metochi* (*BSA* Studies 23). London: British School at Athens.

Reusch, H. 1958. 'Zum Wandschmuck des Thronsaales in Knossos'. In E. Grumach (ed.), *Minoica: Festschrift zum 80. Geburtstag von Johannes Sundwall*, 334–58. Berlin: Akademie Verlag.

Rigsby, K. J. 1976. 'Cnossus and Capua'. *Transactions of the American Philological Association* 106: 313–30.

Rollston, C. A. 2010. *Writing and Literacy in the World of Ancient Israel: Epigraphic Evidence from the Iron Age* (Society of Biblical Literature, Archaeology and Biblical Studies 11). Leiden and Boston: Brill.

Runciman, W. G. 1990. 'Doomed to extinction: The *polis* as an evolutionary dead end'. In O. Murray and S. Price (eds), *The Greek City: From Homer to Alexander*, 347–67. Oxford: Clarendon.

Sackett, L. H. 1973. 'Post-Minoan occupation above the Unexplored Mansion'. *AR* 19: 62–71.

Sackett, L. H. 1976. 'A new figured krater from Knossos'. *BSA* 71: 117–29.

Sackett, L. H. (ed.), 1992a. *Knossos: From Greek City to Roman Colony: Excavations at the Unexplored Mansion II*, 2 volumes, text and plates (*BSA* Suppl. 21). London: British School at Athens.

Sackett, L. H. 1992b. 'The Roman pottery'. In Sackett 1992a, *Greek City to Roman Colony*, 147–256.

Sackett, L. H. 1992c. 'Objects in Bone and Bone Working'. In Sackett 1992a, *Greek City to Roman Colony*, 379–89.

Sackett, L. H. and Grace, V. 1992. 'Stamped amphora handles, sigillata stamps and graffiti'. In Sackett 1992a, *Greek City to Roman Colony*, 137–46.

Salgarella, E. 2021. 'Imagining Cretan scripts: The influence of visual motifs on the creation of script signs in Bronze Age Crete'. *BSA* 116: 63–94.

Sanders, I. F. 1982. *Roman Crete: An Archaeological Survey and Gazetteer of Late Hellenistic, Roman and Early Byzantine Crete*. Warminster: Aris and Phillips.

Sarpaki, A. 2013. 'The economy of Neolithic Knossos: the archaeobotanical evidence'. In Efstratiou et al. 2013, *Neolithic Knossos*, 63–118.

Schachermeyer, F. 1938. 'Vorbericht über eine Expedition nach Ostkreta'. *Archaeologischer Anzeiger*: 466–80.

Schäfer, J. 1992a. 'Amnisos: Die Ausgrabungen: Das "Heiligtum des Zeus Thenatas"'. In Schäfer 1992b, *Amnisos*, 159–85.

Schäfer, J. (ed.), 1992b. *Amnisos: Nach dem archäologischen, historischen und epigrafischen Zeugnisse des Altertums und der Neuzeit*, 2 volumes, text and plates. Berlin: Gebr Mann.

Schefold, K. 1966. *Myth and Legend in Early Greek Art*. Translated from the German by Audrey Hicks. London: Thames and Hudson.

Schoep, I. 2007. 'The inscribed document'. In Macdonald and Knappett 2007, *Protopalatial Deposits*, 131–4.

Schoep, I. and Knappett, C. 2004. 'Dual emergence: evolving heterarchy, exploding hierarchy'. In Barrett and Halstead 2004, *Emergence Revisited*, 21–37.

Seelentag, G. 2015. *Das archaische Kreta: Instituionalisierung im frühen Griechenland (Klio Beiträge zur alten Geschichte 24)*. Berlin and Boston: Walter de Gruyter.

Shapland, A. J. 2010. 'Wild nature? Human–animal relations on neopalatial Crete'. *Cambridge Archaeological Journal* 20: 109–27.

Shapland, A. J. 2013. 'Jumping to conclusions: Bull leaping in Minoan Crete'. *Society and Animals* 21: 194–207.

Shapland, A. J. 2022. *Human–Animal Relations in Bronze Age Crete: A History through Objects*. Cambridge: Cambridge University Press.

Shaw, Maria C. 2005. 'The painted pavilion of the 'Caravanserai' at Knossos'. In Morgan 2005, *Aegean Wall Painting*, 91–111.

Shaw, Maria C. 2012. 'New light on the Labyrinth fresco from the Palace at Knossos'. *BSA* 107: 143–59.

Sherratt, A. 1981. 'Plough and pastoralism: aspects of the secondary products revolution'. In I. Hodder, G. Isaac and N. Hammond (eds), *Pattern of the Past: Studies in Honour of David Clarke*, 261–305. Cambridge: Cambridge University Press.

Sherratt, A. 2006. 'Crete, Greece and the Orient in the thought of Gordon Childe (with an appendix on Toynbee and Spengler: the afterlife of the Minoans in European intellectual history)'. In Hamilakis and Momigliano 2006, *Archaeology and European Modernity*, 107–26.

Sherratt, A. and Sherratt, S. 2008. 'The Neolithic of Crete as seen from outside'. In Isaakidou and Tomkins 2008, *Escaping the Labyrinth*, 291–302.

Sherratt, S. 2001. 'Potemkin palaces and route-based economies'. In Voutsaki and Killen 2001, *Economy and Politics in the Mycenaean Palace States*, 214–38.

Simandiraki-Grimshaw, A. 2010. 'Minoan animal–human hybridity'. In D. B. Coutts and B. Arnold (eds), *The Master of Animals in Old World Iconography*, 93–106. Budapest: Archaeolingua Alapítávny.

Simandiraki-Grimshaw, A. and Stevens, F. 2013. 'Destroying the snake goddess: a re-examination of figurine fragmentation at the Temple Repositories of the Palace of Knossos'. In Driessen 2013b, *Destruction*, 153–70.

Simantouni-Bournia, E. 2013. 'Minotaur: The acclimatization of a Cretan hybrid in the Cyclades'. In Niemeier et al. 2013, *Kreta in der geometrischen und archaischen Zeit*, 382–93.

Small, D. B. 2018. An explosion, not revolution: Recasting issues in the Greek Iron Age'. In Nevett and Whitley 2018, *An Age of Experiment*, 21–9.

Snodgrass, A. M. 1971. *The Dark Age of Greece*. Edinburgh: Edinburgh University Press.

Snodgrass, A. M. 1977. *Archaeology and the Rise of the Greek State*. Cambridge: Cambridge University Press.

Snodgrass, A. M. 1980. *Archaic Greece: The Age of Experiment*. Berkeley and Los Angeles: University of California Press.

Snodgrass, A. M. 1996. 'Iron'. In Coldstream and Catling 1996, *Knossos North Cemetery*, 575–97.

Bibliography

Snodgrass, A. M. 1998. *Homer and the Artists: Text and Picture in Early Greek Art*. Cambridge: Cambridge University Press.

Sporn, K. 2002. *Heiligtümer und Kulte Kretas in klassischer und hellenstischer Zeit* (Studien zu antiken Heiligtümern 2). Heidelberg: Verlag Archäologie und Geschichte.

Sporn, K. 2013. 'Kretische Mythen versus Mythen über Kreta: Zur Einführung von Mythenbildern kretischer Thematik auf Kreta'. In Niemeier et al. 2013, *Kreta in der geometrischen und archaischen Zeit*, 395–408.

Sporn, K. 2014. 'Graves and grave markers in Archaic and Classical Crete'. In Pilz and Seelentag 2014, *Cultural Practices*, 219–41.

Spratt, T. A. B. 1865 (reprinted 2005). *Travels and Researches in Crete, Vol I*. London: John Van Voorst.

Stefanakis, M. I. 1999. 'The introduction of coinage in Crete and the beginning of local minting'. In Chaniotis 1999, *Minoan Farmers to Roman Traders*, 247–68.

Stevens, F. and Simandiraki-Grimshaw, A. 2016. 'Composite, partial, created and floating bodies: a re-assessment of the Knossos Temple Repositories assemblage'. In Mina et al. 2016, *Embodied Identities*, 35–31.

Stocker, S. R. and Davis, J. L. 2016. 'The lord of the gold rings: the griffin warrior of Pylos'. *Hesperia* 85: 627–55.

Strasser, T. F. 1997. 'Storage and states on prehistoric Crete: the function of the koulouras in the first Minoan palaces'. *Journal of Mediterranean Archaeology* 10: 73–100.

Strasser, T. 2004. 'Three axe groups from Neolithic Knossos'. In Cadogan et al. 2004, *Knossos: Palace, City, State*, 61–5.

Strasser, T. 2008. 'Stones of contention: regional axe production and hidden landscapes on Neolithic Crete'. In Isaakidou and Tomkins 2008, *Escaping the Labyrinth*, 155–64.

Strasser, T. et al. 2010. 'Stone Age seafaring in the Mediterranean: Evidence from the Plakias region for Lower Palaeolithic and Mesolithic habitation of Crete'. *Hesperia* 79: 145–90.

Stürmer, V. 1992a. 'Amnisos: Die Ausgrabungen: Die "Villa der Lilien"'. In Schäfer 1992b, *Amnisos*, 129–50.

Stürmer, V. 1992b. 'Amnisos: Die Funde'. In Schäfer 1992b, *Amnisos*, 217–54.

Svoronos, J. N. 1890. *La Numismatique de la Crète Ancienne*, 2 volumes, text and plates. Macon: Protat Frères.

Sweetman, R. 2003. 'The Roman mosaics of the Knossos valley'. *BSA* 98: 517–47.

Sweetman, R. 2004a. 'The changing nature of Knossos: Roman to Late Antique – some problems'. In Cadogan et al. 2004, *Knossos: Palace, City State*, 481–8.

Sweetman, R. 2004b. 'Late Antique Knossos: Understanding the city: Evidence of mosaics and religious architecture'. *BSA* 99: 315–54.

Sweetman, R. 2005. 'Knossos Medical Faculty site: Late Antique graves and other remains (with a contribution from Marshall Joseph Becker)'. *BSA* 100: 331–86.

Sweetman, R. 2010. 'Roman Knossos: Discovering the city through the evidence of the rescue excavations'. *BSA* 105: 339–79.

Sweetman, R. 2013. *The Mosaics of Roman Crete: Art, Archaeology and Social Change*. Cambridge: Cambridge University Press.

Sznycer, M. 1979. 'L'inscription phénicienne de Tekke, près de Knossos'. *Kadmos* 18: 89–93.

Tainter, J. A. 1988. *The Collapse of Complex Societies*. Cambridge: Cambridge University Press.

Tasić, N., Marić, M., Penezić, K., Filipović, D., Borojević, K., Russell, N., Reimer, P., Barclay, A., Bayliss, A., Borić, D., Gaydarska, B. and Whittle, A. 2015. 'The end of the affair: formal chronological modelling for the top of the Neolithic tell of Vinča-Belo Brdo'. *Antiquity* 89: 1064–82.

Thompson, R. J. E. 2019. 'The Ventris–Chadwick correspondence and the decipherment of Linear B: a denier, a dissenter and a dubious conclusion'. *Cambridge Classical Journal* 65: 173–99.

Tilley, C. 1994. *A Phenomenology of Landscape: Places, Paths and Monuments*. Oxford: Berg.

Tomkins, P. 2004. 'Filling in the Neolithic background: social life and social transformation in the Aegean before the Bronze Age'. In J. C. Barrett and P. Halstead (eds), *The Emergence of Civilisation Revisited* (Sheffield Studies in Aegean Archaeology 6), 38–63. Oxford: Oxbow.

Tomkins, P. 2007. 'Neolithic: Strata IX–VIII, VII–VIB, VIA–V, IV, IIIB, IIIA, IIB, IIA and IC groups'. In Momigliano 2007b, *Minoan Pottery Handbook*, 9–48.

Tomkins, P. 2008. 'Time, space and the re-invention of the Cretan Neolithic'. In Isaakidou and Tomkins 2008, *Escaping the Labyrinth*, 21–48.

Tomkins, P. 2016. 'The making of the Kephala Hill and the Knossos community (3600–1950 BC): An overview of the work of the Knossos Kephala project'. Paper given at the most recent Cretological Conference in Heraklion, September 2016. Abstract in *12 ICCS: 12th International Congress of Cretan Studies Heraklion, 21–15.9.2016*, 171. Heraklion: Society of Cretan Historical Studies.

Tomkins, P., Day, P. M. and Kilikoglou, V. 2004. 'Knossos and the earlier Neolithic landscape of the Heraklion basin'. In Cadogan et al. 2004, *Knossos: Palace, City, State*, 51–9.

Trainor, C. 2019. 'Polis, colony and beyond: urban Knossos from Archaic to Late Antique times'. In C. Mitsotaki, L. Tzedaki-Apostolaki and S. Giannadaki (eds), *Proceedings of the 12th International Congress of Cretan Studies Heraklio 21–25.9.2016*. Heraklion: International Congress of Cretan Studies. https://12iccs.proceedings.gr/en/proceedings/category/39/35/814.

Trainor, C. 2021. 'The late Hellenistic wine press excavations from Knossos: The Early Iron Age, Hellenistic and Early Roman contexts'. *BSA* 116: 235–90.

Triandaphyllou, S. 2008. 'Living with the dead: a re-consideration of mortuary practices in the Greek Neolithic'. In Isaakidou and Tomkins 2008, *Escaping the Labyrinth*, 136–54.

Tsoungarakis, D. 1988. *Byzantine Crete: From the 5th Century to the Venetian Conquest* (Historical Monographs 4). Athens: St D. Basilopoulos.

Tzorakis, G. 2021. Ἐπικειμένης τῆς θυέλλας … Η προετοιμασία της κρητικής Αρχαιολογικής Υπηρεσίας εν όψει του πολεμου και οι απώλειες στις αρχαιότητες της Κρήτης κατά τη διάρκεια της Κατοχής'. *Kretika Chronika* 41: 115–42.

Vagnetti, L. 1989. 'A Sardinian askos from Crete'. *BSA* 84: 355–60.

Van den Eijnde, F. 2018. 'Power play at the dinner table: feasting and patronage between palace and polis in Attika'. In Van den Eijnde et al. 2018, *Feasting and Polis Institutions*, 60–92.

Van den Eijnde, F., Blok, J. H. and Strootman, R. (eds), 2018. *Feasting and Polis Institutions* (*Mnemosyne* Suppl. 414). Leiden: E.J. Brill

Vasilakis, A. 2004. 'Τα τοπωνύμια της Κνωσού'. In Cadogan et al. 2004, *Knossos: Palace, City, State*, 493–6.

Ventris, M. and Chadwick, J. 1953. 'Evidence of Greek language in the Mycenaean archives'. *JHS* 73: 84–103.

Ventris, M. and Chadwick, J. 1973. *Documents in Mycenaean Greek*, 2nd edition. Cambridge: Cambridge University Press.

Verdan, S. 2013. *Eretria XXII: Le Sanctuaire d'Apollon Daphnéphoros à L'Époque Géométrique*, 2 volumes. Gollion: Infolio/École Suisse d'Archéologie en Grèce.

Voutsaki, S. and Killen, J. (eds), 2001. *Economy and Politics in the Mycenaean Palace States: Proceedings of a Conference held on the 1–3 July 1999 in the Faculty of Classics, Cambridge* (Cambridge Philological Society Supplementary Volume no 27). Cambridge: Cambridge Philological Society.

Wallace, S. 2010. *Ancient Crete: From Successful Collapse to Democracy's Alternatives, Twelfth to Fifth Centuries BC*. Cambridge: Cambridge University Press.

Wardle, K. 1972. 'Two notes from Knossos'. *BSA* 67: 271–84.

Wardle, K. and Wardle, D. 2004. 'Glimpses of private life: Roman rock-cut tombs of the first and second centuries AD at Knossos'. In Cadogan et al. 2004 *Knossos: Palace, City, State*, 473–80.

Warren, P. 1967. 'A stone vase-maker's workshop in the Palace at Knossos'. *BSA* 62: 195–201.

Warren, P. M. 1981. 'Stratigraphical Museum excavations, 1978–1980, Part I'. *AR* 27: 73–92.

Bibliography

Warren, P. M. 1983. 'Stratigraphical Museum excavations, 1978–1982, Part II'. *AR* 29: 63–87.

Warren, P. 1984. 'Circular platforms at Minoan Knossos'. *BSA* 79: 307–23.

Warren, P. 1994. 'The Minoan roads of Knossos'. In Evely et al. 1994, *Labyrinth of History*, 189–210.

Warren, P. 2005. 'Flowers for the goddess? New fragments of wall paintings from Knossos'. In Morgan 2005, *Aegean Wall Painting*, 131–48.

Warren, P. 2010. 'The absolute chronology of the Aegean circa 2000–1400 BC'. In Müller 2010, *Glyptik*, 383–94.

Warren, P. 2013. 'Middle Minoan III pottery from the town of Knossos: The Vlachakis plot'. In Macdonald and Knappett 2013a, *Intermezzo*, 31–5.

Warren, P. and Hankey, V. 1989. *Aegean Bronze Age Chronology*. Bristol: Bristol Classical Press.

Warren, P. M., Jarman, M. R., Jarman, N. H., Shackleton, N. J. and Evans, J. D. 1968. 'Knossos Neolithic part II'. *BSA* 63: 239–76.

Warren, P. M. and Miles, G. C. 1972. 'An Arab building at Knossos'. *BSA* 67: 285–96.

Waterhouse, H. 1986. *The British School at Athens: The First Hundred Years* (*BSA* Suppl. 19). London: Thames and Hudson.

Waugh, E. 1985 (1930). *Labels*. Harmondsworth: Penguin.

Wecowski, M. 2014. *The Rise of the Greek Aristocratic Banquet*. Oxford: Oxford University Press.

Weingarten, J. 2007. 'Noduli, sealings and a weight from deposits A and E'. In Macdonald and Knappett 2007, *Protopalatial Deposits*, 134–9.

West, M. L. 2007. *Indo-European Poetry and Myth*. Oxford: Oxford University Press.

Westgate, R. 2007. 'House and society in Classical and Hellenistic Crete: a case study in regional variation'. *AJA* 111: 423–57.

Westgate, R. 2015. 'Space and social complexity in Greece from the Early Iron Age to the Classical period'. *Hesperia* 84: 47–95.

Whitelaw, T. 2001. 'From sites to communities: defining the human dimension of Minoan urbanism'. In Branigan 2001, *Urbanism*, 15–37.

Whitelaw, T. 2004. 'Estimating the Population of Neopalatial Knossos'. In Cadogan et al. 2004, *Knossos: Palace, City, State*, 147–58.

Whitelaw, T. 2022. 'Knossos during LMII–IIIB: Dynamism and development'. In A. L. D'Agata, L. Girella, E. Papadopoulou and D. G. Aquini (eds), *One State, Many Worlds: Crete in the LMII–IIIA2 Early Period: Proceedings of the International Conference Held at Khania, Μεγαλο Αρσεναλι, 21st–23rd November 2019* (*Studi Micenei ed Egeo-Anatolici NS* Suppl. 2), 35–70. Rome: Edizioni Quasar.

Whitelaw, T., Bredaki, M. and Vasilakis, A. 2019. 'The long-term dynamics of Knossos in context'. In C. Mitsotaki, L. Tzedaki-Apostolaki and S. Giannadaki (eds), *Proceedings of the 12th International Congress of Cretan Studies Heraklio 21–25.9.2016*. Heraklion: International Congress of Cretan Studies. https://12iccs.proceedings.gr/el/proceedings/category/39/35/816.

Whitley, J. 1997. 'Cretan laws and Cretan literacy'. *AJA* 101: 635–61.

Whitley, J. 1998. 'Knossos without Minos. Review article of H. W. Catling and J. N. Coldstream, Knossos North Cemetery'. *AJA* 102: 611–13.

Whitley, J. 2001. *The Archaeology of Ancient Greece*. Cambridge: Cambridge University Press.

Whitley, J. 2002. 'Objects with attitude: Biographical facts and fallacies in the study of Late Bronze Age and Early Iron Age warrior graves'. *Cambridge Archaeological Journal* 12: 217–32.

Whitley, J. 2004. 'Style wars: towards an explanation of Cretan exceptionalism'. In Cadogan et al. 2004, *Knossos: Palace, City, State*, 433–42.

Whitley, J. 2006. 'The Minoans: A Welsh invention? A view from East Crete'. In Hamilakis and Momigliano 2006, *Archaeology and European Modernity*, 55–67.

Whitley, J. 2009. 'Chapter 14: Crete'. In K. A. Raaflaub and H. van Wees (eds), *A Companion to Archaic Greece* (Blackwell Companions to the Ancient World), 273–93. Malden, MA, Oxford and Chichester: Wiley-Blackwell.

Whitley, J. 2013. 'The Cretan Orientalizing: a comparative perspective'. In Niemeier et al. 2013, *Kreta in der geometrischen und archaischen Zeit*, 409–26.

Whitley, J. 2015. 'Agency and the belly-handled amphora: exchange and society in the ninth-century Aegean'. In N. Kourou, A. Tsingarida and V. Vlachou (eds), *Pots, Workshops and Early Iron Age Society: Function and Role of Ceramics in Early Greece*, 133–53. Brussels: Publications of the Université Libre de Bruxelles; Études d'Archéologie, CReA Patrimonie.

Whitley, J. 2016. 'Burning people, breaking things: Material entanglements, the Bronze Age/Iron Age transition and the Homeric dividual'. In Mina et al. 2016, *Embodied Identities*, 215–23.

Whitley, J. 2017a. 'Chapter 4: the material entanglements of writing things down'. In L. Nevett (ed.), *Theoretical Approaches to the Archaeology of Ancient Greece*, 71–103. Ann Arbor: University of Michigan Press.

Whitley, J. 2017b. 'The end of the tells: the Iron Age "Neolithic" in the central and northern Aegean'. In P. Bickle, V. Cummings, D. Hofmann and J. Pollard (eds), *The Neolithic of Europe: Papers in Honour of Alasdair Whittle*, 24–33. Oxford: Oxbow.

Whitley, J. 2018. 'Citizenship and commensality in Archaic Crete: Searching for the Andreion'. In A. Duplouy and R. Brock (eds), *Defining Citizenship in Archaic Greece*, 227–48. Oxford: Oxford University Press.

Whitley, J. 2019. 'The re-emergence of political complexity'. In I. Lemos and A. Kotsonas (eds), *A Companion to the Archaeology of Early Greece and the Mediterranean*, 161–86. London, Chichester and Malden, MA: John Wiley.

Whitley, J. and Madgwick, R. 2018. 'Consuming the wild: more thoughts on the *andreion*'. In Van den Eijnde et al. 2018, *Feasting and Polis Institutions*, 125–48.

Whittle, A. 1996. *Europe in the Neolithic: The Creation of New Worlds*. Cambridge: Cambridge University Press.

Wilson, D. 1985. 'The pottery and architecture of the EMIIA West Court house at Knossos'. *BSA* 80: 281–364.

Wilson, D. 1994. 'Knossos before the Palaces: an overview of the Early Bronze Age (EMI – EMIII)'. In Evely et al. 1994, *Labyrinth of History*, 23–44.

Wilson, D. 2007. 'Early prepalatial (EMI–EMII): EMI well, West Court houses, North-East Magazines and South Front groups'. In Momigliano 2007b, *Minoan Pottery Handbook*, 49–77.

Wilson, D. E. and Day, P. M. 1994. 'Ceramic regionalism in prepalatial central Crete: the Mesara imports at EMI to EM II A Knossos'. *BSA* 89: 1–87.

Wilson, D. E. and Day, P. M. 1999. 'EM II B ware groups at Knossos: the 1907–08 South Front tests'. *BSA* 94: 1–62.

Wilson, D. E. and Day, P. M. 2000. 'EM I chronology and social practice: pottery from the early palace tests at Knossos'. *BSA* 95: 21–63.

Woodford, S. 1992. 'Minotauros'. *Lexikon Iconographicum Mythologiae Classicae* VI, no. 1: 574–81. Munich and Zürich: Artemis.

Yoffee, N. 1993. 'Too many chiefs? (or, Safe texts for the '90s)'. In N. Yoffee and A. Sherratt (eds), *Archaeological Theory: Who Sets the Agenda?* (New Directions in Archaeology), 60–78. Cambridge: Cambridge University Press.

Yoffee, N. 2005. *Myths of the Archaic State: The Evolution of the Earliest Cities, States and Civilizations*. Cambridge: Cambridge University Press.

Younger, J. G. 1984. 'Seven types of ring construction in the Greek Late Bronze Age'. In C. Nicolet (ed.), *Aux Origines de L'Hellénisme: La Crète et la Grèce*, 83–90. Paris: Centre Gustav Glotz.

GENERAL INDEX

This is an index of classes of material themes, topics, peoples, persons (both mythical and historical) and places outside of Crete (including the Aegean). Only persons who are no longer with us at the time of indexing (Spring 2023) have been included – so Nicolas Coldstream, but not John Boardman. Places in Crete or the Knossos Survey Area have been placed in the topographical index.

Achaean/Achaeans 11, 33, 44, 115, 137, 178, 185, 187
Acropolis (Athens) 48, 52
[administration 88–92]
Aegeus (father of Theseus) 7
Aegina, Aeginetan 70, 149
agrimi (Cretan wild goat) 60–1, 91, 159, 190
Akrotiri (Thera) 49, 116
Alexander the Great (of Macedon) 157
Alexander Severus (Roman emperor) xxi
Alexandria (in Egypt) 159
Alexiou, Stylianos 51
alphabet 147–8, 177–9
Amenhotep III (of Egypt) 12, 121, 189
Anatolia xix, 55–62, 77
andreion 155, 159–60, 173, 184
Antioch (in Syria) 159
Antonine xxi, 14
Apollo (Paian) 124, 149, 156
Apollodorus (and Ps-Apollodorus) 7
Arab (and Arabic) xxii, 4, 15, 172, 174–5, 177–9
Archaic (period) xviii–xxii, xxiv, 12, 23, 49–51, 148–57, 161, 184–5
'Archaic gap' xxi, 151–2, 173–4, 184
Archanes script 89, 179
Argos 152, 156, 185
Ariadne 7–8, 10–13, 18
Aristotle (and Ps-Aristotle) 11, 152, 157, 185
Ashmolean Museum (Oxford), 27–9, 35, 111, 122, 189 ch.2 n.1
Asterios/Asterion (name of Minotaur) 6–7
Athena (goddess) 124, 156
Athens (and Athenian) 1, 5–6, 8, 23, 37, 145–8, 152, 157, 185
Augustus (Roman emperor) xxi, 13, 163–4, 167
axes (including double axes) 61–4, 111, 131

Babylon 125
Bacchylides (poet) 7, 189 ch.1 n.2
basilica (Early Christian) 2, 16, 170–2
bishops (bishopric) 172, 175, 184, 191 ch.5 n.4
Blakeway, Alan 41–4, 49

Blegen, Carl 46–8
boars' tusk helmet 11, 115–16, 135–7
broch (Scottish) 72
Brock, James 49
Bronze Age (in Aegean, as concept) xix–xxii, 1, 3–6, 12, 20–1, 25, 28, 54, 62–77
burials 36–8, 58, 74–7, 92–7, 107, 113–16, 130–7, 139–45, 152, 161, 167–8, 172, 183–4
Byzantine xxii, 5, 15, 51, 175, 178, 185

Caligula (Roman emperor) 164
Caracalla (Roman emperor) 168, 184
Cameron, Mark 49, 190
Capua (town in Italy) 164
Çatalhöyük (in Anatolia, modern Turkey) 60
Catling, Hector W. xxv, 3, 135
Celtic 8
Chadwick, J. 47–8, 119–24
Chalcolithic 61–2
Childe, Gordon 40, 62, 96
chipped stone 57
Christian/Christianity xxii, 14–18, 20, 22 29, 38, 164–5, 170–5, 185
chronology xviii–xxii, 80, 132
Classical (as period) xviii–xxii, 12–13, 27, 50–1, 152–7, 184–5
Classical Archaeology (as subject) xxiv, 16, 37
Classics (as subject) xiv–vi, xxiv
coins 5, 11–13, 28, 156, 166–7, 174, 185
Coldstream, John Nicolas xviii, xxv, 49, 132, 137–48
colonia (as concept or institution) 163–4, 184
Colonia Iulia Nobilis Cnossus xxi, 163–72
Commensality, *see* feasting
Constantine I (Roman Emperor) 15, 170
Constantinople (Istanbul) 15, 19–20, 22
Corinth 37, 157, 164
cremations 135–7, 139–45, 159
Cyclades/Cycladic xviii, 63–4, 146–8, 186
Cydonia/Cydonians, *see* Kydonia/Kydonians in topographical index
Cyrene (or Kyrene, in North Africa) 156

TOPOGRAPHICAL INDEX

These include only sites in Crete, and locations in the Knossos Survey Area (as defined by Hood and Smyth 1981). KS followed by a number (see abbreviations p. xxv) is a cross-reference to the numbers given in the Knossos Survey (Hood and Smyth 1981, 34–62). References to sites in the Aegean, Eastern Mediterranean or elsewhere are given in the General Index.

Topographical Index